EIGHT BALL

DOWN

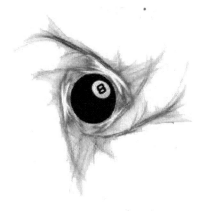

PIG & PHOENIX BOOKS

Pig & Phoenix Books

© AS Thomsen 2015

ISBN 9781520305790

This book is dedicated to my mother.

Thanks to:

Duncan, Johan, Tracy and Becky.

Special thanks to my editor, Alistair Lowde.

Best Wishes,

A S Thomson.

Contents

1

Carl took a long hard drag on his cigarette and slowly blew the smoke upwards into the vampire's face.

The vampire, who, until yesterday, had been a waitress and a recent ex-smoker, snarled back, baring huge fangs before coughing and spluttering furiously as smoke hit her in the face. It triggered a faint memory of craving a cigarette just before an overwhelming blood-lust kicked in around 2am.

The rain pelted down hard on Carl's and the vampire's faces as thunder roared and exploded across the night sky. The clouds crackled and sizzled with a ferocious power Carl had never seen before. His dark brown eyes flicked upwards, past the vampire's face, past the Church spire and into the sky. It looked wrong. It felt wrong. The rain was wrong.

Carl fixed his eyes back on his adversary's watering eyes. "What are you going to do, sweetie?" he mockingly whispered as he held a pool-cue towards her heart. His light brown skin seemed to glow in the pale indigo light emanating from his cue. That was something new. Since when had it glowed?

The vampire wiped away the smoke-induced tears and sniffed. She looked down from her 5ft 10" to his 5ft 2" and was sure she remembered his face. She had seen him in The Pig & Phoenix further down the Lower Richmond Road. He played pool regularly, squatting like a cute little frog on a barrel, watching his opponents with a piercing look. He was short, 30-ish, good-looking and a deadly pool player. Here he was with the same pool cue, about to kill her. She knew she could expect no mercy from the small man standing in front of her. What a place to die, she thought – on Putney Common in

1

the pouring rain, next to the 22 bus stop. This was the spot where she had met the man with green eyes and silver hair. He'd asked her the time and that was all she could remember. That had only been yesterday.

Carl gave her an impatient look. She had only recently turned, he could tell. It was always sad to see the last remnants of humanity leak away – the struggle between two conflicting urges battling it out – the need to go home, watch the telly and have a cup of tea after a long day at work versus an overwhelming desire to slaughter all of humanity and live off its blood! Poor bitch, he thought. She was a fresh one. Soon she would have no human memories. Soon there would be no tea'n'telly. Soon she'd just be a killing machine on autopilot.

"Well, sweetie?" Carl asked, almost gently. It was so much harder to kill a newbie.

'Sweetie' looked down at Carl. She had memories swirling through her head. She remembered her fiancé, the time she went to a Rolling Stones cover band concert, her fifth birthday and then the new desire to kill…getting stronger.

"I haven't killed anyone yet," Sweetie said softly, trying to contain the burning need to rip out his throat – trying to hang onto her remaining humanity.

"But you will…you will," he replied and added: "Do you have it?"

Sweetie put her hand in her pocket and pulled out a small key ring attached to a black ball with the number 8 on it. She didn't understand what all the fuss was about. She now knew that she would never know.

"Hand it over," Carl quietly demanded, his cigarette between his lips.

Sweetie outstretched her hand and dropped it into Carl's. He looked at it a moment and looked at her.

"I…" she managed to say before Carl ran his cue through her heart. She fell to the floor and exploded into flames. He looked back at the ball and scrutinised it and took another drag on his cigarette.

Easy…far too easy.

He reached for his mobile phone and started to text just as a lightning strike missed his head and hit the church wall.

Hmm...Carl thought, and took another drag on his cigarette.

———————————

Johnny was trying to sleep. He tossed and turned, running his hand through his floppy blonde hair, but it was no use. He just could not sleep – even the sleeping mask and one ear-plug were useless (he was deaf in one ear). He had lost $400.00 on internet poker and he was wound up! Yes, yes... there was the problem with the vampires but to lose money – damn. God damn.

He had been playing $1.00 games over a 3 hour period and was down $400.00. Sure it was only about £200.00 but Johnny was deeply annoyed. He had been playing for over a year now and had barely improved. OK yes, the problem with the vampires was starting to get out of hand. Their activity had rapidly increased in the last fortnight, with no explanation. If it continued, he was convinced the price of properties in Putney would rapidly plummet – and he had houses to inherit! If more and more people started to disappear and corpses started to randomly turn up in school wheelie-bins, it was only a matter of time before the middle-classes started deserting. Dear God...no! He was due to inherit two large houses in Putney and the last thing he needed was more vampires. He wanted to get out of mobile phone sales and into the life of wealth. Why now? Why?

It was also true there was the ever so tiny(ish) problem of Johnny being technically dead for the last five years (since turning 37), which he had been hiding rather well. It was another problem that he was one of the four members of the Putney Vampire Killing Society. Normally, activity was pretty predictable – about one vampire-zapping a month and a lot of drinking down The Pig & Phoenix afterwards. However, it was increasing to around thirty slayings per night and it had been this way for the last two weeks. This level of activity would be of great interest to the Guardians and that was the last thing Johnny wanted. They would know that he wasn't fully alive! They would find out he was an almost corpse-walker! But an

3

almost corpse-walker with a degree in psychology, a mortgage, soon to be rich (he hoped – bloody vampires!) with a tiny fiancée who worked part-time in a bookshop. His fiancée was also dropping hints about a wedding and it was all he could do not to make a run for it from all the mounting pressure. But, because of his condition, Johnny was unable to leave Putney for long. Johnny turned over onto his side and sighed dramatically.

So, as long as the house prices didn't collapse and no-one discovered that he was actually 'half-dead', his life should be more than tolerable. 'Tolerable' Johnny sighed dramatically once more. How had it all come to this? To him?

His mobile phone beeped. Johnny read a message from Carl to meet him at The Pig & Phoenix. Johnny climbed out of bed, tore off his sleeping mask, got dressed (black jeans and a black T-shirt – he still had those extra 15lbs to lose but he was over 6 foot and so, of course, could carry the extra weight), picked up his cue and headed towards the pub – his heart sinking and pounding at the same time. He looked at his watch. It was 3.30am.

Lola was 21 years old and for some unknown reason was deeply fascinated by a (long forgotten) former cockney teenage wife of a 1980s rock star. Despite working in a bookshop, she had only ever read one book: 'Love, Rock'n'Tears' by the former teenage wife. Although some had bothered to enquire as to why this was the case, they could soon be found shaking their head and heading for the nearest large gin. Lola also worshipped a celebrity chef and a lanky comedian, both of whom she declared in her loud but squeaky South-London accent as 'Fuckin' Sex Gods' to anyone as and when she felt like it. Lola often had spontaneous fantasies about them or anyone that reminded her of them and would happily announce this to the world. The reason for this was also never known.

Lola was pretty, small and psychotically jealous of any other female her fiancé, Johnny, spoke with. These women would include family members. Johnny would often have to explain why being jealous of his 10-year-old niece was ridiculous but it didn't stop her telling him not to hug her so much. Lola barely made five foot, weighed about six stone and over the last three years had become damn good at killing the occasional vampire. With the recent influx of corpse-walkers, she seemed to be coming into her element. It was entirely possible that she enjoyed it too much. She probably imagined Johnny's former girlfriends while shoving her cue through their hearts. She, however, had no idea that the love of her life was mostly dead.

Lola was lying in bed when she received Carl's text. FUCK! She had been summoned down to the pub. This meant she had to sneak out of the house where she lived on Putney Hill. Lola lived with her mother and hated it. Her mother didn't even know she smoked, let alone that her daughter slaughtered vampires on the side.

Lola picked up her pool cue, crept down the stairs, narrowly missing her cat, Condom, who was one of the worst-tempered animals to exist and probably one of the ugliest cats ever. It was perhaps understandable why Lola despised the creature. Condom hissed at her and clawed at her leg.

"Fuck off, Condom," Lola squeaked. "Or yoo'll get this cue up yer arse. I mean it..." She pointed the cue at the animal and it ran away, hissing.

"Fuckin' animal," she snarled and closed the door quietly behind her before heading down to The Pig & Phoenix.

Bert had just come home to his flat on a small road close to the Lower Richmond Road. It was the last fare of the night in his black cab and he was knackered. He walked up the stairs and grumbled to himself because he could see that 'the Boy' was home.

The Boy was a left-over from his wife, who he was recently separated from and who lived in Portugal. The Boy lived in the converted attic and, although he rarely saw him, he could frequently smell marijuana. The boy didn't work, didn't study

5

and was the bane of his life. If it wasn't for the Boy, Bert's life would be just wonderful.

Bert, who had a kind and well-worn leathery face, sat down in his beautifully white living room, poured himself a large glass of Pinot Grigio and lit up a cigarette. As he watched the smoke drift upwards, he pressed a button on a remote control and suddenly Elvis was singing in the background. He put his feet up and sighed. He was 65 and felt he was perhaps getting too old for all of this kind of thing.

Bert thought about his wife in Portugal and thought about going out there to join her. That was what she had told him. Get out of Putney and come to Portugal. She wasn't coming back to London and as much as he was tempted to go, his wife was unaware that as well as driving a cab for a living, he also destroyed vampires on the side. He had been a cab driver for about 30 years and a destroyer of vampires for about eight. Normally, it was a bit of a giggle – a few drinks, a few killings, a few games of pool and a curry. But this increase in vampires? He had never come across anything like it in his time.

The four of them had been out patrolling the Common (one patrolled the Common while the other three drank at a local pub) and suddenly Johnny had yelled for help. Instead of one, there had been thirty vampires. The next day, there were thirty more and the next and the next. This had been going on for two weeks and Bert was very tired. All four of them were tired but he was a lot older than the others. They were just a small group in Putney – an almost forgotten outpost. They had seen more action in the two weeks than some of the leading Vampire Killing Lodges had in years and it was alarming.

Maybe he really should pack it in. Maybe he should move permanently to Portugal. Maybe he should talk to Carl about leaving the Lodge. That thought made him finish his glass of wine in one glug. It wouldn't be easy.

He felt his mobile vibrate and he looked at the message. Talk of the devil, Bert thought. He put out his cigarette, picked up his cue and left his flat. Destination – The Pig & Phoenix – an emergency meeting with his fellow Vampire Killers. He sighed and thought about glorious sunshine and leaving his mates. Hmm...that would be hard to do. That would be a life-

6

changing decision.

Bert walked along the pavement and headed towards the huge pub resting on the corner of the Lower Richmond Road and a small side road. It was old-fashioned and a bit battered – wooden doors, old windows and it probably needed a lick of paint. Looking at it, you wouldn't think that it was a force of good, that it was the home of 'The Putney Vampire Killing Society'. Your average human was kept in the dark about the battle between good and evil and that, according to Bert, was a good thing. The fewer who knew about them the better! And...also according to Bert...who would believe it anyway? He sighed again, turned up his collar and shuffled towards the Lodge. It must be serious to be called in at this time of the morning, he mused.

The Pig & Phoenix. The former glorious flagship of all the International Vampire Killing Societies. There was a time when the mention of the name 'The Putney Vampire Killers' would have brought a tear to the eye in reverence and a toast from the hardy Norwegian Troll-Biting Brotherhood, a small group of men in Bergen (with reciprocal membership) who, when they weren't drinking merrily, believed Trolls had become aquatic and were now terrorising fish at the bottom of the Fjords. This was never proven, but it never dissuaded them from drinking, getting naked and wrestling anything that got in their way – cats, dogs, statues and on one occasion, a small car.

Over the last forty years, the world's greatest Vampire Killing Lodge, tucked away in Putney in South West London, had fallen into obscurity and even mockery within the International Lodges. Where once they had won the revered Golden Fangs of Madrid, they now had to sit on tiny table 50 (a table that was practically in the men's toilets) at the annual black-tie dinner at a swanky hotel in London. For the last five years they had been awarded the wooden spoon for minimal vampire kills (ever) and a gardening voucher for £10. Johnny had taken the gardening voucher, and bought himself some marrow seeds and a trowel. Gardening had always been a bit of a passion and combined with a few spells he had learnt, he was eager to get going. This decision had, in fact, saved his life.

As to the history of The International Vampire Killing Society: it was a global secret society, which had been hidden in plain sight for hundreds of years. There were 48 Lodges throughout the UK, all of which were disguised as pubs. One of them was now disguised as a singles bar in Leeds, much to the grumbling amongst the real-ale-drinking Vampire Killers at The Crusty Eel in Bournemouth, who greatly disapproved.

Each Lodge covered a certain district and they were responsible for a variety of duties. Some kept the vampire population down. There were other societies that dealt with zombies, werewolves, fairies and pan-dimensional entities. Many of the societies had reciprocal membership and many of the cross-over Christmas karaoke parties had ended up in jeering and punch-ups. The Barnes Zombie Killing Society and the Devizes Werewolf Killing Society had been forbidden to meet up for a minimum of six years.

They were also quite competitive and occasionally provocative. The Glasgow, Liverpool and Manchester Lodges regularly sent plastic stakes and holy water in delicate perfume bottles to Carl at Christmas, as a gesture of 'goodwill'. On one occasion, one of the Irish Lodges hired female strippers disguised as vampires and sent them to serenade the Putney Vampire Killers, during their Monday night meeting (6.30 – 7.30pm). Lola had merely scared them to death when one of them, she thought, was flirting with her man and chased her up the Lower Richmond Road, all the way to Putney Bridge, before stomping back to the Lodge.

As to why the pubs had been called Lodges for the last 200 years, it was quite simple. One of the founding members (one of the greatest Vampire Killers of all time– who started The Great Lodge in Putney) had not been able to get into his local Masonic Lodge and had held a deep grudge. He decided he would call the protecting outposts Lodges. He also decided they would all be disguised as pubs. He liked all things 'pub'. He liked the atmosphere, he liked the banter and he liked the secret cover they provided.

Not all Lodges were the same. Each set of Vampire Killers had different traits. Some killed with stakes, some with guns, some with bows and arrows. The Great Putney Lodge was different for numerous reasons. It had a rich and revered history, was steeped in magic, and it was known that the building itself was alive. This was one of the reasons that made it unique.

Another reason was that no actual person could appoint a Putney Vampire Killer. The Pig & Phoenix chose who it wanted and when. Its decision was final. Not the Guardians, not the UK Executive Committee and not the Global Committee could challenge it. How it had recently appointed its Lodge members (over the last forty years) was via pool cues. There were seven magical pool cues and an enchanted pool table. Five cues had presently been appointed with two left undisturbed and gathering dust in one of the downstairs vaults. There were very few on the planet who knew of their power. The present cue custodians knew very little. The once great and glorious Putney Lodge had been gathering dust on many levels.

There was also a very strict rule book that all Lodges had to abide by. It listed what constituted an emergency, at which point regional Guardians had to be contacted. It then listed all manner of magical devices, ritual procedures, what clothes to wear, fasting, and what to take to the annual Christmas knees-up. It was exhaustive, and over the last 10 years the rules seemed to be expanding. The present rule book was propping up a table in the flat above the pub, where Carl lived. The other rule books were packed in a box somewhere, next to a broken guitar.

Most of the Lodges had regular visits from Guardians, Committee members and even reciprocal members –but not at the Great Putney Lodge. Letters, brochures and invitations seemed to fall lighter on the ground. They were, in many ways, left to their own devices but they always managed to receive the latest growing rule book.

Whereas other Lodges had very strict methods of recruiting Vampire Killers, how The Pig & Phoenix appointed cue custodians was a curious matter. Anyone observing would think that the Lodge merely liked good pool players and had chosen them after each had won a sudden-death pool game, which involved stripping. Some winners had been awarded a cue by Carl. If one vibrated in the vault, he would give it to the winner. It rarely, rarely happened. Only a few times. Now, of the appointed five Vampire Killers, only four met up. One member and one cue were no longer with them. For a Lodge to lose a Vampire Killer and a cue was a very serious matter and it seemed that Fergus had been lost forever.

It was widely believed that the Great Lodge should have replaced the cue but this was never done. How could the power of seven be possible with one cue missing? Why hadn't the Great Lodge severed the missing cue's magic? Without the power of seven, the Lodge was not seen as Great. It was seen as an embarrassment.

Whisperings in darkened corners suggested that the Great Lodge had, in fact, gone slightly senile. Many Lodges left the Great Lodge alone. Some saw it as a much-loved relative who was going batty but was allowed to sit alone, put a tea-cosy on his head and re-enact the Battle of Waterloo.

The Executive Committee did not take this into consideration because, since there were very few vampires in Putney, there were very few to actually kill. There was talk of finding a way to strip the Great Lodge of its right to appoint chosen Vampire Killers and merge the Great Lodge with the up-and-coming Richmond Vampire Killers. They were an elite team put together by the Executive Committee. They were young, fit and eager and got to sit at table 4 at the last Inter-Lodge dinner.

There were those who would see the Great Lodge torn down. There were those who plotted for the removal of the 'worst Vampire Killers ever' – the Great Embarrassment.

The once great Lodge based on the Lower Richmond Road – a stretch of road from Putney Bridge to Putney Common (and rumoured to even go beyond the Putney borders) – a road in the heart of Putney in South West London – had growing enemies.

2

Eric put down the phone, scratched his head and rubbed his eyes in a world-weary fashion. It was 3.30am and his brain was shattered. He'd been talking with his girlfriend in France again. In a nutshell, she was doing his head in. She was moody and demanding and he was getting very little sleep. She wanted him to live there and he wanted the opposite. Eric yawned and poured himself a large brandy. He glugged it down in one and pulled a face.

Eric was 53, had white hair, a long face, was tall and wore small spectacles on his nose. He had kindly, worried features that lent themselves more to humour than sadness.

Eric had bought his house in Putney, just off the Lower Richmond Road, about three years ago. He thought it was a good size, had a garden and was very close to the Thames and to The Pig & Phoenix. He was a keen rower and had joined up with one of the local boathouses. All he wanted now was a wife but his choice wasn't playing ball and he found her behaviour tiresome.

Without a wife, the house felt lonely to Eric and he decided he needed a house mate. A fellow bloke he could drink a few beers with and watch the footie. Someone to bring a bit more excitement to his life. He had really wanted to have a bit more excitement but with a slightly nervous temperament, he had always avoided 'crazy' stuff. Yes, he wanted change but perhaps he was over-cautious. It was most likely due to the strange black-outs he had suffered in his life. He would find himself missing a few hours of time and occasionally strange bits of information would fill his head. One time he woke up

11

and knew a set of survival skills involving an orange, a balloon and a cotton bud. He never knew why and no-one could get to the bottom of it. He would meet strange people, who asked him strange things and then…a black out.

Eric was pulled out of his thoughts by a knock at the door. Very suspiciously, he walked slowly over to it, didn't open it but asked through the wood, in a tone which sounded just a little too agitated, "Do you know what time it is? Who is it?"

He was answered by a man's very deep and gravelly voice: "I've come about the room."

Eric was outraged. What kind of a son of a bitch would knock at someone's door at 3.30am?

"Look…" Eric said angrily. "It's three-thirty in the morning and…"

"Please," the man slowly and softly said, "just open the door." There was a pause. Eric felt a strange feeling of confusion coming over him. He knew that he didn't want to do any such thing and found himself, bizarrely, opening the door and looking into a pair of mesmerizing green eyes. The face was not traditionally handsome but there was a strong masculinity about it. Eric also had to look up at him. He was tall and slender and wearing an expensive suit with an overcoat.

Thunder growled across the sky and in the distance lightning crackled. The rain battered down hard on the pavement and made a constant tapping noise on a metal rubbish bin across the road.

"I've come about the room," the green-eyed man said softly. He unfolded a piece of paper and gave it to Eric. Eric slowly tore his eyes away from the tall man standing in the doorway and tentatively took the paper from his hand. He lowered his eyes and read it. It was the advert he had written to be put in the local corner shop's window.

"Look, I gave the shop instructions to put the ad up tomorrow," Eric protested. "I don't know how you have this but…"

"It is tomorrow," the man interrupted in a slow and compelling voice. He smiled slowly and somewhat seductively.

Eric felt even more confused. None of this made sense.

Why was he even having this conversation? "But it didn't say where I lived. I just named the road and described the room."

The man narrowed his eyes and whispered: "The owners were good enough to tell me where you lived."

Eric shook his head, as it to clear it. "Look...I..."

"Is the room available or not?" the man interrupted casually. "Well...yes, it is...but," Eric spluttered.

"Good. I'll take it," said the man, walking slowly past Eric and into his house, carrying a long thin case and a bag over his shoulder.

Eric closed the door nervously. He felt a shudder go through him as he watched the tall man pour himself a drink and sit down on a large armchair, placing the long, thin case next to him.

3

Carl twiddled with the ring on his fourth finger and looked at Bert, Lola and Johnny. Carl was the owner of The Pig & Phoenix and had built up a loyal following of customers over the years. Every owner of the pub had also been a Vampire Killer and, in effect, ran the Society. He wasn't technically the leader but he seemed to fall naturally into the role.

Carl had pulled down the blinds and set up the pool table before the other three had arrived at the tradesman's entrance. Bert and Johnny lived about three minutes away from the pub – Lola had to come by bicycle, which she hated. Instead of chaining it up, she shoved it next to the large black bin in the little courtyard outside the side door, and hoped that someone would steal it. She gave it a kick for good measure.

"Pile of crap," she said to it and marched into the warm welcome of the pub's interior, her tiny heels pounding into the floor. On hearing the noise you'd think it was heavy-footed man in heels rather than a six stone woman. Her hair was wet and plastered against her face and her tight black skirt and shirt were stuck to her.

She pounded by the pool table and saw that Bert and Carl were playing. The pub was one of the places, if not the only place, that she was loved. Her dark brown eyes, set in a pretty elfin face, looked around for her fiancé. She saw him sitting near the table. He was drinking a pint of cider and smoking a cigarette.

The pub had a large interior, with pictures of Putney throughout the ages hanging on the fading red wallpaper. The ceiling was tobacco brown and the lighting leant a yellow glow to the surroundings. A fruit machine nestled in the corner near to the horseshoe bar and there was a slight smell of stale ale in the air mingled with fresh cigarette smoke.

"Is that the delicate footfall of our sweet little Pixie?" Bert teased and cackled huskily, as he leaned over the table and pocketed a red ball.

"Shut-up, Bert, or I'll seven ball ya," Lola retorted and sat down on a chair opposite Johnny. She took the cigarette out of his hand and took a long drag on it. "It's murder not being able to smoke around me mum's."

Lola had once seven balled Bert, about a year ago, leaving her fellow Vampire Killer to face the consequences of not sinking a single ball during their game. He had to drop his trousers and walk around the pool table and at the time he was wearing superman boxer shorts. The pub was also packed.

"And I don't wanna see them Chicken legs ever again. I'd rather kill a fahsand vampires on me own," Lola said flatly. Bert cackled harder and missed his shot.

"We've got problems," Carl said sternly, as he watched Lola exhale. She looked at Johnny's beer belly, turned towards Carl and said: "Tell me somefink I dunno," as she pointed at Johnny's slightly too tight T-shirt over his paunch.

Bert cackled even harder. Johnny, being deaf in one ear, didn't hear this and was watching Carl at the pool table.

"What?" Johnny asked, suddenly turning his attention to Lola, realising he'd missed something.

"Nuffink. Aren't ya gonna kiss me 'ello?" Lola replied casually and smiled warmly at him.

"What? Yes…yes." He leaned over the table a planted a kiss on her cheek.

"And they say romance is dead. No wonder," Lola whispered. She grabbed Johnny by the collar and pulled in for a long, passionate kiss. She let go of Johnny and he fell back in his seat, looking stunned.

"That's more like it," Lola purred.

Carl leaned on the pool table and chipped a red ball into a corner pocket and moved around to the side of the table.

"So," Bert said. "Go on then, wot is it?" Bert sat at the bar, sipping a beer and watching Carl move around the table. Bert knew that look on Carl's face. Carl was only about 34 years old and a short-arse, but he had an inner strength – a natural leader and an excellent dispatcher of vampires. He'd been running the pub for 10 years and been a Vampire Killer for the same. Bert could tell Carl was deeply concerned and this bothered Bert.

Carl reached his hand into his pocket and threw the small black ball onto the table. There was silence and Bert and Johnny exchanged grave looks of concern. Lola looked all three of them and frowned.

"Well...wot is it?" chirped Lola.

Silence.

Carl burst into laughter. "Oh my God," Carl said as he rubbed his hand over his closely-cropped hair. Carl had an infectious, warm laugh and Johnny and Bert cracked up with him. Both of them were pleased to see him laugh – he didn't laugh so much these days. Lola seemed to be one of the few that could actually make Carl really laugh. Lola, however, just frowned some more.

"Well? ...for fuck's sake...wot is it?" Lola angrily demanded. At 21 years of age and five foot in height, Lola looked like a delicate little elf but she had the temperament of a bad-tempered Viking with a hangover. "I 'ad to sneak out from me mum's to get 'ere and I'm sooo knackered after all these killings so get on wiv it...I mean it."

Johnny sighed and looked at the ceiling – so used to these outbursts he hardly noticed. Bert chuckled.

"'Ow long 'ave yoo been killing vampires, Pixie?" Bert asked in his 30-a-day voice, a cheeky look in his eyes.

Lola, poker-faced, glared back and said: "Don't call me Pixie, yer old bastard." She pointed her cue at him.

This did not offend Bert in the slightest, and in fact he just made a husky gurgling sound while his shoulders shook. Lola just looked at Johnny and said: "Someone tell me wot's goin' on."

"Patience," he said back, like a bored school-master.

"Patience, huh? Fuck that!" She jumped up over the table into Johnny's arms, putting her arms around his neck and planted a kiss on his lips. Carl and Bert rolled their eyes. She

16

certainly was fast and certainly agile.

"Anyway," Carl tried to interrupt this kiss, without much success but he continued talking. "I came by this all too easily."

Bert walked over to the pool table and picked up the small black ball.

"That can't be it...can it?" Bert looked at it in his hand.

Carl looked down on it and said quite gravely: "Well, if it is... we need to hand it over to the Guardians." This news made Johnny break off his kiss.

"No, we don't want them here!" This was exactly what Johnny feared. Under no circumstances did he want the Guardians anywhere near him. Lola looked at her man with adoring eyes.

Lola added: "They're a bunch of metro-sexual mingers. Not an alpha-male among 'em! Not like my Johnny." She landed another kiss on Johnny's mouth, who looked as though the oxygen was being sucked out of his body.

"'Ang about, Pixie. Yoo ain't never met 'em," Bert said gently with that characteristic twinkle in his eye.

Lola pulled herself away from the kiss. "I don't need to meet 'em – I just know." She then lunged back onto the kiss with the helpless Johnny underneath it.

"Well," said Bert, stroking his chin and turning his attention away from Lola, "if it is wot it is...then we need to do wot we need to do." He realised the seriousness of this small ball and it was a matter way, way out their league. Killing a few vampires was one thing – being in possession of 'The' Eight Ball – well, that was something else.

Carl potted another ball and said: "The thing is...I don't think it is what it is. I think it's not what it seems to be."

Lola pulled her face away from Johnny and said: "Wot the fuck are yer on about? I ain't got time for this. Time is money!"

"Chinese Bunny!" the three men impersonated her together.

This infuriated Lola. "I said time is money not Chinese Bunny! Shut-up...I mean it!"

"I mean it!" they squeaked together.

"Stop impersonatin' me!" Lola shouted.

"Stop impersonatin' me!" they all copied.

17

The three of them laughed hard as Lola looked on furiously. Johnny, feeling a little guilty and seeing his fiancée become redder faced, cleared his throat and said: "What do you think it actually is?"

Carl, trying to stop himself laughing, said: "Oo...I think either genuine or...quite an obvious deception."

"Well, which one is it?" Lola sighed, rolling her eyes.

"I don't know. Which is why I asked you here." Carl replied, rolling his eyes back at her.

"Some leader yoo are." Lola groaned and jumped down from Johnny's arms.

"I am not your leader." Carl knew they looked at him as their leader but there was not an elected leader. Yes, he had always been the one who had taken the lead but there hadn't been too much to do. The last two weeks had been a different story and he had taken on more and more responsibility. This night he had told them that he was going out on his own. They were confused that with the increase in activity he would do such a thing, but he had successfully persuaded them. They didn't resent his decision and agreed he must know what he was doing.

"Well, it can't be Johnny. He's too fat and Bert's too old!" She shoved a thumb dismissively in their general direction, grinning at Johnny. Although Lola totally adored her man, she could equally swing into acerbic teasing and swing back into large-eyed, adoring kitten.

"And yoo are too short," Bert added, huskily laughing again, "and angry". Lola stuck two fingers up at him – making Bert burst out laughing. Johnny rubbed his eyes wearily. There were times he yearned for death.

"Oh come on, piglet, where's ya sense of humour? It's OK when yer taking the piss out of me height but not when I mention ya weight!" Lola snapped. Johnny grabbed his belly and grinned.

Appeased by the gesture, Lola turned her attention back to Carl.

"Well, 'ow d'ya normally find out wot it is?" Lola growled at Carl.

"Well, that's why you need the Guardians," Carl answered in a matter-of-fact voice, taking the ball out of Bert's hand. He looked at it hard. Small and black and pretty unremarkable. It was hard to imagine that it was even possible that something so important could be in his hand. "They will be able to tell if this is the real thing or if it is, indeed, a fake."

All four of them gathered around Carl and looked at the ball in his hand. Lola prodded it with a tiny, red nail.

"Hey!" Carl exclaimed. "Watch it."

"Looks like a piece of crap," Lola snarled.

"Yeah, it does look like one of them cheap, girlie key-rings. The Pixie's right," Bert giggled.

"Ow!" he yelled as Lola stamped on his foot.

"So, either way...we've got to call the Guardians," explained Carl.

Johnny sighed with dread. Oh dear Lord...he thought, over and over again. He could feel his palms sweating and a feeling of nausea sweep over him. It would be tragedy for someone with a first class degree in psychology to be struck down in his prime. If only he could run but he couldn't.

"Exactly..." Carl replied. "I don't want to contact them any more than you do but we don't have a choice. Things have gone mental around here and it's just out of our league." Carl took a drag on his cigarette and sat down.

"Yes...but ya still 'aven't told me wot it actually bloody does! I didn't cycle 'ere just to look at a dodgy key-ring." Lola went over and sat next to Carl.

"Maybe it's one of them magic Eight Balls that tells the future...y'know, yoo are goin' on a long journey," Bert roared with laughter as he picked up his cue and played a few shots. Lola gave an outrageous high-pitched giggle.

"Oww. Jesus, Lola," Carl grimaced, shoving his hands over his ears.

"So, wot's so fuckin' amazin' about it then?" Lola, turning to face Carl, demanded.

Lola knew what your standard Eight Ball was. It was that black ball that was potted last in a game of pool and thereby ending the game. If at any point during the game it was accidentally potted, the game would end and be won by the opponent.

Carl looked at Lola and lowered his hands. "I can't believe you don't know. It's like not knowing who Hitler was."

"Who?" Lola asked innocently. Carl swallowed hard. He knew that she could be joking or that she really didn't know. He thought it best to ignore the remark and explain to her the significance of the Eight Ball.

Carl walked behind the bar and pulled out the Lodge rule book, which he had brought downstairs to read and had discovered there was a whole page dedicated to the infamous Eight Ball. He threw the book down on the pool table.

"The Eight Ball is a device that can open up a portal into other worlds. It ultimately holds the balance of good and evil," Carl said softly.

"Maybe we should stick it on ebay," Lola said in a bored voice, looking at Johnny and mouthing the words, 'kiss me' at him. Johnny went to the pool table and watched Bert, shaking his head.

Carl ignored this glib remark and continued. "The device was created hundreds of years ago by one of the first Guardians, who was a very powerful warlock. He created it because there was a Vampire War and he thought he could create a device that would increase chances of good triumphing."

Carl noticed that Lola's concentration was wandering over to Johnny and grabbed her chin and turned it to him.

"At that time, the device was not the Eight Ball...are you listening?" Carl barked, as Lola's concentration wandered.

"Oo...Carl...yer so masterful. Yes, I'm listenin'." Lola purred jokily at him. Carl cast a pleading look at Johnny, who just shrugged back at him. Johnny took a swig of his cider and took a drag on a cigarette.

"It has taken on many shapes over the years. Now, the trouble was that as he was creating it, he had been bitten by a vampire but because he was so powerful, it took a lot longer for him to turn. And, as he slowly turned into a vampire, he was still working on the device which means the device is able to be used by both vampires and warlocks/witches alike."

"Stupid bastard," Lola said with contempt, crossing her arms.

Carl took a deep breath, counted to five and continued: "OK, so the device has not always been the Eight Ball. It has been changed from object to object and hidden out of sight for years. In the 1970s, it became the Eight Ball."

"Yeah, I remember that now. I read it in an old newsletter downstairs," Bert laughed.

"'Ow bloody old are ya?" Lola asked.

"It's 'ard to tell, Pixie. I moisturise nightly," Bert said mischievously. His cheeky face broke in a mass of laughter lines.

Carl continued: "There was a massive debate between Guardians as to whether it should be destroyed or not. However, before the matter could be resolved the Eight Ball was stolen and has remained missing ever since, until now."

Carl held the Eight Ball between his fingers and looked at it hard, his handsome face scrutinising it.

"Well, 'ow d'ya know that's not a key-ring, then?" Lola asked. "It looks like crappy plastic."

"Ah...now this is how I know there's something different about it." Carl smiled warmly at Lola. "Get your cue."

Suspiciously, Lola went over the bar where she had left her cue and picked it up. She walked back over to Carl.

"Ok...point your cue at me." Carl asked.

"My pleasure," Lola said seductively and complied. With the cue in Carl's face, he took the end of it in one hand and moved it towards the Eight Ball. The Eight Ball started to glow a strange blood-red colour as Lola's cue tip started to glow green.

"It's never done that before," she chirped. "Hey, Johnny, Bert – look at this. Me tip's all gone glowy."

Bert and Johnny stepped away from the pool table and joined the other two.

"Blimey," Bert excitedly said. "Can I 'ave a go?"

"Sure." Carl outstretched his arm and, each in turn, they pointed their cue tips at the Eight Ball. Carl's tip glowed indigo, Johnny's blue and Bert's yellow. The Eight Ball's light expanded to about three feet. It also seemed to shake.

"So, it must be real then," Bert said, looking at the light coming from the ball.

"Not necessarily," said Carl.

"How do you mean?" asked Johnny, looking at the red light.

21

"Our cues are magical. It's logical they would react to a strong magical artefact."

The actual extent of the magic they had witnessed so far was merely shoving their cues through vampires' hearts but ever since becoming half-dead, Johnny had become ever-increasingly hopeful there was more magic to be had.

"I think it's a good fake, that's all," Carl said in a concerned voice.

"Why would anyone fake the Eight Ball?" Bert asked.

"Well," Johnny replied in a slightly pompous voice, "As a device that holds the ultimate balance of good and bad and can open up a portal into other worlds, I would imagine it would be highly sought after. A fake would either be created as a decoy or created to con someone."

Carl nodded in agreement. "Yes, I think it's been created to con us."

"But why? There's only four of us...we have the lowest vampire count out of every Lodge of any time. We're hardly important," Johnny said. "We were even awarded the Swedish wooden ash-tray for inactivity at the last Christmas dinner. The bloody Angry Toad in Camden got top prize – again. Smug bastards."

"Well, they always win – don't they," Bert grumbled. "Bloody Camden."

"I hate those dinners," said Johnny.

"I've never been. Why 'ave I never been, Johnny?" Lola turned to Johnny accusingly.

Carl cleared his throat and the three turned their attention back to him. It was bad enough having to go to the dinners – they didn't think the attendees would understand Lola. Female numbers in the vampire killing community were growing, much to the displeasure of many old committee members but Lola – she would probably declare war and get them permanently barred. They had tried to keep all dwindling dinner invitations from her but she wouldn't let it go.

"OK, back to the Eight Ball. Look, being in possession of it doesn't make sense unless it has nothing to do with us but has something to do with the Guardians," Carl explained.

"Huh?" Lola asked.

"OK...in the last two weeks, we have killed about 30

vampires a night. Normally, there's about one a month. Under such circumstances, what should we have done?" Carl asked in a school-masterly way.

Each of the other three looked to the floor – shuffling their feet.

"Well, what we should have done is contact the Guardians," Carl said.

"Oh, yeah…" the other three answered together, sheepishly.

"But, we didn't. We thought it would blow over and besides, nobody wants the Guardians to come stay," Carl said with a sigh.

"No…no…no!" Johnny said emphatically.

"So, what then goes and happens yesterday? A vampire begs me for their life and tells me where the Eight Ball is," Carl began to explain.

"Yeah, pull the other one," Lola snorted.

"My thoughts exactly. So, it told me its story and I killed it anyway. Apparently, a newly turned vampire would have the ball and I was told where to find this corpse-walker," Carl continued in a soft voice.

"When ya put it like that, sounds fuckin' obvious." Lola scowled.

"But wot's the point?" Bert asked, his kind face wrinkling into a frown.

Carl nodded in agreement to the question. What would be the point in conning the Putney Vampire Killers into thinking they had the Eight Ball? Was it another Lodge having a laugh at their expense? Carl could believe it but his gut instinct told him otherwise.

"I think it's all to do with calling the Guardians into Putney. When we didn't call them about the increase in vampire activity, another tactic was deployed. One of the world's most famous artefacts shows up…just handed over…to me," Carl said in a suspicious tone.

Lola saw the perplexed look on Carl's face and blew her fringe out of her eyes.

"Let's just not tell the Guardians. Let's bury it in the garden next to the budgie. Wot they don't know won't 'arm 'em."

Carl smiled at her. He knew that she was trying to appease him but this matter was far too serious to dismiss.

"The thing is, I don't think it's going to be that easy. Someone or something wants the Guardians here. If we don't mention the Eight Ball to them, I think something even bigger will happen. I really think we have no choice but to contact them and warn them," Carl said with a sense of resignation.

"Can't we just post 'em the ball?" Lola asked. "Why do they 'ave to come 'ere?"

Carl picked up the Lodge book and waved it back and forth in front of her eyes.

"Because that's the way it works and there will need to be an investigation..." Carl said softly, looking around the pub cautiously.

On hearing the word 'investigation' Johnny closed his eyes in dread. It was a word that made him cringe.

"They will need to be fed and watered," Bert said, rubbing the back of his neck. "And boy, do they like to be fed and watered."

"Well, they're not staying with me..." spluttered Johnny, feeling a mild panic attack coming on.

"Don't worry. They'll stay here...they'll need to be in a Lodge anyway," Carl said and added:

"So, if we're agreed, I will contact them now."

"Yeah," muttered Lola.

"OK," sniffed Bert

"Suppose," said Johnny in a strained voice.

All four of them lifted their cues and banged them twice on the floor – a gesture of approval.

"OK...looks like I'll be having guests," Carl whispered, looking at his ring and twisting it.

4

The green-eyed man lay back on the bed and stared at the ceiling. He blew out the smoke from his rollie and watched it disperse around him. He looked over to a clock. It showed 4.30am.

The room had Eric's rowing pictures all around the walls, as well as trophies. Green eyes looked around in a slightly amused way, twinkling with malice. He took another drag on his rollie and sat up. He reached under the bed, pulled out a pool-cue case, put it on his lap and opened it. He looked down in pleasure. A blood-red light radiated from the case – making his eyes glow a darker shade of green. In this light, his face took on a dark and twisted look.

He pulled out the two parts of a black cue and smiled while he screwed them together with pleasure. Once connected, it shone and, if his smile could become more demonic, it did. He gripped it between his hands and felt the power radiate through it. The cue tip glinted a dark, blood red.

The green-eyed man walked over to the window, opened it and leapt out. He was on the second floor but no-one below would've seen him land.

Downstairs, Eric looked up at the ceiling and looked puzzled. He pushed his glasses up to the bridge of his nose and continued to look puzzled. He still felt confused about his new tenant and couldn't work out why he had let him stay. If anyone else had turned up at 3.30am, he would've told them to fuck off! He felt odd and thought he had better try and find out some more about the strange man. The first time he left the house, he would take a look around his room.

5

Johnny sat on his hands and watched nervously as the Guardians glugged down their third bottle of champagne. If he could get away with rocking back and forth and singing a lullaby, he would. They had been sitting at the bar, saying very little and drinking. Carl had contacted them immediately and they arrived at 4.45am. Bert, Carl, Johnny and Lola sat at a table nearby, watching them. The Guardians had turned up, said very little, went straight over and perched at the bar and started quaffing champagne. Carl gave them whatever they asked for.

It was now 5.50am on Saturday morning - the morning of the annual Oxford and Cambridge Boat Race and soon Carl would have to open up the pub to his staff. Carl would have six barmaids and a tall Irish chap called Graham working behind the bar today. He would also have two bouncers on the door – which he did every Friday and Saturday evening. The juke-box would be blaring out songs but the usual bar flies would abandon ship until the annual event was over. The tall, thin bus-driver and the small and chubby bus-driver called Cunning Colin and Grumpy Mike would refuse to come in. Why it was they never crashed their buses the following morning after a heavy drinking session was a mystery to many people. One of them had even been bus driver of the year for two years running.

Lola had never met the Guardians before and she was confused. Her piercing eyes glared at the back of their heads. Her fringe was a little too long and her hair was annoying her eyes. She blew upwards, pushing the hair out of the way.

"Do they do anyfink else apart from drink?" Lola asked Bert, turning her huge brown eyes to him. Bert's blue eyes twinkled back at her, wrinkling his weather-beaten face.

"Don't look like it." Bert grinned at her. "Glad they ain't staying wiv me. I couldn't afford it...already got one ponce." Carl chuckled. Johnny nervously smiled and was trying to lower his heart-rate by tapping on his left wrist.

The three Guardians stood up, went outside to the pub garden and beckoned the four of them to follow. They stood up quickly and followed them, exchanging looks of concern. They all sat around a picnic table with an umbrella (which was being battered in the rain) – three on one side and four on the other with Lola sitting on Johnny's knee. Johnny tried to get her to sit next to him but she shoved her way back onto his lap. As it was dark outside, Carl had turned on one of the garden lights.

"Why the fuck are we outside?" Lola whispered to Johnny, who nudged her in the ribs to be quiet.

The garden was a large L shape made up of concrete slabs, and hosted about a dozen picnic tables. There was a flower bed down the right-hand side of the garden, which had numerous attractive flowers growing. It wasn't the most beautiful place in the world but people seemed to like the atmosphere.

Although Carl was thinking about the Guardians and the possibly fake Eight Ball, he was also thinking about Boat Race Day, which was to take place – very soon! As landlord of the pub, there was quite a lot to organise and also quite a lot of money to look forward to. He then remembered how he and Katie used to organise the day together and he had to stop himself there and then. Katie was gone. He must focus.

Carl took a deep breath, twisted the ring on his finger and thought about all the cash he was going to make – all thanks to Oxford and Cambridge supporters. On a good Boat Race Day, he could make about £50,000 – cash. Boat Race Day was a great day for all the pubs and restaurants in Putney. He just needed to keep the champagne flowing and the barbecue going. It was a day when he had a stash of cash and it was a great feeling. That's what he needed to focus on – not the Eight Ball, not Katie – just cash. It was less painful.

The first Guardian, who liked to be called Marilyn, leaned back and took a long drag on his cigarette, or gasper, as he called them. He was in his late sixties, six foot tall, had noticeably dyed black hair to his shoulders with grey roots and plucked eye-brows. His jeans hugged his narrow hips tightly and his black T-shirt showed a tiny beer belly sticking out. He looked over at Jonah, who resembled an old and distant cousin of a giant slug, and who was flicking food off his tight, pink gingham shirt. He also had fixed his eyes on Lola.

"Well?" asked Marilyn in an annoyed voice. "What do you think?" He looked down the table at Jonah. He noticed the huge amount of crumbs on his clothes and felt a little queasy. Jonah, who was absorbed in the food-flicking and ogling, didn't reply. Marilyn exhaled indignantly and gestured to Max to do something.

Max, the third Guardian, who was sitting between the two, crossed his heavily tattooed arms and was slowly smouldering with anger. He turned his head towards Jonah and saw what was so occupying him. While he did this, Lola looked him up and down and thought he reminded her of her 'Sex God' TV chef – except that he looked nothing like him. He had dark cropped hair and a cropped beard and piercing light blue eyes. He was attractive in a battered, warhorse kind of way, Lola thought.

"Chap, can you turn your attention away from women for one bloody moment. Marilyn was talking to you," he barked in a crisp, upper-class accent. Lola liked the sound of his voice and momentarily imagined him naked with a miner's lamp on his head doing star-jumps. The reason for this, was... again, never known.

Jonah took his eyes away from Lola. They were the kind of eyes that had seen far too many whiskeys and the kind of eyes that wanted to see more. "Hmmm?" he murmured, realising that he had been asked a question.

"Well, chap, you know what I think," Max growled to Marilyn, not waiting for Jonah to even reply. "I don't like the sound of this at all. They should have contacted us as soon as activity increased. Those are the rules and rules should be followed. Vampire killing is like Rugby. You can't have people buggering around doing their own thing."

"Yeeeesss," drawled Marilyn, raising an immaculate eyebrow. "I know what you think but I was actually asking Jonah, who appears to be deaf to my voice – again." Marilyn had a curious way of pronouncing his name – JO-NAAR. In fact, Marilyn had a peculiar way of dragging out most if his vowel sounds – especially when disgusted with something or someone – usually someone and usually Jo-naar.

"Is there a curry house near here?" Jonah slurred in a South London accent. He was 6ft 8", nearly as broad as he was tall and had a shock of thick, white, curly hair, which once had been red. He wore thick-lensed glasses that seemed glued to the bridge of his nose. He casually leaned back, rubbing his hands over his belly as he looked around the garden.

Marilyn threw his hands up in despair as Bert, Johnny, Carl and Lola quickly all pointed to the right and said in unison: "Down the road."

"They won't be open, however," explained Carl.

"They will for me," slobbered Jonah.

"Super," said Marilyn, looking at Jonah with total contempt. "Yes, let Gollum eat. It's only been an hour since it last consumed a whale."

Jonah curled his lip, brushed off more crumbs and took another slug of his champagne.

"Tell me, Carl, do you have any good shots behind the counter? I'm in the mood for a little pick-me-up."

Marilyn tapped Max on the arm and pointed angrily at Jonah. Max gestured with his hand to Marilyn to calm down and turned to Jonah.

"Chap, forget about your gut for one moment. This is a very serious matter." Max was glaring at the four of them with bright blue challenging eyes. He was about 50 and his appearance and accent were in direct contradiction. From neck to toe, he was covered in tattoos. However, his accent spoke of public school debauchery, rugby and possibly a favourite distant cousin of the Queen. He was wearing a rugby sweat-shirt and jeans and trainers.

"We can discuss it over a vindaloo," Jonah drooled, turning to look at his comrades. "Why can't we just sit down, have a curry and have a chat about it."

"Oh...God," sighed Marilyn, looking at Jonah with disgust. "Gobble...gobble...gobble..."

"We didn't come here just to eat, chap," Max snapped at Jonah. "We have got to get this investigation going. We must be disciplined about this. I am not carrying you home after a curry blow-out, chap. I'm sorry, chap, but there are limits."

"Oh come on, Max. There's plenty of time to eat, drink and discuss." Jonah slurred his words as he turned his attention back to Johnny, Bert, Lola and Carl. "Wouldn't you four like to go for a curry? Have a little drink – have a little chat? Hmmm?" His smile showed yellowing teeth, and if his watery eyes could've taken themselves off to A&E they would've.

Lola looked at him and shuddered. She could not believe that these three were Guardians. It just did not make any sense. How could Jonah possibly do anything in a battle? What did he do – eat them? Was that his secret power – digestion? Johnny and Bert also caught themselves almost looking at him in open-mouthed horror. Johnny couldn't face the idea of having to watch this man eat a curry. It may even be preferable to turn himself in as a corpse-walker. He tapped his wrist harder under the table. Please make them go...please make them go...he whispered to himself inside his head. None of them had replied to Jonah.

"Well...would you like to go for a curry?" Jonah demanded.

The four of them ummed and erred and looked at each other and back to the Guardians but before they could answer, Max spoke.

"Chap, we need to get this sorted out immediately. Why do you always want to go for a bloody curry?" Max smashed his fist down on the table – making the drinks spill.

"All I'm saying is, let's go and eat. Why are you always so negative?" Jonah said accusingly. "What is so wrong with wanting to have something to eat?"

"Well, some of us like to try and keep our figures, darling," Marilyn cattily remarked.

"Looks like a battle you're starting to lose," he fired back.

Marilyn narrowed his eyes at Jonah and opened and closed his mouth like a suffocating goldfish. "Oh, so you can hear me, can you?" God...how he would love to whip that

30

grotesque bitchy blob.

"Enough. What kind of example of you setting the chaps??" Max gestured, almost dismissively, at the four sitting opposite him.

"No, yoo three stop it!" squeaked Lola. "There's not one alpha male among any of ya. Not like Johnny."

Johnny spluttered, looked at Lola and back to the three Guardians staring at him, and wished he was somewhere, anywhere else. Oh dear God...what was she doing? What was she doing?

6

Sophie lived more or less on her own in a seven bedroom house on Putney Common South. The house overlooked the patch of common where Bert, Johnny, Carl and Lola had been carrying out much of their recent slayings. It was close to the church where Carl had got hold of the Eight Ball and not that far from her local pub, which was next to the 22 bus terminal. It was also about ten minutes away from The Pig & Phoenix.

Sophie's father was a very rich antiques dealer and he moved around the world and was rarely at his London home. Her two sisters had moved out of the family home years ago and so, here she was, at the age of 30, living in a massive, beautiful house apart from the fourth floor – which wasn't quite so beautiful. Her mother had divorced her father years ago and had moved to New York, where she now lived with a Jazz pianist called Blade.

The house had four levels but the top floor had been 'abandoned' many years ago because of a fight between her father and her aunt. Her aunt, who was also a very wealthy woman, had had a room there at the top of the house for a reason Sophie could no longer remember.

One day, about five years ago, a pigeon had flown into her aunt's room and made a nest in a chest of drawers. Her father, on discovering this, told the aunt that she must clear it up immediately. Her aunt, a staunch vegetarian, refused categorically to remove it and then, as the fight went on over letter and telephone calls, Sophie's father made the decision to lock the door until such time as the aunt sorted it out or until he sold the property. So, the door was locked, the pigeon left alone and the fourth floor pretty much left to its own devices. It became known merely as 'The pigeon room' and had been locked for five years.

Sophie's bedroom was on the second floor and in many ways it was a self-contained flat. It had everything in there that she wanted and everything was fine until about two weeks ago. Quite a few bottles of white wine had been consumed in that time and so she could not quite remember the exact date as to when she first started having a feeling that she was not alone in the house. She had really lived on her own for a long time and living alone had never bothered her. However, she had a feeling that there was something around. Just that eerie feeling that someone is watching you and it had become stronger – as if increasing unseen eyes were watching her. It was starting to make her feel very uncomfortable, especially when returning home from The Skipping Goat at the end of an evening.

Then today, around 4.35am, when she was slowing passing into sleep, Sophie heard a sound coming from upstairs. Right upstairs – fourth floor upstairs. There was a loud thump and Sophie's heart began to pound. She felt a cold sweat beginning and that dreaded feeling of 'what do I do?'

There was no way in heaven she was going to go and investigate and Sophie found that she was actually too scared to move. She could pick up the phone and call the police, but unfortunately she wasn't in their good books.

In her inebriated state, starting to have feelings that she wasn't alone, she had made quite a few phone calls to the police in the last week. When the police had come along to investigate, she had fallen asleep. She knew that if she called, it would take at least two hours for them to get to her, if they didn't just ignore her completely. It would be understandable, the reasonable part of her brain worked out. So, what did that leave? Should she call a friend? Should she make a run for the door? And go where? To a neighbour…as all these thoughts were rushing through her head, she heard another thump and, this time, it was on the same floor as her bedroom. In fact, it sounded as if it was just down the corridor.

Sophie managed to crawl out of her bed and made her way,

as silently as she could, into her wardrobe and pulled a jacket over her head. It didn't cover her feet and she shoved a shirt over them. She managed to do this quietly and she took a deep breath and held it. She heard footsteps walking down the corridor and Sophie started to shake with fear. She should call the police…she should call the police…the phone was in her hand but she was terrified.

She heard the walking stop outside her door. She took a deep breath and could feel her heart painfully pounding in her chest. Then the door handle of her room was turning. It was quite a stiff handle and not one that you could open easily. She heard it twist and turn and then it opened. Sophie had never been so scared in her life. Oh God, who was it? What did they want? She didn't want to die.

She heard someone enter into her bedroom and start to slowly walk around. She then heard, and saw through a crack in the wardrobe, somebody standing outside of the wardrobe door. She wanted to be sick. She wanted to scream. Time expanded and contracted all at the same time and it seemed totally unreal that she should find herself in this situation.

The figure seemed to leave and walk away. Sophie had just breathed out slightly when the wardrobe door was flung open. Sophie found herself looking into a pair of green eyes.

"Fergus?" she whispered. "Fergus is that really you?"

7

Max stared at Lola with total disbelief. Johnny was laughing almost wildly in an attempt to over-compensate for Lola, and if he could've crawled away on his belly, he would've done.

"You must excuse Lola. It's the...err...err..." Johnny elbowed Lola in the ribs. Lola merely fixed him with a stubborn look of defiance.

"I mean it, Johnny. This is all rubbish," she snarled with a thumb gesture at the Guardians.

Jonah merely drooled, looking her up and down, and Marilyn was open-mouthed. He had never heard anything like this in his years as a Guardian. He was never overly fond of finding himself as an overseer of the Putney Lodge. He had seen members come and go and dealt with some strange characters but he was starting to think these four were probably a Guardian's nightmare. He had met Carl, Bert and Johnny briefly before at a Lodge dinner. Lola he had never met. She had been a member for three years and had replaced Old Georgie, when he finally had to retire and take up a position in the local bowling club. Former members often joined the local bowling club – a bit like a Dad's Army. As Putney was such a quiet lodge, they really were on the outskirts and didn't even come along on the trips to Amsterdam to meet up at the European award ceremonies.

Bert found the entire situation hilarious and was hiding deep, deep laughter by coughing and taking out a hankie. Carl was momentarily stunned and then immediately said:

"How about I order us in a curry and we can continue this conversation in the vault?"

"What? What did that pipsqueak say?" Max pointed at Lola with his thumb, copying her gesture. His tone was half angry and half amused. He fixed her with his penetrating blue eyes.

"Don't ya know it's rude to point? Wiv yer accent I fought ya would've known that," Lola growled at him. "And can't ya just stop arguing and can't we just get on wiv finding out about this stupid plastic ball?"

"Stupid ball?" Marilyn sniffed at her. "Stupid ball? I can't believe you are actually a Lodge member. What are things coming to?" He threw his arms up in the air dramatically.

"I'll tell ya why I am, it's cos this Lodge chose me after a game of sudden death strip pool, and being a Guardian, yoo should know that," Lola scowled, throwing her hands on her hips.

"I was being sarcastic, dear," Marilyn said and looked as though there was a bad smell under his nose.

"I ain't ya fucking dear. I just wanna know wot it's all about for fuck's sake," Lola barked and blew her fringe away from her eyes.

"Good God, you have a foul mouth on you, chap," said Max.

"Yeah, well – yer kinda sexy, actually," she said and Johnny threw his head in his hands.

This was too much for Bert, who pretended to drop something on the floor and couldn't stop laughing.

"Have you dropped something, 'sir'?" Jonah slobbered with a sarcastic overtone.

Bert realised Jonah was talking to him and shook his head and continued coughing.

Max was actually, for one of only a few times in his life, stunned. He looked to the left, he looked to the right and he looked into his pint glass and was silenced for a moment. He blinked and then he burst out laughing.

"Great Lodge, you are one demented harpy. I pity your boyfriend..." Max whispered and stared at her hard.

"Fiancé, actually...we're gonna be married soon," Lola corrected, turning to look at Johnny. "Wot's a harpy?"

Max found himself begin to shake with laughter. "Is she being serious?"

"Gawd only knows," Bert wheezed between helpless gasps of laughing. "We don't."

"Are yoo laughin' at me?" Lola asked defensively, looking at all the men around her.

"Great Lodge, no," Max replied. "I don't think any of us would dare."

"No, Pixie – not at all," Bert gasped, as if he was recovering from an asthma attack.

"Pixie? You call her Pixie? She's like a crazed goblin with a pitchfork," snorted Max, laughing hard.

"Maybe we could call her Pitchfork Pix," Bert suggested, while weeping helplessly.

"Oi...no-one is callin' me that," Lola declared as she wagged a finger in front of all of them.

"No Pixie," chuckled Bert.

"Pitchfork it is," Max said and threw his head back and laughed.

Johnny was just relieved that at least one of the Guardians hadn't been offended. He was also relieved that not one of them had sensed his half-dead condition. Maybe alcohol dampened their sixth sense. Jonah he figured was far too drunk to notice anything. Marilyn was clearly in a bad mood and Max, well, he hadn't quite figured him out yet. Luckily, Lola had amused him.

Carl had watched this and he also was relieved that no-one had got into a serious row. Lola was just deeply unpredictable. It was a quality they had all become used to. At least she hadn't asked him about the teenage rock star wife and the 1980s. Carl would just have to carry her over his shoulder and lock her in the loo if that happened.

"Are you going to tolerate this behaviour, Max?" Marilyn demanded. "They've broken the rules. They should've contacted us when all these Gee-zahs started showing up." Gee-zahs was a term Marilyn used to describe vampires.

"Well, yes, they should've. However, judging by Pitchfork, part of me can't help feeling sorry for all those un-dead chaps," Max said and roared with laughter.

"Have you taken leave of your senses? We really should punish them," insisted Marilyn.

"Oh, I think that is already taken care of," Max said and winked at Lola, who caught herself momentarily smiling, and quickly replaced it with a frown.

37

Carl nodded his head in agreement and Johnny sighed.

"So, did you say something about ordering a curry?" Jonah asked Carl.

"Well, yes. We could order a curry and go into the vault and discuss the situation," Carl replied. He wanted to move this on as quickly as possible.

"And you have the Eight Ball on you?" Jonah enquired.

"Yes. Do you want it now?" Carl asked.

"Great Lodge, no," Jonah drooled. "Wait until we've eaten."

8

Sophie leaned on her elbow and looked over at Fergus lying next to her. He was on his back, hand behind his head and staring up at the ceiling.

"I thought you had died," she whispered to him. "Why didn't you contact me?"

Without looking at her, Fergus took her hand and kissed it. "I couldn't."

"Are you back for good?" Sophie asked softly.

"No," Fergus answered, still looking upwards.

Sophie looked at him for a while. He seemed a thousand miles away from her and seemed so very different to the man she had known.

Frustrated, Sophie climbed out of bed, reached for a T-shirt and put it on her petite body. She took a cigarette out of a packet and lit it. She sat on the edge of the bed, away from him.

She inhaled deeply and breathed out the smoke.

"So, what do you want, Fergus?" Sophie asked, wanting him to look over at her. "Apart from the obvious."

Fergus smiled his dark smile and turned his gaze away from the ceiling towards the small, blonde woman.

"I need your help" he said in a husky voice.

"What is it? Money?" Sophie asked, expecting the answer to be yes. She knew she could be foolish when it came to matters of the heart and thought she'd get straight to the point.

"No, I need you to deliver some things for me," Fergus said, turning onto his side and looking Sophie directly in the eyes.

"Things? What kind of things are we talking about?" Sophie asked suspiciously. Her eyes looked over the man in her bed and she felt her heart skip a beat in fear.

"Some presents," he whispered.

"Fergus, this sounds…wrong," Sophie said weakly, looking for the right word to use.

"You know me so well." Fergus smiled at her and sat up on the bed.

"What do you want me to do?"

"I want you to give some gifts to a few of your friends," Fergus said, getting up off the bed and walking over to a table, where he had placed a bag. He reached inside and brought out a small, rather unremarkable brown box.

He walked over to Sophie and handed it over to her. She slowly and reluctantly reached out her hands and took the box from him.

"Which friends are we talking about?" Sophie asked quietly, feeling a sense of dread build up in her stomach.

"I want you to give them to Becky, Sarah, Jenna, Holly, Mandy, Jack, Brian and Tara today," Fergus said darkly, placing a hand on her shoulder.

"Why them?" Sophie asked, swallowing hard.

"Because they are your friends," Fergus answered in a matter-of-fact manner. Sophie couldn't look at him. She wanted to run but she lacked the courage.

"Yes, they are my friends and they also happen to all be bar staff," Sophie managed to say in a tiny voice.

"Yes…all the way along the Lower Richmond Road."

Sophie had the horribly gut-wrenching feeling of knowing she was being used and also knowing that she couldn't refuse.

"And why can't you give them to them?" Sophie managed to ask.

Fergus smiled wickedly. "Because I'm asking you to," he replied quietly and gave a slow, half smile.

9

The three Guardians and four Vampire Killers sat around a large, round table in the vault. The 'vault' was beneath the pub and had been there for many lifetimes. The vault consisted of one large room with the round table in the middle of it surrounded by seven seats. There were shelves covered in dusty old books and a flat-screen television in the corner. There were other large rooms. One contained a pool table and the wall was covered in pictures and painted portraits of former members going back hundreds of years. There were also cabinets with trophies in them and on the wall a fishing rod. Beneath the fishing rod was a stuffed 18lb barbel fish.

"It's like somefink out of a Hammer Horror film, innit?"Lola chirped to Marilyn, who was sitting next to her. Marilyn merely raised an eyebrow and said: "Yeessss." He then helped himself to a poppadom.

"Are you seriously telling me that you eat curry off this sacred table?" Max asked, his arms crossed.

"Err...no," Carl answered, looking around uneasily. "We just thought that as you were here, on such an honoured occasion, that we would eat off it."

Lola kicked an empty burger carton under the table.

"Hmm," Max said sceptically. "Because to do so it's absolutely not on, chap."

Johnny kicked an empty polystyrene carton further under the table.

Bert was tucking into a vindaloo. Nobody could even look at Jonah. The noise alone would have stopped the heart of a stampeding bull-elephant.

"So, 'ow do you check out this key ring fing that twat invented?" Lola asked Max. She had decided that Jonah had escaped from a psychiatric hospital and 'the other one' was just annoying. Max, to her, seemed incredibly grouchy – but very authoritative.

"Key ring thing that twat invented?" Max repeated, looking horrified.

"Yeah, that stupid half-vampire bloke. The one who invented the Eight Ball," Lola said. She looked down at her manicured nails. Damn. Two were broken. Vampire killing was costing her a small fortune in manicures.

"Madam," Jonah drooled.

"Yeah?" Lola answered, looking up from her nails to Jonah. Fuck – she'd rather be out slaying a hundred corpse-walkers than be here with this weird fucking bloke.

"Would you pass the lime pickle?" He smiled, showing bits of poppadum in the corners of his mouth.

"Errr...yeah, sure." Lola replied, turning away fast. She grabbed the lime pickle and offered it, without looking back at him.

"Thank you," he said, taking it and momentarily touching her hand. Ahh! Her mind shrieked and for a few seconds as it went to her happy place – a place of rugby players with big thighs, getting their white shorts muddy. She saw steam rise up from a scrum.

"Well, madam. The first thing we will need to do will be to perform a protective ritual," Jonah said slowly, as if he were talking about fixing a washing machine. His voice jolted Lola back to the present moment.

"Wot...now?" she challenged.

"Yes, chap...now," Max challenged back.

Lola narrowed her eyes at him and put her hands on her hips. She looked at all three of the Guardians.

"But yer all pissed," she said in an exasperated voice.

The Guardians looked at each other and burst out laughing.

"You call this pissed?" Jonah slurred, wiping the tears away from his eyes with the back of his hand.

"Yoo bloody well sound it," Lola growled. "I doubt any of ya could play pool."

The three of them went quiet. This was, indeed, a strong insult. To suggest that a Putney Vampire Killer was too drunk to play pool was one thing. To say it to a Putney Lodge Guardian was potential suicide.

"She doesn't drink," Carl blurted out, standing up quickly. "She doesn't know all the rules yet. She didn't mean it." He appealed to the other three. Dear God – there were times when he wished he could just gag her. There just seemed to be no brakes. One tiny foot glued to the accelerator and no bloody brakes.

The three Guardians raised their eyebrows.

"Lola, say sorry." Carl looked at her. His whole face took on a very serious expression. Lola pouted slightly.

"Now, Lola," Carl ordered.

Lola scowled. "OK. I'm sorry," she said quietly. The three of them crossed their arms and frowned at her.

"And this once great Lodge wanted you? It sounds…very… tricky," Marilyn said scornfully, turning to look at Max.

"Oi," Lola pointed in his face. "Yoo listen to me, Marzipan, or whatever ya callin' yerself."

Oh crap! thought Carl.

Marilyn leaned back and looked at the tiny finger pointing in his face.

"Marilyn," Max corrected in a matter-of-fact voice.

"This Lodge…my cue…decided on me which makes me a Vampire Killer and I'm bloody fuckin' good at it…so yoo can just shove ya head up yer arse and fuckin' marzipan off!" she raged, while some of the others wondered what to marzipan off actually meant.

Johnny threw his head in his hands yet again. He hadn't started tearing his hair out yet. He knew it was only a matter of time before this phase began.

Bert cackled heartily and slapped his leg.

Marilyn opened and closed his mouth like a goldfish.

"You can see why they're rarely invited to club dinners, can't you." Max smiled and then gruffly laughed.

Bert took Lola's finger and moved it away from Marilyn. "Come on, Pix. It ain't nice to point. Yoo said so yerself." Lola looked at Bert and her face softened.

"Come on, Pix. Sit down," Bert said softly. Lola slowly

smiled at Bert and sat down. Marilyn grimaced and turned to Max. His expression screamed 'do something!' but Max just looked at Lola and smiled. Marilyn looked outraged. He was about to say something when Jonah started talking.

"The power that flows through your cues is very old and very wise," Jonah slurred as he glugged down a large glass of wine.

"Huh?" Bert said, curious as to this sudden change of subject.

"Madam. You are, of course, right. If this Lodge chose you, it would have good reason," Jonah said. "It doesn't make mistakes, in spite of what many believe," he mumbled, casting a glance at Max and Marilyn.

He continued: "Just as we shouldn't judge you, my dear, by your appearance and apparent lack of any form of grace, manners, intelligence and restraint..."

"...Hey..." Lola protested. She was about to stand up but Bert put a hand on her shoulder and gently held her down.

"...you shouldn't judge us." Jonah looked at her sternly. "We will let that insult go this time. Do not do it again."

"She won't," Carl stated. "You have MY word on that."

"We have all been foot soldiers, just as you are now. And we, all three, earned our roles as Guardians. We are older, wiser and stronger than you can possibly know, Madam. So, please... manners," Jonah said more gently.

Why doncha eat wiv yer mouth closed, then? Lola thought to herself. Tosspot.

"Your cues are a channel for intelligent energy. They are alive and they were meant to be used. They were meant to connect with each and every one of you," Jonah slurred. "The more you use them, the more power they release."

"What?" Bert, Carl, Lola and Johnny said together.

"Not now, Jo-narr," Marilyn whispered under his breath. "Not now..."

"What power?" asked Johnny, taking an interest outside of his growing panic attack.

"Not now, chap," Max growled.

"Wot power?" Bert asked, taking a drag on his cigarette.

"Wot f...effing power?" Lola demanded.

Jonah crossed his arms and sat back and frowned.

44

"I find it so hard to believe that this once great Lodge has been handed over to a group of...incompetents," said Marilyn.

Lola looked at Bert and crossed her arms dramatically. "That's not very nice, is it?"

"No, Pixie," Bert said, smiling at her. "It's very rude."

Carl cleared his throat. "We're not incompetent – this is just a really quiet area. It has been for years."

"Which is why house prices are so good," Johnny added.

Lola looked at Johnny and rolled her eyes.

"Look," snapped Bert. "I really could be at home wiv a glass of wine, listenin' to the King. Are yoo gonna tell us or not? Are ya gonna sort out this Eight Ball or not? I've got a business to run and a ponce to support, so please, gentleman, get on wiv it."

"You chaps really should show us more respect." Marilyn flicked his hair and drummed his finger nails on the table.

"Why? Yoo don't show us any," Lola said flatly.

Marilyn gasped at her.

"So, this bleedin' power. Wot about this bleedin' power? Wot d'ya mean more power?" Bert demanded.

Jonah glugged a mouthful of wine. "Well, you should know that your cues are imbued with deep and ancient magic," Jonah said while dribbling wine onto the table.

"Yeah, yoo said that. Get onto the next bit," Bert asked with eagerness.

"The cue is just a shape. They are host to..." Before he could finish, Bert interrupted him.

"...ancient magic, ancient intelligence...yeah, yeah, yeah... Wot about the power part? The good bit?" asked Bert – his eagerness turning to minor frustration.

"Well, the more you use them, the more power they will give you," Jonah said flatly.

"So..." Bert asked and took another glug of wine. "They give us superpowers, then?"

"Super powers?" Johnny whispered to himself and checked his watch. He knew that he would have to get back to his vegetable patch very soon, before his body started to deteriorate.

"Well," Jonah sat back and devoured an onion bhaji. "I suppose you could call them that, yes."

45

"Why didn't anybody tell me this?" Lola demanded, looking at Carl.

"Hey, I didn't know this," Carl answered back. "No-one told me."

"Wot...not even Fergus?" Lola asked.

"Don't ever say his name to me!"

"Oh, yes. Fergus," Max said quietly but firmly. "Such a shame. Such a disgrace to the Lodge."

"And we were sorry for your...loss." Jonah murmured.

"I don't want to talk about it." Carl leapt to his feet. The room went quiet.

"I do, however, want to talk about super powers," Carl said, his eyes burning with anger, as he slowly sat down again.

Jonah leaned back with his hands across his chest. "Well, dear people, the more you use your cues, the more the ancient magic learns about you. For example, I would suggest, that if you have a mouth on you like a sewer rat, then the magic would provide power of silence." He gestured towards Lola. Lola smiled sarcastically back.

"So...it could be anyfink," Bert whispered.

"Exactly. During great wars, the magic would grow within its warriors. The magic that flows in these cues is the same magic that took the greatest warriors to the greatest heights," Jonah explained.

"Yees," said Marilyn. "And here they are now...wasting away in Putney."

"Well, maybe they're on 'oliday," Lola chirped.

"Holiday?" Marilyn asked incredulously.

"Maybe they're taking a break from all the fightin'," Lola suggested. "It must get borin' after a while."

Marilyn merely arched an eyebrow.

"So," Bert said, his blue eyes sparkling with mischief. "The more we kill vampires, the more powers we get."

"Unique powers. Each person will have different needs," Jonah explained.

"Special needs," Marilyn said under his breath.

"I 'eard that," Lola snarled.

"And it could be anyfink at all?" Bert continued, ignoring Lola and Johnny.

"Yes...anything," Jonah answered.

Bert took another swig of wine. "So...anyfink?"

"Yes!" the three Guardians said together.

"Wot about being able to turn into a cat?" Bert asked.

Max inhaled deeply. "It's not very likely that while killing vampires you'd need to turn into a cat, is it?"

"I like cats," Bert said.

"They are just eating, sleeping and shitting machines, chap." Max said dismissively and took a hard drag on a cigarette.

"I fuckin' 'ate me cat," said Lola.

"I'm sure the feeling must be mutual," retorted Marilyn.

"Children...please." Jonah banged his glass on the table. It then broke.

"It's actually irrelevant right now. The important thing now is the Eight Ball or fake Eight Ball..." Max said.

"Could it be booby-trapped?" Lola asked.

"Very likely, chap – which is one of my areas of expertise," boasted Max.

"But a shock could kill ya – a man of yer age," Lola replied with genuine concern.

Max looked to Johnny, who merely shrugged back.

"I'm 54, chap," Max said in a tight voice, fixing his stare on Lola.

"Exactly," Lola whispered as she nodded wisely.

Max's eyes burned into her.

"Shouldn't we start?" Carl asked quickly, trying to diffuse the tension.

"I'm still eating," Jonah sputtered.

"You're always bloody eating," Marilyn hissed.

"Chaps!" Max bellowed at his fellow Guardians.

"OK," said Jonah, standing up. "Prepare the table."

10

Eric had the strangest feeling. As he sat in bed massaging coconut oil into his left knee, he thought about the man he had let his room to. Although it was in the early hours of the morning and although he knew, logically, that Fergus hadn't left the house, he just felt that there was no-one else around. He put in some eye drops and thought for a moment. He was wondering who the hell Fergus was when his mobile rang.

Pete had passed out in a boathouse on Putney Embankment, dressed as a pirate. Pete was a boat builder and partly owned a classic river launch called Aurora, which had a large open plan deck, could seat around ten people and was moored in Putney.

Pete had taken nine friends that day up to Eel-Pie Island, dressed as pirates, for lunch and a rugby match at Twickenham before returning later that evening to a tiny pub tucked away off the Lower Richmond Road known as 'Stone Henge' – so called because of the bar flies hanging out in the same position year after year. There he drank a few more pints before staggering back to the boathouse and passing out. He had planned to change back into his clothes and catch the 85 bus to Kingston but hadn't made it past the boathouse door.

"Hello?" Pete asked groggily, his long brown plaited wig lopsided on his head. He was still wearing his sunglasses.

Pete was in in his mid-forties, about six foot tall and of slender build. His face was handsome and under the wig had light brown receding hair.

"Eric?" Pete pushed himself up off the floor. He listened for a few seconds. "Mary called? Oh crap...no...no...I'm fine, just passed out in the boathouse."

Pete looked at his watch. It was too bloody early, he was too bloody knackered and drunk to get a bus and go back to his girlfriend. Eric, however, lived only about four minutes away.

"Could I crash over?" Pete hoarsely asked. "Brilliant. Cheers, mate".

Pete pushed himself up to his knees and fell forward onto his face.

"Bugger," he exhaled, as his wig fell over his face and he contemplated sleeping in that position.

He knew he had to get to Eric's. It was Boat Race Day and he had a big job to do. He was piloting the Umpire's Boat. He just needed some rest and he needed to sober up quickly.

He stood up, staggered out of the boathouse and lurched his way onto the Lower Richmond Road. He fell over again.

"Bollocks," he whispered to himself.

11

Candles lined the edge of the sacred table and candlelight lit the vault room. The three Guardians were dressed in long, purple robes with gold trimming.

Carl, Johnny, Bert and Lola sat to one side, watching – Lola's eyes like saucers.

"Wot are they doin'?" she whispered to Johnny.

"Shh," Johnny replied. Lola crossed her arms like a petulant schoolgirl.

"Woz it like this in the 80s?" She asked her fiancé. "No electricity?"

Johnny merely threw his head into his hands. His mind was also on the fact that time was running out for him to get back to his vegetable patch. He reckoned he had about an hour before rigor mortis set into his legs. There was one memorable time when this had happened before – when he first realised he was, in fact, half-dead.

How he happened to be half-dead and kept alive by a vegetable patch was a curious story. Inspired by the marrow seeds and trowel he had acquired, Johnny had become a keen gardener and was also very keen on entering and winning 'largest' vegetable competitions. He had been winning numerous competitions, which was aided by the assistance of rapid growth/life-enhancing soil – a spell he had stolen from a book he had 'found' in the vault.

Cue custodians were not warlocks, as a rule. They were not meant to learn spells and operate in that area of magic. They received magic via their cues and were defenders of good and so it seemed strange to Johnny that the Great

Lodge contained so many magic books and artefacts. Underneath The Pig & Phoenix was like a library combined with a museum and yet few witches and warlocks ever came to visit. It was stamped across the Lodge Rule Book on page one that Vampire Killers were definitely not allowed to use spells. Johnny, a keen reader and student, couldn't help himself. He had felt drawn to the books and over the years he had read many. This didn't mean that he understood every aspect of his readings, nor could he perform the rituals, but he understood a lot of the methodology.

Johnny's stolen spell created magic soil covering about ten feet worth of his garden and everything there grew to massive proportions and also very quickly.

It was very late at night when Johnny heard a noise in his garden. Taking his pool cue from next to his bed, he walked down the stairs and entered tentatively into the garden. He looked up onto the roof – there was a vampire – squatting on the tiles. The vampire looked at him and Johnny looked back.

'Blurble, blurble, blurble" was the sound that Johnny's mind made, which was the closest it could get to making sense. The vampire leapt twenty feet from the roof straight at Johnny.

The vampire was male, looked about 20 years old and was wearing a long red leather coat that really had seen better decades. His hair was brown and greasy and his face was exceptionally pale with an almost yellowish glow in the early hours of the morning.

As the vampire came hurtling at Johnny, Johnny pulled out his cue which crackled in the moonlight. Johnny twirled the cue about his head, which made a whooping noise. (This was a move he had either seen in Star Trek or in a Jackie Chan movie, one he had practiced in the mirror and one that spontaneously erupted from him.)

The cue smacked the vampire across the side of the head and an electric bolt flew out from the cue. It fried the vampire and threw him into the side of the house and he disintegrated on impact. Johnny was also fried and thrown backwards into the vegetable patch. Had he not landed in the regenerative soil, he would have died within minutes. However, the soil was meant for vegetables and not humans. It kept him temporarily alive for about 24 hours and then his body started

51

to die. He later discovered that he needed to sleep on the soil for about five hours.

When he first woke up after the fight, he hadn't realised he had died. It was about 6am, daylight and he was lying on his back in the vegetable patch. What had happened? He couldn't quite remember. There was an image of a massive flash...

Johnny looked to his right and then to his left. He realised he had landed on a giant marrow. He pushed himself up and rubbed the back of his head.

The next night, he was outside doing a top-up spell on his vegetable patch, when he leaned against the wall. He felt a shooting pain in his arm and looked down at his arm and saw that it was starting to rot. He shouted, grabbing his arm – staggering backwards. He then stumbled into the vegetable patch and the pain stopped and his arm healed.

It took him a little while to figure out what had happened and then what he needed to regularly do about it. He was, in fact, similar to a vampire. Instead of feeding on blood, he needed to be sustained by magic.

The Guardians were muttering in gobbledegook, as far as Lola was concerned. They walked around the table one way, then the other way – then they sat down for a glug of wine and a cigarette. What was it all about? She chewed on her thumbnail and looked around the room.

Carl watched on intently. His thoughts turned to Fergus. How could his best friend have betrayed him in such a way? Fergus – a friend since childhood. Fergus – a fellow Vampire Killer. Quite simply, Fergus the betrayer.

Fergus disappeared three years ago. No-one had seen him and no-one had heard from him since. There were rumours, but there were always rumours. What is a world without lies? Carl thought and twisted the ring on his finger. What was a world without Katie?

Bert was singing an Elvis song in his head. He also hadn't clue what all the chanting, incense swinging and the smoking was all about. He thought about Portugal and sunshine and let out a sigh. Then he thought about his cue and magic powers. In his mind's eye he was dressed as a superhero with a cape – 'Super-Bert', that would be his name. He would be able to turn into a giant cat and fly. He chuckled to himself.

Johnny realised his legs were starting to stiffen up and that he needed to get back to his vegetable patch. He was getting concerned and was starting to think up reasons why he would have to leave a very important ceremony. His thoughts turned to food-poisoning. All he knew at that moment was that pretty soon he wouldn't be able to walk at all.

There was an enormous crashing noise – like waves breaking on the beach. The four of them were jolted out of their thoughts.

"Holy fuck!" Lola shouted.

There was a growing amount of smoke coming from the table.

"Booby-trap number one," said Max. "It's always the same." Max stumbled backwards, his hair up on end and his robe on fire. Lola ran over to him, grabbing a bottle of red wine on the way.

"NO..." Max protested but it was too late. Lola covered his head in red wine.

"Yoo should be careful..." Lola mopped his head with a beer towel she found on the floor.

"Stop fussing, woman," Max demanded. Lola giggled.

"I like the way yer called me woman."

"For God's sake, man, control this nymphomaniac," Max barked at Johnny.

Johnny tried to stand up but his legs buckled under him for a moment and almost hit the floor.

"Yer drunk too!" Lola shouted as she helped Max get back to his feet. She dusted him down and he tried to brush her off. She left Max's side, who frowned and ran his hand over his head and looked at it. What a waste of wine, he grumbled to himself.

"I am not drunk," Johnny insisted, trying to get back up to his feet. "And stop harassing that poor man."

"He's old. He needs 'elp" she said, gesturing at Max, whose blue eyes narrowed.

53

"I'm ONLY 54," Max snarled.

"Yeah," Lola nodded with concern.

Marilyn threw back his hood. "WE are going to need some help. The magic surrounding the Eight Ball is very strong." Jonah placed his hands on the side of the table – his hands seemed to glow.

"I don't want to rush you but there is only so long I can actually contain this energy before it blows us all up."

Marilyn also placed his hands on the shaking table and Max rushed over to join them. The combined efforts of all three of them managed to stop the table from violently shaking but it was severely rattling about.

On the middle of the table, inside a crystal jar, was the Eight Ball which was vibrating furiously.

"It's already tried to kill me." Max glared at it. "All of you – over here NOW."

Three of them ran over and Johnny limped.

"What do we do?" asked Carl.

Marilyn replied. "Place your hands on the table and bloody concentrate."

"On wot?" Bert demanded.

"On keeping that ball calm!" Max boomed.

All four of them turned their eyes to the rattling Eight Ball in the crystal jar. Lola stared intently.

The rattling seemed to be getting worse.

"Is this meant to happen?" Carl whispered.

"No," Jonah replied. He took a huge lungful of air and rolled his eyes.

The ball started to rattle faster and faster.

"That don't look too good," Bert gasped.

"Wot's goin'…" Lola began asking before a bolt of lightning from the ball passed through the glass, hit Lola and sent her flying across the room. Bert, Carl and Johnny went after her – Johnny losing balance and collapsing to the floor.

"Don't leave the table!" Marilyn ordered as all three went to leave the table.

"That's my mate!" Bert shouted as he and Carl arrived at Lola's side. Lola's eyes were closed. Carl put his hand on her heart. "She's alive."

"Left a bit," Lola weakly whispered. Carl smiled.

"Don't yoo 'ave warm 'ands," she purred.

"She's fine," Carl said, shaking his head.

"Oh goody – now get over here!" Max roared.

Carl and Bert pulled Lola to her feet. "Sit there." Carl gestured to a chair by the door.

"Like fuck I will." Lola grabbed her cue. "That bastard ball is mine."

Lola's cue started to vibrate. "Holy shit," she gasped.

Lola grabbed the cue with both hands to steady it but it began to violently shake and the cue tip started to glow green.

"Wot the f...!" Lola yelled as a bolt of green light shot out of her cue and went hurtling at the Eight Ball. The energy smashed the crystal container freeing the Eight Ball.

The ball started darting around the room, smashing mirrors, picture frames – everyone ducked as it accelerated at people's heads.

"Bollocks," said Marilyn.

Lola stood on the chair by the door and shouted: "Oi..bally-fing. Over 'ere!"

She grabbed her cue with both hands and swung it over her shoulder like a baseball bat as the Eight Ball went hurtling towards her head. Lola swung and smashed the ball with incredible strength. The ball went flying at an alarming velocity across the room.

Jonah caught it effortlessly in his left hand.

"Whoa," Carl said. "That is incredible."

"What this? Nah...you should try my mother's spotted dick. Now that's something." Jonah smiled.

Bert looked at Lola. "Don't even ask."

"No...your strength. That was incredible." Carl said to Lola, who was looking a little stunned and very much impressed with herself.

"It just flowed through me." Lola looked at her hands. She made a fist and punched the wall. Her hand smashed right through the brickwork.

"Oi...watch my pub!" Carl shouted at Lola, who looked back at him apologetically.

Jonah's fist started to shake. "I'm not going to be able to hold this."

Max grabbed his hands over Jonah's.

"I didn't know you cared." Jonah laughed.

"I don't, chap."

Marilyn also rushed over and put his hands over Max's.

"Isn't it nice...all three of us close like this," Jonah said sarcastically to Marilyn.

"Remind me to poison your kebab," Marilyn replied icily.

All three of them began to shake violently.

"I can't hold this," Jonah groaned.

"Carl, get over here," Max ordered.

Carl grabbed his cue. "All of you, get your cues."

Lola jumped off the chair, Johnny flapped about on the floor and Bert grabbed his cue.

"Johnny, wot's wrong wiv ya?" Bert huskily asked. "Wot's up wiv ya legs?"

"The ball...it...err...hit me" Johnny tried to stand up but his legs had stiffened right up. Bert tried to pick him up. "Jesus... it looks bad."

"Don't worry...just get my cue, would you. Thanks." Johnny attempted to cover up his panic. Bert rushed over to Johnny's cue and brought it to him. As Johnny held it, he felt a strange tingling sensation. He looked down and saw that his legs were disappearing. "Ahhhh!"

Bert looked down. "Ahhh!"

Carl had run over to the Guardians. "What's going on?"

"Johnny's legs...!" Bert shouted. "They've gone."

"What?" Carl cried out.

"Huh?" Lola chirped.

"Stop bleating...it's only magic. GET OVER HERE!" Marilyn yelled.

Bert poked Johnny's legs with his fingers. "They're still there!"

"Help them," Johnny said. "Don't worry about me."

Bert looked at Johnny suspiciously. "Yoo alright, mate?"

"Really, don't worry about me. Get over there. GO!"

Bert ran over to the table and turned his back on Johnny.

Johnny held onto his cue tightly as he noticed that his body was rapidly turning invisible...Thank you, God, he whispered in his mind. If thoughts could squeak and frolic like a happy little lamb, his did.

Bert joined the table.

56

"Point your cues at the ball," Max commanded.

All three of them obeyed. A green light shone from Lola's, an indigo light from Carl's and a yellow light from Bert's.

"Where's the other?" Max demanded.

"He's gawn invisible," Bert said.

"Johnny...we need ya!" Lola shouted.

Johnny, in his invisible state, crawled, with his cue, over to the table.

Their lights were getting stronger and brighter. Johnny crawled to the table, propped himself up and added his cue to the others.

"Johnny, is that yoo?" Bert asked, reaching out his hand and finding himself touching Johnny's elbow.

"Of course it's me!" Johnny protested. Johnny propped himself against the table. He was in pain and didn't know how much longer he could keep conscious.

"I'm used to ya wallet disappearin'...not yoo." Bert cackled.

"All of you...point your cues at it," Max barked.

All four of them pointed and the light from their cues hit the Eight Ball. It felt comfortable for a moment before all their cues started to vibrate violently.

Bert held his with both hands. "Whooooa!" he cried out.

Lola was the only one holding hers with the least effort. She felt the strength surging through her body.

The door to the vault threw itself open and started banging backwards and forwards.

"Close that door! The Eight Ball will make a break for it!" Max shouted.

Bert looked over at the door and with lightning speed, he left his cue in mid-air, ran to the door, closed the door, shoved a chair against it and was back holding his cue.

Wow...speed! He was fast. Super fast.

"Not bad," said Marilyn, looking at Bert.

"WHEN I say let go...let go. ON three," Max barked.

The table shook.

Everyone shook.

"One..." Max looked at Lola. Her face almost contorted with concentration.

"Two..." He looked at a light coming from an invisible cue, held by an invisible Johnny.

57

"Three…!" All of them pulled their cues away.

The sudden pulling away caused an almighty pulse wave which threw everyone to the floor. It also neutralised the Eight Ball. It fell down straight to the table, with smoke coming out of it, filling the room.

It was a few minutes, but Lola was the first up. She leaned over the ball and was about to touch it.

"Don't," Max said, grabbing her hand. "It's dangerous."

"It looks knackered," Lola said to him, taking her hand away. "Is it dead?"

"No. Not even close." Max pulled out a cloth from his pocket and picked up the Eight Ball with it. Marilyn pulled out a small crystal container from inside his robe and Max put the ball in the container, still wrapped in the cloth. Jonah took the container and put it in his pocket.

Bert got to the table. "Super-speed! I've got super-speed. Woohoo!"

"That's great, Bert. I've got super-strength. Which I fink is actually better than yours." Lola giggled at the sight of Bert. His hair was totally dishevelled.

"Nah. Speed any day," Bert said with a cocky grin across his face. Lola smiled and chuckled.

"Wot did yoo get, Carl?" Lola asked.

"Don't know. Nothing seemed to happen like it did with you." Carl shrugged. Why had the others got an ability and he hadn't? At least, not one that he knew about. There were more important things to think about and Lola voiced it with her next question.

"So, now wot?" Lola demanded.

Jonah got to his feet. "We still don't know if it's the real one or not."

"Why not?" Carl asked.

"Because all we managed to do was take care of two booby-traps. This ball, whatever it is, will awaken very soon and it will try to kill us again," said Max.

"Can't ya keep it knocked out?" Lola asked with concern.

"To an extent, yes. But not forever. We are going to have to perform a far more intense ritual and we are going to have to perform it on hallowed ground," Max answered with a deep sigh.

58

"When?" Carl asked.

"Today," replied Marilyn.

"But it's Boat Race Day. There are thousands of people about...day and night. I have a pub to run," Carl protested. No, not on Boat Race Day, goddamit!

"And I've got a cab to drive," Bert added.

"THIS is far more important. This is matter of life and death. This, if it is the real Eight Ball and it falls into the wrong hands, could be the end of the world," Jonah stated.

"Which is far more important that a stupid boat race," Marilyn said sternly.

"Maybe to you. I need to be here. I will not let my staff down." Carl walked over to the vault door. He looked over at a picture of him and Fergus on the wall.

"Well, that's good. How are they going to run a pub... without a WORLD?" Marilyn mocked.

Carl looked down towards the ground. Marilyn was right, of course. His duty to the cause had to come first. They had to find out if it was, indeed, the mysterious Eight Ball. If it was, then it was a major triumph for the good guys. It would also be a triumph for their Lodge. This, somehow, wasn't as pleasing an idea to Carl as he thought it should be.

For years the mysterious artefact had been missing. If it was the Eight Ball, then what would the good guys do with it? Not his problem, he supposed. He was a foot soldier. These decisions were made by those higher up the ranks. He realised that all he really wanted was for life to go back to normal. He wanted to run his pub, slay a few vampires and have a good time with his mates. It had already changed. His friends now had super-powers. He did not. The Lodge would no longer be obscure and he realised that obscurity was satisfying.

"Surely they can run the pub without you. It's only to pull a few more pints and sell hot-dogs. Anyone could do that," Max said, dismissively and also impatiently.

"I accept your offer of help, then," Carl said with a sarcastic, fixed smile.

Lola giggled. "I can see yoo in a chef's hat."

Max looked horrified. "I would love to help you sell burgers but World first, chap. Pub second."

"Well, what time?" Carl was put out. He was looking forward to Boat Race Day. He was looking forward to making lots of money. He was looking forward to having his pub full of people.

"What time what?" Max barked.

"What time are we going to do this ritual?" Carl asked.

"WE are going to do the ritual on hallowed ground this afternoon at 3pm. YOU are going to be on guard, making sure we are all right," Max said in a very serious voice.

Carl sighed. The Boat Race was at 2.30pm.

"God help us," sighed Marilyn.

"Where's Johnny?" Lola asked, suddenly worried.

All of them looked around. He was nowhere to be seen.

"Is he still invisible?" asked Lola.

Johnny had managed, while everyone was thrown to the floor and basically unconscious, to use the last part of his energy to crawl out of the vault. As he was practically dead at this moment, there wasn't enough life in him to be knocked out. He was merely holding on with a grim determination that even surprised him.

As he was crawling up the stairs, thinking I must get home, I must get home, his cue seemed to spring to life. He held onto it for dear life as it levitated in mid-air and dragged him… bump…bump…bump…up the stairs.

He made it to the side entrance out of the pub. It was about 6am and luckily he was invisible. All anyone would have heard would have been Johnny moaning and groaning as he was dragged along the ground towards his home. Keys… keys…he thought, as he approached the front door. His cue tip let out a blue light and his front door was open. He was then dragged through his hallway. His cue opened the back door in the same way and then dragged him to his vegetable patch. 'Thank God' he sighed, as he felt life pour back into his body. His stiff limbs becoming supple. Good cue…good cue…he thought. His cue lay down beside him and Johnny patted it.

The six remaining in the pub were walking around the vault carefully, calling his name.

"Johnny," Lola whispered, as she slowly walked around the vault.

60

"He ain't 'ere," Bert said. "Maybe he didn't just go invisible. Maybe he's disappeared altogether."

"Wot are we gonna do?" Lola asked Carl, with rising panic in her voice. "We're gettin' married."

"Not much we can do. What do you three think about this?" Carl asked.

Marilyn sat down on a chair. "It's hard to say what has happened. However, I have never heard of anyone actually disappearing entirely."

"Nor me."

"Nope."

"I'm gonna call 'im on his mobile," Lola said, panicking. She put her hand in her inside pocket and pulled out a tiny black phone.

"Wot...yoo gonna call the other side?" Bert asked.

"'As anyone got any better ideas?" Lola squeaked.

Lola pulled up Johnny's name, which she had under the nickname Piglet, and called. She waited and waited and then Johnny answered.

"Johnny is that yoo?" Lola shrieked. The others gathered around her. Maybe the afterlife had good reception.

"Are yoo on the other side? 'Ave ya seen Elvis?"

"Oh," she said. She put her hand over the mouthpiece. "He's in 'is garden."

12

Pete knocked on Eric's door. Eric rushed to open it. He came face to face with Pete dressed as a pirate.

"A strange man has moved in and I don't know why I let him," Eric blurted out. "I want to take a look around his room. Although he's in, I think he's out."

Pete gave Eric a quizzical look. "Can I come in?"

"Yes, yes…come in." Eric ushered him in.

"I want to look around his room. Will you help me?" Eric asked with galloping speed.

"What?? I've come over to sleep. I've got a big day today. There won't be time for me to change. Can I borrow some clothes?" Pete asked, heading towards the familiar, dark brown sofa.

"Oh God!" Eric exclaimed. "Are you going to be…y'know… OK?" he asked remembering that Pete was going to be piloting the Umpire's boat for the Boat Race.

"Yeah, yeah, no worries. Sleep needed." Pete lay down on the sofa and closed his eyes.

"The man is just so strange. He seems wrong," Eric whispered. He waited for a reply and then heard a slight, gurgling noise. Pete had gone straight to sleep.

Damn, thought Eric.

He needed to know if Fergus was upstairs or not. He needed an excuse to go into his room. He drummed his fingers on his chin and looked up at the ceiling. He smiled to himself. What a great idea! He thought to himself. He would merely pop his head around Fergus's door and say had he heard a noise and that he was investigating. Simple.

Eric walked quietly up the stairs and came to Fergus's room at the top of the landing. He was going to knock, out of habit, and then stopped. His gut instinct told him Fergus was not in there. He took a deep breath. Put on a ridiculous and pointless smile and opened the door slowly – just in case his gut instinct was actually wrong.

His head popped around the door and he peered inside.

There was no-one in the room. The bed hadn't been slept in. So, Fergus HAD left his room. He was right! The only possible method was by the window. How on earth did he climb out of the window and jump down onto the pavement? More importantly, why would he do such a thing? What is wrong with using the door? The entire Fergus episode made no sense to Eric at all. His was a simple life and this was something that took him far out of his comfort zone. Also, what was he now going to do? Wait for Fergus to return? Would Fergus return? How would Fergus return and what would he say to him?

Eric walked over to the window. It was closed but unlocked. The curtain was open. He looked down the road and the sight he saw made him jump out of his skin. There was a figure, sitting on what looked like a long stick, flying down the road. Eric's eyes bulged in his head as his mind attempted to process the information his eyes were presenting to him. Does not compute. Does not compute.

Eric was torn between staring at the figure getting closer and closer and also rising up towards the same height as the window and the urge to flee. Just get out of here, now! His instincts screamed at him. Go…Go!

As the figure flew closer to the window, Eric ducked down and scrabbled under the bed. His heart pounded violently and he realised his breathing was shallow and fast. He'll hear me. Oh God, he'll hear me, he thought over and over again.

Eric heard a noise at the window and then he heard it open. His head was turned towards the direction of the window. He couldn't see the window but he could see the entire floor area.

He heard the window close but he didn't see any feet on the floor. Then he did. They lowered downwards from the air and then he felt the bed take the weight of someone sitting down. He threw his hand over his mouth to stop a gasp escaping. His eyes moved from left to right wildly as his poor brain was going into overload.

He then heard a noise from downstairs. Pete had gone into the bathroom and flushed the toilet. Eric was relieved for a moment. Fergus could not know that Pete had arrived. Fergus would think that it was him downstairs. What was he going to do now? Stay under the bed? Hell, yes! He would stay under the bed for the rest of his life if he had to.

"I am aware you're down there," Fergus said quietly and smiled slowly to himself.

Eric's face contorted in shock. Maybe he's talking to someone else, his frazzled mind whispered to him.

"By all means, stay under there. I, however, will be going to sleep." Fergus lay down on the bed and closed his eyes.

Eric didn't know what to do. He opened and closed his mouth to say something but nothing came out. He must say something, he must...

"Mice," he said.

"Uh huh..." Fergus replied.

"Big mice," Eric said and coughed.

"I see," Fergus said softly. "Are you coming out?"

Eric was breathing harder and harder.

"No...still looking," Eric said in the strongest voice he could muster.

Fergus put one hand behind his head and smiled to himself.

"Good night," said Fergus.

"Yes, good night," whispered Eric.

13

Lola stomped out of the pub and across the road with the baker's on the corner. It was about 6ish and the street was empty and quiet. The light from the small 24/7 petrol station lit the road up to some degree and she supposed there was the usual man sitting at the cashier window, waiting for someone to show up to buy cigarettes and eggs. She also knew the poor sod would end up being served a can of rice pudding and a loaf of bread.

Lola became aware how loud her stomping heels were and she decided to tip-toe, which slowed her down a little bit. Her brow was furrowed. She was furious with Johnny for leaving the vault.

She stopped dead.

Eyes. She felt eyes on her.

She twirled her pool cue with both hands, like a cheerleader's baton. Come on, yer bastards, she thought. Where are ya?

Her eyes scanned the roofs. She thrust her cue under her right armpit, like a martial arts master and extended her left arm, as she crossed one leg over the other and manoeuvred herself into the middle of the road. She spun fast on her heel, one way and then the other, scanning the horizon. Come on yoo little shits, let's 'ave ya, she thought.

Then there were two vampires in front of her. There were also two behind her.

Lola's thoughts then turned to CCTV. Every street had a camera. Just as she thought that, a bolt of green light blasted out from the tip of her cue and knocked out the two cameras at the end of the road. Good night, big brother.

"'Ello boys," she squeaked.

The two vampires in front of her were actually girls, but she had always wanted to say that line. The girl vampires exchanged looks.

Lola turned sideways, and flicked her head between the two approaching sides.

"'Ello ladies," she said to the two approaching male vampires. They also exchanged looks with one another.

"The only fing I 'ate more than me cat ..." Lola looked up for a moment. "Actually, I 'ate me cat more than anyfink but..." she pulled her cue out from under her arm"...the fing I 'ate second has to be yoo metro-sexual vampires with yer lanky, greasy hair and yer bloody pointy teeth."

Lola started to spin her cue in a large, swooping motion. It made a long whooshing noise. "I know ya can't look in a mirror but yer could make an effort."

The two girl vampires charged her, hissing and bearing their fangs.

"Bring it, yoo bitches..." Lola squeaked.

One girl vampire seemed to launch about 20 feet in the air, making an aerial assault while the other charged her.

Lola leapt upwards and with her new increased strength actually went about thirty feet in the air, missing the vampire, who looked very confused as they passed one another. Lola somersaulted in mid-air, and landed behind the two boy vampires.

She whistled. Not very well – she was not a good whistler, but she still got their attention.

"All of ya. Come on...all of ya at the same time," she chirped. "I mean it!"

The four vampires seemed to line up and walk closer towards her. "That's more like it. Don't be shy."

One broke rank and charged her. Lola charged towards him and shoved her cue right through his heart with incredible strength. There was a crunching noise and then a flash of flame. One down.

Lola's petite body was bathed in streetlight. Her eyes were silhouetted.

Lola extended her arm and beckoned with her hand.

The three remaining vampires seemed to have one single thought to take Lola down together. They all ran forward. Lola leapt in the air and somersaulted behind them. She liked being able to somersault and could see herself doing a lot of it.

"Oi, coffin dodgers..." she whispered.

They spun around.

The three stormed her again. Lola swung her cue back like a baseball bat and when they were almost upon her, she dropped to her knees and struck at their legs, left to right, knocking them all to the floor.

Lola jumped up to her feet.

"Yer not very bright are ya," she said as she shoved her cue through the girl's heart on the right. She went up in flames.

The other two vampires jumped to their feet. The remaining girl vampire threw a punch. Lola deflected it with her cue and then started to spin it faster and faster. The two vampires' eyes followed it round and round. Lola threw it in the air, the vampires looked upwards and Lola threw a punch at the female vampire's head, taking her head clean off her shoulders and sending the flying head onto a butcher's window. It cracked the window and fell to the floor. The last thing it saw was a sign adverting Lamb Shanks, half price.

Lola caught her cue in one hand. She locked eyes with the last vampire.

"Just yoo and me now, buttercup," she said, putting her cue through the heart of the decapitated vampire. The body and head went up in a whoosh of flames.

The last vampire bared its fangs and hissed.

"I'll take that as ya wantin' some more," Lola whispered.

"Well," Lola approached the vampire with her cue over her shoulder. "I want yoo to take a message to whatever mingin', metro-sexual coffin dodger is sendin' ya out night after night. I am well fucked off. I should be married by now."

Lola crashed her cue into the side of the vampire, who hissed.

"Get back in ya coffin..." She hit him again. "Go on...get back..."

The vampire started to back off and flee as she pursued him. "Get back ...go on..." she ran after him as he ran away.

"Fuckin' coffin dodger," she said to herself as the vampire disappeared into the distance.

She straightened her skirt, dusted her jacket and walked towards Johnny's house.

"In 'is garden," she muttered as she stomped down the road, no longer tip-toeing.

14

Sophie looked at the handful of watches in the box Fergus had given to her. Eight slender gold watches. They looked expensive.

Sophie picked one up. The face showed it was 6.15am. She needed to get these watches to eight of her friends, all of whom worked as bar staff in local pubs that lined her pub route home. It started at 'Stone Henge' and zig-zagged its way home to staggering distance across the common. Her feet knew the journey, even when her mind had vacated the building.

Over the years, Sophie had spent a lot of times in pubs in the evenings and had become friendly with the bar staff in Putney. Many had become good friends.

Boat Race Day was an incredibly busy day for all the pubs, bars and restaurants. Fergus had told her to give out the watches **this** morning. He was insistent and she knew he would not be pleased if she disobeyed him. He had made that very clear. Yes, he made her nervous. She didn't know why he wanted her to do this and she was sure that there couldn't be any kindness in the act. It just didn't make any sense to her.

So, she was going to have to contact her friends very soon. That was easy enough. How she was going to explain why she was giving them an expensive gold watch was slightly harder. She'd just have to put it down into being in a good mood. She would pretend she had just received a windfall. She would think of something.

Sophie's thoughts turned to Fergus. She had thought he

had died. Actually, no-one had really known what had happened to him. Yes, she had loved him. No, he hadn't loved her. That didn't matter to her. She knew when he was entertaining himself with her while his thoughts were with Katie. Katie – who chose Carl to be her husband. Katie who had also disappeared at the same time as Fergus had disappeared. No-one knew what had happened to her nor to him. That was three years ago.

Fergus now seemed different. Yes, he looked the same but his character, his confidence, his voice all had taken on a different, darker shade. The humanity she remembered when she looked in his eyes was no longer there. There was a fixed, impenetrable gaze. She searched his eyes to see if there was any of the depth she saw before. There was not.

Sophie was not aware of the Putney Vampire Killers. She was not aware of the secrecy of the order. She had met Fergus at The Pig & Phoenix about six years ago. They had been attracted to each other and they had become casual lovers for about a year.

As far as she knew, Carl and Fergus had grown up together and Fergus had been working for Carl for years. They were the best of friends. Then a beautiful, dark haired woman joined as bar staff. Both men fell like a ton of bricks in love with her. Sophie by now was more in love with Fergus than he with her. It was a stab in the heart to catch him looking at Katie with loving eyes but a mere 'make-do' look in her direction, and Sophie had noticed that Carl looked at Katie in the same love-struck way. The feeling was clearly mutual. Within a year they were married and within a year Fergus and Katie had disappeared. No one knew if they had run away together. There was no note. No message. Nothing. Carl, of course, was devastated. The man with the most infectious warm smile seldom smiled anymore. He seemed to work like a relentless machine.

Sophie had been too nervous to ask Fergus about Katie. She really wanted to know what had happened. Where was Katie? Was she alright? Although jealous of his love for her, Sophie was big-hearted. Her concern for someone's welfare and life outranked jealousy but she was nervous of Fergus. He just seemed wrong. She didn't want to anger him.

70

While her mind was remembering The Pig & Phoenix, her thoughts turned to Tara, Carl's bar manager. Fergus had told her to give one of the watches to her. Tara was a larger than life, blonde haired, mostly foul-mouthed middle-aged cockney woman, who took no prisoners. She had known Sophie for years and, like many people who knew Sophie, felt protective towards her. They saw a small, lovely but lonely young woman who sometimes drank too much and was preyed upon by male parasites. She didn't think Tara would take the watch from her. She would be the hardest to convince.

So, Sophie would call her friends and ask them to meet her early or she would deliver the watches to the pubs herself. She planned to go to The Pig & Phoenix last. If she could avoid a confrontation, she would.

Oh God. She had such a sinking feeling in her stomach. She reached for a glass of wine and took a glug. She had better not go to sleep. She probably wouldn't wake up in time. She picked up the bottle and walked to her living room and prayed that what Fergus was planning wasn't going to hurt anyone.

71

15

Lola found Johnny lying in the vegetable patch in his garden. The garden was large with a green lawn which was bathed in the breaking daylight. Lola found Johnny on his back with his cue next to him. His other hand was around a marrow.

"Wot the fuck are ya doin' wiv that marrow?" Lola asked, her brows furrowed, as she walked speedily over to him. Johnny almost leapt out of his skin, grabbing his chest and turning to face her. He had managed to regain the feeling in his legs and pretty much most of his body. His cue seemed to have helped speed up his regeneration.

"Jesus, Pixie, don't do that," Johnny whispered. "And keep your voice down." He was overwhelmingly delighted it was her and not a vampire. He had hoped that if he had been attacked, his cue could've done something as he was presently just coming out of the equivalent of a coma.

"Wot happened to ya? ''Ow did ya get 'ere? Did ya teleport or somefink?" Lola sat down next to him. "I sometimes fink yoo love ya garden more than me." She said reproachfully. "Even when I stay over, ya sneak out 'ere." Lola looked around the garden. It was very well cared for. There was a large fig tree with a swing attached to it. Johnny's nieces would come over and play on it. Hmmph! Lola thought to that.

"I don't really know how I got here," Johnny lied, pushing himself up on his hands. "I was knocked out and then I was here. I can go invisible. Isn't that amazing?" Johnny put his arm around her shoulder and she put his head on his chest. She let out a sigh. "I woz worried about ya."

"That's sweet," Johnny said and kissed her head.

"Don't tell the others I woz worried," she said and pointed a finger in his face.

"I won't. Of course I don't love my garden more than you." He gave her a squeeze and she sighed and relaxed. She put her little arms around him and squeezed.

"Oww, Jesus! You're crushing me!" Johnny howled. Lola's super strength was still flowing through her.

"Oh, sorry," she said, releasing him. There was a lull in their conversation.

"So, we should get married really soon. We could all die," Lola said with a look of concern. "Yoo could die."

Johnny inwardly sighed. How little she knew. "We will. We'll do it after this is all over."

"Really?" she asked. "Really, really?"

"Really, really," he reassured her and they exchanged a tender kiss.

Lola suddenly looked suspicious. "When ya say when this is all over, do ya mean when we've sorted out this bloody Eight Ball, end of the world rubbish?"

Johnny threw his head back and laughed. Lola looked a little bit hurt.

"Stop laughin' at me, Johnny." Lola looked sad. "Yer always laughin' at me." She shoved his shoulder and he went sliding about ten feet sideways, his hip banging into his marrow and taking the pair of them straight into the fence. The fence took the blow of the force and buckled.

"Ow!" Johnny cried. "Ow!" Lola jumped to her feet and ran over and pulled him out from the fence and onto his feet. He put his arm around her for support. The marrow had been well and truly squished. Lola looked at the mangled flesh and inwardly giggled. She straightened her face for her fiancé.

"Sorry about that. I dunno how strong I actually am." Lola had a thought. She wondered how high she could throw Johnny in the air but then thought better of it. Probably not the best time to experiment. However, her mind was racing with the fun she could have.

"Don't ya fink strength is way better than invisibility. No offence. I mean, I just slaughtered four coffin dodgers. Yer should've seen me. I woz amazin'," she smiled.

"They never stood a chance." Johnny grinned at her, as he

leant down to pick up his cue.

"No they didn't. I can jump really high and somersault and stuff like that. I'm really excited. I can't wait to see wot else I can do."

"I don't remember much about what happened to me," he said, which for the most part was true. As he was getting closer and closer to death, he was focused on just holding on. If it hadn't had been for his cue, he would've perished. Johnny, of course, could not tell Lola this part. His cue was linked to him. It was an integral part of his character. He assumed that this must be the same for all four of them.

"Do you have any other abilities, apart from strength?" Johnny asked. "Perhaps speed reading."

"Oi," she said and smiled. They both laughed.

They started to walk inwards towards the house, Lola supporting a limping Johnny. Johnny felt that energy from his cue flow into his body. As it had laid down beside him, it had absorbed some of the energy from the vegetable garden and it was recharging him – but even faster.

"No, not that I know of," Lola answered. "Maybe we get more abilities. Wouldn't that be great, if we did? Although it did send out a bolt of energy and destroy a camera."

"Why did it do that?" Johnny asked, looking perplexed.

"I woz finkin' that I didn't want me coffin-dodger slaughter on film and it wrecked the camera." Lola shrugged. "Just as well. I wouldn't know 'ow to explain it to the old bill."

"Incredible," Johnny said. "Our cues really seem to be intelligent." Praise the Lord, Johnny thought.

"Yeah, it's amazin'. It sorta does what I fink." Lola grinned.

"Or what you need."

"Do I need me cue to always be strong or am I just strong now?" she asked Johnny.

"I don't know." Johnny answered. "Maybe it's as and when we need what we need." ·

They headed into the house. They both sat down on Johnny's sofa, Lola's head on Johnny's shoulder and each holding their cues. Both closed their eyes. Lola thought about somersaulting and Johnny about a weekend break in Wales where there were no Guardians and no Eight Balls.

16

Pete woke up on Eric's sofa around 8am. The brown pirate tri-corn hat was upside down on the floor next to him. His sunglasses, for some reason, had made it to the other side of the room and were nestling next to a table leg with one of his socks.

Pete was still wearing the dreadlock wig with a bandana – although it was halfway over his face. For a moment he had no idea where he was, and for a moment he thought he had gone blind. Pete had also forgotten, but also only for a moment, that he was piloting the Umpire's boat today. Pete's background was boats, boats and boats. He had rowed them professionally. He piloted them. He made them. He coached amateur rowers and he also, from time to time, piloted the Umpire's boat on Boat Race Day. This was one such year.

Pete looked around the room. The thin white curtains were still drawn but were letting quite a lot of sunlight in. A good day for it, the sobering-up part of his mind told him. Oh God, why did I drink so much? Why? Why?

Pete pushed himself up so he was sitting upright. Ugh! He needed an aspirin and he knew that Eric kept them in a cupboard in the kitchen. Jesus!...ow...he thought as manoeuvred his way off the battered leather sofa. He was still wearing one sock.

Pete walked in a slow, jerky motion to the kitchen. He filled the kettle, which was just a bit too loud for his head. A coffee. A strong, strong...very strong coffee, was needed. He toddled over to the cupboard and found the aspirins. Eric sprang to mind and he took out two mugs. He was probably in bed and snoring like an asthmatic bear with a machine gun lodged in its throat. Pete needed to borrow one of his suits. If he wasn't awake, he'd take one and give it back to him later in the week.

Pete swallowed the aspirins as the kettle boiled. He made the cups of coffee and began to climb the stairs. He got to the top of the landing where Fergus's room was, turned left up three more little stairs and headed towards Eric's room. With both hands occupied, he used his foot to 'knock' on the door, which made no useful noise whatsoever.

Pete pushed the door open with his foot and went into the room. The room was empty.

"Eric?" he said out loud to the house. "Eric?" he said much, much louder.

"He's in here," answered the voice of Fergus.

Pete turned and walked out of the room and went out onto the landing.

"Where is he?" Pete asked in a raised voice, looking around.

"In here," Fergus answered flatly.

"Why?"

"He's looking for mice," Fergus mocked.

Pete knew he had drunk far too much the day before. Even so, this was not what he expected to hear. This must be the new tenant – the one Eric was so freaked out over last night.

"Eric," Pete said loudly. "Eric, are you ok?" Pete asked, moving slightly closer to the door.

"Yes," Eric replied, in a slightly higher than normal voice.

"Umm…should I come in?" Pete asked with a rising sense of uneasiness.

"Of course," answered Fergus. "Come in."

Pete moved cautiously towards the door. "Are you sure it's OK to come in?"

"Yes," squeaked Eric.

Pete approached the door and slowly pushed it open with one of his feet. When he walked in, he saw Fergus lying back casually on the bed, with an arm behind his head. Pete couldn't see Eric.

"Eric?" Pete asked. "Where are you?"

There was a pause for a moment. "I'm…err…under the bed."

76

Pete looked at Fergus directly. "Why?"

"He's looking for mice. What a very conscientious landlord I have, don't you think?" Fergus smiled, making Pete uneasy.

"Well, why don't you come out? I've made you a coffee. And, I need to borrow a suit," Pete said sternly, not breaking eye contact with Fergus.

"By all means, come out...Eric," Fergus said softly. "I'm sure those mice must've gone by now."

Pete watched as Eric slowly emerged from under the bed. Eric looked at Pete but didn't dare look at Fergus. He brushed off some the fluff and dust on his shirt. "Good, good...no, nothing under there. Very, very good."

"Thank you for staying under there all morning. I truly appreciate your diligence."

Pete's brain really wasn't in gear to deal with any of this. He handed out one of the coffees to Eric. "Mice?" he asked.

"Y...yes," stuttered Eric.

"Big ones," added Fergus.

Pete's uneasiness had seriously grown. He wanted to get a suit and get out of there. There was something very, very wrong here.

"You're Pete, aren't you?" Fergus asked.

"Yes...have we met before?" Pete replied cautiously.

"Maybe. I used to live in Putney a few years ago. In fact, a couple I knew used to own this house."

"I bought it about three or four years ago. One of the pub owners sold it to me," Eric spluttered. He didn't really go to pubs a lot and didn't know Carl.

"They were a lovely couple," Fergus said monotonously, even mockingly. "Everyone who saw them said so. This was their bedroom."

Silence.

"Why are you dressed as a pirate?" Fergus asked.

"Party yesterday. I've got to get ready for today, though. Eric can I borrow some clothes?"

"You're driving the Umpire's boat today, aren't you?" Fergus sneered.

"Err...yes. Need to change."

"Really? I think it would be more fitting if you turned up as you are." Fergus smiled wickedly and slowly stood up.

17

Carl hadn't slept a wink. It was 8.15am and the Guardians were asleep in bunk-beds. The vault was prepared for these kinds of situations, although it hadn't been used in a long time. It had just been an age since the Putney Lodge had needed to cater to such esteemed figures. Carl frowned. The Guardians were an odd trio, to say the least. In their own, argumentative way, they worked well as a team. His thought turned to his team. They seemed to work very well together too. Pride. Yes, he felt pride in them.

Bert was sleeping on a mat on the vault's floor and once Lola had heard that Johnny was in his garden, she had marched over there, pool cue in hand, little heels thumping down hard. "In 'is garden...in 'is garden..." was all he could hear as she muttered to herself. There was no stopping her. Well, she could always draw on super-strength, if she needed it. What could he draw on? Where was his power?

He was very concerned about the ritual. It all seemed like an obvious set-up but rituals were rituals. Everything had an order, a process, a place and a time. The Eight Ball to the Guardians was like one note in a symphony. A symphony is not just about one note. It is about the bigger piece. Putney, it seemed, was the bigger piece in this puzzle. The Guardians could not just take the Eight Ball away and stick it in a vault. If it was, indeed, the Eight Ball and depending on the outcome of the ritual, it would have to stay in Putney. One of the Lodge Rules stated that reclaimed or conquered magical artefacts would be housed in the Lodge that found/conquered said artefact/s. In the case of artefact destruction, a replica would be given as a trophy to the triumphant Lodge. How funny to think that this little outpost – well, the once Great Lodge – would become so esteemed again. How sad too. The pub would change. The four of them would have to change too. They were already changing.

Carl was pulled out of his thoughts by his phone jingling. A text. It was Maisie. Blimey, 'The Illustrious Wall Reader of Wandsworth, Battersea and Tooting' herself had sent him a text. She needed to see him and she needed to see him now. She was outside the pub.

Maisie had a mixed reputation for her powers of divination. She was about 50 years old, with medium length brown hair, and a jolly round face that made her look much younger than her years. She stood at about five foot tall. She was wearing a tight quilted jacket, jeans, trainers and was holding her phone. She grabbed Carl's arm.

"The walls are not happy," she whispered.

"Really?" Carl asked with slight bewilderment.

"I have today seen a fish next to a porcupine. It is a warning of a disaster. Disaster."

Carl looked around the street. A few cafés were open and light and dark blue balloons were tied to lamp posts. It wouldn't be long before the helicopter would start hovering above, making a constant racket, as it took aerial shots of the Thames. It always arrived hours before the race and just seemed to be a permanent buzzing noise in the background.

Carl looked as he saw a couple of policemen walk down the road.

"Cup of tea?" Carl asked quickly as he watched the police approach. Maisie's face lit up.

"Oh yeah," said Maisie. "Stuff is happening. It's happening today and it has to be stopped."

"Come in and tell me all about it," Carl said, almost pushing Maisie through the pub's main door.

The pub was empty. Soon his staff would arrive and later there would be a queue outside, some of whom would wait patiently to get in. There were others who would join the queue and in their impatience try and bribe one of the bouncers to get in or lie that their friends were already in the pub. Some would get stroppy and insist that they be allowed in. Carl's bouncers were super-calm Russians.

"No," Mikael would say in a monotone voice, as he looked down from his 6ft 6" height. "No room. You wait."

On Boat Race Day, Putney became saturated with thousands of Oxbridge types. Some roamed in packs and some hunted alone. Some had bred and brought their offspring with them and some were the stereotypical Hooray Henry types that hadn't learnt volume control. Carl smiled to himself. It must be one of the few times of years and locations where Oxbridgitis could be let loose. Oxbridgitis being a condition that some Oxford and Cambridge graduates suffered from. It is the desire to let a stranger know that they went to one of the universities between five and ten minutes of meeting them. "I was on my way to New York last week when I tripped over a suitcase which reminded me of a Professor's suitcase I once saw when I was at Cambridge..." and also, "I took my cat to the vets yesterday where I thought I saw a parrot which reminded me of an old university friend from Oxford."

More points are scored for the most blatant tenuous link suffered by the listener. There is also Oxbridgitis by proxy, where friends and family of someone who went to one of the universities cannot help themselves inform a stranger of their relative's Oxbridge connection – maybe through a bizarre line-dancing accident or possibly through a faulty lawnmower and hedgehog story.

Carl wasn't knocking them. Good luck to them. They all had money to spend and Carl was thinking about all the cash that would be handed over the counter. Thank you...thank you... thank you. The Pig & Phoenix was a cash only pub and the thought that he would be making about £50,000 in one day thrilled him. He figured the other riverside pubs, and pretty much most of Putney's high street pubs, would be making the same. Money flowed through the veins of Putney on this day.

Many of the locals found the entire day a pain. The streets were packed as were all coffee shops. They had to queue to get into their local. Many left Putney for the day or locked themselves in their homes and hoped it would all soon be over. Others saw it as a highlight of living in the area and

80

threw parties.

Carl's bouncers were working all day today and God, did he need them! His wasn't the only pub that would have queues stretching around the corner. The sheer volume of people that came into Putney on Boat Race Day was staggering. Like a plague of locusts, eating and drinking it clean.

Pubs that didn't have bouncers seemed to self-regulate the amount of clients on their premises. The simple fact that no-one could squeeze past the door meant it was now full. Those people stuck in the back of the pub would have to start moving towards the exit at least an hour in advance, armed with supplies and a map. Once out, there was no going back.

Carl closed the door behind Maisie and he asked her to follow him as he walked behind the bar and into the kitchen area. He poured water into the kettle and flicked the switch.

"What's up, Maisie?" Carl asked softly.

Maisie held her hand up, as if to say stop.

"What can I tell you? What can I tell you? The walls are not happy. Not even a little bit." Maisie ran her hand through her hair. She took a deep breath.

"When did they tell you this?" Carl asked, taking two mugs off the mug tree.

"Err...ex-ccooooose me... last night," Maisie said, clutching her chest.

"What did you see?" Carl asked gently. He was never sure about the art of divination but Maisie had come close to the truth on a couple of occasions. He thought 'close' because not all her divinations had fully matured. There were still aspects to be fulfilled. Bad aspects.

How she 'read walls' he didn't know. But then he killed vampires. Their C.V.s would be an interesting read to a psychiatrist.

Maisie was a clairvoyant and was a member of the Putney White Witches. The Putney Vampire Killers and the Putney White Witches were very aware of one another and had joined together in the epic Vampire Wars. In the last few decades they had rarely needed each other's services but all the White Witches drank at his pub. There were three of them and they were a rowdy lot. There was Tarot Kat, who was 60, permanently tanned and was covered in Jewellery and called

81

everyone 'Dahhhling'. There was a bodyguard called Derek, who was 6ft 2", about 40, and who was also a trained psychotherapist. He was often away for weeks at a time but he made enough money to take time out and concentrate on his magical duties. There was, of course, Maisie, who worked as an administrator at an Estate Agents.

Maisie had been the one to warn Carl about Katie. Maisie one night was standing in the smoking shed area of The Pig & Phoenix and she was looking at the brickwork. She saw the standard images she had seen countless times. On the whole, The Pig & Phoenix was a happy and deeply magical building. Suddenly, her eyes locked onto an image of a woman's face. You would have to look hard to see it and she saw that it was in pain. It looked like Katie. She saw another image – one of a swirling portal and one an explosion. Maisie's stomach had turned in fear.

Maisie had slowly walked back into the pub that Friday night. The pub was filling up and she was able to look behind the bar. Katie and Carl had their arms around one another and were looking into one another's eyes and smiling. Her eyes flicked over to Fergus. Jealousy. Yes, deep, dark jealousy was etched into his face.

Jealousy. The most destructive of all the emotions, Maisie thought to herself. Duty was duty. She would tell Carl. She would warn him. She would do what she could. So she did, and sounded probably like a crazy soothsayer after too many pints of lager, but he had to hear her. Perhaps not the thing you want to hear when you are in love and planning a happy future together. He had smiled at Maisie and put it down to eccentricity. He wasn't offended.

They had married. Carl had bought them a house around the corner. Then Katie had disappeared. Fergus too.

Maisie used the walls to focus and channel her energies. She believed that all buildings took on their own personality – that they contained their own consciousness and that if we only listened, they would impart great wisdom. The Great Lodge, however, was so much more.

"Well, what can I tell you, Carl? I was doing my usual meditation looking at my wall and I see a porcupine. Now, the porcupine represents the spirit of Putney. Always has done."

Carl looked quizzically at her. "Errr...OK." He handed Maisie over a cup of tea.

"Cheers, love." They both took a sip of their tea.

"So...yes...the porcupine. It is a positive symbol. It is playful and a sign of wealth and movement. No surprise in seeing that cheeky ole porcupine in Putney but..."

Maisie took another sip.

"But the fish. Again, no problem on its own. It is a sign of fluidity. It can also be a sign of strength. But together..."

Maisie put her hand on Carl's arm. "The two together are catastrophic. We are talking war, death and destruction!"

Carl listened intently. Why a porcupine and a fish would cause such alarm, he had no idea. Then it wasn't his area of expertise.

"The last time I felt like this was with Katie and Fergus." Maisie said quietly. Carl nodded gently. "I think it's part of the same energy."

"How do you mean?" Carl asked, feeling a growing sinking feeling in his stomach. Again, no symbol or action could be read in isolation. He was starting to learn this. To look at all the elements and to read in combination.

"When I warned you that time about Fergus...about his jealousy, I said that something terrible was going to happen with Katie. They disappeared Carl. He took her...I know he took her."

Carl looked at the sink. He watched water dripping from a tap. "Yes, I know."

"And..." Maisie said, looking grave. "He's back".

"WHAT?" Carl shouted. "He's back? Is Katie back? Is she..."

"No." Maisie put her hand over his mouth. "No, she's not."

"Is she dead, Maisie?" he murmured – almost a whisper.

"I've told you before. She's not in the spirit world...and trust me, we'd know. It's like spook Clapham Junction on our house on a Thursday night," Maisie replied warmly and rubbed Carl's arm.

"So where is she? Where the hell is she?" Carl asked softly.

"I don't know, but more importantly, Carl, Fergus is close at hand. Now, what's been going on?"

Carl felt rage rising in his chest. Fergus. Was Fergus back? Where was he?

Carl took a deep breath and briefly explained what had been happening with the vampires, the Guardians. He didn't mention about the powers received.

"Why didn't you tell us?" Maisie reprimanded him. "You should've told us. We do have an old pact, y'know."

"Yes, you're right. I'm sorry," Carl apologised. Yes, the two Putney groups did have an old pact and he should have told her. But things had been going so fast, it was the last thing he had thought about.

"You're forgiven, love. So, it's not a coincidence. Fergus has to be behind this," Maisie said flatly. She turned her attention to Carl, noticing his eyes were a mixture of rage and sadness.

"Why? What possible reason could he have...? It is just madness," Carl said, feeling his heart pound in his chest. Where was Fergus? Where the fuck was he?

"Maybe it is just madness. Maybe it doesn't take any more than that," Maisie whispered tenderly and rubbed Carl's arm soothingly.

"But what is he doing? All I know is there is an Eight Ball that may or may not be the real Eight Ball and the Guardians are performing a ritual today to find out if it is. That's it," Carl moaned in frustration.

"Carl. There is more. There is so much more going on that that. I can tell," Maisie said, holding his arm reassuringly.

"Then you tell me what to do because I have no idea what is going to happen or what I need to do to stop it!" Carl ran his hand over his head. "What on earth am I meant to do? All I know is that I want to see Fergus and kill him."

"What aren't you telling me?" Maisie said, by-passing the rant.

"What do you mean?" Carl asked.

"You're leaving something out," Maisie whispered.

Carl sighed and quickly and glibly explained about the superpowers.

"I see, and you thought this wasn't important, did you?" Maisie asked, raising an eyebrow.

"Hand," she said. Carl sighed, put out his hand and she

smacked it.

"Naughty. Very, very naughty."

Maisie looked Carl up and down and let out a sigh.

"So, you think that you didn't receive a power and now you're sulking," Maisie gently mocked.

"I am not sulking. Today there is a big ritual and if Fergus is orchestrating whatever it is he is orchestrating, what do I have to offer? I don't know what he's planning," Carl stood up and walked over to the sink. He stared at the dripping tap.

"Hmm...Have you been taking low self-esteem pills or something?" Maisie teased.

Carl smiled softly.

"Boo hoo hoo. Now, you stop feeling sorry for yourself and let me tell you something about powers. Not all powers are in the physical body, as it were. You don't need strength or agility. You have those. As for being invisible, that's a curious gift, but useful. Yours is probably something much more powerful than you can imagine," Maisie whispered mysteriously to him.

Carl turned around and slowly walked back towards Maisie.

"How do you mean?" Carl asked, sitting down. She had definitely got his attention.

"I think your power is more magic knowledge based. Not just a super power."

"No offence, but I'd rather have invisibility," Carl huffed, leaning back in his chair.

"Would you now? Are you telling me that you don't want to know where Fergus is? What his plans are? Where Katie is? You don't want to see into the mind of your enemy?" Maisie asked.

"Of course," Carl replied, leaning forward in his chair again.

"Then stop being so prejudiced. I think you received your gifts. You just don't know how to access them yet and I can help you with that," Maisie said, smiling.

"Really?" Carl asked, looking at Maisie with narrowed eyes.

"Yes. Bloody hell. You really underestimate us witches, don't you?" Maisie tutted loudly and swigged down the last dregs of her cup of tea. God, she was going to have to sort Carl out big time.

"Are you talking about clairvoyance? Divination? Isn't all that stuff...witch territory?" Carl looked at Maisie with doubt. This was quite a lot to take in, and in his heart he really wanted an ability such as speed or flying. "Anyway, Vampire Killers aren't meant to use magic in that way."

"What a load of rubbish! Magic is everyone's ability. And, if what I think is true is true," Maisie whispered, "there is so much more going on."

"And what is that?" Carl asked.

Maisie leaned forward and smiled into his eyes. "That you can access the soul of the Great Lodge."

Carl stared at her and was silent.

Maisie changed the mood by saying: "Right, we've got to find out where Fergus is and what he is up to. If the walls are to be believed, the world could end today."

"Oh, so no pressure then," Carl said.

Maisie grinned at him. "Make me another cup, love, and let's have a little channelling session."

18

Bert had spent the early hours of the morning sleeping on a mattress on the floor of the vault. It was actually one of the best night sleeps he had had in years, which annoyed him greatly as he had just spent a small fortune on a new king size bed.

He slowly opened his eyes and rubbed them. There was a moment when he couldn't quite work out where he was and who it was that was snoring across the room. How had he slept through that? He guessed it was Jonah. He was right. He sounded like an overweight and over-sized jungle cat with asthma and flu, who had just attempted running after a gazelle. Jesus – what a racket.

Bert pushed himself up and looked around the vault, which was always dark without the help of artificial light. There were a couple of large purple candles burning on the sacred table. Bert glanced around.

The vault was very handy. Bert supposed it was a ye olde version of a modern day panic room. A bunker of sorts. It could be used for rituals, research (lots of old, magical books) and sleeping people. It was also armed with supplies (it was possible that some World War II tins of food were still lurking at the back of cupboards) but there were also modern day technologies. There was a flat screen, computer, etc. in the attached room.

The bunks pulled down from the walls. There were two lots of bunks and two mattresses. Bert had not wanted to sleep either above or below any of the Guardians and had opted for the floor. Carl had also opted for the floor in solidarity with his friend.

The Eight Ball was still in a box in Jonah's pocket. Bert thought he must be crazy to sleep with such a volatile and dangerous device next to his heart. Well, they were Guardians. They would've been promoted for a reason. They were brave, he had to give them that. They were just...well... not what he was expecting. He had seen them before at Lodge dinners in the city but the Putney Lodge had always been put on an outside table and they never stayed too long. They had become a bit of a joke, he supposed. How things were changing.

Images of the night flashed before his eyes. He could move like lightning. Who would've thought it? He chuckled. He looked down at his cue lying next to him. Anyone looking at it would think that it was just your standard pool cue. It was interesting how so much magic could be hidden in plain sight. Bert wondered what else was hidden that he hadn't seen before. He would start to look at everything with different eyes. Maybe once you started looking, it would become obvious.

He had known that his cue was magical but he hadn't known just how powerful it was. Bert was excited. The fact that there was a very dangerous ritual ahead, combined with Boat Race Day had mostly escaped his memory for the moment. Power. Why hadn't anyone told them? It was true that the Putney Vampire Lodge had been quiet for years but that wasn't their fault. The Lodges before them had done their work well and pretty much cleared out all of the vampire trouble in the 1950s. The next few generations of Lodge members had had it pretty easy. It had also been very dull. What a dilemma. Wasn't it good that the people of Putney were free from the threat of corpse-walkers? Danger was just more exciting, thought Bert. He cackled. Bert, the adrenalin junkie. What a giggle.

Maybe he could fly! Maybe they could all fly on their pool cues like broomsticks. When no-one was looking, he was going to have a try. He grinned and hoarsely laughed. Marilyn stirred slightly in his bunk. Bert put his hand over his mouth and slowly stood up. Where was Carl?

It was hard to imagine that only a few days ago he had

been thinking of going to Portugal. He loved his wife but give up this? It was one of the most exciting things that had ever happened to him. How could he explain this to her?

Bert looked at his watch. It was 9ish. He knew that Carl would start getting the pub ready before people burst through the doors at 11am. The marquee was already up in the garden which would sell cocktails and shelter people from the good ole unpredictable weather. The staff should have already been here by now and it was curious that no-one had arrived for work.

As for the Guardians, they had asked to be awakened at 10am. They had said that they needed to get ready for the ritual and that they would have to perform it on hallowed ground. The nearest church was on Putney Common – where most of the vampire killing had taken place recently.

Bert was curious as to how they were going to do this. Were they just going to wander into the church and take it over by force? Bloody 'ell, thought Bert. The common was swarming with people on Boat Race Day, especially if there was reasonable weather. He just didn't know what to expect. How were they meant to keep the area clear from vampires, with hundreds of people around? How was he going to hide his super-speed?

Bert's thoughts turned to Johnny and Lola. Lola had called him shortly after she had left, to let him know that they were both alright, and had started squeaking about somersaulting. He had said goodnight and Lola had told him that they would be over from about 10am.

Bert would leave the Guardians for another hour and go and
look for Carl. He could murder a cup of tea and a cigarette. Luvverly.

89

19

Lola had been too excited to sleep. She was twirling around on the spot at the foot of Johnny's bed and was giggling. She skipped over to the mantelpiece and looked at the clock on it. It showed the time as 9.40ish. (There were four clocks in Johnny's house and not one showed the right time. This one was ten minutes fast). She picked it up and slightly squeezed it. She had been checking to see if her powers were still with her. As the hours had passed they were fading and it seemed that she was more or less back to normal. Lola was concerned that they would not return at all but Johnny reassured her that they would the next time she needed them. It was 'logical', he explained.

Lola was so ecstatic about being super strong and that Johnny had agreed to marry her once 'it was all over' that she wanted this day to be over as quickly as possible. She had sworn that she would slay anything in her path. Nothing would stop her getting married – not even the threat of the world ending.

Johnny was lying down on his bed and was watching Lola. He hadn't been able to sleep either. He felt in excellent condition. It seemed like a miracle that his cue was able to re-charge his near-death state with energy it absorbed from the vegetable patch. This was going to make his 'half-life' so much easier to maintain. He'd be able to leave Putney for more than 24 hours. Oh joy! Perhaps he could go for a mini-break outside of London for the first time in years. He had no idea how much energy his cue could store. He would have to try it bit by bit.

"Last night was the best night of me life," she giggled. "Don't ya fink it's amazin'? We can go to them award dinners'n'stuff. Ya won't be ashamed of me."

"I'm not ashamed of you," Johnny said gently to her. "We rarely go because it's just embarrassing. We just seemed to be invited so we can be given the booby prize and be mocked by other Lodges."

Lola jumped onto the bed and bounced up and down.

"P'haps we'll get a prize for savin' the world," she grinned and jumped faster.

Johnny grabbed her leg to stop her jumping.

"There is a big day ahead. It's not about prizes. We've got to protect the Guardians. God only knows what's going to happen." Johnny looked worried.

"Yoo really, really fink somefink big is actually gonna 'appen?" Lola looked at him and pouted slightly. The concept that something bad might actually happen hadn't had the time to enter into her mind. She thought about the end of the world for a moment but then her brain went back to its happy place for a few seconds.

"Of course. Look at what's been happening. Look at our powers. It isn't for nothing." Johnny sighed. Lola saw that Johnny was concerned and she jumped down next to him with a thump.

"We're not trained for this," he said. "We could all die."

"I won't let anyfink 'appen to ya. Anyway, if yoo go invisible, who's gonna know where ya are? Yoo could tell us anyfink."

How true, thought Johnny. That was one of the advantages of being invisible. Hadn't his ability saved him already? He would be able to sneak up on enemies. He would also be able to sneak away – if necessary.

"Anyway, the Lodge wanted us. Our cues didn't just want anyone," Johnny said.

Lola thought about this for a moment. "Yoo don't fink it was just because we just 'appened to be the only ones about or somefink like that?" Lola was suddenly worried that it was all a mistake.

They both looked up at the ceiling and back to each other.

"No," he answered reassuringly. "It wouldn't be logical to hand over powers to us if we weren't meant to have them."

91

Lola felt better on hearing this and bounced on her bottom a couple of times. She stopped and frowned.

"Wot bloody git is behind all of this? Why here? Why Putney?"

Johnny put his arm behind his head and contemplated this problem.

"Come on, yer the one wiv a psychology degree," Lola teased. Johnny tweaked her nose and she giggled.

"OK, well...I would say for some reason, someone or something needs to have the Guardians performing a ritual in a certain place and at a certain time," Johnny said.

"Well done, Sherlock," Lola groaned.

"What I mean, Pixie, is that someone NEEDS to have them doing it on this particular day and in this particular location. It has to be on Boat Race Day and in Putney," Johnny explained, pleased with himself.

"'Ow would they know about the Guardians in the first place?" Lola squeaked.

"Well, they would need to have insider information."

"Wot d'ya mean?" Lola asked.

"They would need to know the ritualistic process of the Lodges. They would need to know it from personal experience or from someone telling them about it," he said.

"Why?" she asked. "Why go to all this trouble?"

"Hmm...the Eight Ball is either real or it is a fake. However, on one level it is irrelevant whether it is or it isn't."

"Why?" Lola demanded to know.

"Because the initial 'opening' ritual is the same."

"Huh?" Lola said.

Johnny leaned over and rested the side of his face on the palm of his hand. Lola mirrored him.

"In order to find out if it is real or not, the Guardians are going to have to follow a ritual. From what I know, they open up a portal between here and another dimension but only for a very tiny amount of time. The amount of energy it takes is enormous," he said somewhat nervously.

"So?" Lola asked.

"Well, when that portal is open, there is a rip between here and there. Anything could come through and anything could go out," Johnny anxiously whispered.

Lola frowned again. "So??" She said again but with a growl.

"So, if all you wanted was to have a portal opened up, you wouldn't need the real Eight Ball, would you? You would just need to con people into performing the ritual."

"Ohh...I see," Lola said. "So, someone would do that so that they could come or go."

"Or bring something in."

"Or send it out."

Lola looked down and chewed her thumbnail.

"But who?"

Johnny laid back and thought for a moment. "Hmm...well, Putney has either been chosen because for some reason the location for the ritual HAS to be here OR... it has been *deliberately* chosen by someone for personal reasons."

"Like a grudge?" Lola asked.

"Precisely like a grudge." Johnny answered. Johnny sat quietly for a moment and then his eyes seemed to bulge in his head.

He leapt up. "Oh my God!" he shouted. "Holy shit."

Lola looked alarmed.

"Fergus!" he exclaimed.

"Fergus?" Lola gasped as Johnny pulled her off the bed and grabbed his cue. "Come on, Pixie! Come on!"

Lola grabbed her cue and followed Johnny down the stairs. "We've got to tell Carl."

20

Sophie walked down to her kitchen where she made herself a cup of coffee. She hadn't heard a word from Fergus. She was also incredibly tired but pleased that she hadn't tried to sleep. She would never have got up. Sophie had also been concerned by the loud noises coming from the pigeon room. The scratching and the rustling had been getting louder throughout the early morning but it seemed to be slowing down with the rising sun. It had sounded like a busy railway platform and there was no way pigeons were making that kind of noise. She thought that this must have something to do with Fergus but she was too scared of him to ask. She was also too scared to let anyone else know what was happening.

Sophie looked down into the box of watches. Soon she would be setting off to give them to her friends. She hoped it would please Fergus (or rather, she hoped she wouldn't anger him). She knew in her heart that he was using her and there was an over-riding feeling that this would be the last time she would see him. However, there was always foolish hope and she would cling to that.

Sophie took a glug of coffee, put the box of watches in her bag and went to get her coat. She looked at her Mickey Mouse watch she'd had since she was eight. It was 9.30am when she closed the front door, deciding that she would go to one of the cafés opposite The Pig & Phoenix until the pubs started to open. She stared at her door for a moment. This was it, she thought, and let out a deep sigh.

Sophie turned to look at the common and noticed that there

were more people than usual on it. Putney was starting to fill.

Pete walked out of Eric's house wearing oil skins, covering his pirate's outfit. He was no longer wearing his wig and tricorn hat, but they were in a shoulder bag. As he walked down Weiss Road towards the Lower Richmond Road, the sun glinted on a slender gold watch on his wrist which showed the time as 9.40am. Pete's eyes seemed to be staring into the middle distance as he headed towards his rowing club, where he had been only a few hours before.

Sophie left the common behind her and began to walk up the Lower Richmond Road. It was a beautiful, crisp morning with golden sunlight. Pink blossom covered trees and there was a very gentle breeze. Good weather for the Boat Race, she thought. After a few minutes of walking, Sophie approached the zebra crossing outside a restaurant, which was close to The Pig & Phoenix.

There were a few cars on the road but her attention was struck by a man ...it was Pete...wearing oil skins and walking towards her. She stopped in her tracks and was going to say hello but he just walked by her, as if in a trance. Sophie turned and watched him stride across the crossing and down the road in the direction of the river. She noticed that he had a gold watch glinting on his wrist and a feeling of dread swelled in her chest. She knew Pete. Not that well, but they were on nodding and cheek-kissing terms.

Then, as he disappeared down the road, Sophie saw a blond man and a small woman holding pool cues running up the same road. She heard the noise of loudly clicking heels and giggling. They ran straight across the crossing and towards the pub. Sophie watched as they knocked on the door.

Sophie slowly crossed the road, keeping one eye on the pub, and went into the café. She ordered a white coffee and sat down so she could look directly at the pub. Something was going on there. She didn't know what but curiosity got the better of her. She looked at her watch. She had an hour to go before she started handing out the watches. After seeing how strangely Pete had behaved, she knew the watches were bad news and a pang of guilt hit her heart. However, not enough to make her change her mind.

21

Maisie closed the kitchen door, pulled down the window blinds and lit a white candle she had brought with her. She put the candle down on the gold silk tablecloth that had also emerged from her small black rucksack, the contents of which were like something from a new age market stall. A small crystal ball and a set of tarot cards were plonked down on the table. She also removed a cheese and pickle sandwich and a packet of crisps she had just bought from the petrol station.

"Sorry about that but I'm starving." Maisie ripped open the packet and took a bite. "Do you want half?" she asked in a motherly way.

"No, I'm fine, honest," Carl said. He wasn't very hungry.

"Go on. Have you eaten this morning?" she asked, holding half a sandwich in one hand and proffering the other half to him.

"No...but..." Carl tried to refuse, raising his hand and leaning back.

"You were the same as a little boy. Just take a bite now and you can eat the rest later. I'll leave it for you." She leaned further forward and held the sandwich right in front of his mouth. She flapped it up and down a couple of times, like waving a fish in front of a sea-lion.

"Go on," Maisie urged, grinning encouragingly. "Go on before I do my back in."

Carl found it was easier to agree. He leaned forward and took a bite and swallowed it. Maisie nodded at him, as if to say 'good, isn't it?' It actually tasted really good and he realised he actually was hungry. He took the sandwich out of her hand and started to wolf it down.

"Not hungry, he said," Maisie muttered, as it talking to someone else next to Carl. Maybe she was. Carl looked behind him. He wasn't going to ask.

Maisie took another mouthful and put the sandwiches back in the plastic box quickly.

"Isn't this a beautiful cloth? Kat brought it back for me from India. It's just stunning. Gold is an excellent protective colour," she told Carl, who was looking slightly dubious. He wasn't quite sure if she was talking just to him. He looked behind him again and then back to her. As he finished his last mouthful, Maisie offered him a hand-wipe from a small plastic box. He took and used it.

"Now then. Hands," she said, extending hers to Carl. Carl looked at her hands sheepishly.

"Hands!" Maisie insisted. Carl slowly extended his to hers. She took them in hers. His hands didn't close around hers.

"Honestly. Don't be such a big girl's blouse, Carl," she said. "I'm only trying to help you save the world, after all." She smacked the back of his hands gently and took hold of them again. "Come on."

Carl sighed and gripped her hands. "I don't think it's going to work," he said, feeling embarrassed.

"Err...excooose me," rebuked Maisie. "Are you the witch? Are you?"

"No," Carl answered.

"No, you are not." Maisie rolled her eyes, winking (possibly at him) and grabbed his hands harder.

"It feels silly," Carl said, smiling slightly. He was feeling an urge to chuckle. His mind had actually gone off Fergus for a moment.

"Oh, I see. So, you don't mind running around Putney Common with a pool cue in your hand killing vampires," Maisie guffawed. "Pool cues...honestly..."

"That's different. That's...rugged," Carl explained. "And what's wrong with pool cues? Anyway, they're not really pool cues, are they? They're magical...things."

Maisie laughed. "Magical things, indeed! Stop being so technical, you're confusing me."

Carl tried to pull his hands away but Maisie held onto them. She was surprisingly strong.

"I've seen all of you, in my ball, running around...huffing and puffing. It's ridiculous." Maisie laughed.

"I don't huff and puff. I'm in excellent shape." Carl protested. "What do you mean you've been watching us in your ball?"

"In my crystal ball," Maisie said, taking one hand out of Carl's and patting the ball affectionately. "Much better than anything that's been on the telly in years."

"You've been spying on us? " Carl asked.

"We do not spy," Maisie insisted. "We merely observe. For the common good."

Carl burst out laughing. "For the common good?"

"Yes. Oh, don't worry. It's not like we watch when you are in the bedroom. There are rules, y'know,"

"I wish someone would give me a copy of the rules because right now I am feeling just a bit violated. And why can't you find out where Fergus is, huh? Why can't you look in your spy ball and see where that bastard is?" Carl whispered.

"Oh, listen to you. Like you know how this all works. We've tried searching for Fergus but with no luck. His signal is jammed, as it were. And don't be such a drama queen. And don't flatter yourself," Maisie whispered back. "And why are we whispering?"

"Because my staff should be arriving at any moment, because I have three Guardians in the vault, because I feel silly...and slightly violated," Carl answered.

"Well, let's stop wasting time and getting all precious. Honestly, you were the same as a little boy."

"Just so you know that I do not huff and puff. I am in peak condition," Carl said, defending himself.

Maisie shook her head. "Bert isn't - he should retire. Do you know that he's looked the same for years? A bit like Sid James. It was always hard to tell how old he was."

"Bert has super speed now," Carl said. He would've loved to have super speed or to be super strong. He had seen Bert become a blur in front of his eyes, Lola punch a hole in his pub and Johnny turn invisible.

"Well, he still has to be careful. He's not a young man," Maisie said protectively.

"He is great in a fight. Always has your back," Carl grinned. Carl thought about all the times that he had spent with Bert over the years. He was a great mate. There was something very solid and dependable about Bert.

"And what about the others?" Maisie asked.

"The same. Johnny I always think is going to leg it but he never does. As for Lola...she is on her own planet."

"Yes...I agree with you there," Maisie laughed.

"But, I wouldn't mess with her," Carl said intensely. Lola could be very scary.

"I don't think anyone would want to mess with her, love," Maisie chuckled. "Life wouldn't be worth living if you got in her way, would it?" Carl rubbed his chin.

"No," he snorted. "It wouldn't. I don't know how Johnny deals with her sometimes."

Maisie nodded wisely. "Well, Johnny has his own, unique path." Maisie whispered, and then quickly added, "As we all do. So, good mates. A good team."

"Yes. They were great last night...this morning...you know what I mean," Carl said. Considering they seemed to have handled just about everything thrown at them with remarkable calm, it was quite impressive, Carl thought.

"Only too well. Now, let's get started. Close your eyes and take a deep breath, hold it and then exhale," Maisie said. Her eyes flicked over to the clock on the wall. She was aware that time was ticking along fast. In fact, the second hand had just started speeding up. She held his hands tightly.

Carl closed his eyes and took in a long, deep lungful of air. He held it and slowly, slowly released his breath.

"Again," said Maisie. "I want you to relax into your breathing," she added, looking at the clock.

Carl breathed in again, held it and then exhaled. He felt his body starting to relax as he became less aware of where his body was and more aware of his mind.

"I want you to think of a cube and put yourself in the middle of it. This cube is your protection," she explained, watching the second hand.

Carl imagined the cube. He found it hard to begin with but then as he focused it appeared clearly in front of him. It seemed about fifty foot high and wide and was almost

99

transparent.

"Breathe in and breathe out, slowly," Maisie whispered. "In and out, in and out, calming your mind, calming your spirit."

Carl fell deeper and deeper into a trance. He could see himself in the centre of the cube. He could hear Maisie's voice coming from outside but it seemed as if it was also coming from within the cube.

The second hand on the clock had gone back to normal speed.

"Each side of the cube represents a gateway. Tell me what you see," Maisie whispered as she watched Carl go into a trance before her.

Carl looked at the cube he was standing in. Beneath his feet were stars. The cube appeared to be suspended in outer space. All around him were the stars. It was mesmerising! He was standing in space. He was actually standing in space. It wasn't as if he was just seeing it in his mind's eye. He was seeing it as if it was real.

"Just stars. I'm just seeing stars," he whispered. "This is awesome." Carl smiled. "This is just...wow."

The clock hands had stopped moving. Maisie glanced over to her wristwatch. Her clock hands had also stopped. Time, it seemed, had paused.

Maisie closed her eyes, took a long deep breath and exhaled.

Carl was staring out at the stars when he heard a noise behind him. He turned quickly.

"Maisie?" he asked, as he saw what seemed like the figure of his friend approaching him.

"In the flesh...well, not really, in the etheric, I should say," Maisie smiled. She was dressed exactly the same and standing behind him in his cube.

"This is amazing," Carl said. "How come you're here?" he blurted out without thinking.

"Err...excooose me. Not that hard, actually. Something you'll learn," Maisie answered and walked next to him, her hands tucked into her jacket pocket. She seemed very relaxed and comfortable in this place, like she had seen it a thousand times.

Carl was transfixed. "This is the most incredible thing I

100

have ever seen. It is mind blowing."

Maisie looked out at the stars. "Nice view, isn't it?" she said. "This is where it all starts."

"Huh?" Carl whispered.

"Your journey," she answered. "Think of this place like a … like a bus station or a train station. You are the timetable and the train."

"But I've got a pub to run," he said, lost in his own world. Maisie sighed.

"Yes, in the 3D flesh and blood world you have a pub to run. As you can see, this is slightly bigger than that," Maisie groaned, extending her arm forward towards the stars. "Welcome to infinity and to every limitless possibility," Maisie said in a fake over-the-top American accent. "I've always wanted to say that," she chuckled and nudged him. Carl was too transfixed to respond.

"What am I doing here?" Carl whispered as he walked towards the side of the cube and touched it. It was so very soft.

"What are you doing as in what's it all about, God? or what am I doing in this invisible cube suspended within infinity?" she asked again in her fake accent. Carl didn't seem to notice these attempts at humour. Maisie shrugged to herself.

"What…why…what am I doing in this cube?" Carl asked. "Are we here? I mean…are our bodies here?"

"Yes and no. Our denser physical bodies are in the kitchen. Our lighter, etheric bodies are here," Maisie explained. "Think diet bodies. 1 calorie."

Carl's mind turned to his pub. "Tara will be arriving soon, we don't have much time."

Maisie smiled and stood next to him. "We have all the time we need." She had seen this before with newbies she had brought to the cube. Carl, she thought, was coping very well. No screaming, no shaking, no hair-tearing.

"How come?"

"Let's just say, time has taken a little holiday in your kitchen," Maisie answered.

"Oh," Carl said quietly. He looked around at the stars and they were so beautiful. If he never discovered what his abilities were, this view had made up for it on its own. It was truly outstanding. He felt connected to everything.

"So, my ability or abilities…" Carl said, his voice trailing off.

"Well, you're at the start. It's hard to know what your calling is, but you should have the fringe benefit of being able to remote view anyone and anything from any point of time," Maisie said in a matter-of-fact voice. "However…" before she could finish, Carl butted in.

"Katie," he whispered. As Carl's thoughts turned to Katie, one of the sides of the cube started to go cloudy and a very faint image of Katie came up. She was sitting on a sofa with a cup of tea in her hand and she was smiling.

At least it wasn't porn and sports cars, Maisie thought to herself. How many times had she seen that? Ho ho.

"Katie!" he shouted. "Katie!" he cried, running over to the image. It was about fifty foot high and he stood beneath looking up at her moving image.

"Where is this?" Maisie asked calmly. "Do you recognise it?"

Carl was so overwhelmed to see Katie that his eyes welled up.

Maisie put her hands on his shoulders. "You have to concentrate and control your emotions. Everything moves much faster here. You think of something it will appear."

Carl swallowed. "OK," he answered. "OK." He breathed deeply.

"So, do you recognise this place?" she asked, looking up at Katie.

Carl stared at the image. "Yes," he replied. "It's where we used to live."

Maisie nodded. "Anything else?" she encouraged. "When was this?"

Carl scanned the image. "It was when we moved in, we had just bought a new sofa." Carl smiled.

"But Katie isn't there now," Carl said. "Is she?"

"I wouldn't think so. But you are being shown your house. OK." Maisie rubbed his arm, affectionately. "We have to keep looking deeper. What about Fergus?"

Carl internally growled and the image of Katie disappeared.

"Where did she go?" Carl barked. "I want her back."

"I'm afraid that in here, you're going to have to aim for

neutrality towards Fergus, if we're going to get anywhere."

"Neutral?" Carl asked, his heart pounding.

"Yup, a bugger isn't it?" Maisie said and scratched the back of her head. "Unfortunately or fortunately, depending on your view, anger and resentment will get you nowhere in this cube, love." Maisie chuckled and looked out at the stars. "Anger is a dense frequency. You need to lighten your load in here."

"Lighten my load?" Carl asked incredulously.

"Yup. If you think angrily about Fergus, it will show you nothing. So, you're going to have to be neutral towards him. If you can't be positive, be neutral. It's a good 'beige' starting place."

Carl looked into the universe. This experience should be freaking him out but in his heart it seemed so right. He could see stars upon stars upon stars, stretching out into infinity, above him, below him and all around him.

"This is so beautiful," he whispered.

"Puts a lot of things into perspective, doesn't it?" Maisie chuckled. "It's my favourite thing, next to an ice cold pint of cider of a summer afternoon."

Carl thought about a pint of cider and an image of Maisie drinking came up on the left hand side of the cube.

"Oo, look, there I am." Maisie grinned. "What am I wearing?" She said, looking at a floral dress. "What was I thinking?"

Maisie looked as her image changed into one of Maisie in her underwear. Maisie giggled.

"Oo, Carl, you naughty boy."

Carl looked at the image and was mortified. "I...er...oh... err...shit..."

Maisie was wiping away tears as images of her in various nude poses with flowers, cakes and a bucket interchanged over the side of the cube. "Crap...why is it doing this?" Carl protested. "Don't look, please don't look." Even etheric bodies could blush, it seemed.

Maisie held her sides. "Oh, I'm sorry, I shouldn't be laughing. Control your thoughts for goodness sake. Think of the cube." She watched as an image of her dressed as Batgirl dissolved into nothing. The transparent wall was back.

"Oo, Jesus, that was funny. I haven't seen my wink-wink do that in years," she giggled.

Carl didn't ask. He didn't want to know.

"Can we never mention this?" he asked sheepishly. "Please can we never, ever, ever mention this?" Carl couldn't look at her.

"Of course," Maisie smiled. "You should've seen what happened to me the first time I came here...but that is another story."

Carl was still trying not to blush. There were so many questions, so many things to think about. It was all somewhat overwhelming.

"So, my dear, in order to find Fergus, you are going to have to change your view on him," Maisie said. "At least for the time that we are in here."

"Can't you find him in here? You don't have the same feelings I do towards him," Carl replied.

"Err...excooose me, I told you his signal is jammed to us. God only knows how he is doing it. He has become very, very powerful," Maisie said sternly.

"How could he do so? He was just one of us. He was one of the Putney Vampire Killers. Nothing special."

"Oh enough with feeling sorry for yourself. Even when shown infinity you're still feeling sorry for yourself." Maisie scolded. "Get a grip, Carl."

"Sorry," Carl whispered. "I appreciate all this. It's just...mind boggling."

"How did he do it? I'll tell you how he did it, love, by fast-tracking. He took the fast train to destructive, dark magician land," Maisie explained with sadness.

"He has become a very, very dodgy ceremonial magician," Maisie sighed.

"When you say dodgy, you mean?" Carl asked.

"I mean very, very dodgy," Maisie answered. "I mean magicians who see themselves separate and apart from humanity. They look at themselves as human livestock farmers. They harvest humans and their energy to serve their own evil ends."

"So vampires are?" Carl asked.

"Vampires are also a commodity, just like humans are to them. Think of them as foot soldiers. Things that serve. Things that cause fear. Things that are used in ceremonies both private and public."

Carl turned to look into Maisie's kind and smiling face. "Public ceremonies?"

Maisie snorted. "Oh yes. There's nothing a smug bunch of magicians like more than to perform ceremonies in front of people and include them in their rituals without their knowledge." Maisie shook her head in disgust. "Many dark magicians own brothels and perform rituals in them because they can harvest the denser, darker sexual energy. A brothel is like a fast-food restaurant, which comes, may I point out, with etheric diarrhoea!"

"What? What do you mean by public though?" Carl asked. "That isn't public, though, is it? It's behind closed doors."

"Yes that's right. However, the point of that example is to explain what the purpose of setting up a brothel is. It's to harvest sexual energy. The human livestock go there to shag and create much needed energy for the magician...or really, for the magician's masters. Y'see, the very dark magician operates in the area of anger, rage, lust, violence and fear. He needs to generate these in others to harvest their energy. The more of this generated in the world, the heavier the world's overall frequency becomes. The world gets sick."

Carl chewed his lip. "But how do they do it? How do they get people to join in?"

Maisie huffed. "Not that similar to a Vegas magician. Smoke, mirrors, distraction and entertainment."

Carl frowned and Maisie continued.

"Some rituals are performed behind closed doors, Carl. They are private ceremonies."

"OK," Carl said. He had just been through one and bloody hell, that was one weird experience.

"Now, some rituals take place in public. Some are small and some are very elaborate and clever. Many are watched by people who are unaware that not only are they are watching a ritual but they are actually taking part in it."

Carl gave Maisie his full attention. It was interesting that he had pre-judged her for years as a slightly wacky woman who used to babysit him, and now here he was with her in their etheric bodies, suspended in a transparent cube in infinity discussing ceremonial magicians, all the while actually sitting in his kitchen where time had stood still. And it wasn't even 10am.

"Dark magicians firstly find it amusing to include unaware observers in their rituals. And also, the unaware observers, by agreeing to watch – free will – under the rules of magic, actually become low-level initiates and assist."

"This is a lot to take in. What?" Carl rubbed his eyes. "What do you mean by a ritual? Why DON'T people know they are involved?"

Maisie patted him on the back. "I know it's a lot to take in. Think of it like a con trick. Instead of conning people out of their money, you are conning people out of their energy."

"How do you con someone out of their energy?" Carl asked.

"Where the mind goes, energy flows. When you give your attention to something, energy flows in that direction. One mind is powerful enough. Millions of minds together – that is something else." Maisie sighed.

"So?"

"So, the more energy a dark magician can harvest, the more potent the ritual. If he can direct hundreds, thousands or millions of minds to observe or react to an event, the level of energy released is awesome." Maisie looked saddened for a moment.

"So, it's like being a conductor of an orchestra. He would 'conduct' a public event to create a specific emotional reaction," Carl said, more to himself than to Maisie.

"Yup. Large public events are usually done to create fear. A bomb exploding in a city would create amazing levels of fear. Show the images around the world and you create an even bigger reaction."

"Wow," Carl whispered. He had never thought of negative events like that before.

"However, once you get to know their rules, you can start to predict their movements. Magicians, you see, are bound by names, dates, numbers and locations. They can't just go about willie-nillie doing stuff," Maisie explained. "And that's one of the ways that we can stop them. Knowing their little rules is very useful."

"Why do they need this energy, anyway? What is it for?" Carl rubbed his head and twisted the ring on his finger.

"Good question. The purpose of any dark magician's ritual is to channel entities from another realm or dimension. The magician serves these entities in exchange for supposed power over this realm. The entities have a particular love of human suffering. It is a food to them. And so, offerings of human pain on a small and large scale are made to them, frequently."

"So, if you know what they're going to do..." Carl said.

"We can stop them, yes. If they get their dates and times wrong then the ritual is null and void. If they get the wrong energy reaction, it isn't going to work either," Maisie explained.

"So, that's good isn't it? We...us...the good guys, have been 'blocking' them for years. We must be winning," Carl said hopefully.

"Hmmm...yes. However, with world-wide media, film, TV – millions of people plugged into an emotional manipulator, dark magicians have their fingers on an incredible power source. Times are not the same. The world of technology is the dark magician's new best mate. Sex, violence, greed and death...these images are shown over and over again for entertainment. And what you observe you create." Maisie sniffed.

"So, people are being used to..."

"Create low grade energy for low grade entities who think of us as a food source," Maisie said softly.

"I'll never watch another soap," Carl chuckled.

"Well, with the anger you have in you towards Fergus, you don't really need to, do you?" Maisie said.

"Ouch," Carl winced.

"I'm not trying to be a bitch, but you are going to have to get happier if we are going to get through this." Maisie crossed her arms and arched an eyebrow.

"I can't just switch off my emotions," Carl protested.

"I'm not asking you to switch them off, I'm asking you to be aware of what you are creating when you feel dark thoughts. Now that you know you are adding to the emotional darkness of this dimension you might stop feeling so sorry for yourself and see the bigger picture," Maisie scolded, wagging a finger at him.

"I am no bloody saint. I can't just go around smiling and

107

being nice to everything and everyone," Carl grumbled, feeling slightly overwhelmed.

"I'm not asking you to. I want you, at this stage, to be neutral towards Fergus so we can try and see what the bloody hell he is up to." Maisie shoved her arm around Carl's shoulder and slapped him on the back.

"Well, how do I do that?" Carl asked reluctantly. "And ow – that was hard."

"Well…I'll help you. I didn't bring you to the infinity cube for a cup of tea and to see myself naked with a bucket." Maisie roared with laughter – her eyes closed and her jolly face had turned crimson. She snorted and held her sides.

Carl sighed. "You are never going to let me forget this, are you?"

"God no," Maisie laughed. "Too, too funny." Once again, she burst out laughing. "I'm so pleased mascara doesn't run in here. I'd look like bloody Alice Cooper."

"Oh, Jesus. Let's just get on with this. What do I have to do?" Carl took a step away from her and crossed his arms. He couldn't say to her time was running out because apparently time had stopped.

Maisie managed to control herself. She blew her nose and breathed in.

"OK. List me three things you used to like about Fergus," Maisie said, returning to teacher mode.

Carl closed his eyes. He wondered for a moment that if he closed his eyes within the cube and imagined the cube would he enter into another one. His head couldn't handle that thought right now. His mind was already swirling with the concept of your thoughts and feelings creating your own reality and the responsibility that came with that. Bugger! Double bugger.

Carl then thought of Fergus. He saw his face slowly appear in his mind's eye. Carl found it hard not to get angry and every time he did, the image shimmered and faded. Come on, keep neutral, he said to himself. Don't react. You can do this. He tried again and the image became more solid.

He saw a picture of him and Carl together. It must have been when they were about thirteen. They had been fishing together. Fergus had been on the hunt for a large 18lb barbel in the Wandle River in Wandsworth. The fish had been dubbed 'Moby' and Fergus 'Ahab'. Over a period of five years he pursued this creature, which he eventually caught.

"He's a good fisherman," Carl said. "He is, was, a very patient person. He could sit there by a river and wait for hours."

"Good," Maisie encouraged. "And did you have fun fishing together?"

Carl nodded. "Yes, we had a good laugh but he had so much more patience than me. It's not my strong point."

"Yup. I'd agree with that. But you have such a fertile imagination." Maisie giggled.

"Oi," Carl protested and then laughed.

"Sorry, hon," she apologised. "Come on, that's good. Fergus was a good at fishing and he was a patient person."

"Yes, he used to help me with my homework as kids. He was also a real hard worker. He never slacked off." Carl remembered how hard Fergus would work behind the bar, in the cellar and in the vault. He had been a member of the Lodge and because times were quiet he had spent a lot of time reading the books down there and there was a massive collection down there. There were books on ancient magic and magical history that had to be hundreds of years old.

The Lodge members at the time of Fergus's disappearance had been Carl, Fergus, Bert and George. The table in the vault could seat seven, there were seven pool cues and there could be seven Lodge members at any one time. The Lodge and the cues chose the members. It had nothing to do with a voting committee.

When Fergus had disappeared he had taken his cue with him. He had stolen it and by doing so had broken a fundamental law and dishonoured the Lodge. A stolen cue was a sin.

After Fergus had disappeared, old Georgie had retired from the Lodge. He had handed in his cue and joined the bowling club, where there were numerous ex-Lodge members. Within a month, Johnny and Lola had replaced Fergus and George. When Fergus and Katie had disappeared, it had been Bert that had held everything together. He had held him together. He didn't want Bert to retire. He never wanted Bert to retire.

109

"So, he's was good at fishing, he was patient and a hard worker. Excellent. Open your eyes." Maisie instructed. "So… the fish. It makes sense. OK, I want you to think of that fish, Moby. It represents neutrality towards Fergus. If any bad thoughts about Fergus try to break through, make the fish bigger and bolder in your head."

"OK," Carl said softly. "I'll try."

"OK, turn and look at one of the walls."

Carl turned to his right and looked out into the stars. Maisie stood behind him.

"Now, focus on the fish." Carl thought of Moby the barbel. It represented a time when he and Fergus were best mates.

A fifty foot image of the fish started to shimmer on the wall, as if it were a superimposed screensaver.

"Excellent," she said. "Now, keep looking at the fish and I am going to ask questions. But…and I mean, but…keep looking at the fish."

"OK, I'll keep looking at the fish," Carl answered.

"Right. Now…" Maisie placed her hands on Carl's shoulders. She took a breath.

"Where is Fergus?" she asked, looking up at the screensaver. "Where is Fergus?"

The fish just seemed to swim happily around the large transparent wall.

"Nothing is happening," Carl complained.

"Shh," Maisie retorted. She took another breath.

"Where is Fergus?" she asked again.

The wall seemed to be receiving interference, like an old television set. The image of the fish shook and then the wall went fuzzy, blocking out the stars.

"What's happening?" Carl whispered. "Where's Moby?"

"We're breaking through the block," Maisie whispered back. "Keep your eyes peeled. This isn't going to be like a movie. There may just be fragments of information and keep thinking about Moby."

"Where is Fergus?" Maisie asked again.

A fleeting image of Moby returned, then the fuzziness and then an image of Eric's house. It was only there for the briefest moment.

"That's my old house," Carl blurted out.

110

"Yes, we saw that before," Maisie replied. "Keep focused."

The fuzziness had returned. Then there was a fleeting image of a slender gold watch. Then the image of Moby returned and changed back to the fuzziness.

"What was that?" Carl asked. "And don't say a watch."

"Clues, Carl," Maisie answered. "Keep the link going."

Moby swam around the giant wall and then a very brief image of Tara appeared.

"Tara?" Carl said loudly. "What's Tara got to do with any of this?"

"Shh," Maisie ordered. "Just keep focused and keep watching."

An image of the Thames came into focus. It was Boat Race Day. The teams were racing. Then there was an enormous explosion on a boat following the teams. People screaming – chaos.

"Jesus," Carl gasped. "Was that a bomb?"

"Looked like it. Keep focused, love. You're doing really well."

Another image came up. It was of a brown bag. In the bag was a stash of money. Carl saw himself handcuffed by the police.

"What?" Carl shouted. "That's never happened."

"Has somebody not filled in their tax return?" Maisie teased.

"That has never happened. What is this?" Carl protested.

"Fish," Maisie said calmly. "Think of Moby."

Carl was trying hard to control his emotions. The screen went all fuzzy again.

"Come on, Carl. Think of Moby. We are doing so well," Maisie said. She rubbed his arms gently. "Come on, love. Let's go again."

Carl closed his eyes, thought of Moby. He opened them and there he was, swimming around.

"OK. Show us more. Show us Fergus," Maisie asked. "Show us Fergus."

The screen turned fuzzy once again. There was an image trying to break through. It was of Putney Common. It was swarming with vampires. There was a fight. Bert, Johnny, Carl and Lola battling them in what seemed like overwhelming odds.

"Wow," Carl said, breathing out slowly. "That's a lot of

111

corpse-walkers."

Suddenly, the cube shook violently but briefly. "Whoa," Maisie gasped as she stumbled to her left. Carl staggered into the wall.

The image on the wall disappeared and all sides of the cube went fuzzy, blocking out all of the stars.

"What was that?" Carl asked, his face pressed against the wall.

"I don't know," Maisie answered nervously, slowly walking back to where she had previously been standing.

The cube shook again, as if it has been hit by a blast. Carl fell to the floor and Maisie fell onto her back.

"We've got to get out of here...now," Maisie ordered, trying to push herself up. There was another heavy blast and the cube rocked. Maisie tried to get up again.

"How?" Carl shouted. He was on his hands and knees. He raised his head and looked over at Maisie who was about ten feet away from him. Maisie's hair was over her face and she was like a turtle on its back, kicking her arms and legs about trying to get up. There was another blast.

"Kitchen!" she shouted, sliding across the cube on her back before smashing into the wall. "Take us back to your kitchen."

A loud, deep buzzing noise broke through the quiet cube. Maisie threw her hands over her ears. "Take us back," she cried. "For God's sake, take us back!"

"What?" he yelled. He shoved his hands over his ears. The buzzing was getting louder. He got to his feet and ran across the cube towards Maisie as an image started to break through the fuzziness behind her. It was Fergus's face. The image was faint and flickering.

"Fergus," he whispered, reaching Maisie and pulling her up to her feet. "Fergus!" he cried and pointed behind her. Maisie turned and saw a fifty foot face of Fergus flickering faster and faster on the wall, getting stronger.

"Fergus, you bastard!" he shouted.

"Don't get angry," Maisie commanded, putting her hand in front of his face. "Don't" she said. "Don't look, Carl."

"What are you doing?" he protested. Another blast hit and the buzzing got louder.

Maisie put her mouth to his ear and shouted. "Kitchen. Close your eyes. Think of your kitchen!"

Carl closed his eyes. The temptation to open them was enormous. He started to think about him and Maisie holding hands in his kitchen. He saw the small wooden table with its green checked tablecloth and two cups of tea on it.

Maisie looked up and saw Fergus's fifty foot face coming through the fuzziness. His image then appeared not on just one side of the cube but all of them. Fergus's face was furious. This wasn't just an image, it was clearly Fergus looking at them. The images were getting stronger.

"Think about the kitchen. We are in the kitchen," Maisie said as she tried to steady her emotions. She held out the palm of her hand towards Fergus. The image began to flicker again.

"Now!" she shouted, looking as if she was in pain.

The image of Fergus began to seriously weaken. "Do it now. I can't hold him back forever," she panted.

Carl was trying hard. He looked at the kitchen in his mind's eye again and again. The buzzing was getting louder. He shoved his hands over his ears and dropped to his knees. Another blast hit the cube and he went flying forwards into the wall.

He could faintly hear Maisie shouting at him to hurry up.

He imagined the pub, he imagined his bar, he imagined Boat Race Day and then he imagined Katie. He opened his eyes but he was still in the cube.

"It's not working!" he roared.

Maisie was breaking into a sweat. "Keep trying."

Carl closed his eyes again. He thought about Lola, then Johnny and then Bert. He smiled at the time Bert had sat down on a chair and it had collapsed. Carl had laughed his head off.

The shaking had stopped. The buzzing had stopped.

When he opened his eyes, he was holding Maisie's hands in the kitchen. She opened them.

"Well, that was fun," she said, opening her eyes and putting her hand to her chest. She breathed out.

"Holy fuck!" Carl exclaimed, leaning back on the chair and rubbing his head slowly.

Maisie smacked his hand. "No swearing."

113

"Sorry," he said, leaning forwards. "Was that really Fergus?"

"Yes. Strong little bugger, isn't he?" Maisie sniffed. She looked at the clock on the wall, the hands still weren't moving.

Maisie stood up slowly and walked over to the clock. She looked at her wristwatch. It wasn't moving either.

"That's very odd," Maisie whispered as she tapped the face of her wristwatch with her nail. "Time isn't moving forward."

"What?" Carl asked with a half laugh. "What do you mean?" He stood up swiftly and moved to Maisie's side.

"When we went into the cube, time stood still here. It's like a timeshare apartment scheme."

"Of course, what was I thinking?" he mumbled.

"But...time has still stopped," Maisie said. Her face looked concerned and she ran her hand through her hair. Her kind, round face looked confused.

"What...everywhere?" he asked, sounding concerned.

"Time should have stopped just in this room until we returned."

"So, this room has no time?" Carl asked, trying to work it out.

"Yes. It's like a stasis pod," she explained. "We've got to get time moving again in this room."

"Why?"

"Otherwise it will always be 9.45 on this particular day forever in this room," she answered authoritatively.

"I take it that's bad," Carl said. He could feel the tension mounting in his chest.

"It ain't good, love," she whispered. "Although it's 9.45 forever in this room, it will start to leak out."

"A time leak?" he gasped. Oh God, how was he going to tell the Guardians about this?

"How do we fix it?" he demanded, feeling a huge sense of personal responsibility. He could see Max's fuming face in his mind's eye and it wasn't pretty.

"I'm going to have to go back into the cube," she stated. "Fergus has clearly got some very dodgy mates. *I've* got to fix this."

"So, when we walk out of that door?" he asked apprehensively.

"We walk into a different time zone," she answered. "Time

114

is running normally out there."

"So, anyone who walks in here?" Carl sighed, closing his eyes for a moment.

"Mustn't," she replied. "No-one apart from you and me are allowed in here."

"Why not?"

"Because everyone else was doing something else at 9.45am. We can't put them in another location at the exact same time. It will kill them," she warned.

"But its Boat Race Day!" he shouted. "How the hell am I meant to keep my staff out on Boat Race Day? I can't tell them my kitchen has a time leak that could kill them."

"You're gonna have to keep them out. Your vault should have a few bits I need," she said.

"Shall we tell the Guardians?" he asked anxiously.

"Are you crazy? They're going to prepare to open a portal," she rasped and shook her head to emphasise her point.

"And you're going to try and close one?"

"Oh the irony," Maisie murmured.

In all the confusion, Carl had forgotten about the images he had seen. "Hang on!" he cried. "What about all that stuff with Fergus? The house, the watch, the bomb…"

"You've got your work cut out for you, haven't you?" Maisie said.

"But what does it all mean?" Carl asked. He was clearly agitated. "The house…what was that about?"

"Well, my little duck, that location came up twice. Maybe that's where he is," she advised and smiled at him.

"But why? What sick reason could he possibly have for doing that?" Carl frowned.

"I think you just answered your own question. Because he is twisted. That was where you lived with Katie. It was something he never had with her."

Carl's dark brown eyes looked down at his feet then up to the clock.

"What time is it out there?" he asked, nodding his head in the direction of the light blue kitchen door. It had a calendar of the England Rugby team hanging on it.

"Seeing as no-one has walked in and died, it must be quite close to 9.45am. The gap between the two times will get larger, however," Maisie cautioned.

"He knows we know, doesn't he?"

"Yup," Maisie answered firmly. She walked over to Carl and gave him a hug,

"There's something else about time leaks," she said in a low voice. "It's a slight side effect." Maisie chewed her lip and raised her eyebrows.

"Yeess?" Carl asked, raising his eyebrows back at her.

"Do you have any gloves?" she asked in a matter-of-fact tone.

"Yes, I do. Why?" Carl replied slowly.

"Because you're going to need them." Maisie said. "So will I. We're both contaminated."

"What do you mean, contaminated?" Carl barked.

"We are part of this time leak," she whispered in a conspiratorial manner.

"We are?" Carl whispered back. This was just getting worse, he thought.

"Yes, when we go out there…part of us will still be stuck at 9.45," she stated this as if it were the most normal thing in the world to explain.

"So?" Carl demanded.

"So, if you touch anyone, you could kill them."

"WHAT?" Carl bellowed. He grabbed Maisie by the arms.

"Shhh!" Maisie said. "Get a grip, Carl."

"Are you fucking crazy? Don't touch anyone. How can I not touch anyone? What about my face – people kiss me!" he shouted.

"Ooo…get you! No part of you must touch someone else," she ordered and pointed at him to emphasise her words. "The same with me until I fix this."

"How are you going to fix this?" he asked, running his hand over his head.

"When Fergus attacked the cube we didn't have a chance to break the link properly between here and there. There is a cord connecting the two. I am going to go back and cut it."

"How long will *that* take?"

"How long is a piece of string?" Maisie replied dryly.

"How the hell am I not meant to touch anyone? I hug and kiss people all the time," Carl blurted out.

116

"Well stop being sooo kissy-kissy," Maisie chided. "Put on a mask or something. Say you've got flu. And cover your head."

Carl sat down at the table and banged his head a few times.

"Yes, that will help, love," Maisie chuckled.

Maisie sat down opposite him and banged her head as well. She laughed.

"Maisie, this is crazy. What about that bomb, the watches..." he said. "Me being arrested."

"The positive thing in that image is that copper didn't die from touching you, did he?" Maisie said optimistically.

"Hooray, I stop killing people with frozen time and I get arrested." Carl sighed.

"Anyway, that was just one possible future – there are an infinite amount of possibilities. As we were tuning into Fergus, it's probably more to do with his vision for you."

"So, Fergus is probably at my old house. I'll just go around there and touch him. Won't that end all this?" Carl said, getting up and breathing hard. "If I kill him, won't this all stop?"

"And Katie?" she questioned. "What about Katie? He must know where she is."

"I'll make him tell me," he said.

"Maybe...maybe not," she cautioned.

"I need to find out about that bomb. It was on the Umpire's boat," he said. How the hell was he meant to stop a bomb on a boat?

"You're going to need to talk with the others. You've got your work cut out for you," Maisie whispered.

"And all those vampires. That fight," Carl said. "There were hundreds of vampires. There's only a few of us."

"Carl, we are going to walk out that door. We have to quarantine the kitchen and we have to cover ourselves head to toe," Maisie instructed and patted his shoulder.

Carl ran his hand over his head and then twiddled the ring on his finger.

"Costumes. We have loads of Halloween costumes and masks," he stated. "Upstairs in my flat."

"Ok, we're going to go out there. You're going to get the costumes, then I'll go to the vault. Step by step, we'll do this,"

117

she said softly.

Maisie and Carl shook hands.

"Ready?" she asked as they walked to the kitchen door. Maisie gripped the handle.

"Ready," replied Carl.

"Good luck," she whispered and kissed him on the cheek.

"You too," he said, as Maisie opened the door.

22

Pete walked into his club boathouse, which was an unremarkable low-rise building overlooking the river. There were numerous rowing clubs next to one another on the river bank and they were always packed on Boat Race Day. You could always see people cramped together on the balconies, swigging Pimms and laughing too loudly. As the long stretch of the road from Putney Bridge to the small play park would be swarming with people by the early afternoon, the balcony was probably one of the best places to be. It certainly had one of the best starting views of the race.

On the opposite side of the river was Bishop's Park (in Fulham), famous for being 'that place used in The Omen', where Patrick Troughton, who played the priest, got impaled by the church spire.

All that could be seen from Putney's side of Bishop's Park was a long, long line of huge trees, and if you looked to the left, you could see the stadium lights of Fulham Football Club. As the race pulled in around 250,000 people to the river to watch, giant screens were erected on the river bank so people could watch the entire race. As a big, sponsored event, it was now broadcast to millions of people at home.

This annual boat race between The Oxford University Boat Club and The Cambridge University Boat Club had been a tradition since the time of the Great Vampire Wars – about 150 years ago. Many great Vampire Killers had taken part both legitimately and illegitimately in the race and some even claimed they were responsible for its creation. This differed to the official human view that the idea for the race had originally

119

come from two friends – Charles Merivale (a student at Cambridge) and Charles Wordsworth (a nephew of the poet William Wordsworth), who was at Oxford. The great Vampire Killer 'Mick The Torch' (studying Classics at Cambridge) claimed he had started the event when he tauntingly rowed eight of his kills past one of the most evil Vampire leaders known only as 'Sid The Impaler' (studying Theology at Oxford). Sid The Impaler retaliated by rowing eight impaled corpses of Vampire Killers past him and the tradition was apparently born.

The human version claims the tradition began in early 1829 when Cambridge sent a challenge to Oxford and over some time the race ended up taking place in Putney, generally on the last Saturday of March or the first Saturday in April between competing eights (eight rowers using sweep oars and steered by a cox). The Great Putney Lodge inhabitants were incredibly proud of this tradition. In the 1960s, one of the Putney Vampire Killers, known as White Ball Psycho Jools, put on a three-day festival and had to be restrained by seven Guardians from going on a celebratory streaking and killing spree across Clapham Common.

As for the course, following am 'S' shapes from east to west over 4 miles and 374 yards (6.779km) from Putney to Mortlake, passing Hammersmith and Barnes – the Mortlake Lodge (The Rusty Kettle) demanded it end there so they could get the punters in, and heartily welcomed both 'blues' supporters with Cambridge in light blue and Oxford in dark blue.

However, Pete's mind was far away from the race as he looked vacantly in front of him. He pushed the keys into the door, climbed the stairs and walked into the large bar area. It had a musky smell combined with the smell of varnish. The walls of the bar were covered in pictures of individual rowers and rowing teams from yesteryear and present day. There was even a picture of Pete on the wall with his arms around a group of people.

Pete sat down on a chair and opened his bag. Inside it were about 100 small plastic Eight Balls. They looked exactly the same as the one that at that moment was resting next to Jonah's chest.

120

Pete picked up a handful of the key rings and vacantly wandered towards the men's toilets. He went into one of the cubicles. He stopped in front of the toilet, took the lid off the back of it and dropped an Eight Ball into it. He did this with the other cubicle and then also with the women's toilets. Four of the key rings had been used.

Pete wandered into the main room – a very large room that could be used for conferences, dining, dancing, etc. It had access to the balcony which ran alongside it. This room had also been prepared for the Boat Race. There would be a few hundred people that couldn't fit onto the balcony (but that still wouldn't stop them trying). However, a large screen had been placed on the wall to accommodate those denied the prime spot. Those that smugly had watched the start from the balcony would barge into the room in an attempt to try and watch the end of the race. By 2.30pm, the club would be packed.

Pete attached a key ring behind the flat screen. He then walked like a zombie out onto the balcony and put an Eight Ball in a flower pot.

He wandered back into the bar and sat down. He took off his oil skin jacket to reveal that he was, indeed, still dressed as a pirate. He zipped up the small bag with the remaining Eight Balls and put the little rucksack onto his back. He then put his oil skin jacket back on. He sat their vacantly. He felt a little electric shock from the gold watch on his wrist and he closed his eyes.

Pete was the only person in the club. Soon there would be others. Soon there would be hundreds.

23

Carl rushed upstairs towards his flat as Maisie turned the other way and headed downwards towards the vault.

"Don't touch anyone!" she shouted, as she disappeared from view.

"There's no-one up here!" he cried. "How can I touch anyone?"

"Just don't," she said. "I'll see you here, by the bar, shortly."

Carl pushed open the door to his flat. It was a cramped, two bed flat and in one of the rooms he had a large basket full of costumes. For years the pub had hosted parties and the fancy dress costumes had mounted up. He threw open the lids and started pulling them out quickly.

Gorilla...no. Spiderman...no. Don't even know what that is...no. Coconut bikini...why? No...no. He needed to cover all of his body – so did Maisie. Then he came across two identical outfits. He sighed. They would have to do. He put them down on his bed as he rummaged for two pairs of gloves.

He looked at the outfit on the bed. Better get it over and done with.

Maisie was running down the stairs when she came across Bert coming up them. Maisie stopped dead in her tracks when she saw Bert coming up, cue in hand. Bert stopped when he saw her. Maisie's face was alarmed.

"'Ello, Maiz," he said, with a cheeky grin and a twinkle in his eye. "Whatcha doin' 'ere?" He took a step nearer.

"Stop, Bert," she said, putting a hand up. "I've been contaminated by a time leak, if you touch me you will die."

"Mornin' to yoo too," Bert said and chuckled. "A time leak? Wot d'ya mean? Like a gas leak?" He scratched his head and looked over at the slightly red-faced woman in front of him.

"Err…excooose me. No, not like a gas leak," she said then added, "Actually, a bit like a gas leak, yes, in that it can kill you."

Bert rubbed his eyes.

"Look, Bert. Don't go into the kitchen. Time has stopped at 9.45 in there. Don't touch me or Carl as we were in there when it stopped," Maisie garbled and started to fan herself. "God, I'm having a flush."

Bert scratched his head again. "Don't go into the kitchen, don't touch Carl and don't touch yoo," Bert repeated. "Shame," he said and winked at Maisie. Maisie burst out laughing and sat down fanning herself.

"Behave yourself, Bert. You're a married man," she cackled, her face getting redder and getting slightly sweaty.

"Err…yoo alright?" Bert asked with concern.

"Oh this…just the change, love," Maisie whispered. "Nothing to do with time leaks." Maisie took a piece of paper out of her pocket and started to fan herself.

Bert looked a bit uncomfortable with that information. "Yoo know there are three Guardians down there asleep," he warned.

Maisie nodded as she continued fanning herself. "Oh, yes, Carl told me. I just need to get some bits and pieces from down there. Then I've got to go back into the infinity cube and patch up the time leak."

"Right," Bert said, not understanding a single word.

"Carl is up in his flat getting costumes so we can cover ourselves up so we don't kill anyone," she said.

"Right," Bert said and nodded, pretending he understood what she was saying. "Don't go into the kitchen? I wanted a cup of tea," he sighed.

"Well, go to the caff across the road. Just don't go in the kitchen," Maisie ordered, furiously fanning herself and standing up.

"You gonna be OK?" he asked.

"Yes, of course. Just another thing. Fergus is behind it all."

Bert frowned. "Don't surprise me," he said solemnly. He

123

gripped his cue. "We now 'ave powers, don't we? Does Carl know?"

"Of course. He was in the infinity cube with me when he attacked."

Bert closed his eyes. "I definitely need a cup of tea."

"Well go on. Get me one too and I'll see you upstairs in a few minutes," Maisie said, pushing herself flat against the wall. "Come on, get past."

Bert leaned back, putting as much space between her and him as he could. Bert got by her and started to jog up the stairs (he was trying to see if he still had his super-speed). Maisie wolf-whistled after him.

"You've still got it, Bert," she teased.

"I never lost it," he cackled as he approached the door leading to the bar.

Maisie fanned herself some more and headed down into the vault.

Bert opened the door and went into the bar. As he did, he heard a knock on the public door. He jogged over.

"Who is it?" he asked.

"Me and Piglet," Lola squeaked.

"Who?" Bert laughed.

"Don't fuck about," Lola threatened. "I'm super strong now, remember?" Lola knew that her powers had temporarily subsided but she was still very excited from all the recent events.

"Yoo'll 'ave to catch me first," Bert said dryly as he opened the door and let them in.

"We know whose behind this," Lola announced and jumped up on Bert. Bert picked her up and twirled her around.

"So do I," he said. Lola frowned and jumped down. She crossed her arms petulantly. Johnny looked put out.

"So do I," said Carl, who was standing behind him. The three of them spun around to see their friend dressed head to toe as a nun. On top of his wimple there was a mask of Elvis (that he could pull down over his face) and he was wearing ski gloves. In his right hand he held his cue. In his other glove was a lit cigarette.

"Forget the tea, I'm goin' for a brandy." Bert walked over to the bar, shaking his head and scratching the back of it hard.

124

Johnny and Lola stood open mouthed.

"I know what you're thinking," said Carl, taking a drag on his cigarette.

"No, I really don't think you do," mocked Johnny.

"I know this looks strange."

"Is it 'alloween today?" Lola asked.

Carl smiled at Lola. Again, he wasn't quite sure if she was serious or mucking about. "Look. Fergus is behind all of this," Carl said quickly.

"Yes, I know," said Johnny, feeling slightly deflated that Carl knew this. He thought that he was the only one to have worked it out. He and his first class degree in psychology.

"We worked it out," Lola chirped. Johnny inwardly sighed.

"There are other problems," Carl warned. "I don't really know how to explain it all but, in a nutshell, there's a time leak in the kitchen and it's bad news, which is why I'm dressed as a nun."

Johnny leaned against his cue. "As a psychologist, you had better give me a more rational explanation or it's the pretty pink pills and an ambulance with a flashing light for you."

Carl took a long drag on his cigarette while Bert poured himself a very large brandy and took a swig. Carl exhaled, thinking hard and fast about how he was going to explain the situation.

"Look, it seems my power is witchy, magical-type stuff. Maisie had seen a fish next to a porcupine on the wall and the next thing I knew I was in an invisible cube in space, Fergus attacked and now the kitchen is stuck at 9.45 and is leaking out," Carl blurted out without drawing breath.

Johnny exchanged looks with Lola.

"I can somersault," she said. "Really high."

Carl raised his eyebrows at her.

"That's really helping your case now, is it?" Johnny said to Carl, getting a cigarette out of his pocket and lighting up. Bert took another glug.

"Look, if you go into the kitchen, you will die. If you touch my skin or Maisie's skin, you will die." Carl said. "It's that simple."

Carl took another drag of his cigarette. "Maisie is going back into the kitchen to patch up the time leak. She's just gone down to the vault to get some stuff and then she'll be back."

Johnny started to feel slightly normal about his half-dead status. Lola merely frowned and chewed her lip.

"Fergus is back and he's got all kinds of dark powers." Carl explained about the visions he had seen in the cube – the house, the gold watch, etc.

There was a pause.

Johnny, Lola and Carl all slowly sat down around the table, resting their cues against the table. Bert was standing behind the bar, having another glug of brandy.

"Anyone else want one?" Bert asked, raising his glass. The three looked over at Bert.

"Hell yes!" Johnny cried.

"Yeah," said Carl.

"Just an orange juice," Lola added. "No ice. Ta."

"Look, the Guardians will be waking soon." Carl said. "We don't have a lot of time."

Lola looked at Carl's face poking out from the costume and she began to find it very funny. She tried to suppress a laugh. A high-pitched squeak emerged.

"Ow," Carl winced, covering his ears "God, Pixie, your laugh."

"Oh shit," Johnny said suddenly. "Are you going to tell them about all this?" They had already been in enough trouble with the Guardians.

Carl leaned back in his chair, rubbed his stubble and looked up at the ceiling. "Maisie says that we shouldn't tell them about the time leak."

"Wot about all yer visions?" Lola asked. "Are ya gonna tell 'em about those?"

Bert walked over with their drinks. He put them on the table and Johnny immediately picked his up and glugged down the brandy. Lola sighed. She picked up her orange juice and took the smallest sip and replaced it on the table. Carl picked his up with both his gloved hands and took a glug.

Bert went back to the bar, picked up his cue and returned to the table. He put his cue next to the others.

"If I tell them about the visions then I am going to have to tell them about the leak," Carl said.

Bert sat down with Johnny and Lola. Carl was in isolation

on the other side of the table.

"I don't think they'll be too happy to find out we've been mucking around with time," Carl warned.

"Yoo mean, you've been muckin' around wiv time," Lola said, taking a cigarette out of her pocket and lighting up.

"OK, I've been mucking around with time," Carl replied.

"Look, the Guardians will be performing a ritual this afternoon at the church. We have to find out if Fergus is at my old house. We've got to find out about the Umpire's boat and those watches. I also saw Tara in my vision," Carl explained.

"Big Tara? Tara your manager?" Bert asked.

"Yeah, Tara," he replied.

"What has she got to do with any of this?" Johnny asked.

"I don't know," Carl sighed. "I just don't know but I don't think I would have been shown her if it wasn't really important." Carl took another sip. "She'll be here soon. I'll just...have to keep an eye on her."

"Wot d'ya want us to do?" Bert asked.

"You three are going to have to go over to my old house and see if Fergus is there. I would go, I really want to go, trust me, but I can't leave here," Carl growled. "I am going to have to keep everyone out of the kitchen, run this pub, and keep the Guardians happy."

"And explain why ya dressed like a penguin," Lola added.

"Yes, Pixie, and explain why I'm dressed like a 'penguin'," Carl said.

While they were talking, the tips of their pool cues started to glow. Lola was the first to notice it.

"Look," she pointed. "Look," she said excitedly. The other three looked to where she was pointing.

"Why are they doin' that?" asked Bert.

"I don't know," panicked Johnny. "Carl?"

Carl shrugged. "God knows," he said, looking at the four cue tips that were each throwing out indigo, blue, green and yellow lights.

"The last time they did that was with the Eight Ball, before the Guardians came," Johnny stated, feeling his pulse begin to quicken.

"I know," said Carl.

Outside the pub at that moment, a hooded figure walked by,

127

wearing dark glasses and head lowered in the sunlight.

Sophie had been looking at the street and pub ever since she had seen the two people with the pool cues go inside. Her heart started to pump harder when she saw the hooded figure walk down the street. She would know his gait anywhere. It was Fergus. He was heading towards the common.

24

Maisie crept down the stairs until she came to the vault door. It was made of oak and covered in carved symbols and markings, including elegant graffiti from former Lodge members dating back years. Maisie gripped the large gold handle and slowly started to turn it. The door hinge creaked and Maisie held her breath. She pushed it slowly and it creaked again. She paused once more before opening it just enough for her to squeeze through. The first thing that hit her was the noise of the snoring. The second thing that hit her was the smell of incense, smoke, beer and stale curry. Maisie wrinkled her nose. Ripe! She waved her hand in front of her nose.

The room was dark but the two large candles were still burning on the vault table. She squinted trying to take in who and what were where. Her eyes began to adjust to the darkness. She saw two sets of bunk beds that were pulled down from the wall. She could see three bodies. They all appeared to be asleep and one was snoring like a maniac. On the floor were two untidy mattresses where Carl and Bert had slept.

Maisie needed to get into the adjoining room, where all the magical books and artefacts were kept. She would have to step over the mattresses and creep by the bunk beds. There was one particular thing she was after and that was a staff. A staff made of holly wood. All staffs used by powerful magicians were made of holly wood (and known as the holly wood) and this particular staff had belonged to a very, very powerful white magician indeed. Like many other objects in the adjoining 'magic' room, the staff was a neglected treasure. A hundred years ago this vault had seen heroic Vampire Killers and White Witches work alongside each other. The Putney Lodge had been a shining beacon to all other Lodges around the world. However, the life and vitality had slowly been drained out of it but now, after decades of stagnation, changes were occurring. Maisie could feel it and see it. Powerful Vampire Killers were emerging and they were working alongside a witch. As it should be, thought Maisie.

Maisie tip-toed over the mattresses placed near to the bunk beds. As she was lifting up her right foot it got caught in a blanket and she fell forward, coming nose to nose with Max. A centimetre closer and she would've touched him. She would've killed him! Maisie's eyes went wide with horror. He hadn't woken. Thank God. She heard Marilyn turn over on the top bunk and she heard the rattling snores of Jonah on the other set of bunks.

Maisie pushed herself away from Max as quietly as she could. He muttered. Maisie slowly stood up on her feet and tip-toed over to the room. She put her hand on the handle and turned it slowly and quietly.

The room was completely sealed away from the rest the vault (a panic room within a panic room, she thought). There were no windows so no light could get in or out. She entered into the room and closed the door behind her and suddenly she was in pitch black. She reached her hand to the side and flicked the switch. Overhead fluorescent lights flickered on and settled.

The room was large indeed and cluttered. There were shelves upon shelves covered in books and artefacts. There was a table in the centre, covered in closed and half-open books. It was like an ancient mini-museum. Maisie hadn't been here in years. She had been here only a couple of times about thirty years ago as a young witch as part of a White Witch coven tour. The Pig & Phoenix and the vault had been a highlight to her and she remembered this room well. She had also seen it recently in her crystal ball. In fact, she had seen the staff twirling in the crystal only the other night.

Maisie walked towards a shelf. It was covered in all types of things. Books, a bronze naval compass, a map, a bouquet of silk flowers and there, behind them, lay the staff. It was about four foot high, smooth and dark. It was nothing special to look at. Maisie picked it up and walked back to the table and laid the staff down on it. She closed her eyes, breathed deeply and started to wave her hand over it back and forth.

There was a crackling and a hissing noise. The lights overhead began to flicker and a wind started to blow in the room. Papers flew off from the table and the staff started to glow. Maisie continued muttering and the hissing got louder. A cloud of blue light started to come out of the staff growing up to the ceiling. The wind kept blowing and the lights flickered.

The blue light started to form an image. It was blurred at first and then an image of a blonde woman looking like a Nordic Viking warrior holding a large axe appeared. She was about nine foot high.

"I am the Guardian of the Staff and this had bloody better be good," she snapped in a posh English accent.

25

Fergus walked across the common. Although his face was obscured by a hood and sunglasses, anyone looking at his body language would say he was angry. He walked towards Sophie's house and let himself in, aggressively marching up the stairs, higher and higher until he reached the top floor – until he reached the pigeon room. As he approached the door he could hear a cacophony of high pitched squeals. He grinned evilly to himself. He stood outside the door, took out a mobile and made a call.

Carl glugged down the rest of his brandy and put the empty glass down on the table. Lola stood up, grabbing her cue, and skipped over to the middle of the bar area. She started to twirl her cue like a majorette's baton.

"Right, let's find out if he's at yer old house," she said. "I can 'andle it on me own."

Carl was about to answer her when his mobile phone began to ring with the theme tune from the 1970's children's show, 'Rainbow'. Carl stood up and started to pat down his nun's habit with gloved hands. He then pulled off a glove with his teeth, hoisted up the long black material and grabbed his phone out of his right hand pocket. The caller ID said: 'Fergus'. Carl's heart pounded. He still had his old phone! No way.

Johnny saw Carl's face contort into a mixture of shock and anger.

"Carl, you OK?" Johnny asked.

"It's him," Carl whispered, staring at the caller ID.

"Who?" Bert asked, looking worried.

"Fergus," Carl answered. He saw that the time was coming up to 10am on his mobile. He looked at his wristwatch. The second hand was ticking forwards and then one second back. Bollocks! He was slowly starting to leak time.

Lola ran over. "Well fuckin' answer it then," she squeaked. "I'll fuckin' answer it."

Lola took a step nearer. Carl backed off.

"Don't come near me, Lola..." he warned. Carl pressed a button and put the phone to his ear.

"Yes?" Carl asked, chewing his bottom lip. He put his hand up to stop anyone coming near him.

Lola mouthed 'put it on speaker' but Carl dismissed the idea with a wave of his hand. Bert frowned.

There was a pause. Nothing was said for a moment. Then Carl heard a deep, dark voice. He recognised it but it had become warped. It had a resonance that was pure evil and it sent a chill down Carl's spine.

"Hello Carly," Fergus said mockingly.

Carl stared ahead out of the window. He saw sunlight hit a tree covered in blossom and he was determined to focus on it and keep his mind neutral. He didn't reply to the childhood nickname Fergus had called him.

"So," Fergus's voice said. "You've been playing around in an infinity cube."

"What do you want, Fergus?" Carl asked coldly. Johnny, Bert and Lola all turned their ears towards him. As Johnny was slightly deaf it was a pointless exercise but it was one of those instinctive things.

"Is that any way to talk to an old friend?" Fergus taunted.

"What do you want, Fergus?" Carl asked again, staring ahead.

"It seems you've developed a few skills since I last saw you," Fergus sneered.

"As have you," Carl replied. "Just a shame we're on opposite sides of the coin, isn't it."

"Oh no, this is much more fun. I suppose the Guardians are with you, ready to get down to the common this afternoon."

"What do you WANT, Fergus?" Carl demanded.

Fergus chuckled. "I thought I'd give you some help, for old

time's sake."

"It still seems you have a good sense of humour," Carl said. "What help could I possibly need from you?" Carl whispered, trying to keep his attention on the blossom.

Fergus chuckled again. "I didn't recognise your new band of nobodies. I suppose George hung up his cue and started playing with his balls."

"Well, he didn't dishonour himself, and our Lodge, by stealing a cue. It's wasn't yours to take, Fergus," Carl said with a steely voice.

"It doesn't seem to mind. I've managed to make a few modifications," he replied icily.

"Give it back, Fergus," Carl warned. "Give it back while you still can."

"How noble of you, Carly. But it isn't quite that simple."

"Why, wouldn't your masters like it? What's the deal, Fergus? Who have you made a bargain with?" Carl snarled.

There was silence.

"I'll tell you what I think," Carl said. "I think you are scared. I think you've made a promise to some nasty...what shall we call them...demons? I don't think you factored in how powerful we would become. I think you're scared that we just might stop your little...offering."

There was a pause.

"Aren't you going to ask me about Katie?" Fergus asked darkly.

Carl inhaled deeply, calming himself. "Why should I ask you? You'll only lie."

There was another pause.

"Don't you want to know where she is?"

Carl looked at his three friends in front of him. "You know what, Fergus? I'll find her without you. You made a bad mistake underestimating us and you will regret it."

"It's too late, Carly. You'll never stop my plan. It can't fail. Whatever you do, it'll just help me," Fergus sneered.

"If you weren't scared of me, of us, you wouldn't be calling me, would you? I know what your plans are and we are going to stop you." Carl stopped the call and looked down at the phone in front of him.

"Lola, get over to my old house," Carl said.

134

"Do ya fink he's there?" Lola asked. "Cos I'm ready for that twat."

Carl smiled at her. "No, Pixie. I don't think he's there but I think he's done something there. When I was in the infinity cube with Maisie, she told me that dark magicians needs to cause pain and chaos. It's an offering to their masters. A favour for a favour or energy for a favour."

"Yoo wot?" Bert asked, standing up and getting hold of his cue.

"Fergus is serving up a menu of pain, chaos and despair for his clients," Carl explained excitedly.

Johnny gave him a knowing look. Lola just stared at him.

"The bomb, the fighting, my house with Katie, it's all designed to create pain. It's like...it's like...a starter, main and dessert," Carl said.

"So?" Bert asked. "But we wouldn't 'ave known any of this if yoo 'adn't been in that cubey fing."

"Infinity cube," Carl corrected.

"Yeah, that fing," Bert answered.

"I worked it out that it was Fergus," bragged Johnny. "I used psychology and not magic."

"We worked it out," Lola said.

Johnny sighed. "OK, we worked it out."

"And we're gettin' married when it's all over," she added.

"Yes, and we're getting married when this is all over."

Bert shook his head and laughed. "Good luck to ya, Johnny."

"Oi," Lola snapped. "Watch it, ya old git."

Bert laughed his head off. Lola grabbed her cue and shook it under his nose.

"That's a powerful weapon. A little pixie like yoo should be careful," he said, also grabbing his cue. Lola's elfin face became thunderous. Her large brown eyes almost seemed to glow and her brow furrowed. Bert looked like a cheeky schoolboy.

"Do ya 'ave a death wish?" She asked, violently shaking the cue. "Do ya, old man?" She raised her cue as if it were a sword.

"Wot...a little pixie like yoo? Hurt moi?" Bert teased, fanning himself like a Victorian lady who had just heard a scandal involving her daughter and the vicar.

"Yeah, me and Cindy," Lola said, swinging back the dark brown cue in her baseball stance – knees bent and bottom out. She blew her fringe out of her eyes.

"Who the 'ell is Cindy?" Bert asked, swinging his cue behind his shoulder, jokily copying Lola – sticking his bottom out.

"Err... can we focus? Err...Fergus. End of the world?" Carl said, trying to intervene.

"Shut it! Yer a frozen penguin and ya can't touch us," Lola said. Johnny merely shook his head, once again. Carl rubbed his eyes.

"Cindy is me cue," Lola stated proudly, taking a step nearer to Bert. Bert laughed hard and took a step closer to her.

"Yer can't call ya pool cue Cindy," he spluttered.

Lola swung her cue at Bert, "Really?" she challenged as Bert prepared to parry the blow.

The two cues struck one another and there was enormous crashing noise, like a lightning strike. Bert went flying backwards one way, his cue flying out of his hand, and Lola the other – also losing her cue.

Johnny, unluckily for him, was in the way of Lola's flight. Luckily for him, she weighed six stone. Bert skidded along the floor and crashed into the Ladies' toilet door. With the weight and speed of him, he slammed the door open where he continued skidding into the wall. Unfortunately, there was a hand dryer on it, which he set off and which blasted his head with hot air.

Johnny went flying backwards into the wall, which took the wind right out of him. Lola appeared to be physically fine, if stunned by the sudden blast.

"Ow," said Johnny, wincing. Lola looked spaced out. That was twice she had blasted backwards in under 24 hours! She wasn't happy about it.

Carl sat down and lit another cigarette and shook his head in a mixture of resignation, frustration and fear. He felt that the outside world was ticking along normally. There were people already on their way to Putney to see the Boat Race. Families were having breakfast and his staff were only a few minutes away from coming into his pub to work. Here he was, dressed as a nun because he was contaminated with a time leak. Fergus was out there, leaking out evil. Plotting and scheming. A mere puppet to serving evil overlords.

Carl rolled his eyes upwards towards the heavens and he did a double take. His cigarette fell out of his mouth and onto the table.

The two cues were hovering about five inches below the ceiling. Carl leapt to his feet and pointed by jabbing his finger upwards. The other three were too incapacitated to notice Carl's quiet but frenzied action.

"Look!" shouted Carl. "Look!" he said, jabbing furiously.

Lola looked up and her jaw dropped. She aggressively pushed herself off Johnny, who was grimacing with pain. "Ow," he whispered again as her hand pushed up from an inappropriate place.

Lola, slacked jaw, walked underneath where the cues were hovering.

"Oh my God," she huskily whispered. "Piglet, look at this." The two cues were about two feet apart but side by side and static. "Wot 'appened?" she asked. "Why are they up there?"

Bert slowly pushed himself up to his feet. He had also had the wind knocked out of him. His lower back hurt, his hair had been blown all over the place and the top of his scalp was burning from the hand dryer.

"Wot woz that?" he asked, rubbing the back of his head and staggering forward.

Johnny peeled open his crunched-up eyes and focused on Lola. He upwardly followed her eye line. He gasped slightly. It wasn't *such* a shock to him as the others to see a hovering cue. His cue had, after all, dragged him home and saved his (half) life. He did feel guilty about not telling the others but he couldn't afford to reveal his secret. Maybe one day. Maybe after all that was happening they would accept him.

"Wow..." he said with fake surprise. He pushed himself up, taking deep breaths. He felt like he had gone two ten rounds with a boxing kangaroo. His ribs and back ached and his knees cracked.

"'Ow are we gonna get 'em down?" Lola asked.

"We *have* to get them down," Carl said, rubbing his stubble. "Tara will be here soon. She can't see this." Carl was

137

determined that he was not going to cancel Boat Race Day. He didn't care that he was leaking time, that there were floating cues and Guardians asleep in the basement vault.

Bert walked over to Carl's side. He saw the cigarette on the table. He picked it up and put it back in Carl's mouth. The danger of Bert getting that close to Carl seemed to escape the pair of them. "Smoking is dangerous," he said and cackled. Carl grinned for a moment, then his eyes went wide and he swallowed.

"So is putting a cigarette in the mouth of a man that can kill you with a single touch," Carl said quietly.

Bert clasped his hand over his mouth, like a naughty schoolboy who had just said a rude word in front of a teacher. "Shit! I forgot!" he exclaimed, taking a large step back. Then taking another step back. That was the closest to instant extermination he had ever been.

"Look up there, look at them," Carl said, licking his lips and trying to forget what had nearly happened. The idea of nearly killing Bert by accident was too terrible to contemplate.

"Why are they doin' that?" Bert asked, taking another smaller step away.

Johnny gently walked over to Lola, holding his right side and rubbing the other. "Maybe they don't like fighting each other," Johnny suggested, still taking deep breaths.

Carl and Bert walked over to join the other two.

"What, they're protesting?" Carl asked.

"They are alive," Johnny said. "Maybe they don't like being smashed into one another. I know the feeling."

"'Ow are we gonna get 'em down?" Bert croaked.

"Wot do we do? Send flowers?" Lola squeaked. "'Ow do ya apologise to a cue?"

There was silence for a moment. Each one of them thinking hard about their predicament. Lola jumped up and down in excitement, clapping her hands. "Ooo…I know wot to do. I know wot to do."

"Let me get on ya shoulders." She turned to Johnny. "I fink I can reach 'em."

"My shoulders? My back's knackered!" he protested.

"Heroes don't get bad backs," she whispered at him, narrowing her eyes. In all the films she had seen, heroes

138

always seemed to be super fit and immune to pain. Johnny was a hero to her but he didn't seem to be immune to pain.

Johnny, feeling the pressure to impress his fiancée, picked Lola up and put her on his shoulders, grimacing as he did. He would need an entire night in his vegetable patch before long.

Lola stretched and strained upwards but she couldn't reach them. She needed at least another three feet.

Bert turned to look at the contorted face of Johnny and the strained face of Lola – her tongue sticking out as she stretched upwards.

"I ain't putting yoo on me shoulders," Bert said to Carl.

"Even if I wasn't leaking time, I wouldn't accept," Carl replied dryly. Bert chuckled.

"Stand on ya toes," Lola ordered down to Johnny, as she stretched as high as she could. Johnny stood on his toes. But it really didn't help the gap of three feet.

"Jump," she said. Johnny sighed and started to jump – each landing hurting his ribs. The jumping also didn't help with the gap.

"Bert, would ya pass me one of them other cues?" she asked. Bert was momentarily surprised to be included in this performance but quickly moved over to the table and picked up Johnny's cue. He passed it up to Lola, accidentally knocking Johnny's nose as he did.

"Sorry, mate," Bert said to Johnny.

Lola reached up, extending her spine and her arms to their maximum stretch and tried to get the cue over the top of 'Cindy' and pull her down. However, all she managed to do was tap the other cues. Johnny's cue started to shake in her hands violently. It broke free out of her grip and went to hover next to the others.

"Fuck," she said. Her eyes narrowed. "Fuck, fuck, fuck!" she growled. "That's not fair," she barked at the cues, shaking her fist. "Wot's wrong wiv ya? Wot's ya problem?" She ran her fingers through her hair in wild frustration and kicked her legs.

"Ow," said Johnny.

"Sorry, piglet," she said. "It's them fuckin' cues, wot's wrong wiv 'em?"

Bert and Carl exchanged looks. Neither had a clue why the cues were behaving in this rebellious way. Carl cast a glance towards his cue, which was still resting next to the table.

"I ain't givin' up! I'm gonna try and jump up and pull one down," she informed the others with determination.

"Ok, Pixie," Bert said, placing his hands on his hips.

Lola carefully pulled one knee up onto Johnny's shoulder and wobbled to keep her balance. She stretched her arms upwards and with a short, hard push jumped upwards. She grabbed hold of one of the cues but she failed to pull it to earth. It still hovered there with her dangling.

"It's stuck," Lola shouted. "It's fuckin' stuck." She kicked her legs to try and get some energy flowing through her.

"Maybe that's not your cue," Carl suggested. "Move along." Carl couldn't tell from that distance whose cue was whose. Perhaps the cues would only respond to their custodians.

Lola reached over to the next cue, grabbed it and swung over. She held on and tugged it. It was her cue – she recognised its markings and the familiar feel. Suddenly there was a slight tremor in her body.

"Somefink's goin' on," she said. "Whoa...it's shakin'."

The cue started to vibrate. It jerked two feet forward and stopped. Lola squeaked, "Fuck." Then her cue started to move forward very slowly and steadily with Lola hanging on.

"Bollocks," she yelped. "Wot's goin' on?"

"'Ang on, Pix. It's on the move," Bert wheezed.

The cue moved forward to the end of the pub, with the three men slowly following behind, transfixed. The cue suddenly flipped 180 degrees, spinning Lola quickly. "Eek!"

It then lowered slowly and stopped about ten feet off the ground.

"Wot's it doin'?" Lola demanded.

"You can jump off if you want," Johnny said.

"Or you could climb onto it," Bert mused. As it was no longer just hovering underneath the ceiling, he realised she could get onto it. Then a light bulb went off in his head. "Pix, climb onto it!" he cried excitedly.

"Wot?" Lola barked. "'Ow can I do that? I'm not a fuckin' Russian Olympic gymnast."

"Hey, I thought you could somersault," Carl teased.

"I can somersault. I woz super strong when I did that!"

"Go on, you can do it," Johnny said encouragingly.

"Why?" she snapped.

"Just do it, Pix," Bert said. "Yoo'll see."

Lola put in a concentrated effort to swing herself up onto the cue – to straddle it. Her first attempt achieved little more than swearing and leg thrashing but on her second attempt, with even more swearing and leg thrashing, she managed to swing her leg over and sit on it, holding it and leaning forwards for balance. Her face beamed with pride. The three down below applauded. Lola giggled. The cue was still hovering and Lola looked around the pub.

"It's great up 'ere," she laughed. "Yoo look funny down there. Yoo look small."

"Now wot?" she asked, looking at the men standing below her. She wiggled her feet. "This is brilliant. I love it."

"Try and move forward," Johnny said.

"'Ow?" Lola replied.

"Think about it," Johnny advised. "Remember, the security camera? Remember wanting to remove it and your cue destroying it. The cue responded to your thoughts."

Lola furrowed her brow and started to think about the cue moving forwards. Her cue moved forward slightly. "Wow," she said with a big, broad grin. She giggled. "Wow, that woz amazin'," she beamed as she started to move slowly forwards.

Bert grinned. "Atta girl."

"I'm flyin'," she said, as she started to move forwards. She giggled again. "Look at me, I'm flyin'."

Lola was flying slowly towards the end of the pub. When she reached there, she thought about it turning around and it did. It quickly flipped again and Lola had to grip hard so that she wasn't thrown off. When she got her balance, she thought about flying back the other way and the cue started to move.

"That looks fantastic," Carl said. "But I'm so sorry, you've got to stop, Tara will be here soon." In fact, all his members of staff should've been here already.

"I want a go," insisted Bert, not listening to Carl. "My cue's up there. If Pix can do it, then so can I," Bert said, looking up at his hovering cue.

"And me," said Johnny. "I want to fly too. Don't you? Forget Tara, this is far more important. This is flying. Flying!"

Carl looked over at his cue. It wasn't hovering. It was still next to the table – unmoving. No, it hadn't been used aggressively towards another cue. Was that why? Did cues protest? Did they get resentful and temperamental? Maybe they were similar to or reflected the characteristics of the people they chose to be their custodians. Maybe Lola and her cue were as 'unique' as the other, he thought.

However, his cue had also been in the kitchen with him when time stuck at 9.45. Maybe that was the problem. Maybe it had something to do with the time leak. Maybe the other cues were keeping away from his cue to protect themselves from death. These thoughts went around his head as he watched Bert climb onto a chair. Of course, they were all going to be excited about flying! On a practical note, he also needed them to get their cues down from the ceiling.

"Bert, what are you doing? Why don't you just think to it, like Lola did," Carl suggested. Johnny grinned at Bert, who grinned back. They both closed their eyes.

Johnny thought to his cue and it slowly, slowly started to lower down and come next to him. The same happened with Bert's cue. The two of them opened their eyes and looked at the cues hovering next to them at hip height. They both seemed to have the same thought of who could be the first to fly. They flung their legs over and thought of moving upwards. Their cues obeyed and it was a slightly painful experience for both men.

"Ow, bloody 'ell," griped Bert, wincing. "I'm gonna need paddin' down there."

"Jesus," Johnny said, looking as if he had just sucked a lemon. "Magic is painful."

"But a right laugh," Bert added, as the two of them floated upwards towards the ceiling. Bert went too high and hit his head.

"Ow, down...down..." he ordered. There was no response. He had to think the words...'down...down' and he went lower.

Johnny was jerking about, like a car stalling. Lola, meanwhile, was moving forwards with more confidence and gracefully. She pulled up next to Johnny. "Great, innit?" she said and added: "Beep beep. Beep beep!" as she moved past him, turned and stopped.

"Err...yes..." Johnny said as he jerked forward and stopped. Bert lowered down from above and pulled up next to Lola, who looked at Carl and beckoned him with her hand to join them.

Carl watched his three friends hovering. It was an incredible sight to behold and he felt that sense of pride in them. He also felt an incredible sense of wonder. Who knew you could fly on a pool cue?

"Come on Carl," Lola squeaked. "Grab yer cue and 'ave a go."

Carl inhaled. He looked at his cue. If it was also affected by the time leak then he would have to cover it up as well. He grabbed it and marched behind the bar. There were black bin bags in a cupboard and some duct tape. He put his cue on the counter, unravelled two bin bags, shoved the cue in each end and taped it up loosely. Meanwhile, Johnny moved jerkily by the counter, Bert was twirling slowly and Lola was moving backwards. He could hear the high-pitched giggles of Lola and the laughter of the others. Carl wanted to play too!

Carl looked at the bagged up cue on the counter. He closed his eyes and imagined it hovering. He opened his eyes but nothing had happened. He tried again and this time it started to hover before him. The biggest smile broke out across his face. His heart pounded with happiness. "Wow," he said with wonder. "Just wow."

He walked back to the other side of the counter, keeping his eye on the cue as he did. He took a step deeper into the public area and thought about his cue moving over to his side. It sped over quickly. Carl burst out laughing with delight. He pulled up his habit and stuck his leg over. He thought about moving upwards and he slowly did. He also experienced a modicum of pain. "Ouch," he groaned.

He thought about moving forwards towards his friends and he started to glide. He moved swiftly and calmly forward but couldn't stop. He headed straight towards a bunch of light and dark balloons stuck to the wall. "Noo...not the balloons!" he cried as he hit them and smashed into the wall. Two loudly popped, making the others jump. "Wot woz that?" Lola gasped.

"My balloons!" Carl yelled. Lola turned her cue around and looked at Carl, dressed as a nun, flying on a pool cue with a balloon wrapped around his neck and started to giggle loudly and continuously.

Bert turned to look at where the bang had come from. He was starting to get the hang of flying very quickly. He figured years of driving a taxi around London, practically on mental auto-pilot, had given him an advantage. His cue responded to his commands very quickly.

Bert caught sight of Carl and he guffawed. Johnny, who was still jerking about, but getting better, also turned and looked at Carl. "You couldn't make this up," he muttered to Bert.

"Yup," he said. "Truth is stranger than fiction."

"Yoo need an 'and, Carl?" Bert cackled, as he flew over next to Carl. Carl gave him a knowing look. "Yoo'll never guess who I 'ad on the back of me cue last night," he joked. Carl grinned.

"You going to Kensington?" Carl asked. Bert pursed his lips and shook his head. "Nah, ain't goin' north of the river, mate."

Bert reached over to the balloon around Carl's neck and broke it free from the string. Carl thanked him and started to loosen the remaining string. Bert bounced the balloon on the back of his hand.

Lola pulled up next to him and he tapped the balloon over to her. She tapped it back to Bert who tapped it over to Carl.

Johnny managed to jerkily move up next to them. Carl tapped the balloon over to Johnny, who managed to tap it back in the general direction of the other three. Lola caught it.

"I can't believe this," Carl said. "Things are just getting weirder and weirder." Johnny managed to fly up to the left side of Lola, so that all four of them were lined up in a row. Carl, Bert, Lola then Johnny. They were hovering about fifteen feet off the floor.

Lola looked over at Carl. "I want a costume too."

"I'm only dressed like this because I have to," Carl complained.

"I wouldn't mind dressin' up," Lola squeaked. By the look in her eye it would seem that her mind was set on this idea.

"Why?" asked Johnny. He knew that look.

"It looks like fun," she said in a far too innocent voice. "Why don't we all dress up?"

"No," Bert and Johnny flatly said together. Lola frowned but before she could say anything Bert began to speak.

"Race ya," Bert said to the others with a cocky smile.

"Where to?" Carl asked, feeling a sense of competition rise in him.

"Hmm...to the other side and back."

"Let's do it," chirped Lola. She was going to win this!

"Hell yeah," agreed Johnny.

Carl smiled. "On three..." he said. "One..."

All four of them leaned forward onto their cues. Lola's eyes were narrowed and facing the other end of the bar.

"Two..."

Johnny looked over at Bert, who looked back at him, pulling a face. Johnny mouthed 'loser' at him.

"Three..."

On the word three, Bert went storming off ahead, followed by Carl, then Lola, then Johnny. Bert was like lightning. He reached the wall fast but failed to stop in time and crashed into it with a thud and fell to the floor. Carl reached the wall without smashing into it but had difficulty in turning around. When Lola pulled up, she managed to turn but too quickly and she swung under her cue, clinging on. Johnny tootled over in his own time, touched the wall, smiled at Carl who was still having difficulty turning. Johnny took his time to turn, but he did and headed off slowly back the other way.

"No way!" shouted Bert, sitting on the floor with his cue next to him, as he watched Johnny slowly but carefully head back to the other side and win. "We'll never 'ear the end of this."

"That's just shameful," griped Carl, still trying to turn.

"That's cos he's an alpha male and you two ain't," Lola said, clinging on.

Carl and Bert both rolled their eyes. Bert mouthed the words 'alpha male' to himself sarcastically.

"I am the winner," shouted Johnny as he touched the wall. "I deduced you three would fail and I was right," he said in a cod-Austrian accent and laughed.

"Shut up, it's only cos ya slow. Yer degree got nuffink to do wiv this," Bert groaned at him.

"Au contraire," said Johnny. "You clearly never read the hare and the tortoise," he lectured, stroking an imaginary beard.

"The hare, a pathological narcissist with a possible drink dependency, believes he is better and faster than the tortoise – himself possibly suffering from low esteem and repressed hostility towards society."

"Someone shut 'im up," pleaded Bert, standing up and thinking to his cue to hover. Hmm… he thought. A hover cue… if only he could sell them. He'd make a fortune.

"Not the professor voice, don't do the professor voice," warned Carl, managing to turn his cue around slowly.

"I like the professor voice," purred Lola. "It's sexy." She quickly lowered down to the floor. When she was safely deposited, she swung her leg over her cue and started to rise. Bert had also stood up and managed to climb back onto his cue.

"Everyfink's sexy to yoo," Bert teased, rising up next to her.

"Yer not sexy to me," she said, looking over.

"Thank gawd for that. You'd bleedin' kill me!"

"Yoo fink I'm sexy, doncha, Carl?" Lola said matter-of-factly, turning to face Carl.

"Yes, Lola, I think you're sexy," Carl said in a bored voice back to her. It wasn't the first time he'd been asked this. It wouldn't be the last.

"Hmmm…" was all she said. "Yer quite sexy, but not as sexy as Johnny."

"Thanks," Carl said as he glided forwards towards Johnny.

"No offence," she chirped.

"None taken." He turned to look at her.

When Carl pulled up next to Johnny, Johnny had a fixed, fake superhero grin splashed across his face. "I won," he boasted and broadened his smile.

Carl nodded wisely then pulled a balloon off the wall and whacked Johnny over the head with it. Johnny, in response, pulled another balloon off the wall and whacked Carl back. Soon, they were both hitting each other and laughing.

Bert and Lola pulled up next to them. Bert pulled a balloon off the bunch and handed it to Lola, who whacked him over the head. Bert grabbed a balloon and hit her back. Soon, all four of them were darting about, chasing each other and whacking each other with balloons and laughing hard.

"Just what is going on here?" boomed the voice of Maisie. They all stopped dead and crashed to the floor.

26

Eric slowly opened his eyes. He felt disorientated and sleepy with a dry throat and a growing thirst. He groggily looked about him, his senses slowly returning to him.

It took him a few moments to recognise that he was in his living room and that his thin white curtains were still drawn. He could see that the sun was burning hotly outside and its light was pushing its way into his living room.

He realised he was sitting upright but that there a strange sensation in his mouth. There was something in it. He tried to spit it out but his mouth was gagged! Eric let out a muffled scream. He jerked his body only to find that he was bound tightly, his hands behind his back and his ankles tied together. He was also naked. A horrible sense of ice-cold fear trickled down his spine.

On his lap was tied a picture of Carl and Katie on their wedding day. He looked down at it and it made no sense to him whatsoever. He screamed again into his gag. His fear was growing and his heart was pounding. He tried to stand up but he couldn't move. He was bound to the sofa.

As he began to scream, there was a crackling noise above him. Eric's eyes darted upwards and there was a tiny black cloud, about an inch long, growing about five feet above his head. Eric screamed harder and harder and the cloud started to slowly expand. He started to hear a very low demonic growling noise coming from the cloud and his eyes widened in horror.

Eric writhed furiously to try and move but he couldn't. He looked wildly around and saw that there was a large pile of small, plastic Eight Balls about four feet away from him. His heart pounded violently and he passed out.

The growling stopped and the small cloud stopped growing.

Maisie marched over to Carl, her hand on one hip and the staff in the other.

"What is going on here? It's like a children's birthday party," Maisie chastised, waggling the staff in front of her.

"We can fly," Lola said, grinning. Lola didn't really know Maisie that well. She had met her and the other two friends in the pub a couple of times and Bert had explained to her that they were witches. She didn't really know what to make of witches as the only ones she had heard of were in stories.

"Err...excooose me, young lady. Yes, I can see that," Maisie scolded. Lola pouted slightly but couldn't stop grinning. She felt exhilarated from the flying and couldn't imagine anyone upsetting her at the moment.

"And Fergus called," Carl announced.

"I see," Maisie said sternly. "And what did he have to say for himself?"

"He called to taunt and threaten me," Carl replied matter-of-factly.

"I see," Maisie huffed. "You seem remarkably calm at that."

"He is a lonely, bitter coward. He has no friends and no laughter," Carl said, looking affectionately at his friends.

"He's dangerous and he has very powerful masters, Carl!" Maisie shouted. "He is not to be underestimated. He is planning...God only knows what. We are going to need courage, cunning and, above all else, luck!"

Her speech went some way to still their excitable mood.

"What's that?" asked Carl, pointing at the staff Maisie was holding.

"Never you mind. It's something I need to stop the time leak. You've told them, I suppose," Maisie asked. "Otherwise you'd look pretty stupid wandering around dressed like that."

"I've got one for you too," Carl grinned sarcastically.

"Well, on second thoughts I won't be needing it. What I do need you to do is to tape up the door after I go in. Don't let anyone go in. Also, if you see anyone coming out of there, who isn't me, don't touch them."

"What do you mean, anyone else other than you? Who are you expecting?" Carl asked, feeling slightly concerned.

Maisie smiled sweetly. "I'm just covering all eventualities. You know what can come through when you have an open time wound?"

"Actually no, I don't," he said. What on earth could come through?

"Shouldn't we tell the Guardians about this?" Carl asked.

"No. Just let them get on with their preparation and the ritual as per normal. This is what Fergus clearly has been planning. Let's see if you can alter his plans," Maisie said.

"You gonna be OK, girl?" Bert asked.

"Course I am, hon," Maisie winked.

"Aren't you a little bit impressed that we're flying?" Carl asked.

"Course I am. Can't wait for a ride," she chuckled and smiled over at Bert. Lola clocked the look between the two of them and looked at Bert with a huge grin. Bert grinned sheepishly back. She mouthed 'Bert' at him in a shocked manner. He shrugged.

"I'm going in now. Only Carl can come in as he is affected by the time leak." Carl nodded over at her.

Carl moved over to her side and hugged her.

"OK. Well, I leave it in your...capable hands, the four of you. It's almost time to wake up the Guardians. Ten o'clock wake up call, it's alright for some!" she barked as she walked towards the kitchen door.

"Hopefully, I will come out of the door in only a few minutes of your time," she said as she opened the door. "Wish me luck."

"Good luck!" the four of them cried together as Maisie closed the door behind her.

150

27

Fergus sat upright in a large circle made with blood. Black candles covered in inscriptions flickered all around it and they gave off a revolting smell. Fergus was naked and his face was covered in red symbols made of blood. At his crossed legs lay his cue. It was a paler colour than previously – closer to the colour of the other cues.

After his call to Carl, Fergus's eyes glowed with a demonic rage. They seemed barely human, devoid of all goodness. He jumped down a flight of stairs and strode into a large room with a wooden floor. He pointed his cue at the curtains and they closed.

He cut his hand with a knife and coated his cue with it. Fergus's cue was no longer black. It was a grey colour and this greatly disturbed Fergus. The blood offerings he was forcing it to absorb were not lasting as long as they used to. He could sense that the cue was growing in strength and resistance.

The cue absorbed Fergus's blood, turning it a darker shade of grey. Fergus smiled wickedly at the corrupted cue in his hands but his expression changed when the cue almost immediately turned back to a paler colour. He growled and yelled in frustration.

Fergus had forced his cue – a host to a magical, living entity whose purpose was to serve good – into an instrument of evil. He had started to slowly corrupt it when he was still a Vampire Killer. His jealousy of Carl and Katie had led him down a toxic path. In his rage and resentment, a pathway had opened up in his mind which whispered evil promises to him

151

and he had listened. He had listened to the dark voices of hungry demonic entities, wanting more and more pain, and they had made him a promise – a conditional promise of everything he wanted.

He started to chant in a low, deep voice. A wind started to blow and swirl around the room. It gave off a foul smell as it whipped around his head and above the circle faster and faster. Fergus's chanting increased in speed as the wind howled around the room, blowing shelves over, and throwing chairs against the wall.

Lightning struck the cue and it went flying across the floor. Lightning struck it again and again. The cue was smoking with the force of the blasts but it was undamaged. Fergus opened his eyes to see where it had gone.

He looked upwards at the swirling energy above his head. The face of a youngish female with long hair appeared in the clouds. Her eyes were white and her skin looked like it was covered in fish scales. Her teeth were pointed and she had a forked snake tongue.

"It is not time," she hissed. "Why do you summon us?" A lightning bolt hit the cue again.

"Why are you doing that, my Mistress?" he asked, looking over at the smoking cue.

"It is changing. Can you not see?" she hissed. "It is fighting you. It grows stronger."

"It serves you," he said, bowing his head.

"It disgusts us," she sneered. Fergus thought he saw a fishtail flick behind her head, but he couldn't be sure.

"They are stronger than you anticipated, Mistress. They know too much," he warned.

"They are nothing. We are everything," she snarled. "We cannot fail. You will not fail us."

"They have developed powers, they know about me. They know about the infinity cube."

"We can sense a disruption in time," she said. "A disruption which does not serve us. A disruption you caused," she hissed, her black tongue flicking angrily.

"I was trying to stop them," he whispered.

"You risk the wrath of the Time Police. You are foolish!"

There was a huge thunderclap and a huge gust of wind

blasted Fergus's face.

"Time Police?" Fergus asked.

"Yes. The witch must contain the leak. You must not stop her."

"But what if she discovers more?"

"Once she has stopped the leak, we will trap her there forever in eternity. Forever on her own. Never to grow old and die. Never to love. The madness, the agony will be her offering to us." She began to cackle hard. "How she will serve us."

"It begins," she said. "The Guardians awake," she cackled as another lightning bolt hit the cue.

28

Max was the first to open his eyes. His bright blue eyes darted around the vault. He saw two unmade mattresses to his left and the smell of curry was in the air. He grimaced as he sat up. He was struck by the noise of Jonah snoring. Great Lodge! Revolting.

He looked at his watch. It was 9.55am. He lay back for a moment and thought about the day ahead. The ritual would have to be performed at 3pm (as laid out in the Vampire Lodge handbook). They had all the instruments they needed for this in his bag. All they needed was the hallowed ground and the ritual should be straightforward enough. If it was THE Eight Ball, then the Putney Lodge would have to buck up its ideas and get match fit. It would be a huge responsibility housing such a powerful magical item. He didn't think the four present custodians were up to it quite frankly.

If it was THE Eight Ball, then he might have to consider having them stripped of their powers and having other custodians assigned. Yes, it was true that cues chose their custodians from anyone from any background but there were ways of separating the two. Perhaps it wasn't playing fairly but there was a bigger picture at stake. It wasn't as easy as just transferring Lodge members about. He couldn't just transfer other people into the Putney Lodge and transfer the other four out. Everything was bound by strict rules and regulations and, on the whole, Max was a stickler for those. However, there were ways of stripping powers, if it was absolutely required.

Once the whole Eight Ball rigmarole had been sorted out, he could return to a more civilised Lodge – one where they were fairly normal – and he could get on with his teaching. He was, at heart, a military historian and soldier. He had studied the tactics of just about every magical soldier/leader since records began. He had loved being a foot soldier. He also enjoyed the Guardian class he had been elevated to but everything had its price. His price was to give up being on the ground level.

He knew the richness of the history of the once great Putney Lodge. The founder Vampire Killers were legendary. They were held up as almost demi-gods in Lodge history but these four...hmm... he thought. What a contrast. All of them were undisciplined and as for Pitchfork – he smiled. He knew he should be furious with her but he couldn't help but laugh at her volatile nature. He had never come across a Vampire Killer like her before. He would loathe to see her stripped of her powers. As the Putney Lodge had been left alone for so many years, no one had noticed this particular brand of individuality and rebelliousness existing on the outskirts. Maybe it was just as much the fault of the Guardians. The whole Eight Ball episode would put them on the map, whether it was real or not, however. A double page spread in the newsletter would be guaranteed. Focus would be upon them.

He stood up, stretched and looked down at Marilyn snoozing. He leaned down next to his ears, breathed in and shouted "Wake up!" next to him. Marilyn leapt out of his skin.

"You complete bastard!" he yelled at him. Max burst out laughing but neither the yelling nor the laughter had done anything to wake Jonah up.

Max walked over to Jonah and looked at the slobbering mess in front of him. Max grimaced again.

"Wake up!" Max shouted in his ear. Jonah opened his eyes. "Mother?" he asked, before he realised where he was. Max look horrified and walked away.

"Ah...a cigarette is needed," Marilyn said, taking out one out of the box and lighting it. "Good," he said, sitting up. "Yessss," he sighed, exhaling.

"What do you think our lovely four have been up to?" Max asked, taking a cigarette out of his packet and lighting it.

"Those four? Dread to think," Marilyn scoffed. "Probably

accidentally blowing up the world and not mentioning it," he said sarcastically. Max had expected the reply. He knew Marilyn had little time for them, if any.

"How's the Eight Ball?" Max asked Jonah. Jonah pushed himself up and reached into his pocket. He pulled out the container. His shirt fell momentarily open to reveal a chest that was tattooed with all manner of insignia and symbols.

"It behaved itself all night," he said. "Do you think it's real?"

Max took a drag on his cigarette. "I don't know," he said in a very stern voice. "All I can tell you is that very dark and powerful magic surrounds it. Real or not, it's dangerous."

"It makes me rather nervous that it *isn't* real," said Marilyn. "Some geezah is up to no good."

Max nodded. "Yes – I know what you mean." Only a very powerful creature could go to such trouble.

"We need to be heavily armed for this evening," advised Jonah. "I can't imagine those four being much good in a battle. They have no experience, especially if we're up against some sinister corpse-walkers."

"We can't just call in other Lodges. It's not done," Max barked. "It's *this* Lodge's problem."

"But this is very, very serious. They're green," Jonah protested.

"What about faith? I know you never really had much, but has it gone completely?" Marilyn asked Jonah. "Don't you think this is probably meant to be?"

"Oh, don't start. Smoke your fag and shut up," he gibed. Marilyn was about to launch a tirade at him when Max spoke over him.

"I believe in the power of good magic," said Max. "If we start meddling, thinking we know better, we might interfere with the great plan."

The other two thought about this for a moment. A great plan was at the core of their magical faith.

"They did kinda find the Eight Ball...possibly," said Jonah, giving them some credit.

"Lodges have been seeking it for years," Marilyn added, reluctantly.

"It's probably more likely that it found them. And that's the problem," objected Max, frowning as he looked down across

156

at Marilyn.

Jonah leaned back and started coughing. Marilyn wrinkled his nose in disgust.

"What about all the people that will be out and about today?" Marilyn asked.

Max thought about it for a while. "One – we create a mind wipe," he suggested. Marilyn pulled a face.

"Two – film set," Max offered as an alternative. Marilyn grinned. "That is always so much fun."

Jonah groaned. "It's always the film set with you two."

"We like pretending it's all a film," Marilyn huffed.

"But you always do it," Jonah said.

"Well, what do you suggest chap?" Max asked, sounding slightly annoyed.

"I don't bleeding know," Jonah sighed.

"Then film set it is," Max confirmed, nodding to Marilyn.

"I hope you've upgraded the program," Jonah grumbled and belched loudly.

Max scowled, giving Jonah an indignant look. "I like the old program."

They were interrupted by Bert coming down the stairs. The three of them looked over at him.

"Oh, I see yoo three are up," Bert said. "I was just comin' to wake ya,"

"Well, as you can see we are awake," Marilyn said.

"And we're very hungry," slobbered Jonah, yawning and rubbing his belly.

Bert scratched his head. "Err...three English breakfasts?"

All three replied with a yes.

"Do ya want it served down here?" Bert enquired, looking at the three men hopefully.

"Great Lodge, no. We'll eat up there," Max snapped.

"Hair of the dog," said Jonah.

"What, at this time?" asked Marilyn with an air of disgust.

"Stop whingeing, you're such an old woman," Jonah sniped, waving his hand dismissively.

"I am not old," Marilyn hissed, pointing threateningly at Jonah.

Bert turned his back and started walking back up the stairs, leaving the noise of the bickering behind him.

29

Lola had been determined to wear a fancy-dress costume. She had taken the other nun's outfit meant for Maisie and put it on. It was too big for her, with the habit hanging over her feet and her little face peeping out from the wimple.

Lola had loudly protested that they should all dress up because Carl being the only person in costume would look suspicious to the Guardians. There was some merit in this argument, Carl had to agree. Johnny and Bert had exchanged resigned looks.

"I wanna be Elvis," declared Bert quickly.

"I look more like him that you do," insisted Johnny, posturing and curling his lip.

"I sing more like 'im," Bert argued, knowing this would rile Johnny.

At this point, Carl had intervened and sent Bert downstairs to wake up the Guardians. He also explained that there were no Elvis costumes upstairs, only the Elvis mask he was using. There was a gorilla costume and a superhero outfit that would probably fit Johnny better than Bert and that was that.

"Gorilla," Bert muttered as he went off down to the vault.

Carl sent Johnny upstairs, who was pleased that he got to dress up as a superhero. Carl had forgotten to mention that the superhero costume was in hot pink.

"Lola," he said, turning to his fellow nun. "I need you to go over to my old house. You know where it is?"

"Yup," she squeaked and smiled. "This is gonna be great." She giggled.

158

"Are you actually looking forward to this? It's could be very dangerous," Carl said with concern.

"I know, but I'll be super strong again, won't I, if fings get bad? And I can fly." Her eyes lit up and she let out a high-pitched laugh – a laugh that could've taken out a gang of trolls at a thousand paces.

"Good luck to you. Call us within 20 minutes of leaving here," Carl winced, covering his ears. "If we don't hear from you, we're coming over."

Lola smiled. "I'd hug ya, but ya might kill me."

Carl chuckled.

Lola picked up her cue, walked over to the pub door and opened it. It was bright outside. She put on her large black sunglasses and turned her face upwards. "Turned out nice," she said as she closed the door behind her.

Sophie was still sitting in the café looking intently at the road and the pub. She was deeply anxious about Fergus walking by. Her instincts told her he was heading towards her home but she knew she couldn't go and check on him. Why was he going there? She was too scared to find out.

Her eyes were attracted back to the pub when she saw a tiny woman come out dressed as a nun, holding a cue. It must've been the same woman she saw go in there only a short while ago. Perhaps it had something to do with a promotion, she explained to herself. Probably a new beer or something. She looked at her watch. She still had time to keep an eye on the pub before she started to hand out the watches. She was starting to dread it more and more.

Lola pounded her tiny heels down hard on the pavement. She was clutching her cue and she had a huge smile on her face. She was rushing towards Weiss Road, which was only a short distance away. Her mind raced with all the things she would do to any opposition. She was hoping there would be lots of opposition as she wanted to feel that super strength racing through her and she wanted to fly again.

She turned the corner into Weiss Road and very soon she was outside Eric's house. The door was black and it had a large brass knocker on it. There was also a small doorbell to the right hand side.

Lola reached up to the door knocker and whacked it very

loudly, twice. There was no reply. She rang the doorbell and waited. Again, there was no answer.

She looked around her, there were a few people walking down the street. Putney would soon be swarming with people. When she was sure that the people had passed by, she thought to her cue to open the door. It sent a little light bolt out and the door swung open.

Lola entered into Eric's house and slowly closed the door behind her. She walked quietly forwards and looked to her right. There on the sofa was Eric.

Lola paused and looked at him hard. Lola had never seen this man before, let alone naked and tied up. She couldn't tell whether he was alive or not and her heart started to beat a little faster.

The house was quiet. She could hear the hum of the fridge coming from his kitchen and the ticking of a clock on the wall next to her. Eric didn't appear to be moving. Lola gripped her cue with two hands and placed it over her shoulder slowly. She was hoping that her super strength would return to her right now. She cautiously took another step towards Eric, and a floorboard creaked. She peered into the room and cast her eyes around.

Lola saw that there was something flat, like paper, tied to Eric's lap, but she couldn't tell what it was. She walked slowly into the room and glanced around. She was startled to see a large pile of small plastic Eight Balls piled up near to him. They looked identical to their Eight Ball. She took a step closer to them and knelt down before them. She reached over and picked one up – it just looked like another crappy piece of plastic! Suddenly, she heard a murmur behind her.

Eric was slowly raising his head, muttering. Lola put the Eight Ball back and turned to him. She knew that she had to untie him, and quickly, but she was crap with knots and people always seemed to untie knots easily in films! Sod it, she thought. She pointed her cue tip at the rope and a small bolt of energy shot out and zapped apart the ropes around his ankles. Behind her was small clicking and rustling noise but she was too focused on Eric to notice it.

Lola moved behind him to untie his hands. Her cue shot out another bolt of energy and his hands were free. The rustling and clicking noises became louder. Lola's eyes scanned the room – her eyes zooming in on the pile of Eight Balls, which appeared to be moving around each other. Lola's jaw slightly dropped and she felt a surge of energy pass from her cue to her. Oh yeah, she thought, feeling the energy move up from her feet to her head.

Eric made another small murmuring noise and his eyes started to flick open. As they did, a tiny black cloud began to form, once more, above him. Lola clocked this instantly. She had never seen anything like that before either. The clicking and the buzzing of the Eight Balls became more frenzied. She turned her attention to Eric. She must get him free and to safety. She pointed her cue at the remainder of his restraints and zapped them. Lola noticed the photo stuck to his lap – it was Carl with Katie! Oh, yuk! she thought. Creepy and wrong!

Lola tapped Eric on the shoulder. Eric murmured again. There was a crackling noise like a brewing storm above them and the clicking from the Eight Balls got faster.

"This ain't good," she whispered to herself, as she looked over to the Eight Balls that were slowly separating themselves into two piles. "Fuck," she whispered. Lola slapped Eric's arm. "Naked man, wake up," she said.

Eric slowly opened his eyes. His memory of Fergus, the cloud and being tied up flooded into his head and he jumped up screaming, tearing the photo off his lap and throwing it to the floor.

"Shut up!" Lola shouted. "Shut the fuck up!"

Eric turned and looked at the tiny nun with a pool cue in her hand and screamed again.

"Stop screamin'. Yer gonna be alright!" she hollered. "I'm 'ere to 'elp."

"What are you?" he asked, pointing a finger at her and backing away.

"A shop assistant," she answered. "Why are ya naked?" she asked, trying to avoid looking at his 'todger'. Eric's sense of prudishness kicked in and he was more alarmed by his nudity for a moment than by the small cloud forming and the moving Eight Balls. He cupped his hands in front of his manhood.

"T-t-the man, the man that was here, he's e-e- evil," Eric

161

stammered, his eyes glancing wildly around.

"Which man?" Lola asked.

"He flies on one of those...!" he shouted, pointing at her cue. "You're like him. You're evil."

"I'm rescuin' ya, ya knob 'ead," Lola said. "He can fly?"

"I saw him, flying down the road and then...then...Pete. Where's Pete?" Eric shrieked, looking around. "What did he do with him?"

"I dunno who the fuck ya talkin' about," said Lola. "But I 'ave to get yer outta here."

"Where are you taking me?" he asked.

"Somewhere safe," she said.

"I don't trust you," he squealed. "You want to kill me!" Eric went running out of the room towards the stairs to the landing.

"No, don't run away!" Lola shouted after him. "Come back!"

There was a dark humming noise coming from the Eight Balls. Lola slowly turned her head in their direction. Half of them were hovering above the ones on the floor. Both piles were vibrating furiously. She looked up at the cloud, it was starting to grow in size and lights were flickering about in it.

"Bollocks," she whispered.

There was a splitting and a cracking noise. Something was happening to the Eight Balls. The plastic was cracking. Lola stood transfixed as she saw the ones on the ground split their coating and hatch what seemed like razor sharp spider legs, while the ones in the air seemed to sprout long and silver wings, looking very sharp and very deadly. Lola slowly placed her cue over her shoulder. She just needed to get out of the room, close the door, get the naked man and take him to safety.

Lola took a step back and the Eight Balls moved closer. She took another step backwards and they moved closer still. Any moment, she was going to bolt to the door. She took a deep breath, turned and ran. She slammed the door, only to hear the noise of dozens of metallic wings and legs slash at the door, quickly slicing away the wood in what looked like a frenzied knife assault.

Lola ran up the stairs. "Where are ya? We've got to get outta 'ere, now!"

162

Lola could hear the slashing noise downstairs and the crackling noise growing. It was only a matter of minutes before they slashed their way through the door.

"Naked man, where are ya?" she shouted. Lola ran into his bedroom. She opened the wardrobe and looked under the bed. He wasn't there. She ran into the room ahead, which had been Fergus's room. A shudder went through her. She could almost feel him in there. The room had taken an imprint of his evil energy and she was sensitive to it. She opened the wardrobe and looked under the bed. Eric wasn't there.

"Ya stupid twat, where are ya?" Lola shouted. She ran into the bathroom and pulled back the shower curtain. There she saw Eric cowering.

"This ain't 'elping us, is it?" she said.

"Get away from me, get away from me," he cowered, going foetal.

"Christ's sake, get up," she ordered. She reached down and with one little hand grabbed under his arm and pulled him effortlessly up and out of the bath. It was hard to tell who was the more surprised.

"You're not human," he shouted. "Help! Help!"

"Shut up!" Lola yelled at him.

"Help, help!" Eric shouted louder. Lola, getting flustered, pulled a fist and punched him out cold.

"Bloody beta males," she said.

The bathroom door was suddenly assaulted with a wave of frenzied slashing. The Eight Balls had hacked their way out downstairs and were trying to break in through the bathroom door. The door was pierced over and over again.

Lola looked frantically around her. The bathroom was small and there was no way out.

She looked down at the tiled floor where Eric was sprawled out. She pulled him up with one hand and rested his slumped body against hers. With her other hand, she smashed her cue down with incredible strength and the floor cracked.

The Eight Balls were almost breaking through the bathroom door – their razor sharp legs and wings slashing furiously.

Lola smashed her cue down again and again, breaking the

floor. There was a ripping, cracking sound as the floor started to give way. Lola straddled her cue with one hand, pulling Eric's arm over her shoulder.

The bathroom door was almost shredded away. Lola's heart was pounding.

"I 'ope yer insured," she said as the floor fell away. She jumped up and her cue was hovering above the hole. Lola looked down to where the plaster had covered the sofa.

She accelerated downwards through the hole back into the living room where the cloud was now about a foot long and crackling violently. The room was darker than before and there was a smell of sulphur in the air.

The cloud shot a lightning bolt at Lola's cue, missing it by centimetres. She gasped as she turned to look at the cloud, seeing a pair of white eyes fleetingly pass by inside. The frenzied scratching upstairs was getting louder. They're breaking through! They're breaking through!

A lightning bolt hit her cue, sending it spinning towards the wall at alarming speed. Lola shoved out her fist as they went hurtling into the wall and crashed her entire right arm through it – stopping them in their tracks. Luckily, she was still on her cue and still held Eric over her shoulder. Another lightning strike hit the wall next to her, blasting a massive hole in it. Lola looked through the hole and saw that there were French doors leading into the garden via the kitchen. She smashed a fist against the wall, making the hole bigger and flew through it down the kitchen towards the French doors.

She jumped off her cue, zapped the doors open and started to drag Eric to the bottom of the garden, where she shoved him into his shed. He fell to the floor, with his nose resting against a pot of unused paint and a tennis racket.

She turned and ran back into the house. There were deadly flying and crawling things and she had to stop them. She stormed into the kitchen and she stood there with her cue over her shoulder. Heading towards her were the Eight Balls. Lola inhaled deeply, tightened her grip and prepared for battle.

The first wave came by air. About ten flying Eight Balls accelerated at her head, she swung, taking three down with her cue, sending one flying and smashing two. Another flew at her cutting her right arm. It was fairly deep but the pain was deadened by her strength and by the adrenalin pumping around her body. Another and another bombarded her body, clipping her and shredding part of her costume.

Then a wave of spiders swarmed towards her while she was still trying to defend herself from the flying assault. She randomly aimed her cue at the floor, sending out energy blasts and managing to hit a couple of them. Another flyer cut her arm and a spider cut her leg. She smashed her cue down hard, smashing two and clipping another.

"Fuckin' bastards," she shouted, swinging her cue around her hair and smashing another three. The assaults were getting faster and faster and dozens were attacking her.

Lola was smashing and blasting what seemed like an overwhelming swarm when she saw a blur move across the room. A couple of Eight Balls fell out of the air and hit the ground, then two spiders seemed to just smash to pieces all by themselves. Lola whacked another Eight Ball and was about to hit another one, when it seemed to explode in the air all on its own. She stood there as spiders and flyers were smashed before her eyes until there were none left. She stood there clutching her cue, panting.

"'Ello, Pix," said Bert as he materialised next to her, dressed as a gorilla.

"Bert?" Lola asked, breaking into a huge smile.

"In the flesh," he grinned. She gave him a huge hug and then frowned.

"That weren't twenty minutes," she grumbled, looking annoyed. "Yoo didn't trust me."

"We was worried about ya," he protested. "Thank gawd I come over."

"I woz winnin'," she stated. Bert gave her a knowing look and pointed at her arm.

"Yer been 'urt," he said in a concerned voice.

"This?" Lola questioned, looking at her arm. "Nah! I'll live but fanks."

Bert thought that Lola looked a bit shaken up and was wiser than to challenge her further on it.

Lola leaned backwards and took a deep breath, closing her eyes. She suddenly opened them.

"Bert, there's a naked man in the shed. He woz tied to the sofa wiv a picture of Katie and Carl stuck to 'im," she garbled.

"Dodgy," he said.

"And there's a cloud in there, Bert. A cloud wiv eyes and lightnin' and…"

"No cloud, Pix," Bert said. "But, just ran round the 'ouse. Great to be agile again."

"There's a man in the shed…" Lola began again.

"Slow down," he pleaded. "One fing atta time…one fing atta time!"

Lola stopped and was about to start again when Bert was distracted. He looked at all the smashed Eight Balls on the floor – there must have been about fifty of them.

"Wot the 'ell are they?" he asked. "They're Eight Balls…like ours…but there are dozens of 'em." He shoved his trainer into the remains on the floor, which was covered in legs, wings and smashed plastic.

"That's wot I woz tryin' to say," she said. "They're like ours but wiv razor legs and wings."

"Are there any more of 'em?" Bert asked, looking around.

"They'd probably be tryin' to kill us if there were," she retorted. Bert gave her a 'don't be cheeky' look and Lola looked a bit sheepish.

"Wot if there are fahsands of 'em out there somewhere?" he asked. "Jesus wept. Wot if fahsands are let loose? They would mow people down. No-one would stand a chance."

"God, Bert, ya don't need fahsands, a few would do it," Lola remarked. "One of them fings is lethal."

Bert rubbed his eyes and scratched his face.

"Ours 'as got to be a fake too. It looks just like these," he said. "We 'ave to tell the Guardians. They mustn't do that ritual, Pix."

"But they 'ave to, they said so, it's that handbook fing,"

Bert sighed. Bloody rules and regulations – they were the bane of his life.

"But our one woz much 'arder than these. Ours woz booby-trapped. Even three Guardians couldn't break into it," Lola said, kicking some of the debris across the room.

Bert nodded. "Where's this naked bloke?"

"He's in the shed," Lola replied, pointing through the

French doors to the bottom of the garden. It was a very pretty garden with a large apple tree, a mown lawn and lots of flowers.

"Why's he in there?" Bert asked, peering down the lawn.

"I put 'im there," Lola answered blankly and Bert sighed.

"Woz he naked when yoo first met 'im?" Bert teased, winking at her.

"Oi. Yes, he woz. I don't want ya tellin' Johnny I've been up to funny business," she warned, pointing a finger in his face and slapping his arm.

"Would I?" Bert grinned and Lola stared at him threateningly.

"Yoo make any shit up and I'll get yer back, old man," she said wagging her finger dramatically at him.

Bert cackled and Lola smiled at him. He asked her what had happened and she explained everything, including the part about Fergus flying.

"So, the cheeky shit can fly, can he?" Bert said. "Damn."

"Yeah, but wot the fuck is that cloud fing?" Lola demanded. The cloud thing had unnerved her the most. Floating white soulless eyes and lightning strikes were no fun at all.

"I ain't got a clue, Pix," he said, shaking his head. "This is all a bit more than our vampire nights used to be, huh?"

Lola nodded. It was hard to believe it was only a few weeks ago when life moved at a much slower pace.

"Wot are we gonna do with naked man?" she asked, shoving her thumb in the direction of the shed.

"Well, we can't leave 'im 'ere, can we?" he said. "Wot if that cloud returns?"

Lola looked concerned. "We're gonna have to dress 'im," she advised. "Bert, yer gonna have to dress 'im."

"Why me?" Bert challenged, looking alarmed at the prospect of this.

"Coz yer a man and I'm engaged," she explained, smiling sweetly at him and batting her eyelids furiously.

"Err...yoo can knock that off for a start. I find yoo being this nice more frightenin' than a common full of vampires," Bert gulped, backing away slightly from her, as she clung onto his arm.

"Oi," said Lola, slapping him across the arm. "I am always

167

nice."

Bert cackled hard at her. "Pixie, I ain't dressing 'im."

"Well, I ain't dressing 'im neither," she said stubbornly.

"We can't just leave 'im, can we? And we can't take 'im back to the pub naked, can we?"

Lola batted her eyelids some more and Bert sighed with resignation.

30

Maisie placed the staff on the kitchen table. She held each end of it, closed her eyes and began to deepen her breathing. She focused her mind on the cube and allowed herself to fall deeper into a trance.

Maisie saw the cube in her mind's eye and then it slowly turned into a solid image, like a photograph. She walked into it, looking down and around at the stars surrounding her. Her eyes darted over to one of the cube's transparent sides. There was a crack running down the centre of it and spreading outwards and down to the corner. Maisie nervously walked over to it and touched it, tracing the crack before stopping. Her face was gravely concerned as she saw a thin silver cord trapped in the corner of the crack stretching out into infinity. This was the strand of time that Fergus's attack had trapped like a coat belt in a car door.

Maisie knew it wasn't going to be long before the Time Police showed up. They patched up time and placed any offenders into the rehabilitation zone. There wasn't a trial and there was no debate. Their word and prescribed punishment was their choice. Most frequently, they sent people into a penal colony dimension where time moved excruciatingly slowly. The idea of this was to make any offenders against time aware of the seriousness of their misconduct – being made aware of the very delicate nature of time by forcing the offender into slow, thick energy (like treacle) they believed created a greater understanding and respect. They probably also found it very funny.

Maisie's heart pounded as she held the holly wood tightly

and waved her hand over it. There was a crackling noise and lights flashed off it. Smoke rose up and the Staff Guardian appeared.

"Yes?" asked the Staff Guardian, materialising (this time) as a shortish blonde woman next to Maisie. She held an axe over one shoulder and sipped a glass of white wine. Maisie raised an eyebrow.

"I was going to say it's a bit early for that, but..." Maisie gestured around the cube.

"Oh dear," said the Staff Guardian, moving over in a wisp of smoke to the crack and materialising again. "Someone's for it."

"Yeah, me..." said Maisie. "Unless you can help me."

The Staff Guardian had technically belonged to one of the Putney Lodge founders. He had been a very powerful Vampire Killer and warlock and one of his specialities had been experimentation with time travel. The Staff Guardian, who had great knowledge of a great many things, stubbornly refused to assist him with his experimentation with time travel. He begged, threatened and pleaded over the years and eventually gave up on this topic. He eventually called less and less upon the Staff Guardian, leaving her to her own stubborn devices and stuck her down in the vault. The Staff Guardian hadn't minded at all and was perfectly content not to be bothered with mortals and their boring limited lives.

"I said I would try and help you. You didn't mention the minor point of also breaking your cube. Are you even allowed in this cube?" she demanded indignantly.

"Yes," Maisie said. "We are all allowed cubes."

"Hmmm," said the Staff Guardian suspiciously. "In my day, only the few were allowed the privilege."

"Things have greatly changed, thank God," replied Maisie.

"Clearly. Bloody incompetents," she muttered. Maisie rolled her eyes and sighed with exasperation.

"Don't lecture me, just help me...please," Maisie pleaded.

"Mortals shouldn't play around with time," the Staff Guardian said in an arrogant tone. "This is what happens. You've threatened the safety of your planet and beyond," she sniffed, looking down at the silver cord.

"That little cord is the potential destroyer of your universe.

What were you thinking?"

"Look, we were attacked by a very powerful arsehole," Maisie rasped. "Please would you cut the cord before the Time Police show up and punish me."

"A period of reflection might do you good."

"I was only trying to help. It's been a long time since you've been around but things have changed. The world is in danger because of a crazy, jealous man with very powerful friends," Maisie replied, desperately trying to justify the situation.

The Staff Guardian kneeled before the crack to take a closer look. "The trouble is, if I remove that cord, this cube may shatter."

"If you don't, this cube definitely will break," Maisie argued.

"Hmm…typical," she grumbled. "Bloody typical of someone like you to put me in this position," the Staff Guardian snorted.

"Can you do it?" Maisie begged, avoiding the insult.

The Staff Guardian gave Maisie a hard look. "The question is, can I do it without the cube shattering and the Time Police showing up? That is the real question you wanted to ask."

"OK…yes. But please hurry…" Maisie begged harder.

The Staff Guardian grinned, turned into a wisp of smoke and passed through the side of the infinity cube and out into space. She materialised next to the cord, swung her axe upwards and was about to chop when they both heard over a loud hailer the voice of a woman with a strong New York accent: "Put down your weapon and step away from the time cord."

Maisie's heart almost burst out of her chest. "For God's sake cut it!" Maisie shouted. The Staff Guardian looked around her and couldn't see anything.

"Cut it!" Maisie screamed.

"Step away from the time cord," came the booming voice.

"Up yours!" the Staff Guardian shouted and cut through the cord. The cord fell away and disappeared before Maisie's eyes.

An enormous blue and black triangle materialised behind the Staff Guardian. Maisie's cube was like an ant next to an elephant. Maisie's jaw dropped. Holy shit! The Staff Guardian turned around, swung her axe over her shoulder, looked upwards and gave them the finger. "Bollocks to you."

"Get back here!" Maisie shrieked.

The Staff Guardian looked the enormous triangle up and down with contempt. She raised her right hand and a glass of wine materialised in it. She glugged it down in one, then chucked it away – the glass disappearing instantly as she did.

"I say BOLLOCKS, that's what I say." The Staff Guardian gave the cube the finger vigorously and Maisie felt a panic attack coming on. She slapped her hands against the side of her cheeks and froze to the spot.

"Bollocks to them. Who the hell do they think they are with their enormous triangle telling me...ME...what to do?" The Staff Guardian turned around to look at Maisie and gestured with her thumb at the triangle.

"Please...just...don't provoke them," Maisie begged, although knowing that this was probably far too late.

"I will not be bullied or told what to do by brain-dead Time Police. Most of them are insane. Well, you would be wouldn't you, if you spent your time roaming the tunnels of time like a rat in a sewer," she growled. "RATS!" she shouted at the triangle, "RATS!"

"Oh Jesus!" Maisie cried, gripping her hair and her stomach sinking.

"So sorry to have already forgotten your name...Donald is it? Anyway, it's really time for me and my axe to go and play." The Staff Guardian grew to about nine feet tall but still miniscule next to the blue and black triangle. She threw back her head and let out a battle cry and went running across space at the triangle laughing maniacally.

Maisie could not actually comprehend this mental action but genuinely felt a strange feeling of admiration for the Staff Guardian. Maisie watched as the small figure ran closer and closer to the triangle until she was out of sight. There were dozens of flashes across space as the Time Police fired on the tiny figure.

Maisie suddenly realised that if she was going to make it back to the kitchen, then this was going to be the only moment she had. She could not afford to be arrested by the Time Police. She was going to have to use the diversion of the Staff Guardian's kamikaze attack and run for it. She was torn between wanting to help the Staff Guardian and needing to help Carl and the others.

Unfortunately, infinity cubes were places of teaching and reflection. Anger, fear – any lower end emotions just didn't have any effect on the cube. The cube was capable of many wondrous things but only with an elevated state of mind. Maisie's mind right now was like a crazed bear smelling bacon cooking on an open fire – she was firing on instinct and her instincts were telling her to flee. Her breathing was heavy, her mind was racing, her eyes being drawn again to the flashes shooting out of the triangle. They clearly hadn't stopped the Staff Guardian...yet.

Maisie was going to have to get calm and get calm fast. She closed her eyes and tried to block all the sights around her. She started to think about the kitchen again.

"Do not try to escape. You cannot escape," the same female voice boomed out.

Maisie's eyes jolted open and a bolt of energy hit the cube. Maisie looked over to the crack, it was starting to split further. "Shit!" Maisie screeched. "Shit!"

A high-pitched siren blasted out, vibrating through Maisie's head and body. This was making concentration impossible. Maisie fell to her knees, clutching her ears. She tried closing her eyes again to concentrate.

"You cannot escape. You will not escape," the voice boomed out.

Maisie leaned forward, doubled over, trying to block out the noise so she could concentrate. Her senses were being bombarded.

Then there was silence. There was a crackling noise over the loud hailer and what sounded like a woman yelling and then nothing. The triangle also stopped firing. Maisie raised her head and looked out across to the triangle. Nothing stirred. She turned to look at the crack – it was spreading.

Maisie stood up, her mind racing. She breathed hard – she knew she had to get back to the kitchen. She had to get out of the cube before it was destroyed and her with it.

The loud hailer crackled again and there was what sounded like another scream. Maisie walked closer to the edge of her cube and looked out as if this would somehow explain what was happening.

There was another crackle and another scream and a blast. Maisie listened intently, trembling somewhat.

The loud hailer crackled again. Someone cleared their voice.

"Greetings, Donald. I did warn them but they gave me no option. If they are really foolish enough to go around telling me...ME...what to do, well I really have no choice but to teach them their place," came the haughty voice of the Staff Guardian. "Idiots, all of them. IDIOTS".

Maisie's jaw dropped. How the hell? Maisie felt a sense of relief and wonder. She then felt fear. The Staff Guardian had attacked and taken over a Time Police ship. God only knows what punishment there is for that.

"I would suggest, oh lowly mortal, that you take this opportunity to leave," the Staff Guardian commanded.

Maisie nodded to herself.

"Yes, I'm sure you're thanking me. I was great," the Staff Guardian boasted. "Mr Axe was brilliant too. Maybe that will teach them how to behave themselves."

Maisie sat down and crossed her legs. She looked at the crack, which was splitting quite dramatically. She needed to get out fast.

Maisie closed her eyes and thought about the kitchen as she heard the Staff Guardian shout over the loud hailer: "To victory! To victory!" followed by laughter. Maisie couldn't help but smile. She couldn't help but like the Staff Guardian as the sound of her singing faded and she heard the ticking of the kitchen clock. Time was on the move again. She wondered what time it was on the other side of the door.

31

People started to stream past the window of the café where Sophie sat. It was 10am and the Lower Richmond Road was already starting to buzz with families and children wandering by. Some were possibly on their way to Leader's Garden, the little play park with swings, tennis courts and a café next to the river while some were on their way to cafés and shops.

Sophie looked over to the restaurant across the road. It already had people sitting outside, drinking coffee and sitting in the sunlight. A waiter brought out two English breakfasts and placed them down in front of two men who looked like rowers. They laughed loudly as they both went to grab the ketchup bottle. Next to them were a man and his young daughter who kept pointing to the balloons tied to the lamp post and batting her eyelashes at her father, who was trying to explain that she couldn't have one. Arms were folded dramatically and a big pout followed, until the waitress put a bowl of ice cream in front of her. Hands then clapped and a huge smile formed.

Sophie sipped her cappuccino and took a bite of her hot buttered toast. She had always loved to people watch and this was a spectacular day to do so. As she thought this, a clown walked by holding a bucket and collecting for a charity. Sophie figured that he and that tiny nun wouldn't be the last.

Two couples also walked by the window, looking as if they had escaped from 19th century rural England, carrying plastic bags which were clanking with bottles and talking extremely loudly. On the opposite side of the road, a young mother smoked a cigarette while pushing a baby with pierced ears.

175

Sophie shuddered. Babies with pierced ears alarmed her.

Sophie looked back over to the pub. In the near distance, she saw the nun approaching. There was someone dressed as a gorilla next to her and this time she was pushing a wheelbarrow. She couldn't quite tell what was in the wheelbarrow but it looked like a very large dummy or something under a duvet. On top of the duvet were two pool cues. She heard a squeaky voice say: "Penny for the guy, penny for the guy," as she pushed the wheelbarrow by a couple who gave her the oddest look.

The nun and the gorilla knocked on the pub door, which was opened by another nun with ski gloves and stubble. What on earth were they promoting? The little nun seemed to be very strong and she seemed to lift the wheelbarrow up a step into the pub. The gorilla waved at the other two and walked across the road towards the café where Sophie was sitting.

Bert entered the packed café. He needed to get the Guardians their English breakfasts but the kitchen was still out of bounds. Time leaks? Blimey, he thought. He still couldn't get his head around that.

A yowling, injured woman masquerading as a singer blasted out on the radio as all eyes turned to Bert and then quickly looked away. He realised how conspicuous he must appear. He swallowed and walked over to the counter where the two waitresses stood. As he often had a fry up in the morning before he started work, he knew both the girls.

A voluptuous girl with light brown skin, thick wavy hair and glasses laughed, showing dimpled cheeks and smiling eyes. The other smaller woman had shoulder length thick brown hair, a fringe and almost black eyes. She also laughed.

"Banana smoothie?" she asked in a northern accent and the two of them cackled.

Bert pulled back the gorilla mask, which was attached to the back of the costume, and revealed himself to the girls. They cackled again and asked him what on earth he was up to. He thought quickly and explained that it was all a bit of a giggle and everyone was dressing up at The Pig & Phoenix. The girls exchanged looks and seemed excited by that, saying that after they shut later in the day they would dress up

176

and join in. Bert grinned encouragingly and then ordered three English breakfasts. He explained that there was a bit of problem with the kitchen over the road and that could he have them to go. They smiled and ruffled his hair. Bert blushed slightly and ordered a coffee while he waited.

He looked around for a seat. There was one next to a small lady with glasses with a box on the table. He walked over and asked the girl if it was OK to sit down. Sophie smiled and said it wasn't a problem. In fact, she was curious to find out what all the dressing up was about.

"Why the costume?" Sophie asked.

"This?" Bert said looking at the pretty girl next to him. "This is fresh off the Milan catwalk." He chuckled huskily and she smiled. He chuckled some more and looked sheepishly away. He thought he recognised her from the pub. His memory wasn't quite what is used to be for faces but she did look very familiar. So many people came and went and some stayed to forever become part of the furniture, propping up their favourite corner and repeating the same actions and conversations.

"And the nun?" she asked. She also thought that Bert looked familiar but Bert had one of those generic faces. It was his twinkling blues and his husky laugh that people mostly remembered on first meeting him.

"Err...all a bit of a party...y'know...a giggle. The Boat Race an' all that," Bert said. "Yoo watchin' it?" he said smiling and looking at the box on the table. It was brown and had a lid that was loosely closed. He felt a tingle go down his back. It was the first time he had ever had that kind of feeling from looking at an object. Sophie noticed his eyes were on the box and she shifted in her seat uncomfortably.

"Nah," Sophie said, putting her hand protectively over the box. "Not that interested but I'll probably watch it in one of the pubs." She forced a smile and took a sip of her cappuccino.

"Good luck gettin' in," he said. "Why not watch it over the road?" he asked, gesturing with his twinkling eyes towards the pub.

"I'll be popping by later. I need to see someone," she nervously said and cleared her throat. At that moment, a little girl opened the door and ran into the café laughing. Sophie

177

was startled for a moment, turned and knocked the box off the table. Bert's reaction was superfast as he caught it as a blur, looked inside, and put it back on the table. Luckily all eyes were on the little girl, who jumped up and down at the counter while her flustered mother entered into the café, carrying a tricycle behind her and admonishing her for running.

"Who?" asked Bert, relieved no-one had caught him speeding. He laughed for a moment at that to himself before he processed what he had seen in the box. Watches. Gold watches. Carl had told them about a gold watch from his vision.

"Oh, a friend. Tara," she murmured, her attention turning back to Bert. She looked back at the box, it had moved. She shuffled it closer to her and put her hand over it again.

"I know big Tara," he said. "Been mates a long time?" Bert knew that he had stumbled onto a jigsaw piece and he his heart began to pound. Tara had been part of Carl's vision too.

"Oh, years…y'know," Sophie replied in a soft voice. "I used to drink over there a lot but not so much anymore."

Bert started to recognise her.

"She'll be arrivin' shortly, why not pop back wiv me?" Bert asked. "Save yoo the 'assle of tryin' to get in later." He put on his most non-threatening happy voice, which sounded just a little bit too strained and he blinked just a bit too innocently. It was an odd combination and one which slightly alarmed Sophie.

"Oh no, it's fine, but thank you," Sophie insisted, putting the box on her lap.

"Go on, come back wiv me. Come and see Tara before it gets too crowded." Bert now sounded more desperate, which he noticed and tried to compensate for with a large, fake smile. This concerned Sophie even more.

"No, I'm fine. Thanks but I'll be over there later." Sophie didn't like this change in his manner and his fluctuating, pressurising tone of voice. Bert noticed her withdrawal and tried to compose himself.

"Wot's ya name?" Bert asked, softening his tone.

"Sophie," she whispered and cleared her voice again, holding the box tightly.

"I'm Bert," he grinned. Just then the dark-haired woman

with the fringe voiced loudly that his breakfasts were ready. Bert nodded over to her direction. "Cheers," he said and turned his attention back to Sophie. "I've got to take these over there. Are ya gonna still be 'ere in a few minutes?"

Sophie blushed slightly. "Look, I have a boyfriend and..."

"Oh God, no, I'm not tryin' to chat you up nor nuffink. I woz tryin' to 'elp, y'know." Bert blushed to the tips of his greying hair. "Wiv Big Tara and yoo, y'know."

"Oh...I see...it's just that...I don't know you and..." Sophie mumbled, feeling embarrassed and nervous. She did need to see Tara but she wanted to see her last. She was mildly obsessive-compulsive and breaking a pattern truly unnerved her.

Bert stood up and said: "Look, I'll be back in a few minutes. Stay...ok?"

"Why?" Sophie asked, feeling more and more uncomfortable. It wasn't so much that an oldish man dressed as a gorilla was trying to chat her up, it was the fact that she knew he had sensed something.

"Cos I need to talk to ya about somefink. Please be 'ere when I get back," Bert gently pleaded. He knew he had to get the breakfasts to the Guardians before they started to ask too many questions. This girl was part of what was going on and he couldn't let her just slip away.

"Sure," said Sophie, forcing another smile.

Bert turned around and walked over to the counter, took out some money from inside his gorilla costume and picked up the three stacked plates covered in foil. He turned around to head towards the door and say goodbye to Sophie but she had gone, leaving a ten pound note on the table.

Shit, thought Bert.

179

32

Lola plonked the wheelbarrow down on the floor next to the fruit machine. Carl stared at the pale, naked foot sticking out from under the duvet.

"Errr..." Carl murmured. "What is that?" Carl asked, pointing at the foot.

"Wot does it bloody look like?" Lola chirped. "It's a bloody foot attached to a bloody naked man." She pulled back the duvet to reveal Eric's face.

"What is he doing here?" Carl demanded. "He can't be here. The Guardians will be up here any second."

"Well, that's too bad. Wot woz I meant to do, leave 'im while that cloudy fing or them flyin', 'ackin' Eight Balls went for 'im?" Lola growled. Carl noticed that Lola's nun costume had serious tears all over it.

"Are you OK?" he asked gently and touched her arm with his gloved hand before he fully registered what she had said.

"Yeah, fanks for askin'," Lola said sarcastically and looked worriedly at his hand. Although his gloved hand protected her from his contamination, he pulled away.

"Flying, hacking Eight Balls?" Carl asked – his soft brown eyes hardening. "What do you mean flying, hacking Eight Balls?" The tone of his voice darkened as a sense of anger rose in his chest and a desire to fight pounded through his veins.

"Flyin', 'ackin' Eight Balls wiv razor legs," Lola snarled as she pulled up the duvet and reached carefully inside. She pulled out bits and pieces of the destroyed Eight Balls.

"What the fuck!" cried Carl. He picked up a razor sharp leg

with gloved fingers. He slowly shook his head as he inspected the barbed limb. He touched the corner with his glove, making a small tear in it. It could easily go through flesh like a hot knife through butter. As he held the limb before his eyes, Lola continued talking.

"Yeah, there were dozens of 'em…flyin', crawlin'…slashin' through everyfink," she scowled. Carl's jaw dropped when she told him about the photograph of him and Katie, the cloud, and everything else that she could think of – including Bert's small part of helping her, not that she needed it.

Carl inspected the legs more closely. These hatched out of Eight Balls? He was getting angrier and angrier. How many were there out there? Thousands? Millions? Weren't vampires bad enough? Now flying and crawling killing machines? Were these going to be released today on crowds of people? He knew Fergus had become twisted – controlling vampires was evil enough but at least their killing was driven by a need to feed. These devices were designed to create terror and murder innocent people. They weren't killing to survive a wretched and cursed existence.

"Are we gonna tell the Guardians?" Lola asked as her eyes diverted to the Men's toilets where Johnny emerged dressed in a shocking pink lycra superhero outfit. Lola released a piercing high-pitched giggle.

"Don't…just don't," he pleaded as he looked over at the two nuns and the wheelbarrow. He clocked Eric's foot and unconscious face but was instantly drawn to Lola's torn costume. He ran over quickly and put his arm around her and gave her a kiss on the forehead.

"You OK, Pix?" he asked, running his finger down her little nose.

"Yes, I'm fine. Don't fuss," she said. "Just cos I'm small." Johnny and Carl exchanged looks – they weren't going to rise to that one.

"What happened?" Johnny asked with concern and Lola quickly explained excitedly, enjoying telling her story. Johnny seemed horrified at the thought of Lola being attacked by the Eight Balls. He also felt a huge sense of pride in her ability to cope beyond his expectation and sheer relief that she was alive. He felt gratitude towards Bert.

181

While he had been deciding on his costume, Bert had grabbed his gorilla outfit and, without telling him, followed Lola. Johnny felt ashamed that he hadn't been the one to have followed her. How was he to know about those killer Eight Balls? Then another thought crossed his mind. They were a team. They were each responsible for the others, regardless of their personal relationships. Bert had as much right to look out for Lola as he did.

Carl scrutinised Eric's face. "He's the bloke I sold our house to," he said. Despite the killer Eight Balls and the cloud, the image that disturbed him was of his and Katie's picture being placed on Eric's naked lap. It was so very, very creepy.

So, this was the starter course of an evil energy offering? Well, they had stopped the first sacrifice − a sacrifice which involved him and Katie at some warped level he couldn't even begin to understand. What kind of fucked up bargain had Fergus made?

Carl was also troubled by the amount of killer balls left in the house. Surely, one ball would've taken care of killing one man? The excessive amount had to be for their benefit. Fergus must've thought they would've all turned up and stood no chance against dozens of killing machines. It actually sounded desperate. Fergus must fear failure, Carl thought and smiled. He must fear failing his masters.

"So, are we gonna tell 'em?" Lola asked Carl. Carl breathed out and ran his gloved hand over his face.

"They are sticklers for the rules," he said. "They have to perform the ritual at a certain time regardless."

"Well, fuck the rules. They're not 'elping anyone, are they? There the reason we're all in the shit." She kicked the wheelbarrow and dented it, jolting Eric who momentarily opened his eyes and closed them again.

"The handbook states..." Carl said but was interrupted by Lola.

"I 'ain't never seen a copy of this book and it sounds like a pile of fuckin' bollocks shit crap fuckin' arse wipe bollocks," she growled and placed her hands defiantly on her hips.

"You were given one...arse wipe bollocks?" Carl asked, throwing his head back and laughing. "Arse wipe bollocks," he repeated and laughed harder.

"The book has no pictures," Johnny said to Carl, who burst out laughing himself.

"Oi, watch it, fatty," she snapped, prodding him in his belly, which was protruding out in the tight lycra.

"Ow!" Johnny exclaimed. Lola had forgotten her strength again. Although she was getting used to the subtleties of the energy – when it started to pour into her, when she was resonating it fully and when it was starting to subside – she was still adapting to it. Right now, she could break someone's hand by shaking it. If code red was the term associated with being fully charged then she was in code orange. It was actually slowly dawning on her that she needed a bit more self-control around people and things when charged up.

"Serves yer right," she said to Johnny, as he rubbed his belly. "And yoo stop laughin' at me," she barked at Carl, who had tears in his eyes. "It ain't funny." Carl bit his lip and tried to compose himself.

"They already think we're a bunch of flakes," Carl said. "I don't know what they'd do if they knew about..." Carl gestured around the pub and at them, "everything." Carl burst out laughing again. It all seemed too much and too funny. Johnny was also cracking up and Lola was the only one not laughing. She tried to get the conversation back on track.

"Well, it's not as if they're gonna do anyfink, is it?" she said sternly. "Wot can they do to us...so wot if they fink we're flakes, fuck 'em," Lola growled again.

Carl managed to compose himself, followed by Johnny, who still had shaking shoulders and looked down at his feet. The seriousness of the situation returned to Carl and he needed to get his fear off his chest.

"We didn't have the powers we do now. Maybe..." Carl began, but was spoken over by Lola, who was beginning to fume.

"...Yeah, well, it's our power now, innit?" Lola said. "Wot are they gonna do about it?"

"We didn't have powers to take away before, did we?" Carl suggested and Lola scowled. She turned to Johnny, looking for an answer.

"They can't take anything away from us," said Johnny. "It doesn't work that way. THEY do not have the authority or right to do that." He pointed downwards towards the vault.

"I know, but there are so many regulations," Carl said. "Regulations we've...y'know."

"Fucked up," Lola stated.

"Yeah...fucked up," Carl said.

Johnny put his hands behind his back and started to pace up and down. "You think they may try and...take away our powers?" Johnny asked. The horror of having his invisibility and his new-found life recharger taken from him made him start to panic. He started to tap his wrist furiously.

"Yoo 'avin' a moment?" Lola asked.

"I'll be fine," Johnny whispered, staring ahead. "Just fine."

"So, after all this...yoo fink they're gonna take our powers?" asked Lola. "Like fuck they will. I'll fight 'em all."

"Ok, Tiger...relax," Carl said, looking at Lola, who was starting to twirl her cue above her head, making a large whooshing sound. "I don't know if they are...I've just been getting more feelings about things."

"Me too..." agreed Lola. "I could really feel an evil presence in naked man's 'ouse. I've never felt that before."

Johnny thought about it for a moment. He couldn't say that he had noticed getting any more subtle feelings. He had been so joyous about the thought of having a mini-break for the first time in years that he hadn't been paying that much attention.

At the moment, there was a kick against the door three times. Carl ran over and opened it. It was Bert, who marched in carrying three plates, covered in foil.

"For their Highnesses," Bert said quickly. "They want 'em up 'ere." He plonked them down on the counter and turned to face Carl.

"Look, I just met a little bird called Sophie in the caff. She only had a box of gold watches on 'er and she knows Tara," he garbled.

"Sophie?" Carl said. "I know Sophie...short with glasses?" Bert nodded. Carl knew exactly who he was talking about. He knew Fergus had been casually seeing her and she still came to his pub occasionally.

"Yeah, well, she had a box of them watches," Bert said,

sounding flustered and agitated.

"Is she still there?" Carl asked.

"Nah...I ballsed it up, didn't I. She legged it. She knew I knew somefink." Bert was furious with himself.

"Shit. Where did she go?" Carl demanded.

"Dunno, mate," he groaned. "Wish I did," he said, rubbing his forehead and taking out a cigarette.

"How many watches were there?" Carl asked, grabbing the packet out of Bert's hand and taking a cigarette out. He chucked it back and Bert caught it.

"About six," Bert replied, putting the cigarette in his mouth and lighting it.

"She used to go out with Fergus. We've got to find her," Carl said lighting his. They both inhaled at the same time and blew out.

"She'll be comin' 'ere, won't she? She said so," Bert said, trying to find a silver lining to the predicament.

"Yeah, but when? Who is she going to give those watches to? That's what it's about," Carl growled, angry that a lost chance had slipped through their fingers.

The private door, which led down to the vault, banged opened and out strode the three Guardians, deep in conversation with one another and not even noticing the gorilla and nun standing in front of them. Carl turned to the three plates and quickly pulled the foil off them, scrunched it up and threw it behind the bar.

"Oh yes, you can smell hot, fat grease a mile away, can't you!" Marilyn hissed in the direction of Jonah. Jonah ignored this and just walked over to the bar and grabbed one of the plates and took it away to a table. He pulled a face of a nagging wife as he passed by Marilyn.

"Do you mind, dear? I happen to have a ball of mass destruction next to my left nipple," he said. Marilyn scrunched up his nose in contempt.

"Tooo much information! Tooo much information!" Marilyn boomed.

"You're such a humourless old fart," Jonah said. Marilyn opened his mouth in horror and made two fists, which shook in rage by his side.

Carl realised they needed cutlery and vaulted over the side

185

counter, where a pot holding knives and forks wrapped tightly in paper napkins was kept. Next to it rested a plastic box packed with sachets of sauces and vinegar. Carl grabbed three sets and whacked them down on the counter along with the box – drawing Max's attention.

Max, who had plonked himself down on a stool, realised Carl was dressed as a nun. He stood up, walked over to the side counter, and looked Carl in the eyes without any expression and asked if he had any tartar. Carl grinned, nodded and handed him a cruet set.

"Thanks, chap," Max said and headed back to his seat.

He turned his head to the left where Bert was standing and was greeted with an exaggerated smile. Max stretched his head to look across the pub and saw the lycra-clad Johnny, who also had a huge fake grin plastered across his face. Lola and the wheelbarrow were obscured by the counter and a coffee machine. Max inhaled, shook his head and said nothing. He sat down and started to tuck into his food.

Jonah noticed he needed cutlery, but realising it would hugely aggravate Marilyn, picked up a sausage and bit it in half. Marilyn closed his eyes and swivelled on his heel to face the bar. Carl instantly offered him a drink.

Marilyn finally opened his eyes, saw Carl and smiled slowly, if not slightly flirtatiously. "Why are you dressed like that?" his grin widening as he pulled up a stool next to Max.

"Boat Race. Bit of fund-raising, y'know," Carl explained, putting on an innocent and carefree tone.

Johnny saw Eric stirring in the wheelbarrow. His eyes widened and he nudged Lola. Lola gasped, which drew her attention to Max. He stood up so he could get a better look across the bar at her.

"Ah, Pitchfork. Dressed as a nun? Don't know how you have the nerve." Max chuckled.

Lola, who was distracted by Eric, looked up quickly towards Max and waved. "Hi," she said nervously. "'Ow are yoo today?" she said, stumbling for words.

Max answered, "Very well, Pitchfork, in spite of having to sleep next to a snoring walrus and a whingeing old woman."

"Kinky," Lola quipped as Johnny grinned inanely and edged towards the wheelbarrow.

Max guffawed. "Hardly," he said and smiled, catching the eye of Marilyn whose face was less than approving of this flirtation. Max composed himself and turned his attention back to his breakfast.

Marilyn delicately nibbled on a piece of toast and said to Carl, "I say, this tastes rather good, actually. I expected…shall we say…a disaster."

Carl smiled sweetly at him. "Well, we do try our best. Glad you like it, Marilyn. So…your drink? Perhaps some champagne…?"

Marilyn smiled, "Oh yes, I'm always up for some… champagne," he said, turning to look at Max who whispered to him, without looking up: "YOU, behave yourself, chap."

Marilyn asked quietly, "What?" Max continued eating and said: "Just don't chap. There's no time for that."

Marilyn slowly crossed him arms. "Hypocrite," he whispered and turned to smile even more broadly at Carl. "Yes, champagne would be soooper."

Carl asked if the other two wanted some as well.

"Just put down the bottle on the table," said Jonah and his chest rumbled with laughter.

"One each," Marilyn said and Carl nodded.

"Sure," he said quietly. "Of course." What was he thinking!

Eric began to open his eyes. The first things he noticed were a fruit-machine and a pool table. Ow! His jaw hurt. It felt swollen. His head was groggy and he found it hard to focus. He knew that he was lying down in some fashion and he tried to raise his head, murmuring as he did. He then felt himself moving, as his line of vision moved from a pool table to a toilet door, which also had a sign saying 'exit' over it.

The door was opened by a pink-clad arm and then he was being pushed through a long corridor. Another door was opened and he was pushed into an old cloakroom, which was now used for storage. He groggily looked over to see a masked superhero in hot pink.

"Where am I?" Eric asked with a croaky voice, unable to see brilliantly without his glasses.

Johnny put his hands on his hips, threw his head back and said cheesily: "I am Captain Cupid. Have no fear, human, you are safe." He thought (attempted) humour might go some way towards putting Eric's mind at ease.

Eric focused on the slightly protruding belly and the vacuum cleaner he was plonked next to. "Who?" he asked. "What am I doing here?" he asked nervously. "Why are you dressed like…that?"

"Don't you remember Mike's stag night?" Johnny lied. "What a great night. God, we drank soo much. I'm surprised if you remember anything from it at all. Actually, when some people drink they hallucinate and even forget friends they've known for years – like me."

Eric looked around and noticed he was in a wheelbarrow. He also noticed he was naked. He let out a scream.

Johnny threw his hands over his mouth. "You mustn't scream," Johnny whispered which made the muffled screaming worse. "Please don't. You're safe…" but the muffled screaming didn't stop.

"Oh bollocks," Johnny sighed, as he picked up his cue from the wheelbarrow and pointed it at Eric. A bolt of blue light came out of it and knocked Eric out.

"Sorry. Really sorry," Johnny said but hoped it would keep him quiet for at least an hour or so. They really needed to dress him but Lola hadn't picked up any of his clothes. Johnny supposed that he would have to go home and get some of his. There was also the option of fancy dress. The only costume left upstairs was a coconut bikini. He couldn't do that to the poor man, it just wouldn't be fair. It really, really wouldn't be fair.

"What was that?" Max barked when he heard what sounded like a scream.

"What was what?" Carl asked.

"Sounded like a scream," Max said.

"I didn't hear anything. Did you?" Carl asked over to Bert.

"No, mate. I 'eard nuffink," Bert replied innocently.

"Lola?" Carl asked.

"Wot?" she squeaked.

"Did you hear anything?" Carl asked and beckoned her over to Max's side with his eyes.

"No," she said and hurriedly walked over next to Max. "I 'eard nuffink at all."

"'Ello," she said to Max, smiling widely and grabbing his

188

attention. Marilyn was busy drinking and eyeing up Carl, whereas Jonah was immersed in his food.

"Hello Pitchfork," Max said. Lola said nothing but caught Carl silently urging her to say something.

"'Ow is yer mother?" she asked, not knowing what to ask.

"My mother is in the south of France living with a trembling, in-bred Pekingese rat-dog called Jason," Max said with derision. Lola nodded wisely. "I 'ate me cat, Condom" she moaned. "And it hates me." Max nodded back to her.

Straining to think of something else to say, she forced out: "Are ya looking forward to this afternoon?"

"I think it should be pretty straightforward. Nothing much to worry about," he said, smiling at her. "Things will then change forever for you four." Lola again nodded wisely but was miles away. She was wondering where Johnny was and what had happened to Eric.

"Why is your costume torn?" Max asked suspiciously, pushing his finger through one of the tears.

Lola was momentarily caught off guard and then answered:" I am a...zombie...nun." Max gestured for her to continue.

"Err...Actually, Barnes 'as a zombie problem, which ain't our problem, cos we kill vampires, as y'know..." Max nodded indulgently and Lola continued: "...and so we dress up as zombies from time to time...outside Barnes pond...just to... err...annoy the zombie killers," Lola said. "Which we do."

"It really doesn't surprise me," Max said. "Nothing would."

Lola was running out of things to say. She looked over at the juke box on the wall.

"'Ow about some music?" she asked, dashing over to the machine, wanting to escape the gnawing feeling of embarrassment swirling in her belly.

"Rock'n'Roll, chap. No bloody boy bands," Max said.

Lola tapped in the code that gave ten credits and started to choose some songs. An Elvis Rock'n'Roll song blasted out across the pub.

"Good choice," Max remarked, starting to sway as he ate.

"Nice one," chimed in Bert, shuffling around in his gorilla outfit, getting into his groove. Bert loved to dance and genuinely didn't care what kind of spectacle he made of

189

himself.

"What is he doing?" asked Marilyn, nudging Max. "Looks like he's having a fit."

"God knows what any of them have been up to, chap. They all look guilty as sin this morning," Max said flatly.

"Really, I can't say that I noticed anything peculiar," Marilyn replied.

"That's because you're a self-obsessed drama queen, chap," Max shot at him. "You wouldn't notice a twenty-foot tap-dancing centipede if it broke through that door and sang 'somewhere over the rainbow'."

Marilyn narrowed his eyes. "Is that right?" he said. "You think I wouldn't notice that, do you?"

"He's right," chipped in Jonah, who had still dispensed with using cutlery and was eating a piece of bacon.

Marilyn pushed himself elegantly up from the bar, picked up the bottle of champagne and poured himself a glass.

"Well, let's see if YOU notice…this." Marilyn glugged down the champagne and slammed the glass down on the bar. He raised his hand out in front of him, closing his eyes and inhaling deeply and then let out an enormous belch. Max practically spat out his food from laughing.

"And you call me disgusting," Jonah mocked, chewing a mouthful of mushrooms and roaring at the same time.

Marilyn gave Max a filthy glare and aggressively shoved his arm out in front of him. He shut his eyes and took in an enormous lungful of air.

Bert was still shuffling around to the King, oblivious to his surroundings. He loved music – it just got into his soul and he couldn't help but feel the power of rhythm surge through him. He grooved joyously as he opened his eyes and, with terror, leapt ten feet backwards. A giant yellow centipede with a top hat and tails was tap-dancing in the bar, next to him. Having never seen a twenty-foot tap-dancing centipede before, Bert's mind had no check-list to compare it to. He hollered: "Wot the fuck!" and promptly fell backwards, grabbing his chest and staring at the incredible spectacle before him. It was the little tiny tap shoes that got him the most. Half the legs had tap shoes with tiny yellow bows and the rest held tiny black canes with yellow butterflies on them.

190

His face was like a cartoon character with two large round eyes and a grinning red mouth with perfect teeth. It was singing something but Bert couldn't hear.

Max guffawed with laughter, Jonah chortled, almost choking for a moment and Marilyn grinned, as he looked proudly at the illusion he had conjured before him. Oh, that would teach Max – oh, yes!

Marilyn's Guardian class ability was the power of illusion. He was exceptionally talented and able to generate three-dimensional soft images. They appeared to be real and solid – perfect in every detail – but anyone could put their hand through them. He could create pretty much anything he put his mind to but, as with any ability, they took up a lot of energy. He couldn't maintain them indefinitely.

Lola, who was still selecting tracks on the juke machine, heard Bert yell. She spun around and leapt backwards herself, hitting her head on the machine. She didn't notice the pain – she was utterly transfixed by the centipede. It was dancing in tune to the music. She glanced around to the Guardians, two of which were laughing their heads off and one of which was smugly nodding at her. Judging by their reactions, she instinctively knew there was no danger but her heart pounded against her chest.

Carl was totally gobsmacked. A glass slipped out of his hand. It smashed and he didn't notice as he leaned across the bar and stared.

Lola, whose stubbornness often outranked her need for self-preservation, took a step closer to the giant centipede, reaching out her hand. She smiled in childlike wonder and amazement as she walked tentatively closer, taking little steps – her eyes locked onto the centipede's face, which was smiling and had glowing rainbows for irises. Lola was slack-jawed. The centipede was the height of the room and about five feet across. She stretched her head back and looked up, reaching out a hand above her and went to touch it. Her hand went right through the image. She grinned and giggled. It was amazing. She swiped her hand through the image again and walked straight into the centre of it.

"It ain't real," she shouted over the music. "Wow," she added. She walked out of it, looking it up and down. Bert was

191

still transfixed by the vision.

"Wot is it?" he shouted, pointing at the benign tap-dancing cartoon.

"It ain't real, Bert," she said. "It's fake...look." Lola twirled around and jumped into the image and then jumped out of it.

At that moment, Johnny had left the unconscious Eric, still naked, in his wheelbarrow and headed back into the pub, holding his cue. He first heard music blaring out. He next saw what he thought was something huge moving in the corner of his eye. He turned the corner of the pub and saw Bert on the floor pointing upwards, and Lola jumping in and out, giggling, of a giant dancing centipede. He instantly turned invisible and fell backwards.

Carl vaulted over the counter and approached the image. "Incredible," he said to himself, as he watched Lola jumping in and out of the creature. The centipede looked totally solid. He turned back to Marilyn, who was looking smugger than a millionaire who had just won the lottery and asked: "Are you doing this?"

Marilyn nodded. "Of course, darling," he boasted. "You don't think walrus breath could do this, do you?" He gestured over to Jonah, who was wiping tears away from his eyes.

"How?" Carl asked.

"All part of being a Guardian," Marilyn replied enigmatically.

"That is just one of the most amazing things I've ever seen," Carl said. "Just amazing,"

"I've seen better," Max jibed. "But that's good, chap."

"What else can you do?" Carl asked.

"Pretty much anything I can put my mind to," Marilyn replied.

"That's where the problem lies," Max snorted.

Marilyn narrowed his eyes at him. "Sneer, sneer, sneer!"

"It's a very good centipede and you should be very proud," Max said patronisingly. "Gold star," he added as Marilyn grabbed the champagne bottle and started to pour another glass.

"I forgive your jealousy. Engineering is no match for the power of illusion," Marilyn said dismissively. Max waved him away with a hand and laughed, continuing with his eating.

"So, how large...I mean...can you create buildings, St Paul's, that kind of thing?" Carl asked with wonder.

"I could, but not for too long. The smaller the better. It's not often I say that," he said and grinned.

"So, you can copy anyone...their voice...everything?" Carl asked. He was completely blown-away by Marilyn's ability. Would they get a skill like his one day?

"Yes, providing I know what their voice sounds like."

"How long for?"

"Hmmm...about twenty minutes," Marilyn replied.

"Can you create flying mice in tiny black suits? I've always wanted to see that," Carl blurted out like an excited child.

"Really?" Marilyn asked flatly. Carl nodded.

"That's just weird," Marilyn remarked and Carl shrugged.

"I don't usually do requests," Marilyn said. "But...as I am in the mood...why not?"

Marilyn extended his arms, breathed in and out. Carl turned and watched the centipede flicker in and out of visibility, as Lola was still jumping about. She stopped and watched the unstable image around her morph into a dozen white mice with dark glasses, wings and black suits fly around her head. She jumped up and swiped at one – her hand going through it again and she laughed.

"This is better than sex," she said loudly. Bert was still transfixed but couldn't help but giggle. He pushed himself up onto his feet.

Johnny, meanwhile, had recovered from his tiny black-out and also got back onto his feet, only this time he was looking at flying mice. He walked over to Bert's side, his eyes staring at the illusion.

"What is going on?" Johnny asked – as if it wasn't bad enough being half-dead.

"They ain't real," Bert explained. "Like a hologram or somefink," he added. "Apparently, it's better than sex."

"Huh?" Johnny asked and looked over at Lola who was jumping up and swiping at the mice.

"Better than sex, apparently," Bert repeated with a wicked twinkle in his eye.

Johnny scratched his head. "Oh, cheers," he said as he stared at the mice.

"How...?" Johnny asked as he approached the flying mice buzzing around Lola's head. Lola looked over to Johnny slowly getting nearer, his eyes mesmerized by the illusory mice.

"Ain't they brilliant!" she exclaimed.

"How?" he asked.

"Marzipan, I fink," she replied and Johnny turned towards the Guardians and Carl. Max was eating at the bar and not giving any attention to the illusion while Jonah was chewing as he brushed new dandruff off his shoulders. Carl and Marilyn appeared to be talking.

Johnny turned back to the mice. He reached up and he swiped his hand through one that was flying over his head. He felt nothing at all. He looked harder at the image and realised the attention to detail of the projected images was extraordinary. He could see little sequins on their suit collars and one had a gold tooth.

"Amazing. I wonder if he can do anything he likes," Johnny said as he tried to put his hand through another one.

Bert had pushed himself up and nervously walked over to Johnny and Lola, while staring at the mice. "Look at 'em," he said. "They look real."

One flew down so that it was nose to nose with Bert. "Alright, mate," Bert chuckled. The mouse pulled out a machine gun and giggled in a high-pitched voice. It turned towards the other mice and started firing flowers at them. Roses, daffodils, lilies all flew out from the barrel and suddenly hundreds of petals of all colours and shapes were swirling around in the air as the mice dissolved. Lola was enchanted by all the colours swirling around her.

"I want this for me weddin'," she said and jumped up into Johnny's arms and kissed him. "Wouldn't it be fantastic? I want flyin' mice for me bridesmaids."

"No, Lola," Johnny sighed. "People wouldn't understand." Lola jumped down from Johnny's arms and ran over to Marilyn.

"Yoo are amazin'," she said and giggled. Marilyn smiled smugly, raised a glass and sipped from it. "D'ya wanna come to me weddin'?"

Johnny and Bert watched as the petals wafted down to the floor, covering it in brilliant colours and then they gradually disappeared. They were both truly impressed with this

194

performance.

They turned and walked over to join Lola and Marilyn.

"That's just outstanding," complimented Johnny.

"Nice one, mate," Bert said. "Yoo almost gave me an 'eart attack."

Marilyn loved the attention and seemed to glow with pride.

The kitchen door suddenly burst open and Maisie came running through the door. She looked around her. The Guardians looked her up and down. Max scowled. Jonah sniffed the air.

Maisie ran over to Carl and grabbed his shoulders.

"What year is this?" she demanded.

33

Sophie had made her escape from the café as soon as the strange gorilla man had turned his back on her. She felt that she had been busted and she needed to get away as quickly as she could. Damn! She had told him that she would be seeing Tara in the pub later. Damn!

Sophie paced down the road at high speed and took herself to another café at the end of the street. She bought a soft drink and moved right down to the back of the premises, tucked away in a corner. With the amount of people in there, it would be hard to find her. She looked over to the couple sitting in front of her. They were holding hands and seemed to be in love. Sophie looked down at the box of watches in front of her, sighed and bit her nails.

She pulled out her mobile phone and made a call to her friend Sarah, who was the bar manager at The Cat and Trowel. Sophie had the idea to have her eight friends, who were all destined to receive the watches, to pass by the café and pick them up from her. They all worked on the Lower Richmond Road, so there was no hardship and it was perfect timing as most of them would be on their way to their pubs. She just didn't want to run the risk of running into gorilla man or any of his friends.

"Hello, Sarah. It's me. Look, can you pop by the café near the bridge? I've got a present for you. You are? Brilliant...see you in five," Sophie said and internally sighed with relief. She noticed hordes of people walking over the bridge wearing light and dark scarves. The helicopter was buzzing overhead. People were pouring into Putney. Boat Race Day was beginning.

As Maisie gripped Carl's arms, Max stood up and scowled, looking at the two of them suspiciously. Carl licked his lips nervously – his mind racing for an explanation. Maisie was panting and bending forwards, trying to get her breath.

"Hello, Auntie Maisie," Carl said, putting his arm around her. "How are you today?" he asked. He turned to the others. "This is Auntie Maisie, she's helping out in the kitchen, extra staff, y'know."

"Super breakfast," praised Marilyn.

"Loverly," slobbered Jonah.

"Yes, very good, chap," agreed Max. Maisie raised her head and looked at them. She put her hand to Carl's face.

"It's you. You're young," she panted.

"Yes," said Carl, guiding her to a calendar on the wall, showing the date and year. "It's Boat Race Day, today. Remember, Auntie?"

Maisie grabbed the calendar and clutched it to her chest. "Thank God, you have no idea...just no idea..."

Carl whispered in her ear. "Is it fixed?"

"Is what fixed?" Maisie asked.

"The time leak." Carl replied with a stony glare.

"Oh, yes...yes...but that's not the problem. It's your kitchen," Maisie babbled. "It's ..."

Carl twiddled with the ring on his finger. "What?"

Maisie was getting her breath and pointing towards the kitchen.

"Well, what?" Carl demanded. "What's going on?" He noticed that Max was still looking at the two of them and Carl put on a sweet smile and rubbed Maisie's arm affectionately.

"Tell me what the hell is going on. You just left here about fifteen minutes ago."

"Fifteen minutes," she puffed. "Fifteen minutes...is that all?" she asked. "You have no idea where I've been..." Maisie wheezed, looking around the pub with a look of happiness breaking out across her face. She smiled with relief.

"Maisie, what is going on?" Carl really needed to know.

"Oh, hon. I don't know where to begin," she said. "She changed her mind. She didn't let me go..."

"Just tell me," Carl insisted.

197

"Your kitchen is…errr…" Maisie said. She didn't quite know how to put it.

"Yes…go on…" he urged.

"Well, it's…a kinda …err…refugee camp."

"Excuse me?" Carl asked, grinning even more wildly.

"Ummm…some of those on the run from the Time Police are staying in your kitchen."

Carl looked up at the ceiling and then around the pub. He wasn't sure that he could take this in.

"The plus side is that you don't have to wear this anymore, do you?" she remarked, grabbing his sleeve and shaking it.

"Oh, that's the least of my worries," he protested. "I thought a naked man in a wheelbarrow was bad enough. That's nothing. That's just a mere flirtation with stress."

"You what? Look, they're not going to be there for long," she whispered and smiled inanely at Max, who was still looking over with accusatory eyes while tearing a piece of toast with his teeth.

"How do you know how long they're going to be there? How many are there? Why are they there?" Carl growled while falsely smiling.

Maisie pretended to laugh as if Carl had said something outstandingly funny. "Come with me, I'll show you," she said. Carl shot her a look which was less than appreciative. "Come on," Maisie demanded.

"You deal with it," Carl said stubbornly.

"Come on and see. You need to see this," she insisted, grabbing his arm and pulling him towards her.

"Hey," he frowned.

"Come on, Carl…otherwise I'll tell everyone about me and the batgirl costume."

"That's blackmail," Carl said.

"Yes, yes it is…now move your arse," she snapped.

Maisie pulled Carl towards the kitchen door. Luckily the music was still blaring out in the bar otherwise they would've heard Carl scream when he looked into the kitchen. Max heard the door slam. He cast a very, very suspicious look and glugged down his champagne.

The public door knocked. Johnny looked at Bert, who looked at Lola. Bert shrugged and shuffled over to the rhythm of the music to the door. What a morning, he thought. As mornings go, this was one for the diary. He opened the door and there was Big Tara.

"Oi, oi..." she said. "Wot's all this?"

Tara was about 43 with long blonde hair and blue eyes. Her face had a mischievous quality and wise eyes that belied her age. She was on the heavier side which didn't prevent her from wearing tight clothes. Take her or leave her, that was her motto. She was wearing a black V-neck T-shirt and three-quarter-length faded blue jeans.

"It's fancy dress, Tara. Didn't Carl tell ya?" Bert asked cheekily and laughed huskily.

"Don't yoo flirt with me, Bert," she chided.

"Moi?" Bert said, as he opened the door. "I wouldn't dream of it." He grinned. Tara ruffled his hair as she walked by.

"Yeah, yeah, yeah and the rest, mate," she chuckled.

"Ooo...'ello," she said to the others. There were three unshaven men drinking champagne and eating breakfast and Bert, Johnny and Lola wearing costumes.

"Is it really fancy dress?" Tara asked. "Carl said nuffink to me."

"Didn't he?" Bert asked. "Strange," he mused. "Look Tara, can I ask yer somefink?"

"No, I won't fly to the South of France with yoo and live on yer millionaire's yacht," Tara sniffed. "I'm quite 'appy with me lager, chicken and chips."

"Nah, nuffink like that, Tara. I wanna ask ya about that little bird, Sophie," he said, grinning.

"Blimey, this place smells of smoke. Open those doors, would ya?" she asked Jonah, as she pointed to the large back doors that led into the garden. Jonah looked around him to see who she was talking to.

"Sophie, wot about 'er?" she asked, turning her attention back to Bert and frowning.

"Where is everyone?" she demanded. It was one of the busiest days of the year and there were no members of staff about. Max glanced over at Marilyn, who nodded conspiratorially back at him.

"I met her earlier and she said she needed to give you somefink," Bert explained, ignoring her other question.

"Lucky ole me," Tara winked as she walked towards the bar, followed by Bert. She walked by Max and clocked the three of them each had a bottle of champagne.

"Wot's the occasion?" she asked Max, opening the side counter and walking through. Jonah in the meantime had gestured to Lola to go and open the back door. She was annoyed at this but complied with a scowl.

"This chap? To celebrate Cambridge's win today," he bragged.

"Yoo ain't won yet," Tara jeered. "I'm more of an Oxford girl, meself."

"Really, chap?" he asked with a disapproving sniff.

"Yeah, I went there right after leavin' me bleedin' Swiss finishing school for young ladies," she said flatly. "Where's Carl?" she asked looking around. "I've got a ton of fings to sort out. Where is everyone?"

"Tara, he's just…away for the moment…I need to ask ya about Sophie," Bert said.

"Wot about her?" Tara snapped.

"Do yoo 'ave her number? Can yoo call her?" Bert asked, putting the emphasis on 'yoo'.

"Yes, I 'ave her number and no, why should I call 'er?" Tara said, with suspicion. Bert was trying to think of a good reason for this and looked a bit flustered.

"Yoo ain't got yer eye on her, 'ave ya?" Tara sniggered. Bert shook his head vigorously.

"Wot would Mrs Bert say?" Tara teased, seeing that Bert was beginning to blush.

"It's nuffink like that. It's just…she really needed to see ya," Bert said. Tara stopped what she was doing, gave Bert a long hard stare and then reached into her bag, which was still swung over her shoulder. She looked at it. She had a text from Sophie. Johnny at this moment had joined Bert at the bar.

"That's funny," Tara frowned. "She's sent me a text." Bert was excited by this.

"Wot does it say?" Bert asked.

"Don't privacy mean nuffink to yoo?" Tara growled, looking at Johnny. Johnny raised his hands in apology and walked to the other side of the bar where he, Lola and Eric had been earlier.

"Go on, Tara. Is it about a present or somefink?" Bert asked hurriedly.

"Yeah, actually, it is," she said.

"Go on, tell me. I wouldn't ask if it weren't important."

Tara raised her eyebrows and read the text again. "She wants me to go and meet 'er in a caff and pick up a present."

"Which caff?"

"Is she in trouble?" Tara asked. "Why d'ya need to know where she is?"

Bert thought about it for a moment. "She over-paid me that other night, I want to give 'er the change."

Tara roared with laughter. "Are yoo 'avin' a giraffe? That's priceless that is." Her laugh was deep and thoroughly wicked. Bert blushed and was starting to become lost for words and an excuse.

Bert's eyes bulged when he saw Johnny's face materialise behind Tara's shoulder. He read the text, turned to Bert and winked. He then disappeared again.

Tara clocked Bert's strained expression. "Yoo alright, mate?" she asked.

"Yeah, yeah…no worries," he said. Great! Johnny had the information. "Look, ya know wot. Don't worry about it, I'll catch up wiv 'er anuvver time." Bert grinned and shrugged.

"Yoo ok?"

"Yeah, yeah…great music," Bert said and shuffled off, leaving Tara looking as if Bert had grown two heads.

Bert shuffled over to the other side of the bar, where Johnny had re-materialised.

"Where is she?" Bert asked.

"She's down the end of the road in the café by the river," Johnny replied.

"We need to get those watches off her," Bert said excitedly.

"I'll go," volunteered Johnny. "Incognito."

"Wot? Yoo'll go there invisible 'n' everyfink?"

"Yes," Johnny said. He still felt bad about the danger Lola had been put in and part of him wanted to make up for it. He also really wanted to go out and use his invisibility power.

"It's gettin' busy out there. People will bump into ya," Bert warned. "Yer still solid, ain't ya?"

"I'll have to be creative, won't I?" Johnny answered. "I'll

201

sneak out the back way. Hopefully, I'll be back before anyone notices."

"I wouldn't worry mate," Bert joked and chuckled.

"Cheers," Johnny said, grinning at him. "Just cover for me, if anyone asks," he added as he headed towards the back door. It was the same exit with the corridor and the room where Eric was presently unconscious.

"Bert, you're going to have to dress our guest," Johnny said, suddenly remembering Eric's predicament.

"I ain't dressin' no naked man," Bert insisted. "I don't mind killin' vampires but I ain't doin' that."

"Bert, you have to. I've knocked him out but he will come around soon," Johnny said. "What are you afraid of?" he mocked, putting on his pseudo-Austrian accent.

"Knock it off, Professor," cautioned Bert. "No man wants to do that."

Johnny pushed the exit door open. "It's why you *don't* that is interesting, hmmm." Johnny laughed. "Come on, Bert." Bert sighed and nodded in resigned agreement. Johnny nodded, saluted and walked into the corridor. He passed by the spare room housing Eric, poked his head around the door – he was still unconscious – excellent, thought Johnny, as he continued towards the back door. He grabbed the handle, paused for a moment and closed his eyes. When he opened them he had turned invisible. He pushed the door gently and squeezed through the smallest gap he could manage (he didn't want to freak out any passers-by that might see a door spring open and close on its own accord).

The day was bright and there was a slight breeze in the air. He reached his hand out before him just to check that he really was invisible, as a slight paranoia crept over him. He was. He threw his leg over his cue, straddling it and thought to it to rise up in the air. He found himself lifting up and up to the height of the large silver birch tree next to him. He brushed one of its branches, alarming a blackbird which flew away, squawking. Johnny's heart pounded with the sheer joy of flying. He could see over the houses, down the road and the river a little way to his left. It was a moment he would never forget in his (half) life.

He thought to his cue to move forwards and he found

himself slowly and jerkily flying towards the café, which was about a five minute walk away from The Pig & Phoenix. He was by no means a fast and competent flyer and he was nervous about falling off. He slowly flew above the Lower Richmond Road before dropping some height and manoeuvring towards the pavement. He reminded himself that he was already half-dead and he was sitting on a cue charged up with life energy. His chances of resurrection, should an accident occur, were very good indeed.

He felt free. He wouldn't need to catch a train anywhere for a mini-break! He was invisible and he could fly. He should've been thinking more about the dangers they were to face but he was grinning from ear to ear, gaining a bit more confidence before he arrived at the café.

He hovered above the road, looking down at the cars and the café. Johnny looked over to the bridge and decided he really, really needed to practice just a little bit more. He had time. His cue turned 90 degrees to his left and he faced the Thames. There was a magnificent vision of Putney Bridge with the sunlight glinting on it. To his right, there was St Mary's Church – an Anglican Church steeped in history – dating back centuries, and across the water there was Bishop's Park. He hovered for a moment taking in this view. The only drawback was the buzzing noise of the hovering helicopter – way up in the air. He didn't know if he had the guts, at his stage, to go that high. He figured that he probably would in time. It would be irresistible not to.

He looked down the river bank and the connecting roads. There were numerous large lorries and trucks, housing television crews and equipment, which would broadcast this event all over the world.

People were already gathering along the river bank. Some were walking their dogs, others just strolling by and some were sitting on benches. The High Street behind him was buzzing with people, making their way in streams towards the river. Many, he could tell, were waiting for the pubs to open at 11am. He was someone who loved the Boat Race. He knew it was good for the economy of Putney. He supported Oxford. He hadn't studied at any of the Oxford Colleges but if he had had the choice, and had had the grades, he would've gone!

He slowly flew forwards until he was hovering above the Thames at the same height as the bridge, which was an arm reach away. The wind blew against him as he took one hand off the cue and slowly patted the bridge. He felt filled with utter happiness and liberation. He smiled broadly and looked down. The river looked cold and he could see fast and dangerous swirling currents but the excitement of adventure spurred him onwards. He turned in the direction of Hammersmith and flew forwards slowly investigating the riverbank, the pavement and the pubs. Unfortunately, two low-flying ducks were unaware of his presence. One clipped his head, spinning him around and forcing him to hold on violently. Feeling unnerved, he retreated very quickly back towards the pavement and reminded himself that he needed to fulfil his mission. Operation Steal Gold Watches from Sophie!

Johnny flew cautiously towards the café until he was hovering about thirty feet above the ground. It felt weird looking down on peoples' heads. The part of him that was still seven years old imagined dropping water balloons on them. However, he was a fully mature and grown-up man and would never stoop to doing such a thing (not without Bert's help, anyway). He lowered down and angled himself so he could look through the door. The tables were packed and there was a queue of people waiting for their takeaway coffees. His mind itched. How on earth was he actually going to do this? It seemed Bert had a point.

The door was wide open but there was quite a narrow gap. Johnny looked at the café's ceiling. It was high. If he could fly through the door at the right moment, he could then aim towards the ceiling and hover there. He could locate Sophie and steal the watches.

Johnny waited for five minutes before opportunity came his way. There was a lull on the coffee queue – just one woman. Johnny dropped down and flew through the gap in the door, clipping it with his foot and slamming it behind him, startling people. He flew upwards and hit his head on a lamp. There was a clonking noise and the light began to swing. A young man, reading a book on ghosts and hauntings, glugged down his coffee and left the café at alarming speed.

Johnny edged away from the swinging light. It was weird having all eyes turn upwards but no-one see you, he thought. He looked around and saw Sophie tucked away in the corner. She had a box on the table and a girl with chin-length blonde hair was sitting opposite her. He saw Sophie give the blonde girl a watch, who in return hugged her and started to leave. Johnny was torn between following her and getting the box. He flew over to where Sophie was sitting and realised that he would need to create a diversion before any more watches were given away.

He thought towards his cue. A small energy bolt was released and Sophie's glass shot off the table, smashing on the floor. Sophie's instinctive reaction was to gasp, bend over and attend to the wreckage. As she did that, Johnny dropped down, swooped up the box and shoved it under his arm, making it instantly invisible. Sophie sat up. Panic set in. The box had gone. Oh dear God! Fergus would kill her. She felt an urge to cry and an urge to run. She didn't know what to do or what had happened.

Johnny hovered near the door area, which was once again open. Opportunity was gracing him yet again and he was able to fly out, clipping a hat off someone's head and knocking an ice-cream off a child's cone. He had the box. How many watches had she given out? He hoped it was only one. He floated upwards to see where the blonde girl had gone to. He got a fix of her walking towards one of the pubs nearby. She pulled out keys and let herself in. So, she worked there. He pondered for a moment. Tara worked at The Pig & Phoenix as the bar manager. That was the link. Pubs. These watches must be meant for people who worked in the local pubs. But why?

Johnny slowly flew down the Lower Richmond Road back towards The Pig & Phoenix. The others would be so proud of him. Yes, he hadn't fought slashy spider things but this was a very important part of the jigsaw puzzle. Fergus would not be expecting that and he assumed that Sophie would have to break the news to him. He knew that psychologically Fergus would have to retaliate. How violently he didn't know. They had upset his plans and his ego would not be able to take the blow.

205

Johnny hovered above the pub and slowly landed by the silver birch tree, noticing that the blackbird had returned to the branch. Johnny landed, climbed off the cue, grimacing slightly – flying was not a painless occupation.

He pushed open the side door and strode into the corridor like a conquering hero. As he passed by the old cloakroom, he decided to check in on Eric. Unfortunately for Eric, he was actually beginning to stir. Johnny pointed his cue at him, fired another blue bolt of energy and knocked him out once again. "Sorry, mate," he whispered. "Doesn't last as long as I thought."

He walked into the bar, only to be missed by a lightning bolt. "Fuck!" he shouted as he dived forwards, as another bolt of lightning shot over his head.

34

Carl slammed the kitchen door behind him and threw his back against it. He clamped his hands over his mouth and stared at the creatures around his kitchen table. Some were drinking tea while others were gambling on what looked like two alien insects racing across the kitchen table.

One of the creatures sitting down appeared to be a six foot tall praying mantis, but wearing a double-breasted blue suit and reading a newspaper. He gave off the air of a businessman and seemed oblivious that he was sitting in a strange kitchen. Opposite him was a shimmering, almost transparent, yellow mist. It was about two foot in length and occasionally sparkled, letting out a high-pitched squeaking noise followed by a crackle. Next to 'it' sat a small, female humanoid who wore a massive cream-cake of a dress befitting a 19th century American southern belle. She looked wistful and fanned herself gently as her dark ringlets fell around her heart-shaped face. "My, oh my," she repeated softly.

One of the two gambling was a four foot high ball of shocking pink fluff but with stubby arms and two bright pink glowing eyes. He also appeared to be hovering about a foot off the ground. His opponent was a large bird-like humanoid but with a flat cap and a pipe and wearing a tweed jacket. He had arms and hands but they were covered in white and blue feathers. His face was a cross between a man and a bird, with human eyes but with a beak housing teeth. He was quietly cheering on his insect as he sucked on his smokeless pipe.

Carl just stared. His heart pounded in his chest like a Rio de Janeiro carnival in full swing. There was another figure sitting next to the bird man, but he or she was wearing a black robe which hid their face and body.

Maisie appeared at his side and rubbed his shoulder gently. "You OK, little duck?" she asked.

Carl just shifted his eyes towards her. He shook his head and looked back at the spectacle before him. Maisie rubbed his back.

"They're not going to be here for long," Maisie said, trying to sound light and cheerful. "Honest," she added. At that moment the microwave oven made a 'time's up' beeping noise. The door flew open and a large beam of light burst out from inside it, projecting the image of a ten foot high and five foot wide striped red and white portal. Carl clamped his hands even harder over his mouth.

The six visitors paid no heed whatsoever as a nine foot Viking woman with an axe stomped through the portal with a small floating half-naked man next to her. He was approximately two foot high and he had long red hair. He wore a loincloth and a small necklace.

"That will teach them for telling me…ME…what to do. Who on earth do those bastards think they are? Low-level parasitical bullies!" the Staff Guardian growled before going into hostess mode.

"Hello everyone. This is Zagdoon," she said, pointing at the floating man next to her. Zagdoon waved at the others, who interrupted what they were doing and casually waved back. The southern belle fanned herself and batted her eyelids at him.

"Zagdoon was arrested for accidentally punching a hole into a neighbouring dimension without a permit." she said. Zagdoon nodded wistfully and clutched a hand to his chest.

The two gamblers looked at him and applauded. The praying mantis saluted him with his cup of tea and the yellow mist made a continuous popping noise. The hooded figure didn't move at all.

Carl just stared, unable to take his eyes off the scene before him. The Staff Guardian noticed the small nun across the room.

"What is your name, sister?" she called over to Carl, who had temporarily lost the power of speech. Maisie stepped in.

"This is Carl," explained Maisie, putting an arm protectively around his shoulder.

"Odd name for a nun," the Staff Guardian replied, materialising a glass of white wine in her hand and taking a large mouthful.

"Yes, if he was a woman...durhh," Maisie said, mocking the Staff Guardian in a very familiar fashion – almost like a long-time married, bickering couple.

"Don't start witch or I'll drop you off in the nearest time-loop," she threatened, pointing her axe at Maisie.

"Err...excoose me! You already tried that once and it didn't work," she groaned, slapping her forehead. "Anyway, is that the last one? They can't stay here. It's toooo dangerous, you nutter."

"Do you know how many prisoners there are out there? Do you?" the Staff Guardian demanded dramatically. "People and concepts," she said, gesturing to the yellow cloud, "are being banged up in hell holes across dimensions and time for no good reason at all by a group of self-appointed fascists. Well, I, for one, am not having it! Not now, not ever...never!" She raised her axe in the air and the group cheered.

Maisie rolled her eyes. "But they can't stay here. You are going to have to take them somewhere else. Somewhere where it is safe for...not just them...but for us," Maisie pleaded. "I told you I would help you but this can't go on."

"Oh moan, moan, moan! Moan, moan, moan, moan, moan!" the Staff Guardian mocked. "Me, me, me ,me. Me!"

"I do care about fighting the Time Police and I will continue the fight but this kitchen cannot be a refugee camp. It just can't," Maisie protested. "Right, Carl?"

Carl just stared at the nine-foot woman.

"First of all, this is not a kitchen. It is a Lodge. It is THE Lodge. The flagship, the Great Lodge. It stands for the individual. It stands for creativity. It stands for freedom. It does not stand for cowardice and self-interest, witch," the Staff Guardian boomed. "Why can't they stay?" the Staff Guardian challenged, pointing her axe in the direction of Carl.

209

Carl opened his mouth nervously. "There are three Guardians out there who think we are barely competent. If they see…this… it could be the end for us…" Carl said.

"And who is us?" she asked, throwing her axe over her shoulder and marching forward towards him. Carl looked up, startled. He tried to step backwards but he was already against the door.

"My friends…the other Vampire Killers," Carl said, licking his lips nervously.

"Ahh…you are custodians of the cues," the Staff Guardian said, breaking into a smile.

"Yes," he blurted out, glad that she was smiling. He had never seen a nine-foot woman enter a room via a microwave oven before. The way the last few days were going, he was sure this was probably something he should be getting used to.

"I know the Protectors well," she murmured, looking out into the middle distance dramatically. "They are most excellent creatures."

"The Protectors?" Carl asked, suddenly wondering why she was actually dressed as a Viking but thinking better than to ask.

"Yes, the Protectors. A group of seven Protectors. Your seven staffs…cues," she said in a matter-of-fact voice and as if he should easily understand this reference. Carl knew they were magical artefacts in disguise but he had never heard them called 'the Protectors' before. This information resonated at a deep level with his heart. It felt true.

"Well, there are four of us and one of the cues was stolen years ago by a man…who was my best friend…who wants to destroy me and possibly the world," Carl explained, knowing it must sound totally incompetent.

"He stole a cue? What?" she hissed. "Where is he?" she demanded, lowering her axe down and holding it close to Carl's torso. Carl gasped. It was one big, sharp ole axe. In a volatile explosion, she might either deliberately or accidentally cut him in two.

"He's close by. We're onto him but God only knows what he is planning. Whatever it is it is deadly," Carl said in a low voice, trying unsuccessfully to edge away from the axe.

210

"Is that why the Guardians are here?" she asked, pointing her chin in the direction of the bar, taking another glug of wine.

"Yes, it's all about the Eight Ball. They have it…or they have a copy," Carl explained while his heart pounded.

"The Eight Ball? *The* Eight Ball?" the Staff Guardian asked. "I didn't even think it was in this dimension anymore. I thought it had been hidden," she said, looking upwards as if wondering whether she had accidentally left her pet dog in a park. "I really didn't think it was here."

"It doesn't matter. They are still going to perform their ritual this afternoon."

"Why?" the Staff Guardian questioned aggressively.

"It's in their rule book," Carl whispered, extremely nervous of the blade that was inches from his chest.

"What rule book?" she asked, raising an eyebrow and her lip curling.

"The Lodge rule book," Carl said as lightly as he could possibly muster.

"Sod that book. I know how the book was started. I was there!"

"You were?" he asked with genuine curiosity. Who was this…creature?

"Yes. We were all drunk," she grinned, lowering her axe to her side. Carl closed his eyes with extreme relief. "It was about a hundred years ago in The Kitty Club in Mayfair. Great days."

"Huh?" Carl said, flicking his eyes open. The Staff Guardian seemed to be slightly annoyed by Carl's lack of understanding. She looked down into Carl's alarmed face and decided it would be best to tell him in a slow manner – a manner in which you talk to a child with learning difficulties.

"The Lodges were disagreeing over how large their districts were. So, to stop Lodges encroaching on other Lodges, some rules were created. It was a way of stopping internal bitching," she explained, but could see by the blank expression on Carl's face he was in need of further child-friendly explanation. She leaned further forward.

"Also, there was a power balance thing so the time rule thingy was created to make Lodges declare their conquest thingies. What it was really about was potentially a way of

211

getting your hands on another Lodge's goodies," she explained and patted him on his wimple, forcing it down over his eyes.

"What do you mean?" Carl asked, pulling his wimple back up and looking slightly put out. She kneeled down next to him and put a hand on his shoulder, practically forcing him to the floor. The Staff Guardian sighed. She decided she would just explain and if he couldn't keep up, well that was just too bad. She had other prisoners to rescue across space and time.

"The Lodge who find any serious magical artefact have claims on it for their Lodge only. However, they have to make a claim on it by proving it is what it is within a certain time. The claim is logged, by calling in the Guardians for verification, and they check it out," she said flatly before adding with an air of suspicion: "There is no actual magical hour required to check out its authenticity."

"They said it had to be performed at 3pm," Carl protested. "It's in the handbook. I've seen the handbook. We've all seen the bloody handbook," he said angrily and hoped that she would take her giant hand off his shoulder.

"It wasn't originally there," she said with conviction. "Someone must've added it at some point –probably to get hold of some item." She looked down at him and put her hand on his other shoulder, forcing him to the floor. He winced as he knees hit the ground.

"Like many regulations, no-one really knows why they're there and suddenly they are ancient and wise rules from mythical forefathers. Someone was probably drunk and added it for a bet," she remarked with booming laughter near to Carl's ear. He winced again.

"So, they could perform the verification ritual at any time?" Carl asked with his ear ringing. Was it true that the some of the rules were a result of nothing more than greed? He could understand having some kind of rules, to keep things in some sort of order, but adding rules for greed or to steal an item off a neighbouring Lodge, it just seemed against the spirit of the Lodges.

"Yes, well done, you got it in one," she said and patted him on head again, pushing the wimple back down over his eyes. She stood up, taking her hands off his shoulders and he exhaled with relief and leaned forward.

"How can I get them to stop the ritual?" Carl angrily asked while re-positioning his wimple and rubbing his ear. The Staff Guardian looked down at the small man as if he were a complete idiot.

"Err…why do you want them to stop? Also, you just let them think it's later," she snapped. "And YOU are more than capable of doing that. Tick tock. Tick tock," she added, moving her finger from left to right.

"What?" Carl demanded, standing up "How can I possibly do that?"

"Thought projection for a start," the Staff Guardian replied, once again looking at Maisie in exasperation. Maisie raised a hand to pacify her.

"I can't do that," Carl protested.

"Oh yes you can," came a voice from the table. Carl looked over to the hooded figure who threw back his cowl. Carl gawped. There, sitting down, was an older version of him with white hair and beard.

Maisie rubbed Carl's arm gently. "Carl, I'd like you to meet…Carl."

The older Carl stood up and bowed. "Carl is from another dimension. He was rescued from a penal colony," Maisie said. "He was arrested for selling time pop lollipops. You don't want to know."

The older Carl walked over. "How's it going, mate," older Carl said as the younger Carl twiddled the ring on his finger and ran his hand over his face. "Luckily for me these ladies busted me out. They are totally brilliant," he said and winked at Maisie, who grinned. The Staff Guardian arrogantly nodded in agreement and took another glug of wine.

"What the hell are time pop lollipops?" Carl asked, his mind racing. He really didn't know what else to say as he looked at the older version of himself. There were a million questions he should be asking about everything but where the hell would he or could he start? Another dimension? Nine foot Vikings? Bird, tweed-jacket man?

"Oooo," Maisie said. "Maybe you shouldn't tell him that," she warned older Carl.

"They are fantastic," older Carl said. "If you're anything like

213

me, then you'll be able to make them one day."

"I don't even know what they are. I don't even know who you are."

Maisie stroked Carl's arm. "He's just an older version of you from another dimension. He's on the run, love. That's it."

"Oh, I see. Silly me, I should've realised," Carl said. "Everyone...thing...is on the run from the..."

"Time Police," Maisie said.

"And...this woman...is?" he asked, gesturing towards the Staff Guardian.

"Is a very powerful spirit and time operator," Maisie explained. That was only half the problem, she thought.

"Why is she dressed as a Viking?" Carl asked.

"Why are you dressed as nun?" the Staff Guardian asked back, narrowing her eyes and pointing her axe at him.

"I was leaking time," he replied.

All the creatures at the table turned and gasped. Older Carl shook his head. "That is a major crime," he whispered. "That can end a universe, that can."

"It can?" Carl asked.

"Oh, yes," older Carl replied.

"But it wasn't our fault. We were attacked by...a lost friend," he sighed. "By a warped magician."

"Oh, that's not good for either of you," older Carl whispered. "You may need to go on the run with us."

"There is no way I am going on the run from Time Police. I have a pub to run and that's all there is to it," declared Carl.

"I used to run a pub," older Carl said. "I was married to Katie." On the mention of the name Katie, Carl's eyes turned softer.

"Katie?" Carl asked. "Did she...was she...taken...from you?"

"Yes," older Carl replied. "Yes, I got her back."

"You did? How?"

At that moment there was a high-pitched beeping coming from the microwave. The Staff Guardian growled and swung her axe over her shoulder.

"Everybody out, everybody out. Back to the ship." she ordered. "You too, witch." The Staff Guardian marched over to the microwave, pressed a few buttons and the red and white

214

striped portal beamed out. "We've got to move, everyone. Come on."

The creatures around the table stood up and one by one they moved into the portal and disappeared sighing and popping. The Staff Guardian called over to older Carl and Maisie.

"I'm coming, I'm coming, don't fuss," Maisie moaned.

"Oh do shut-up," the Staff Guardian barked. Maisie curled her lip at her as she turned towards Carl.

Maisie hugged Carl. "I'll see you soon. I've got to go with this nutter. Unfortunately, I promised to help," she added as she walked away. She stood in front of the portal, waved at Carl and said to the Staff Guardian: "You need special care, you know that, don't you?" Maisie said. The Staff Guardian booted her butt gently through the portal. "Many have tried," she snorted. "You with the beard, come on," she ordered.

Older Carl reached into his robe and pulled out a long thin sweet. "This is a time pop lollipop," he said, pressing it into Carl's hand. "It may just help."

Older Carl ran towards the portal. He winked at Carl and jumped through the red and white stripes. Carl looked upwards at the Viking.

"Onwards and upwards," she smiled, raising her axe in the air. "This is not the end!" she cried. "It never ends!" She laughed maniacally and jumped through the portal, which closed promptly behind her.

Carl stood alone in the kitchen, holding the sweet in his hand and feeling slightly shell-shocked.

35

Johnny crouched down as a large lightning bolt struck the toilet door behind him. He instantly turned invisible, rolled forward, dropping the box of watches, and hid behind the pool table for cover. Another lightning strike hit the pool table. It was on fire. Startled, Johnny glanced around him.

Bert ran around the corner of the bar in a blur, his pool cue aimed at the cloud, sending a bright yellow bolt at it. The cloud absorbed the energy and crackled loudly. A strike, then another, then another trailed the blurred Bert as he ran around the table, returning fire into the cloud again and again. Lola had followed Bert's trail and jumped on her cue, flying towards the cloud, sending dozens of bright green bolts of energy into it. As she passed it, a strike hit the back of her cue, throwing her halfway across the bar, spinning her around at incredible speed. Lola held on for dear life as the world swirled in front of her. She gripped her cue, closed her eyes and clenched her teeth so hard she thought her jaw would break.

Max and Marilyn stormed over as Jonah remained at the table, eating. Max glared at the cloud. He had encountered their kind, years ago, when he had been a young Vampire Killer. They were called 'The Quilloks' and he thought their butts had been spanked and removed from the Earth a long time ago...by him.

"The Quilloks," he growled. What the hell was one of their kind doing back on earth? The Quilloks – the fish demons – a demonic race that promoted and fed on human pain.

Marilyn raised one hand, closed his eyes and created

dozens of Vampire Killers with cues which sprung randomly around the pool bar, drawing the fire of the cloud, passing right through them and scorching the walls.

"Jonah!" Max shouted. "Get your backside over here." Max's incredibly loud Sergeant-Major-style shout cut through the music. Jonah waddled over slowly, like an old-fashioned gunslinger who was sizing up their opposition. He seemed calm and unimpressed. As he approached the chaos in front of him, he merely appraised the situation with a sense of indignation.

A lightning bolt hit Max on the chest, but incredibly leaving him uninjured. His rugby shirt was steaming and half destroyed. Fuck! It was his favourite England shirt! His chest was bared, showing it covered in dozens of tattooed magical symbols. Another strike hit him on the chest, bouncing off, but thrusting Max backwards. Another one hit and another one. Max was backed into the counter. Then his attack ceased, as lightning bolts were drawn by hologram Vampire Killers running by. Max raised his head and glared at the cloud.

"I am slightly miffed, chap," he said to the cloud, as he pushed himself firmly up off the counter and forwards. At this moment, Johnny aimed his cue at the large black cloud hovering below the ceiling and fired blue bolts of energy at it.

"Don't fire at it!" Max shouted over the noise and chaos. "You're fuelling it!"

Bert didn't hear and continued firing as did Johnny. The cloud crackled louder and grew bigger.

"You're giving it ammunition," he warned. "It's an energy demon! For fuck's sake, stop!" he shouted. Johnny turned to Max. "Stop!" he shouted again. Johnny stopped firing but Bert continued zooming around and around the pool table at super-speed, zapping the cloud again and again. All anyone could see was a blur and feel a blast of wind. Bert just couldn't hear him.

"Jonah!" Max yelled. "Do it!" Jonah merely gave him a slightly indignant look. He reached out his hand, turned it over and began to chant. The cloud flashed red as a huge crash of thunder blasted out. White eyes flashed in rage across the cloud, followed by a violent, thrashing tail. Jonah chanted harder, turned his hand over and made a slow, pulling

217

motion.

The cloud rumbled again as it began slowly stretching towards Jonah. It crackled violently and let out a series of random lightning strikes.

Lola had just stopped spinning and held her head, feeling sick, just as a bolt missed her chest. She had luckily managed to stay on her cue and flew quickly up to the ceiling to escape and appraise the situation. The cloud was stretching towards the fat Guardian and Max was topless with a smouldering shirt. Lola liked the way he was ordering everyone to stop firing! Blasts striking the cloud drew her attention away from Max's tattoos and she followed them to a blur running around the table. She knew it was Bert and he was the one firing.

Although he was going too fast to hear Max, the speed of his movement was actually putting the pool table fire out. Lola suddenly noticed there were dozens of other people running about. There was something wrong here.

The cloud stretched further and further towards Jonah, getting thinner and thinner. It had stopped firing lightning bolts and seemed to be struggling against the force of Jonah's gravitational pull on it. Jonah muttered chants and pulled his arm closer to him, the resistance of the cloud making his arm shake.

Johnny was trapped against the pool table by the huge wind blast caused by Bert. He was running so fast that he was starting to cause a twister, reaching upwards towards the cloud, which was now stretching across the room and downwards into the twister. The cloud let out an unearthly shriek. Lola, instinctively knowing a wounded cry, flew over towards it and shoved her cue straight through it, as if stabbing a vampire though the heart. It did nothing to the cloud.

"'Ow am I meant to kill it?" she yelled.

Max ordered Marilyn to do the same as Jonah, who extended his arm and began to chant. The pull on the cloud was greatly increased and part of it was now only a few feet away from the two of them. Max instructed Marilyn to start walking to the right and in doing so, pulled part of the cloud in the same direction, starting to split it in two.

218

Johnny knew he had to stop Bert firing. The only thing that he could think of was of sticking out his cue, but he thought at that speed, it might send Bert flying and seriously damage him. Although, Johnny thought, if Bert has super-speed then he really should be able to stop at super-speed as well. What a choice.

"Stop firing!" Max shouted again, but Bert still didn't hear. Johnny sighed. He knew there was nothing for it. He closed his eyes, as if to already say sorry and stuck out his cue. Bert went flying, crashed arms first through the toilet door, straight down the corridor, braking just before he hit the exit door. Johnny vibrated with the force of Bert hitting his cue. He guessed he was lucky he hadn't broken his arm but thank God his cue was filled with vegetable-patch healing energy!

Marilyn walked further to his right and the cloud stretched with him. Although Bert had left the bar, the twister was still doing a good job of pulling the cloud downward and trapping Johnny against the side of the pool table.

Max observed Marilyn and when he saw that the tear in the cloud was enough, he walked slowly into the wound. He winced as a lightning bolt struck him but his magical protection was strong. They bounced off again and again but the force of the impact was horrendous. Max winced and he walked further and further into the wound.

Carl had rushed out of his kitchen on hearing what sounded like explosions. He shoved the time pop lollipop into his jeans under his habit and ran out of the kitchen. There was nobody on that side of the bar. What he saw on the other side of the bar was, however, chaos. There were burnt streaks all over the wall and all over the floor. He saw a large black cloud being pulled in two and also downwards by what seemed to be a tornado. His pub! Boat Race Day! His pub! He ran over between Jonah and Marilyn. They both had closed eyes, extended arms and were chanting. In the centre and walking forwards was Max. He was being heavily blasted as he walked towards the cloud.

Carl's instincts got the better of him. He knew he had to protect Max. He took his cue and ran after him and, pushing in front of him with his cue, smashed away blasts from Max's path. The strikes had force but they seemed to be getting

219

weaker as they appeared to be now under the cloud. Max looked upwards and Carl followed his lead. Carl could see what looked like a huge fish tail about five feet above them.

Max looked at Carl. "Do everything I say," he ordered. Carl nodded and blocked another strike.

Max took a deep breath and slowly began to extend his hands above his head. He slowly pulled the two sides of his hands together and two separate tattoos made the image of a perfect circle with a square in it. He began to chant. The cloud began to visibly vibrate. Max continued chanting. The tattoos began to glow and he parted his hands.

"Put your hands up," he commanded. Carl looked slightly perplexed but obeyed, putting his cue under one arm.

"I didn't ask you to follow me in here, chap. But too late," he said. "Turn the sides of your hands to face me." Carl obeyed. Max leaned over and put the sides of his hands with the tattoos against Carl's. There was a burning sensation and light glowed off both their hands, lasting only a few seconds. Carl pulled his hands away and quickly inspected them. He had exact copies of Max's tattoos of the circle and square.

"You will die in here without them, chap," he warned. "Now, do I as I do."

Max raised his hands up towards the cloud. Carl copied and Max began to chant, making both their tattoos begin to glow. Max pulled the sides of his hands together and Carl followed his lead. More chanting followed and their tattoos began to glow bright white. The cloud began to vibrate and flicker between black and red. Giant white eyes turned downwards and looked at Carl.

"You will die. Katie will die," it hissed at him. "We have Katie. We will kill her."

Carl was stunned to his core. All he could think of was that they had her and they would harm her. He felt a rage beginning to burn deep in him.

"It's tricking you, chap. Demons lie," Max said. "Don't listen and that's an order."

Carl nodded but it was almost impossible not to listen. He knew they had seduced and recruited Fergus – his best friend. They taunted him with Katie. Maybe they did have her. Maybe Fergus didn't have her at all. Maybe he never had her.

Perhaps they had lied to him to control him and this was part of their plan. He tried to remember Maisie's teachings about remaining neutral and not feeding the energy of demons but this was too much.

What were they? Judging by Max's behaviour and instruction, he knew exactly what he was dealing with.

Max and Carl both held their hands up toward the cloud and Max began to chant louder and louder. Carl felt a powerful force trying to separate his hands apart and his body began to shake. He felt his brow sweat and his body getting hotter.

The cloud swirled and crackled and white eyes passed beneath the cloud, looking at Carl and then at Max. "We will kill you all. We will kill all you love," it hissed.

The white glow from Max's hand started to permeate outwards and Carl saw the same was happening to him.

"Do as I do," Max barked looking at Carl, who nodded intensely back at him.

"Good," he said, looking back into the cloud. The white light from both their hands touched the underbelly of the cloud. The eyes turned purple and glared down. The cloud started to vibrate faster and faster, causing obvious pain to it.

"Why are you here?" Max demanded. The cloud laughed deeply. Max began to separate his hands increasing the width of the light. Carl followed his lead. The cloud shrieked as Max parted his hands wider, and began to map two half-circles with each hand.

"Why are you here? You will tell me," he threatened as the cloud vibrated and changed into a multitude of colours.

"You will all pay," the cloud sneered. "Mistress will make you pay," it said, as the eyes turned black.

"Ahh, your mistress. And what precisely is she planning?" Max demanded, as he drew his hands closer together, almost touching. This action made the cloud scream. "Tell me," Max ordered. The cloud was turning red and black.

"An offering," it taunted. "An offering worthy of Mistress and you will all die," it mocked as the cloud crackled and vibrated. Max glared at the cloud.

"Sorry, chap. Not going to happen," Max said and pulled his hands together, completing a circle with them. A burst of light cut right up and through the cloud, piercing it. Carl copied.

The resistance he felt was enormous. His hands shook and he pushed them together, sending another bolt of light through it. The cloud vibrated violently and screamed.

As Bert walked back through the toilet door and into the bar, he saw a stretched vibrating cloud before it exploded and threw him and knocked everyone flying. It knocked Bert straight back through the door and onto his back.

"Bugger," he groaned.

.Max was thrown into Marilyn but Jonah withstood the blast. Johnny was still trapped next to the pool table and Lola was thrown against the wall and fell off her cue. Her super-strength stopped her from injuring herself.

Carl smashed against the wall on the other side of the pub. Tables and chairs were flung into the air and the mess was incredible. It really did look as though a bomb had gone off.

"My pub!" Carl shouted, as he looked around and a beer mat floated down before him. Just before he could say anything else, Tara returned up from the beer cellar. She dropped the glasses she held in her hands and just stared in front of her. All she could see was mess and a twister over the pool table.

Max pushed himself slightly embarrassedly off Marilyn, who had been winded by Max landing on him.

"Now you know what it's like to be in a scrum, chap," Max said to Marilyn. He saw Tara standing there gawping at the mess.

"Marilyn," he called, indicating over to Tara with his head. Marilyn rubbed his back and nodded.

"Yeeesss," he said. "Holiday is needed," he whispered under his breath as he limped gently over to Tara.

Max turned his attention over to Carl, who was just open-mouthed looking at the wreckage around him.

"They're called the Quilloks," Max explained. "They are fish demons. I last saw them when I was a young man and I thought I had banished them. Obviously not."

"What do they want?" Carl asked, pushing himself up and looking at the twister. It was starting to calm down but he could see beer mats and bits of wreckage swirling around in it. Johnny was trapped by the side of the pool table and clinging on.

"Pain and death," he answered flatly. "They are from another dimension, chap." Max extended his hand to pull him up, and Carl accepted.

"Why?"

"They are different creatures to us," Max answered. "And they do not negotiate. You cannot reason or bargain with them. They are evil."

Carl ran his hand over his hair, taking in the mess around him. "Who is this...Mistress?" Carl asked, picking up a chair, which promptly fell apart in his hand. Carl winced and dropped it to the floor. Max walked over to Carl and put a hand on his shoulder.

"She is a truly evil bitch," Max replied. "Truly evil," he added and patted his shoulder.

Lola pushed herself up off the floor and looked around her. It looked as though a herd of stampeding drunk elephants had ploughed through the bar.

Bert had finally managed to get himself back onto his feet. God, his back! he complained to himself. This was one of the moments when Portugal appealed – a beach and a ridiculous drink with a pink umbrella in it. Portugal, he thought, whimsically. Ah, Portugal.

"What is she?" Carl asked, taking off his battered nun's costume. Max also took off his shirt, revealing a body covered in tattoos.

"What are all those?" Carl asked, pointing at his chest.

Max smiled. "Take a look at your hands," he told Carl. Carl obeyed and looked at the tattoo he had on the sides of his hands.

"I got all these in the same way you got that, chap," Max said. "Each one needed for a different battle."

Carl inspected the two half-circles and square the tattoo made. "This kills them?" Carl asked. Max snorted with laughter. "It takes a bit more than that, chap."

"How many of these creatures are there?" Carl demanded, noticing that Marilyn had just put his hand over Tara's eyes and she had sat down on a chair in a trance. Carl was beginning to see just how powerful these men were.

"In total? They are a race. Millions, I suppose. They come from a dimension close to here but they cannot manifest here

223

for long – not without a lot of human energy," Max explained. "The fact that a low-level soldier attacked here makes no sense at all. It's not part of their tactics," Max said, looking around at the carnage. "There's something I'm not seeing here," he muttered and looked Carl directly in the eyes. "Is there something you're not telling me?"

The twister on the pool table was calming down enough for Johnny to be able to stand up. He felt slightly sick and he felt a little dizzy as he pulled himself to his feet. He saw that the pool table, their pool table, was severely burnt. He felt a pang of loss and stared at the charred mess. It also stank of smoke and it was steaming. He saluted it and put his hand to his chest.

Bert staggered over to Lola. "Yoo OK, Pix?" he asked her, his hair on end and his face slightly flushed.

"Yeah, yoo?" she asked back, taking off her wimple and shaking her fingers through her hair. That felt good.

"Yeah," he replied, rubbing his back and his neck. "Wot 'appened?"

Lola thought about it for a moment. "That cloudy fing went night-night."

"Yeah?"

"Yeah," Lola answered.

Jonah waddled over to the pool table and stood next to Johnny, who was staring down with sadness at the smouldering green baize. He patted Johnny on the back. Johnny turned and looked at him but didn't feel the usual queasiness – the recent events seemed to have removed the previous overwhelming revulsion.

"Look at this mess," Johnny sighed. "Poor Carl," he said and cast a glance over to Carl and Max, who, judging by their faces, seemed to be in a very intense conversation.

"You should've seen what happened to my pub in Islington back in the 70s when a gang of pan-dimensional trolls demanded 5,000 packets of peanuts. The mess...the mess..." Jonah smiled, showing his yellowing teeth. Johnny shuddered slightly.

"You owned a pub?" Johnny asked, turning to look at Bert and Lola, then over to Marilyn and Tara. Marilyn was whispering in her ear. God only knew what he was saying to

224

her! He figured he must have her under some kind of hypnotic spell. He obviously had the ability to put people instantly into a trance.

"God, yes. We all did in our time. It's all part of the job, young man," he replied.

"I see," Johnny said. "Is there any part of your job that is able to clear up this mess?" he asked whimsically.

"Not us," Jonah replied. "We could do a bit but not much."

"What could you do?" Johnny asked.

"It's all very mysterious. It's called...a dustpan and brush," Jonah answered and laughed indulgently at his own joke. Johnny grimaced and looked back down at the table. He put his hand on it and thought he felt a tremor. He put his other hand on it and waited again. The table really started to shake.

"Err...people," Johnny said, backing away slightly. As the music was still playing and everyone seemed to be immersed in their own conversations, no-one seemed to hear him. Johnny tapped Jonah on the arm and pointed at the table. "It's shaking," Johnny whispered over to him.

Jonah leaned over and put his hand on the table. "So, it is," he replied casually and crossed his arms. "They have a habit of doing that – especially when set on fire by demons."

Johnny noticed there was a mist forming over the table. At first he thought it was just smoke from the fire but this smoke was a light soft green and it was coming from one of the pockets. Then, from each of the pool pockets, a different colour mist began to rise up slowly. Violet, blue, yellow, green, indigo and orange smoke began to rise up into the air, reaching about six foot. Johnny stared in wonder but didn't feel afraid. Jonah merely crossed his arms and looked at the table with slight boredom.

"Lola!" Johnny called. Lola turned to see who was calling her and was stunned to see the mists coming out of the pool table. She tapped Bert, who also just stared at the mist. Lola then grinned and ran over. For some reason, she also didn't feel afraid.

"That's so pretty," she said, watching the mists rise up about eight foot. They seemed to form human shapes but they lacked definition. Johnny stared hard to see if there was a face behind their 'hoods' but he just couldn't see anything!

225

When the six figures rose up, a smaller seventh mist, a red colour, materialised from the centre of the table. Its light seemed paler than the others and at first flickered in and out of sight. The other six sent a light beam its way and it visually grew stronger. When it turned a richer colour, it took its place before the orange mist. It was still smaller than the others by about five feet but it already appeared more vibrant.

The mists began to move around the table, slowly at first and then getting faster and faster.

Not again, thought Johnny. I'll puke!

Carl and Max immediately stopped talking and watched. Jonah smugly smiled and went over to a chair and sat down, brushing crumbs off his clothes. Marilyn was still with Tara, who now stood up and walked over to the other side of the pub as if nothing was happening at all. Bert, dazed, also approached the table and stood next to Johnny and gently slapped him on the back. Johnny turned for a moment and grinned before returning his attention back to the mists.

The mists were now moving so fast that their individual colours were blurring into a white light moving around the table. The light became brighter and brighter forcing everyone to squint. It became so bright everyone had to cover their eyes and finally they had to turn their backs on the table as the light began to expand rapidly into the pub.

As the light touched a chair, it appeared to fix itself – legs, arms and seats rushed together at enormous speed from across the pub. Scorch marks across the walls disappeared, returning everything into its former state, including Max's shirt. The whole pub was bathed in white light and then it stopped as quickly as it had begun.

Carl was the first to open his eyes. To say he was surprised and very happy would be an understatement. It was hard to tell which he was happier about – his pub being fixed by a white light or that he would be able to open on Boat Race Day. He just couldn't believe it. Everything…everything!...was back to normal. He looked around with an enormous smile plastered from ear to ear.

Lola was next to open her eyes. Her beloved pool table was back to normal. The green baize was back to its former glory but there was something else. Lying on the table was a cue rest. Lola looked perplexed. It definitely wasn't there before, she thought. She was sure of it.

"Don't we 'ave one of them already?" she asked out loud, apparently ignoring the fact that the entire pub had been put straight by a mysterious force. Johnny tentatively reached down and picked it up and inspected it. It looked unremarkable – like an average cue bridge.

"What the hell just happened?" Johnny asked, looking around to the others. Bert was scratching his head and looking somewhat confused.

"Don't you know your own cues when you see them?" Jonah asked, looking even smugger.

"Our cues?" Lola squeaked.

"Yes, Pitchfork," Max chipped in. "The Protectors."

Lola frowned. "Yoo wot?"

Marilyn had returned at that point from his dealing with Tara. "The Protectors," he said. "The ones who give you your powers," he said and added under his breath: "God help them."

"Wot's goin' on?" Bert asked.

"There woz seven of 'em," Lola explained. "Seven coloured floaty mist fings."

"Well, there are seven cues, dear," Marilyn said. "One to seven…simple maths."

Lola narrowed her eyes and was kicked by Johnny in a warning not to say anything too explosive back. Lola smiled sweetly, which greatly unnerved Bert.

"One woz nicked," she said with clenched teeth. Marilyn raised an eyebrow. "So, why were there seven? Why woz he 'ere?"

"Looks like the missing cue is getting stronger, doesn't it?" Marilyn said. "Which is very good news."

"And also raises some questions," said Max, crossing his arms and walking over to Johnny.

"Wot d'ya mean, stronger?" Bert asked Marilyn, scratching his head some more.

"What questions?" Carl asked Max, following him to the table, knowing exactly which questions he would ask. Carl just needed to think about how carefully he was going to answer them.

227

"Well," Marilyn said. "The fact that seven were able to make it here at all shows that the missing cue is nearby and as all cues are linked..."

"Huh?" Bert asked.

"Huh?" Lola added.

"The more power you generate the more power the stolen cue and the other cues receive. It's not rocket science!" Marilyn sighed and wandered next to Max to take a look at the cue rest.

Bert and Lola exchanged looks.

"What is this?" Johnny asked. "I mean, I know what it IS. But...what is it?"

Max took it out of his hands and looked at it fondly. "I haven't seen one of these for a very long time," he said and smiled.

"That's nice... but wot is it?" Lola demanded.

"This, Pitchfork, is very, very special. Very special indeed," he said, holding it up to eye level and looking it over.

"So, wot is it, for...ffff...flip's sake?" she asked, shoving her hands on her hips and glaring at him. "Can't someone just say?"

Max couldn't help but smile and tried to suppress a laugh. Marilyn noticed this and shot him a glare, which did little to help Max's twitching lips. Jonah, meanwhile, leaned back with his hand behind his head and closed his eyes. He belched and thumped his chest.

"The best way to describe this, Pitchfork, is as a guest," he explained. Lola frowned.

"Wot kind of guest?" she asked. "A lodger? An Australian aunt? Wot d'ya mean?"

Max handed the cue rest over to Lola. She looked at it. It was a standard wooden cue rest. It was about five foot long with a metal cross-piece at the end of it. Cue rests were used as an extension to a cue, especially when the cue ball was obstructed by other balls.

"One of the cues...the Protectors...is missing. There have always been seven cues but right now, there are six only. However, madam, now there are six and a guest." Max said.

"That's still no clearer," Lola moaned. "Who is this guest?"

Carl took it out of her hands and also looked at it. "There were seven figures, Lola." he said.

228

"One was smaller than the rest. That was Fergus's cue. His cue – the seventh Protector...somehow...made it back here for a while and all of them left us this," Carl said with a smile and he handed it over to Johnny. He closed his eyes, trying to feel any energy coming off it.

Lola turned to Max and looked into his blue eyes. She still had a perplexed look on her face. Max smiled at her and put a hand on her tiny shoulder.

"Although Fergus has stolen a cue – a Protector – they were able to come here together as a creative force and they healed their home – this building – and left a gift. Think of this cue rest as a substitute player, if you like. It's not a cue, exactly, but essential to the game from time to time. A game could be won or lost with it," Max said.

Johnny opened his eyes and handed the cue rest over to Bert. Johnny turned to Max. "But there are only four of us and we each have a cue."

Bert added: "And that git Fergus nicked one."

Lola huffed: "And there's two gathering dust in the vault."

"So, who is meant to use this? We have two spare already," said Johnny.

Marilyn gave a haughty look. "It is all part of the great plan," he said. "If we knew the answers to all these things, we'd be billionaires in the Bahamas."

"You could get a new van, chap," Max said to Marilyn. "The Marilyn Mobile needs a re-vamp."

"Don't remind me, dear," he replied. "My suspension is shocking," he said to Carl.

"Yoo mean, ya dunno," Lola said derisively to Marilyn, who raised his eyebrows at Lola and pursed his lips.

"All things happen for a reason. This..." He pointed at the cue rest. "Is here for a reason."

"Well, I wish they came with a fuckin' instruction manual," she said, stomping over to the bar. Marilyn looked as though he was about to turn her into a toad or obliterate her from the universe altogether. He was about to say something when Max interrupted.

"Good flying," Max said. "How long have you been able to do that?" he suspiciously asked.

"A few 'ours, actually," she replied nonchalantly.

"Hmmm..." Max said. "Your powers have grown enormously in only a short time."

"Which means," Jonah interrupted, "That a lot of things have been happening."

"That you haven't told us about," Max added.

"That's rich comin' from yoo. Why did no-one ever tell us about this stuff? Why woz yoo all keepin' our powers so fuckin' hush hush, then?" Lola demanded.

"It's part of the great plan," Marilyn answered as if talking to an idiot. Lola frowned at Marilyn, her face moving from anger to fury.

"I'd like to know who wrote this fuckin' great plan because they need a kick up the bleedin' arse!"

The three Guardians stared at her hard. Marilyn pointed his hand at her and was about to do something when Max stepped in and lowered Marilyn's arm. "Don't, chap," he said. "None of them have been properly instructed."

"That can't go unpunished," complained Marilyn.

"We are here for the Eight Ball, remember?" Max said. "Pitchfork does have a point."

"So, you're on her side, are you?" Marilyn asked with an indignant sniff.

Carl stepped in. "Please...can we not do this. You want to know what's been going on, fine. I'll tell you. But it's not Lola's or anyone else's fault. If you want to blame anyone or take it out on anyone, then take it out on me."

Max looked at Carl with admiration. Marilyn crossed his arms and Jonah eyed up the bar. He had just noticed a range of vodka bottles on the top shelf behind the bar.

"So, Carl, what has been happening here? I take it you can all fly?" Max asked.

"Can you?" Carl asked back.

"It took us a long time to learn," he said. "And it took you less than a day. What does that tell you?"

Johnny stepped forward. "That the danger out there is immense."

Max nodded. "It also says, there have already been some very recent incidents that have rapidly accelerated your abilities."

Johnny looked down at the floor and saw the box he had

230

dropped when he rolled into the bar. He also suddenly remembered that there was still a naked man in a wheelbarrow down the corridor. How much was Carl going to tell the Guardians?

36

Sophie felt sick. She stared at the table in front of her. The box was gone. The watches were gone. She couldn't tell Fergus. She wouldn't tell Fergus. She felt truly scared.

Her face had gone chalk white and slightly green. Five watches had been stolen. She had managed to give out three but she knew that wasn't part of Fergus's plan. All the watches were to be given away.

Beads of sweat began to build up on her forehead. She looked over at the counter where the waitresses were standing. There were napkins on there. She needed to wipe her face. She stood up and shakily walked to the counter. She smiled weakly and took a handful and wiped her brow, taking off her glasses and also wiping some of the tears that had welled up there. She stared absently at the menu board behind the waitress and bit her nails.

The waitress came over and asked her if she wanted anything to eat but Sophie said no and weakly asked the waitress if she had seen anyone take a box or if they had accidentally removed the box. The waitress shook her head. She asked her colleague in Portuguese and she also shook her head. Sophie searched the faces of all the people at the different tables. They were as they had been. They weren't responsible. She knew it in her gut.

The waitress asked if she wanted to pay up. Sophie absently nodded – she wanted to get out of there and run for her life. The waitress told her the amount and Sophie took a five pound note out from her purse and walked out of the café without waiting for any change.

232

Thoughts of the morning rushed through her mind. She had seen Pete with a similar watch on his wrist only a short time ago. A man dressed as a gorilla had tried to get her to go to The Pig & Phoenix. He knew Tara and she hadn't been able to give Tara a watch. She put her hand into her pocket and pulled out her mobile phone. She didn't know what to do. She was torn between calling Fergus and smashing her phone and running for it.

She stood outside the café, stunned. People walked around her and asked her to move. She staggered to the side of the road. Her mind turned to Tara. She liked Tara. She felt safe with Tara and that man said he knew Tara. There had been something odd about that man. He had gone into The Pig & Phoenix. As she thought about him, her legs absently started to walk her in the direction of the pub.

People brushed by her as she slowly walked down the road. She didn't notice the sunlight and the breeze she had paid attention to earlier, as she walked closer towards the pub.

Shortly she was standing outside the large building on the corner. The window shutters were still pulled down. For a moment it sounded as though there were explosions coming from inside. She tried to look in for a better look but those shutters were solid.

Sophie walked over to the large wooden front door. She pushed against it but it was locked. She knocked gently against the door but there was no answer. She knocked more loudly. It was opened by Tara.

"Tara?" Sophie asked. "I....I..."

"Wot is it, mate?" Tara asked with a cheeky but dismissive look across her face.

"Umm..." Sophie began. "About my message. About my present," she whispered. "I'm not going to be able to give it to you. I'm so sorry," Sophie said and burst into tears.

Tara looked concerned. "No worries, Soph. No worries. Look, come inside ya daft cow," she said kindly, putting an arm around her and bringing her into the pub.

Sophie walked in to see that it was empty. "There's no-one here," she said. "Where's the gorilla man?"

"Who?" Tara replied. "Gorilla man? Wot were ya drinkin' last

233

night?"

Sophie smiled through her tears and looked at Tara. "I'm in a lot of trouble," she said, wiping away her tears.

"Hey, wot's all this about? A present for me? Don't be so silly," Tara said with tenderness and took her to a table and sat her down.

Carl and the others stood on the other side of the bar and watched this. They had heard the knock and watched as Tara, under a hypnotic spell, had walked over to the main door. Marilyn had raised his hand out in front of him and begun to breathe in deeply.

When Sophie had walked through the door, they were clearly in plain sight of her but she couldn't see them.

"Why can't she see us?" Bert asked, walking closer to Marilyn. He wanted to see what was going on and it confused him that the little bird, Sophie, couldn't see him.

"It's an illusion," Jonah said.

"Wot is?" Bert asked, turning to look behind him. The others had also gathered around Marilyn and were looking directly ahead at Sophie and Tara but neither of them noticed them. Johnny held onto the box with the watches in it. He sensed evil from them and felt guilt at seeing the girl he had stolen them from so very distressed and obviously scared.

"It's an illusion, dear," Marilyn said, lowering his hand and giving off a very smug look around him.

"Of wot?" Lola squeaked.

"Of an empty pub," Marilyn answered, putting his hands in his pockets. Marilyn had created the illusion that half the pub, where they were all standing, was completely empty. He was also able to mask some degree of sound but not always 100%. However, it was sufficient to mask them all and their conversations.

"She can't see us?" Bert asked, grinning somewhat.

"No, dear" Marilyn sighed, checking the nails on one of his hands.

"It's like being a spy," Lola said. "But better. It's like 'avin' an ice-cream but wiv hundreds and fahsands and two chocolate wafers," she added. Carl looked at Bert, who looked at Johnny and they all shrugged at one another.

Carl was holding the cue rest and he felt it shudder slightly in his hands. "Hey," he said, holding onto it tightly. "It shook." Johnny reached down and held onto the cue rest. He closed his eyes. In one hand he had the watches and in the other he had the cue rest. Good in one hand and evil in the other. He could feel the energy difference between the two. The watches felt heavy, especially behind his eyes, as if a migraine was forming. Whereas with the cue rest, it felt light, it felt like a warm glow spreading throughout his body.

"You're right. It is shaking," Johnny said. "Gently though. Doesn't feel bad or anything."

"Didn't know you were an energy expert," Jonah said. "Like me."

Johnny turned to Jonah. "I'm not. It's just that, I know that one of these things feels good and the other bad."

Lola and Bert both nodded towards Johnny. They had both had similar experiences. It was as if they were becoming greatly sensitive to their surroundings and objects.

"We're gonna end up in a monastery, I can feel it, Pix..." Bert said and cackled. "They only place where we can stand it."

"A buildin' full of men?" Lola asked, who thought about it for a moment and started smiling.

"Don't yoo start," Bert said, sighed and looked back to Sophie.

Carl felt the cue rest start to vibrate more vigorously. "Why is it buzzing?" Carl asked.

Max reached over and took it out of his hands. He closed his eyes and held it tightly. "Looks like it's ready," he said and started walking towards the other side of the bar.

Sophie was talking with Tara when she saw a dark-haired, bearded man appear suddenly in the middle of the bar and walk in her direction. Sophie's jaw practically collapsed to the floor and she hit Tara on the arm and pointed. Tara turned her head and looked but saw nothing at all.

"Wot ya doin'?" Tara asked. Sophie just pointed at Max. "Wot ya pointin' at?" Tara saw that Sophie was alarmed and agitated but she did not see the man walking towards Sophie with a cue rest in his hands.

Sophie stood up and started to edge away from him.

"Hello, chap," Max said. "Chin up, nothing to worry about."

Sophie backed into the main door and fell onto her behind. Tara watched Sophie back into a door and fall down but she didn't see Max.

"Are you dead?" Sophie asked, looking up.

"Only before 10am," Max replied. "I'm not a morning person."

"Where did you come from?" Sophie asked, trembling. "You weren't there before."

"Actually, I was. Actually, we all were," Max said. He reached his hand down to her and she nervously accepted it and he pulled her up. Tara did a double take when she saw Sophie invisibly pulled to her feet.

"Wot's goin' on? Tara asked, obviously freaked. "'Ow did ya…'ow did ya do that?" she backed into a bar stool and knocked it over. Marilyn at this point also emerged through the illusion and walked over to Tara but she couldn't see him. Marilyn put a hand on her shoulder and told her to sleep. She did – instantly.

Max felt the cue rest buzz almost in a frenzy in his hands. He looked down at Sophie, who seemed to be terrified – staring at Marilyn and the unconscious Tara.

"It seems, chap, that you have been chosen," he said to Sophie with a gentle smile. Sophie looked at Max as if he had just escaped from an insane asylum.

"F…for what?" she nervously asked, her eyes darting around the pub – looking for an exit.

"Good…good philosophical question. For what, indeed. However, let's just say…for good," Max said and handed the cue rest, open palmed, to Sophie. Sophie wasn't sure what to do. She wanted to get out of there. She felt so scared.

"Take it," Max urged. Sophie licked her lips and tentatively reached out and took the cue rest from him. Humour the loony, she thought.

"Good…good…" he said and patted her on the head. Marilyn wandered over to her, hands in his pockets and an electric cigarette in his mouth. He exhaled water vapour and put a hand on her shoulder.

"Trying to give up, dear. I smoke a real one, then a fake one," he explained. Sophie nodded. She was in a mad house. Jonah then emerged through the illusion and

236

waddled over to her. Sophie shuddered at the sight approaching her.

"Welcome to the fold, little girl," he slurred and patted her on the other shoulder.

"Hello..." Sophie whispered. Her body jerked suddenly. "Whoa," she said. Her legs, stomach and torso started to feel strange. A warm, tingling feeling was passing through her. Her fear was starting to subside and instead she started to feel a calmness.

"What's going on?" she asked. "I came here to see Tara."

"She's fine, dear," Marilyn said. "Just a bit of hypnosis. Nothing serious."

"But you knocked her out," Sophie whispered.

"Exactly. Nothing too serious," Marilyn said and looked at Max quizzically.

Max took Sophie gently by the arm and led her to a table. He pulled out the chair and gestured for her to sit down. She did so, holding the cue rest and looking around the pub nervously.

"Welcome to the Putney Vampire Killers," Max said. Sophie laughed out loud.

"It's not funny, chap," Max barked. "This pub is a Lodge and you have just joined the ranks. Congratulations." He extended his hand and she gently took it. He shook it vigorously.

"You must have a lot of questions," Max said. Sophie's mouth just hung open.

"No...none. None at all," she mumbled and smiled. "May I leave now? Thanks... for the present. I needed one of these...things." She tried to stand up but Max leaned over and gently pushed her back into her seat.

"I understand that you may be feeling somewhat confused," Max said softly. Sophie merely shook her head and decided that to say nothing at all was possibly the best policy and then she could run for it.

"You see, chap, there's been a lot going on and I know you must be feeling slightly...odd about all this...I don't even know your name. What's your name, chap?" Max asked, reaching over and touching her hand gently.

Sophie pulled her hand away. "Sophie...my name is Sophie," she answered. "Who are you?"

Max introduced himself and the other two Guardians. First with Marilyn, who had put on a pair of black shades and was puffing on his electric cigarette and then with Jonah, who stared at her and smiled, wiggling sausage-like fingers in a wave.

The four Vampire Killers decided to stay behind the illusion and watch Sophie and the others. Johnny opened the cardboard box and picked up one of the five watches. He handed the box over to Bert, who opened it and looked inside.

"There's some missin'," he said. "There was about six or seven of 'em." He took a watch out and passed the box to Lola, who took one out and inspected it.

"Nice bit of gear," she commented. "Could pay me rent for a year wiv that."

Bert cackled. "Yeah. Sometimes it sucks being the good guys." Lola giggled and nodded.

Johnny inspected the watches more closely. He saw that there was writing inscribed on it. It was in Latin, and being a good public schoolboy he had a faint memory of totally mangled and mashed-up Latin in the back of his mind. He tried to interpret it. The first thing he understood was that it had something to do with money. In fact, that was the only thing he understood.

"I think it's some kind of enchantment," Johnny said, looking at the wording. It reminded him of his vegetable patch spell – but he had a thirty-year-old Latin dictionary to help him find out what the hell it was all about.

"An enchantment? Wot do yoo know about magic?" Bert asked him mischievously. Johnny felt a slight sense of panic and brushed Bert off with a wave of hand.

"Oh, nothing...just common sense. Lots of writing in Latin...can't be good news, can it?" Johnny cleared his throat and inspected the watch some more.

"It's ain't a bomb, is it?" Lola asked. "Cos Carl saw those explosions' n' stuff," she added, looking at the exquisite watch in her little hand. She wagged a finger at the watch. "Yoo better not be a bomb," she said to it. "I won't be 'appy."

"I don't think it's a bomb, Pixie," Johnny said. "I wouldn't be standing here so casually, if I thought it was."

This made sense to Lola and she put the watch on. "Ok...

238

so...that funny writin' is Latin, is it?" she asked.

Johnny nodded his head. "I'm not an expert, Pix, but..." he closed his eyes tightly. "You know what...my gut instinct on this...this is a form of...I think...of mind control," he explained.

Lola looked blankly at Johnny and turned to Bert.

"That's lucky for us," she said and giggled. "We ain't that bright, are we?"

Carl and Bert grinned. Johnny looked slightly offended. He had a first-class degree in psychology!

"Are we gonna show it to 'em...?" Bert asked. Carl breathed in deeply and shrugged. It seemed to him that they had no choice.

Max could see that Sophie was terrified of him. He smiled at her and said: "I think it would be lot easier if we do this the very fast way."

He gestured for the other two to come over to his side. "Trust me, this isn't going to hurt." The three of them leaned over to her. Max placed two fingertips on her forehead, Marilyn placed two fingertips on her left temple and Jonah two on her right.

Sophie felt her eyes quickly close and saw a stream of images flash into her head. It was as if somebody flicked thousands of photographs one after the other into her mind at lightning speed. She could make out some of the individual images but thousands were pouring into her mind, bypassing her consciousness. As they poured in, she began to feel an understanding about who the three men in front of her were. She began to know about the Lodges, the history – the Vampire Wars, Guardians, demons and about the cue rest she held.

The Guardians stood back from Sophie. She slowly opened her eyes and looked into their faces.

"What was that?" she asked, rubbing her forehead.

"Oh...that was a thought ball," Max answered. "Think of it as a fast information download, like software into a computer."

"I see," Sophie said, her fear beginning to pass out of her but she felt tired – as if she had been reading in poor light for about ten hours. "Why have I been chosen?" she asked. She thought of Fergus. She thought of the watches. Wasn't she part of the problem? She was definitely no hero.

239

"That, young lady, is out of our hands," Jonah said.

"Yes," said Marilyn. "Or it would be very different if we were in charge," he added, looking at Max. Max ignored this remark and patted Sophie on the head again.

"Warriors and heroes come in every form," Max said with a smile. "This..." he gestured towards the cue rest, "...is all about courage."

"I'm not brave. I'm not courageous at all," Sophie sighed.

Max patted her on the arm. "This Lodge chooses well."

"If not bizarrely," Marilyn sniffed and turned to Jonah. "Do you think Lodges can go senile?" Jonah rolled his eyes. "Shut up, you silly mare," he replied. Marilyn narrowed his eyes but Max clapped him on the shoulder.

"Not now, chaps," he reprimanded. "Sophie here needs to meet the others."

As Sophie stood up, she felt more information bubbling up to her consciousness as if she had always known it for years and she now knew who Max was talking about.

"Oh...them...!" she cried. "I've met one of them. I've seen the tiny nun...with a wheelbarrow!"

"Marilyn," Max said, gesturing in the direction of the other side of the pub. Marilyn got his meaning, raised his hand and the illusion disappeared. Standing in front of Sophie were the four Vampire Killers, three of them with gold watches and still in fancy dress.

"The watches!" she yelled. "You've got my watches!" she cried and began to run over. Carl noticed Max's face, which was beyond accusatory.

"We can explain," Carl said.

"You better," barked Max. "What wheelbarrow?"

240

37

Fergus stood up from the circle. He looked cautiously over at the pool cue lying on the other side of the room. The once dark colour was now lighter and a golden inscription was now forming down the side of it. He had watched the cue disappear from the room for a few minutes and return. When it returned, it was almost back to its original colour and the inscription had arrived. Fergus knew that his control over the cue had lessened. He wanted to see the glinting inscription. No, he needed to see it.

Fergus walked cautiously over to the cue and it darted away from him to the other side of the room. Fergus stretched out his arm towards it and began to chant, summoning it to his side. The cue shook, as if resisting the pull coming from Fergus. Beads of sweat built up on Fergus's top lip. He breathed out, expelling air forcefully and dropped his am to his side.

"Come to me!" he shouted at it. The cue stayed the same. The gold-coloured writing glowed brightly and the cue remained still. Fergus took another walk towards it and it hurtled to the other side of the room. Fergus let out a scream in rage. "Come to me!" he ordered but the cue refused to move.

Fergus returned to the circle he had been sitting in. He closed his eyes and held out his palm. He chanted and on it appeared an athame, a black-handed ritual knife. He held out his other palm and cut it. He turned his hand upside down and dripped the blood into the circle. As the drops hit the floor, they pulled together and formed a small pool.

Fergus muttered and chanted. The blood floated up to eye level and it began to stretch into a thin, thin layer – almost transparent. It stretched outwards to about six feet and floated in front of him. The thin layer took on an elastic quality and it began to change into different shapes before him – a circle, a cube, a triangle, repeatedly. It then turned into a large bull whip, floating before him. Fergus stood up and reached down and held the handle. A magical blood whip – a whip that could be used on magical creatures in this dimension and those in the etheric, non-physical worlds. It was about nine foot in length with a large handle and the end of it was forked.

Fergus raised it above his head and cracked it in the direction of the cue. The cue darted out of the way of the whip, which shot out seven nearly transparent red balls, locking onto the darting cue like homing missiles and chasing it across the room. The cue smashed through the door and headed up towards the top the house – towards the pigeon room. The cue smashed against the door, as if trying to get inside and as it did, the seven red balls paused and aimed at it. The cue started to ram repeatedly against the door. Six balls hurtled at the cue and it managed to dodge them –four of them smashing into the door, damaging the wood. Loud squeals began to quicken from inside the room.

The cue moved up towards the ceiling, the six balls following it while the seventh went in the other direction, towards the floor. It then accelerated upwards at the cue and as it did, the golden inscription glowed and the ball evaporated on impact.

Fergus had followed behind them and he was now at the top of the stairs. He cracked the whip and another seven red balls came flying out of it. The cue flew directly at Fergus, forcing him to duck. It then turned towards the door again and began to hammer at it.

Thirteen balls followed the cue and bolted at it at alarming speed. The thirteen balls hit the door as the cue pulled upwards, and the combined impact broke a hole in the door. A dark red light burst out from the crack in the door and the noise of the squealing was frenzied from inside. The red light hit the red balls and they exploded in mid-air.

Fergus rushed towards the door. "No...!" he shouted. "It

isn't time!" The squealing got louder and louder and the light started to push further out onto the landing. The cue had turned and moved down the stairs.

Fergus turned away from the door, closed his eyes and began to mutter. When he opened his eyes, they were white. "We have to move now," Fergus said, turning towards the red light pushing outwards. He raised his hand above his white eyes and pulled the red light towards his hands. When it touched his hand, his entire body began to turn a dark red colour. He raised his hand above his head and the light moved up and out from him. It went through the roof and up into the sky. He began to chant and as he did there was a crackle of thunder and a large black cloud began to form over the house. Rain began to fall and the cloud began to spread across Putney.

38

Sophie held the cue rest in both her hands and waved it threateningly at Johnny. "Why did you take them?" Johnny blocked the cue rest with his cue and pushed it down to the floor. Sophie looked furious, hurt and confused. She rubbed her left temple with her fingers and closed her eyes.

"Probably to stop Fergus from killing people. How's that for an answer? Why were you working for him?" snapped Johnny. Sophie looked at the people surrounding her. Their faces were a mixture of puzzlement, especially Lola, who looked as though she was trying out a cryptic crossword for the very first time, and resentment, especially Johnny and also Carl. More of the thought ball was opening up as the download reached her conscious mind, integrating new information with her own memories.

"Because I was too scared to do anything else," Sophie sadly replied and rubbed her forehead.

"A coward," Marilyn said and sucked on his electric cigarette. Max glared at him.

"If you like, yes..." Sophie softly said as she felt a surge of energy pass through her from her cue rest. When she thought of Fergus and the watches she found that the stomach-churning fear was leaving her and an urge to confront him was rising. "It's strange..." she said. "I feel...different."

"We're all different 'ere, love," Lola said with a frown and Bert huskily laughed.

"Yoo ain't wrong, Pix," Bert said, rubbing her hair affectionately.

"Oi!" Lola threatened him. "Watch it, Bert."

There was a crash of thunder overhead. "Holy shit," Carl said. He ran over to a window and pulled up the shutters. Rain started to pour down from the sky at an alarming speed and quantity. "What the hell is going on?" Carl asked as he watched the rain smash against the glass. He saw people running for cover, their T-shirts drenched, and then he saw people blur as they moved at incredible speed. Carl looked over to the clock on the wall...time was accelerating forward. The large clock hand was starting to move around quickly. The clock showed 11 o'clock and he saw hundreds of people enter into his pub, blurring as they moved.

"Time is speeding forwards," he gasped. As he turned around, he shockingly saw the other Vampire Killers and Guardians had disappeared as people moved around and through him at alarming speed. The clock showed 1pm, then 2pm until it hit 2.30pm. The television was on in the corner of the pub and people were crowded around watching it. Everyone was moving apart from Carl, who was stunned and tried to shield himself as people seemed to be moving through him.

The clock stopped at 2.30pm. The pub was full of people but his friends were nowhere to be seen. The cheering and the applauding started as the Oxford and Cambridge rowers were at the start of the race. Feet stamped, drunken men shouted, ladettes hollered and girlies delicately applauded. Carl was disorientated. Feeling his head spin, he balanced against the wall until someone knocked into him as they made their way to the toilet.

"Sorry, sister," a South African man with a bald head and beard said. "I didn't see you there," he added before turning to his friend and continuing to complain about the food in England. Carl rubbed his arm as he turned to look out of the window. The rain was drizzling but nothing like the thunder storm only a few moments ago. Well, hours ago. He realised he was still dressed as a nun. Some people suddenly noticed him. "Hello beautiful," a tall man with glasses said to him. "Fancy a drink?" he said, putting a drunken arm around Carl.

"Get out my pub, you're barred," Carl said without flinching. The man looked crestfallen.

245

"You serious?" he asked. Carl smiled and shook his head. "Don't be silly. I'm just not that kind of girl," he said. The man smiled and staggered away. Carl dropped his smile and looked slowly around the pub. He reached into his pocket and pulled out his mobile phone. He tried to call Bert. No answer. It was the same with the others. He walked through the pub, looking for his friends. He checked the garden – nothing. Maybe they had gone down into the vault. He made his way there but it was empty. His heart was pounding. It appeared he had been taken forward in time – was it a trap? Was it something to do with Maisie? He walked into the adjoining room, where the Staff Guardian had been living for years and sat down. He turned on the television set and changed channels until he found the Boat Race showing.

The teams had set off and they were neck and neck. The helicopter angle showed the bend in the river, the teams, and a flotilla of about twenty boats following behind, one of the boats belonging to the Umpire, and behind that a combination of the press and privately owned boats.

Carl turned down the sound. He needed to get his thoughts together. What was going on? Why had he been brought forward in time?

Suddenly there was an enormous explosion on the television set. One of the boats – the Umpire's boat – had exploded. The shock wave had blown the two teams out of the water and threw debris like bullets in all directions. Carl leapt to his feet and turned up the sound. The TV crew were in shock and then transmission was ended.

He ran out of the vault and up the stairs, only to see everyone rushing out of the pub and down to the river. Some people were screaming, some people wanted to go and get a better look. Carl tried to stop them from running but it was futile.

Soon his pub was nearly empty. Tara was flicking around channels to try and hear the news. Carl knew it was Fergus. He knew he had murdered innocent people for the sake of creating an effect – for the sake of creating energy for his masters. Millions of people would now watch this horrific event and their anger, shock and fear would fuel demons.

He needed to get a message to his friends. They were, he

246

figured, somewhere back in time. They would be looking for him. He wanted to leave them a message and warn them but he was too far ahead.

He took off the fancy-dress costume and stood there in his jeans and black T-shirt. He put his hand on his hips and noticed, sticking out of his back pocket, the time pop lollipop. He brought it up to his eye-line. He could feel through the packaging that it had been broken in two – a clean break. He unwrapped it and looked the thin red sweet in front of him. He took the two halves and pushed them together and then apart to look at the break. He didn't even know what it was or how it was supposed to work.

Carl then saw that on the back of the wrapper was a large set of instructions. It looked complicated and Carl sighed. As he held the sides, he decided that he would glue the two halves together with his spit. He would lick one side and stick it to the other.

He took one of the halves and licked it. It tasted of strawberry. The next thing he knew, a large strawberry bubble was starting to form around him. As the pub was mostly empty and no-one was looking in his direction, they didn't notice the large red bubble with Carl inside start to float to the ceiling. When it hit the ceiling, it popped and Carl fell to the floor. Only it wasn't the floor of his pub. There wasn't a pub at all. He landed on the ground.

Carl found himself sitting on the original Lower Richmond Road – one that was built by Romans and one that had a Roman soldier walking his way.

39

Lola's eyes darted all over the pub. "Where's Carl? Where'd he go?" One minute he had been looking out of the window and then he faded in front of her. She turned towards Max, whose face was unreadable. He walked over to the window and looked out. It was raining and people were rushing for cover. He closed his eyes and breathed in. His face looked concerned.

"What is it?" Johnny asked. "What's happening?" He walked over to Lola and put an arm protectively around her shoulder.

"Where's Carl?" Bert asked. He felt a mixture of confusion and a stomach-churning feeling of dread.

Jonah waddled over to join Max at the window. Max looked at Jonah as he rolled up one of his sleeves to reveal the blue tattoo of a nautical compass. He swept his arm across the area where Carl had been standing. Max rolled up his sleeve to reveal the same compass. Max copied Jonah's movements. Both tattoos glowed red, then indigo then turned black.

"Fluctuating..." Jonah said. "Heavily..."

"He's moving...randomly..." Max said gravely.

Bert wandered over towards them and looked at their tattoos. "Wot ya doin'? Where's Carl?"

Max turned his bright blue eyes towards Bert's and answered. "Oh, he's here, chap..."

"I fought Johnny could go invisible..." Bert said, fretting. "Carl can as well?"

Max walked away from the window, looking at his tattoo as if he were using it as a Geiger counter. He stopped at the pool table and walked back to the window.

"Well, wot is it?" Lola demanded.

"Where's Carl?" Sophie asked. Lola looked at her accusingly but Sophie felt a rising sense of courage growing within her.

"He's been abducted," Max answered flatly. The others all exchanged looks of bewilderment and concern. "By who?" Bert asked, gripping his cue tightly. He had a very good idea and he felt his anger rising.

Marilyn sucked in on his electric cigarette and walked over to the other two Guardians. "So much for poker night tonight," he said dryly. Lola cast him a catty look and was about to say something when Johnny put his hand over her mouth.

"Please...where is he?" Johnny asked, as Lola mumbled something obscene through his hand.

"He's here – just in another time zone," Max answered, looking around the pub.

"Zones..." Jonah added as he looked at his tattoo. For a moment it turned a yellow colour. "Oh, now that was interesting," he said. "He was very close to us then."

Sophie asked very quietly: "Why is he in another time zone?"

"Because someone put him there," Max answered, looking at his tattoo.

Sophie looked sad. "Fergus?" she asked. Max looked up and nodded. "Yes, or at least...some friends of his."

Lola bit Johnny's hand, who yelped and shook it. "But why 'im? Why not us?" Lola demanded.

"He is obviously seen as a strong threat," Jonah answered. "But why? Why more than us?" Jonah asked Max. Max shook his head in reply.

"Well, 'ow do we get 'im back?" Lola chirped. "'Ow do we get Carl back?"

"Time abduction isn't like ordering a pizza, Pitchfork," Max snorted. "To say it's complicated is an understatement."

"So, wot's wiv' 'em tattoos, then?" Lola asked. "Wot are they doin'?"

"Many years ago, we dealt with a time demon chap, who had the rather irritating habit of throwing people either five

249

minutes into the past or one hour in the future," Max explained. "It doesn't sound like much of a problem but the chaos it caused. These tattoos are a very powerful sigil," Max added. Lola looked confused and then asked. "Who's Sybil?"

Max briefly explained the meaning of a sigil to Lola – which is a magical symbolic spell, designed for a specific purpose by combining other magical symbols and shapes together. When she looked at him with large, confused brown eyes, he went on to say that it was going to a buffet and putting your own combination of foods together for a particular diet. Lola nodded wisely and patted Max on the arm.

"So, where in time is Carl?" Bert asked. "'Ow do we get 'im back?"

Jonah looked at his tattoo and it started to change from yellow to green to blue. Jonah shook his head in bewilderment. "I've never seen anything like this," he confessed. "It's as if he is frantically leaping across time."

"That doesn't make sense, if you were going to send someone out of time to get rid of them, you wouldn't keep zapping them everywhere, would you?" Max said to Jonah. "You wouldn't need to. Just introduce them to a friendly dinosaur and goodbye chap."

Just as he said that, a faint image of Carl appeared between them. Max stepped back immediately.

"Carl!" Bert cried. "Carl, mate...where are ya?" He ran over and looked at his mate, who was practically invisible before him. Bert put out his hand and it went right through him. Jonah looked at his tattoo – it was fluctuating between the blue ink of the tattoo and yellow.

"He's almost here," Jonah said. "A few seconds out of sync with us."

"Carl!" Lola shouted. She saw Carl mouth something and his voice was very quiet.

"What's he saying?" Johnny asked. They all stared at Carl and tried to hear what he was saying. He seemed to be shouting it and then he faded away.

"Come back!" yelled Bert. "Come on mate!"

Max put a hand on his arm to steady Bert and to keep him focused. "What did he say?"

"Gunfire?" Lola asked. "Did he say gunfire?"

250

Sophie was looking at his mouth intently. "No, he said 'Umpire'." Sophie had become very good at lip-reading as a result of being nosey. She loved to people watch and she had learnt to eavesdrop at a distance. "He was saying stop the Umpire's boat. I suppose he means the Boat Race," Sophie suggested. The others looked at her cautiously. "The Umpire's boat? No?" she asked.

"I think you're right," Max said and smiled at her encouragingly.

"'Ow do we do that? 'Ow do we get to the Umpire's boat anyway?" Bert asked, looking at the empty space where Carl had been.

Sophie smiled. "I know who it is. Isn't that funny...isn't that strange."

Johnny asked. "Why is that funny?"

"Because I saw him earlier on wearing one of Fergus's watches."

Max smiled. "It's like a jigsaw...all the pieces coming together." He looked at the other two Guardians. "Faith..." he whispered..."Faith."

40

Carl leapt to his feet at the sight of a Roman soldier accompanying a cart trundling down the paved road. There were none of the familiar buildings around – there were trees, trees and more trees and rain – lots and lots of rain. Carl ran for the cover of a tree and was lucky the soldier hadn't seen him. He quickly stole a look as the soldier and cart passed by – he seemed young, very miserable and was constantly squinting. Bad eyesight, Carl guessed.

The soldier turned his face towards the sky and he shook his head as the rain splattered down on him. Carl recognised that look – bloody weather. He knew it well. He felt that on Boat Race Day when he'd set up a barbecue and everyone rushed inside and bought peanuts.

Carl looked frantically around him. Where the fuck was he? There were cows grazing where his pub should be. He could see the familiar river Thames within sight and there were shapes of people – Roman soldiers in the distance. Romans! He thought. Shit! If their faces looked anything like their friend's they'd all be deeply pissed off and desperate to get home to warmer weather. The time pop lollipop must've brought him here. Just how exactly did these things work? He had licked it to stick the two halves together…that must've been it. Licking it activated it. Carl still had the sweet it in his hand and had put the wrapper in his pocket. He pulled it out and began to read it.

The first thing Carl noticed was the outside of the plastic wrapping. It was black and red and was sponsored by what seemed like a green squirrel wearing a monocle. On the monocle were lots of little pictures of different time eras. Carl turned to the back of the wrapper, which was black and the writing was tiny and white. Carl heard the trundling of the cart continue as he frantically read the instructions.

The large tree gave him some cover as the rain stormed down on him. Lightning struck the tree and a branch fell down before him. There was another lightning strike, then another. Holy, holy shit...he was under attack.

Carl ran out from the tree and started to run down the road as laser bolts – not lightning – started to follow him. He ran in the direction of the Roman soldier, who by this time was wiping a small tear mixed in with the rain away from his eyes. Carl ran by him and another laser bolt hit the cart, blowing it up. "Run!" shouted Carl at the shocked face of the solider.

The soldier thought this was a typical thing to happen to him and blamed numerous gods for his current predicament. Instead of following Carl, he shook a fist up at the sky. That was, unfortunately, the last thing he saw. Carl just heard a shriek and the explosion of a bolt hitting the ground.

"Stop, fugitive," the deep voice of an American woman called out. Like fuck he'd stop running! Carl ran into a large area of trees and wasn't that surprised he was continuously shot at. "Bollocks...bollocks!" he shouted. Who the fuck were they? Before he could answer that, they answered him.

"You are wanted for the violation of seventeen thousand time laws. Come out quietly," the voice said. Carl frowned and his heart pounded.

"This is the Time Police. Come out from the trees and into the road," she ordered. Carl looked at the lollipop in his hand. He had managed to decipher some of the tiny white instructions. It was something to do with the amount of licks (and the flavour) which decided where you went in time. The time bubbles didn't last long. They would pop you in and pop you out of time zones.

Here goes nothing, Carl thought, as he gave a big lick down the side of the sweet. He was then floating up inside a strawberry-coloured bubble, becoming scared that he would float up into the sight of whatever was firing on him. He fears were correct...he floated up into the sky to see an enormous triangle hovering there. "Oh shit," Carl said and popped out of

Roman Putney, just a laser bolt missed him.

Carl fell to the ground again and this time was back in the pub, but he was now in the garden. The era seemed closer to his time zone but different. Carl realised it was the hair and clothes. Oh God...he thought. It looked like the 1960s. The garden was about half full and no-one had seen him pop into the garden. He slowly walked towards the door and opened it. It was a different colour – the door was red and the walls were covered in horrific wallpaper. However, this was a Lodge. It always had been – which meant there would be a Vampire Killer in charge and there would be a vault!

Carl made his way to the bar. He could see that his shaved head was getting some very odd attention. He looked behind the bar and was momentarily knocked out. It was, without doubt, a very young Max. Max the Guardian. Carl had never known that Max had worked at The Pig & Phoenix and he definitely hadn't mentioned it. The 1960s had been one of the quietest times for vampires in Putney, which had been the start of the 'mocking'. There hadn't been a great deal for the once great flagship to do in the 1960s. Maybe everyone, including the vampires, were just stoned.

Carl turned his attention away from Max and walked towards the area where he and his friends had been standing before he was abducted. He stood away from people and it was just as well as he popped right out of their existence and back into the pub, just after the Umpire's boat had exploded.

It seems he was brought back to this time zone, despite his other time excursions via the lollipop. He also now had Time Police on his tail and they meant business. Seventeen thousand violations – how?!

He took the wrapper out of his pocket and looked at it again. He read it. Some of it made sense, some of it seemed insane. He held the lollipop in one hand and, reading the instructions, he gave a series of licks. He floated up into a bubble and popped back into the pub – except it looked like a Victorian pub. He recognised it from pictures hanging on the pub wall in his era. This was the height of the Vampire Wars. He couldn't resist but walked over to the empty bar. The smell...the smell...so familiar and at the same time different.

Carl had the feeling of a 'time pop' coming on and found himself back just after the boat explosion. He tried again and this time he could see his friends but they seemed like ghosts to him.

His friends had obviously seen him too and gathered around. Sophie was there too, looking intensely at his mouth. He tried to shout at them about the Umpire's boat but popped right back to just after the boat explosion.

Carl was determined to keep trying. Just as he was thinking this, the back door which led to the toilets opened and a hysterical naked man ran out. Eric, it seemed, had woken up.

41

Marilyn had left to go and pick up his van. Johnny, Sophie and Bert were standing outside the pub waiting for Marilyn to pull up next to them. Max and Jonah planned to stay behind and man the pub. Lola had been fuming that she hadn't been selected to go over with the others to the boathouse to go and find Pete. A face like thunder was an understatement. She tore off her nun's costume and crossed her arms and glowered at Max. He explained that her strength was very likely needed and smiled at her. She lit up a cigarette and fumed. "Why the fuck is Sophie goin'?" she demanded.

"Because she's needed," he answered, taking the cigarette out of Lola's mouth and smoking it himself. She gawped at him and he laughed.

"Behave, Pitchfork," he said gruffly as she stuck two fingers up at him.

Bert and Johnny had changed back into their jeans and T-shirts. Bert had become rather fond of his gorilla outfit, whereas Johnny was somewhat delighted to no longer be clad in shocking pink lycra. They stood outside, looking at all the people streaming by. Bert stared up at the helicopter. He loathed the noise and told Johnny this, who nodded in stern agreement.

There was a screeching noise as a three-quarter-silver painted van stormed around the corner and stopped right outside the pub. The van had seen better days – Marilyn clearly hadn't got around to painting all of it. The name Marilyn was stencilled down the side of it, combined with a picture of him in drag on the side.

256

"Ahh...that's why he's called Marilyn," Johnny said. "I did wonder."

"Huh?" asked Bert.

"He's a drag queen," Johnny explained. "Although I thought they had more inventive names."

"Maybe he's a tribute act," Bert suggested and Johnny nodded again. Sophie was still making sense of the thought ball as information was moving up into her consciousness.

"Don't just stand there like a bunch of tarts, get in," Marilyn said. Bert pulled the sliding door and yanked it open. The three of them climbed into a mixture of a dressing room and an arsenal of weapons.

"I didn't realise show business was so dangerous," Johnny remarked.

"Punters can get...frisky," Marilyn said as he put his foot down on the accelerator.

"It's only around the corner," Sophie advised. "We could walk there," she added, gripping onto the side of the door for support as Marilyn sped down the road. Sophie was thinking that they were going to miss their turning but many of the roads were blocked off by the police to stop drivers getting down to the river, where thousands of people would be gathering.

"We're not going to be able to get there. We should just walk," Sophie said, as they drove further down the Lower Richmond Road.

"Don't be such a boy," he snapped at Sophie. "Amateurs."

Marilyn parked down towards the Common, close to where Sophie lived. Johnny and Bert both shuddered at the same time and Marilyn turned around to them.

"You can feel it, can you?" he asked. Bert and Johnny shivered and nodded at him.

"Yes. Pure evil. It has a particular resonance, does it not?" Marilyn looked across the Common. Sophie felt an enormous pang of shame and guilt.

"I live there. That's where Fergus...came to see me," she said quietly. She shuffled in her seat and held on to the cue rest. Marilyn raised an eyebrow.

"You're not the first boy to be seduced by a bad egg," he said. "And you won't be the last."

257

Sophie smiled weakly at that and looked at the frowns of the two men opposite her.

"So, is this where Fergus is hiding out?" Bert asked angrily. "Maybe we should just pay him a visit."

"Not that simple," explained Marilyn. "You're forgetting the Eight Ball, my dear. We need to perform a ritual here later. And there he is, sitting like a spider next to the church. What a complete whore."

"So, if we take 'im out now, it'll all end. Let's get in there," Bert urged. "Then we can get Carl back."

"No…that's not the plan, dear," Marilyn stated. "We're going to go down to the river and park."

"But we can't," Johnny protested. "There won't be any place we can park. People will see us."

"As I said earlier…amateurs." Marilyn closed his eyes, breathed in and began to chant. He stopped and looked around smugly at them. Bert and Johnny shrugged at him. Sophie, still feeling guilty, said nothing.

"What's happened?" Johnny asked. Marilyn sighed and shook his head and started up the engine, muttering angrily under his breath.

Marilyn started to move the van, and as he did a woman walking by saw a police van pulling off down a side road and towards the river. Bert noticed that they passed by a police car, whose occupants did nothing at all to stop them.

The penny dropped in Johnny's mind. "Clever," he said. "Very clever," he added as he looked around some more at the contents in the back of the van. Two red feather boas were draped over a box of crucifixes and a crossbow. Behind him was a rail rack attached to the side of the van and a dozen or more dresses hung there. There were shoes, hats, stockings and a stuffed lion that had definitely seen better years.

"Wot is?" Bert asked, also looking around him and feeling very uncomfortable surrounded by male/female undergarments. He cleared his throat as he saw a garter on the floor.

"He's created the illusion of this being a police van," Johnny explained. Bert nodded wisely once again but his thoughts were on Carl and on Fergus being so close. Why couldn't they just go and set fire to him or something? All these rules

258

and regulation, they just seemed to be more obstructive to him than helpful.

"Good trick," Bert said. Marilyn didn't turn around but mouthed 'trick' to himself indignantly and shook slightly. He pulled open the glove compartment and shoved his hand into the bag full of sweets. These amateurs would not be good for his figure, he just knew it.

They pulled up just opposite the boathouse and all eyes turned in its direction.

"This is the one," Sophie said in a hushed tone.

"I know," the three men said together, as a chill went down their backs.

259

42

Lola looked in the mirror above the fireplace in the pub and straightened her hair with her hands. She was very angry that she hadn't been allowed to go off with the others and was deeply pissed off that Sophie – Sophie who had helped Fergus and Sophie who had just joined them and had been given a cue rest – not even a proper cue but a cue rest – had been chosen over her. She blamed Max and felt full-blown resentment but then thought of Carl and felt a pang of concern. Carl...where was he now? She hoped he was OK and that they would get him back safely.

She pouted at herself like a fashion model and put on her bright red lipstick. Putting on lipstick always made her feel better but she was dissatisfied with the result and frowned at herself. She took a brush out of her handbag and attacked rather than brushed her hair, flattening her heavy fringe over her dark, pencilled eyebrows. She was starting to feel a little better and some of her gargantuan tension was drifting away but something else just had to come along and spoil it, she thought.

The reflection of a dark-haired young woman appeared over her shoulder. Lola quickly turned around but there was no-one there. Lola turned around again – she did this for about a minute, like a fast-spinning, stuck record and then worked out if was more beneficial to stop than to continue. So, she stopped – and felt a little sick. She rubbed her forehead and then turned her eyes towards the woman standing behind her.

The woman looked as though she was in her mid-twenties

and she was very pretty. As Lola looked at her, her clothes changed. She wore a wedding dress, then jeans, then a baseball cap – honestly, no consistency of fashion, Lola thought – although not precisely with those words. It was a little harsher – a lot harsher – involving something to do with a bin-bag, a dead fox and some curling tongs.

For a moment Lola thought it was one of the Guardians having a laugh with her – maybe it was one of Max's abilities or that Jonah bloke. She turned around again and could see the two men were on the other side of the bar, deep in conversation. Jonah had taken out the Eight Ball from inside his shirt and had handed it to Max. Max held it up to the light and was inspecting it. His face seemed grim. He handed it back to Jonah, who did exactly the same, holding it up to the light and looking at it intensely. What did they think they were going to see – a tiny gnome in rubber? Lola then wondered if gnomes actually existed. She grinned as her eyes widened in excitement at this thought before quickly turning her attention to Tara.

Tara was behind the bar taking glasses out of the dishwasher. Although Lola was in Tara's line of sight and waved at her – she just did not see her. She also did not see Max or Jonah. Marilyn had done his job well. He had programmed Tara's mind to block out what was directly in front of her. Tara just could not see her or the Guardians – they were operating outside her range of perception. Marilyn's ability to mesmerize had amazed Lola more than the tap dancing centipede.

Lola turned her eyes back into the mirror and looked at the woman again. She did look familiar to Lola. She wasn't someone she had met but she seemed so…so…Christ! Lola thought. It was Katie. It was Carl's wife! Of course…the wedding dress, she was trying to communicate with images who she was. What on earth was she doing in a mirror?

Katie smiled as Lola nodded back furiously at her and stuck up a thumb.

"I get it!" Lola squeaked. "Yer Katie, yeah?" Lola asked and the image of Katie nodded back. She began to speak but Lola couldn't hear her. First Carl and now her – why was sound always affected?

261

Katie paused and held up a mirror. It looked like a standard rectangular mirror but it was actually made up of ten pieces held together. She folded it so it formed a decagon – a ten-sided shape. Lola had no idea what on earth this was meant to mean.

"And..." she growled. "Wot am I meant to do wiv that?" she demanded. "Can't ya just give me yer mobile number? An email address? Wot does that mean?" Lola moaned in exasperation. Katie opened up the mirror again and tapped on the seventh one along and then tapped on her own chest. She mouthed: "Me" and then tapped on the seventh mirror. "Seven" she said and then turned her head, looking scared, and disappeared.

"Oh, well...that's just great!" Lola snarled. "Wot the fuck woz that all about? For fuck's sake this is startin' to get on me tits." She sighed. "Max!" she shouted. Max frowned and looked over.

"What, Pitchfork? We're busy," he barked. "And we're going to need you. Stop admiring yourself in the mirror, woman."

Lola pouted and threw her hands on her hips. She grabbed her cue and stomped over to Max and Jonah.

"It just so 'appens, Mr tattoo-pants, that I've just seen Katie," she huffed. Jonah laughed his head off at this name.

"Carl's Katie?" Max asked.

"No, Katie fuckin' Price. Of course, Carl's Katie!" Lola cried. Jonah laughed even harder. Max arched an eyebrow as Lola explained about the mirror and the number seven and Max frowned even more.

"It's more complicated than I thought," Max said, scratching his beard. "I didn't realise she had been taken there. I didn't know anyone could escape long enough to send a message."

Lola pulled a face. "Well, she did, so that's good, innit?" she asked. "'Ang on, escaped from where?"

"A penal colony," Max replied. "Like a hall of bloody mirrors but a hall of bloody dimensions. God only knows how she managed to send a message. God only knows who put her in there, but I can guess."

"Who?" Lola asked.

"The Quilloks," Max answered. "My old friends, the Quilloks.

Looks like demons keep personal grudges too, doesn't it."

"'Ow do we get 'er out?" Lola squeaked.

"That is witch territory," Max answered. "We need experts."

"Wot are yoo, then?" Lola asked.

"Technicians," Max answered gruffly. He then changed the subject and put the Eight Ball down on the pool table.

"Pitchfork, I want you to smash your cue down as hard as you can on this ball," he said. "I have an idea."

43

Carl tried to calm down Eric, who was attempting to run towards the main door. Carl reluctantly looked at his cue – he had to stop him and that meant zapping him – poor man! He knew that he shouldn't and he knew that it was wrong, but what else could he do? A naked, screaming man coming out from his pub would just not be good for business. Also, it appeared that Eric was in the same time zone as he was. For some reason, Eric hadn't been woken up hours earlier by the others and he was in exactly the same present time as Carl. Why? Carl thought. Why would this man be in the same time zone as himself?

Carl chased after him, put a hand on his shoulder and attempted to calm him down with soothing, if not slightly patronising words. Eric was having none of it and slapped his hand away like an elderly spinster aunt who accidentally found herself wandering into a drunken rugby stag do. Carl yanked his hand back and watched as Eric continued rushing towards the door.

Carl sighed and looked deeply apologetic. Holding his cue down by his side, he flicked his wrist like a quick draw gunslinger. A bolt of indigo light flew out of the cue tip, knocking Eric to the floor but not knocking him out. Carl walked over and stood next to him.

"I am so, so sorry," Carl said. "But today hasn't that been that great for me either."

Eric pointed up to him. "You're all evil!" he shrieked. "I've seen you…I've seen …" Eric trailed off.

"No, we're the good guys. Don't you remember me? You

264

bought my house off me?" Carl asked. "Carl? Remember?" Carl remembered Eric, although last time he hadn't been naked and screaming in his pub.

Eric squinted up at Carl. Yes, he did seem familiar to him and there was something about that that did seem to have a slight calming effect.

"Let me get you some clothes and let me get you a drink," Carl said. "I know you've had a hard time but, trust me, it is nothing in comparison to the day I'm having."

Carl extended his hand. Eric nervously looked at Carl's hand and looked back up into Carl's kind brown eyes. He tentatively put out his hand and Carl pulled him to his feet.

"How did I get...here?" Eric asked, as Carl jumped over the bar. Carl was slightly reluctant to answer that in full and covered his response with a question.

"Whiskey?" Carl asked. Eric nodded nervously and walked over to the bar. He was now very aware of his nakedness and his eyes darted around the pub, looking to see if anyone else was around. They weren't and Eric felt a certain amount of relief. Not much, but a bit.

"I...really...really...need...some...err..." Eric spluttered, pointing down at his body. He looked around again, just in case he had missed any spectators the first time but the entire pub really was empty.

"What...day is it? Is it still..." Eric panicked, grabbing a bar towel and holding it over his groin.

"Boat Race Day? Yes, it still appears to be today," Carl answered. Yes, it was today but in the future just after the explosion on the Umpire's boat – about three hours in the future. Carl had been sent to a time where he couldn't stop the explosion but witnessed it happening. Why? Why not tomorrow or five hundred years in the past? Was it all about mocking him and tormenting him?

"What's going on?" Eric asked. "I...I..."

Carl handed over the drink and gestured for him to glug it down in one. Eric obeyed and Carl took back the glass and refilled it. The same action was repeated and Eric started to feel ever so slightly better.

"Look," Carl said. "It's pretty complicated and I don't have all the answers. I'm telling you this because for some reason you and me are in the same time as one another."

Eric looked at Carl as if he had just announced that he was, indeed, Napoleon and that everyone had to marry an ice-skating badger. Carl could definitely read the 'edge gently away from the nutter' look on Eric's face and knew that he had some quick explaining to do.

"Look, I know you've had a really bad time and I...we...are so sorry..." Carl said gently.

"Who is we?" Eric asked. "Little voices in your head?" Eric laughed, almost hysterically and indicated that he wanted another whiskey. Carl brought a bottle over to the bar counter but before he could put it down, Eric pulled it out of his hands and took an enormous swig.

"Steady, mate," Carl warned, pulling the bottle away from him.

"No, not little voices in my head," Carl said and leaned forward. "There's no easy or gentle way to tell you what is going on. Quite simply, we are the Putney Vampire Killers and you and I have been sent about three hours into the future."

Eric nodded wisely at him and pulled the whiskey bottle back from Carl and continued glugging. "Of course...of course...what was I thinking? That makes perfect sense to me. How do we get back to our time?" Eric slurred slightly and giggled.

Carl looked up at the ceiling. How the hell were they going to get back? Carl grabbed the bottle back from Eric, who seemed to have a silly smile appearing across his face.

"Well, I have a time lollipop, which I...from another dimension gave to myself," Carl explained and Eric nodded along in agreement. Carl continued: "...and so far I've popped back to Roman times, Victorian times and the 1960s but not for long. Lollipop time isn't stable...y'know?" Carl asked and Eric nodded quickly.

"Sure...sure..." Eric whispered.

"Somehow, we've got to find a way to stabilize time...do you understand?" Carl asked.

"Absolutely," Eric slurred. "Anything you say, VK."

"VK?" Carl asked.

"Vampire Killer," Eric explained and hiccupped.

Carl was about to continue when there was a banging

noise. It sounded like a door being rammed or knocked loudly. Carl left Eric for a moment and went to inspect where it was coming from. He saw that the private door leading down to the vault was being knocked from inside. Carl knew that there had been no-one down there. Maybe there was someone else from his time down there that had also been sent forward.

Carl opened the door and came face to tip with a hovering cue. One of the two unused magical cues had decided to make its own way up the stairs. Carl stood back as it flew around the corner of the bar and hovered next to Eric.

"You have got to be kidding me," Carl whispered. "No way... not him."

Eric turned to look at the hovering cue and saluted it with the whiskey bottle. Carl twiddled the ring on his finger and walked slowly over to Eric's side. It seemed one of the cues had chosen its new owner. Oh dear God, Carl thought.

44

Marilyn lowered his head and began to chant once again. Sophie thought his voice had quite a melodic and soothing tone to it. It sounded like the voice of someone who had learnt to sing. She had no idea what he was saying but it sounded good to her.

Sophie looked over at the boathouse and at all the people crowding around the river. The flash storm had disappeared as quickly as Carl had. More of the thought ball download was passing into Sophie's mind. Not just information about the history of Lodges but there was something else there. It was at the back of her mind – it felt like a knowing – a knowledge of something. Something she needed to know – something to do with life or death.

She noticed Marilyn had stopped chanting. He turned around to the three of them.

"OK, kittens, time to play," he purred and opened the side of his door. The others copied him and entered onto the street. Someone came over to Sophie and asked her the way to the park. Sophie ummed and erred for a moment and then pointed down the road. The woman said 'thanks officer' and wandered off. Ahh, thought Sophie. I see. People are seeing us as coppers.

Sophie cast her eyes nervously over to the boathouse and she could feel evil emanating from it.

"What's in there?" Sophie asked Marilyn, who lit up a cigarette.

"A new experience for you," he said. "And an old one for me," he added without looking at her.

Marilyn led the way across the road, avoiding people and children as he did. The three of them followed behind, carrying their cues and cue rest. It was obvious that the public could not see them as they really were.

Within seconds they were outside the boathouse. Marilyn reached out to turn the handle. The door was locked. He clicked his fingers and it opened and he gently pulled the door towards him. Marilyn gestured to the others that they follow him and he put his finger over his lips.

"Quiet," he mouthed.

Marilyn crept up the stairs, which squeaked beneath him. Marilyn gritted his teeth and scrunched up his eyes. Why did stairs always have to squeak?

Sophie followed behind him, followed by Johnny and then Bert, who was walking up the stairs backwards, keeping a watch behind him. Johnny was starting to fluctuate between visible and invisible. Trouble was close. His instincts were already kicking in and protecting him.

Sophie clutched her cue rest as tightly as she could. More images and information rose up into her consciousness. Images of vampires…images of wars…images of pirates. Pirates? Female pirates. What on earth did pirates have to do with anything?

"Pirates," Sophie whispered, turning around to Johnny, who was oscillating. Sophie clamped her hand over her mouth.

"What?" Johnny said quietly. Sophie shook her head.

"Nothing," she whispered. "Nothing at all."

"Did you say pilates?" Marilyn asked in a hushed tone, turning his head towards her. "I'm looking for a good class."

"Oh," Sophie whispered. She had joined a mad house. "A new gym has opened on the high street," she added softly. "Women only though". Marilyn shot her a look, which Sophie immediately understood.

"No…not that you couldn't join…" Sophie said, grimacing at the hole she had just dug herself into.

"Wot about pirates?" Bert asked, as they climbed further up the stairs.

"I don't know….I just know that this has something to do with pirates. Female pirates," Sophie explained.

"Saw a movie like that once," Bert said and cackled.

269

Sophie smiled gently. "Not like that kind of movie."

"Well, wot?" Bert asked, as they climbed higher up the stairs, almost reaching the top.

The boathouse was quiet. The only sound came from them – whispering and squeaking. Marilyn was still smoking his cigarette.

"They'll smell that before they see us," Sophie said when Marilyn blew out the smoke.

Marilyn turned around to face her. "I agree with the pirates," he said.

"You do?" Sophie asked. "You do?" she repeated. Marilyn nodded and inhaled his cigarette again.

"You must've have got more from me in that download than a history class. Part of my instincts, it seems."

They reached the top of the stairs and were faced with double doors.

"Ready?" Marilyn asked. That question was enough to turn Johnny completely invisible.

Marilyn pushed the doors open and saw a long corridor in front of him.

"Hmm," he muttered. He chanted under his breath, creating an illusion that they were not there – an empty corridor.

"One should always travel under cover," Marilyn said as he started to walk forwards and entered into the bar area. He saw that Pete was slumped over the table.

Marilyn walked over and looked at his wrist. Pete had on one of the gold watches. Marilyn put his fingers on his neck to see if he was alive, which he was.

"It's so cold in here," Sophie whispered.

"Yes," Marilyn replied. "I know."

Marilyn opened up Pete's jacket and saw the harness. The one holding dozens of Eight Balls.

Bert inhaled. "I've seen them buggers before." Bert held his cue up. "They're flyin', spider, razor fings."

"You've seen these, have you?" Marilyn asked suspiciously. "I knew something had been going on."

"They are really, really dangerous," Bert said, looking as if he'd let the cat out of the bag.

"Let's get them off him," proposed Johnny. Sophie couldn't see him at all. Even his cue had disappeared.

"Wait," Marilyn warned. "Not yet. Let's look around. Look at everything. In every corner."

"Why's he just slumped there?" Sophie asked. "He looks like…"

"A puppet?" Marilyn suggested.

"I was going to say he looks dead…but yes…a puppet," Sophie nodded as she stepped closer to Pete.

"He is a puppet," Marilyn said. "Waiting for the puppet master to start pulling the strings."

"He…the puppet master doesn't know we're here?" Sophie asked.

"No, she doesn't."

"She? But Fergus is…"

"Another puppet," said Marilyn.

Bert zoomed off at lightning speed to take a look around the main hall. He zoomed out onto the balcony and found an Eight Ball in the flower pot. He leaned over it and whispered.

"There yoo are, ya little bugger."

He leaned forward and prodded it with his cue. There was silence for a moment, followed by a cracking noise. The Eight Ball in the flower pot began to crack. Bert looked forward and held his cue ready for the spider creature.

A spider creature did not crack out. What cracked out, in fact, was a tiny female pirate. Bert stepped back and scratched his head. He heard other cracking noises come from all over the boathouse.

Sophie looked at the dozens of tiny female pirates jumping out onto the table, armed with cutlasses. It was one of the most incredible things she had seen – dozens and dozens of tiny female pirates seemed to pour out from every area of the boathouse.

"But they're tiny," said Johnny and laughed.

Marilyn backed off. "For the moment," he warned. "We can't fight them. Don't fight them!"

"Why not?" Sophie asked.

"They multiply and grow big. Really big."

"But we can't leave them here," Johnny said. "They'll kill people."

"And keep growing," Marilyn said.

"Onto your cues," Marilyn ordered. Johnny and Bert jumped

271

on and started hovering. Sophie looked at her cue rest and looked panicked.

"I don't know how to fly," she said worriedly.

"We'll double up," Marilyn said, looking directly at Bert.

"Bert, I'll double up with you," Marilyn grinned. Bert looked very uncomfortable. Johnny smiled to himself and zoomed over next to Sophie. All she knew was that she was pulled by an arm and onto an invisible cue. She sat sideways on it and gripped Johnny's midriff for dear life.

Marilyn followed suit and Bert looked as though he'd rather fight a thousand pirates, naked and blindfolded, than this.

They hovered above the ground as the female pirates swarmed beneath them, jumping up and down and hollering at them.

Marilyn turned in the direction of Sophie, who was now also invisible. "This one is for you, dear," he said.

Sophie stared at him as if he had gone stark raving mad.

"Oh no...no...no..." Sophie stammered. "I have no idea what to do..."

Marilyn smiled. "Yes...yes, you do."

45

Lola looked at Max and scowled at him.

"Yoo want me to smash me cue down on that Eight Bally fing?" Lola thrust her hand on her hip. Max nodded sternly and gestured for her to come over with a head movement.

Lola walked over slowly and suspiciously. "Yoo want me to try and smash open a fing that could bring about the end of the world?" Lola asked, drawing closer to the Guardians.

"Yes, chap." Max held her stare as she wandered over, a look of incredulity stamped on her elfin face.

Lola arrived next to him. She looked between him and Jonah.

"Why, in fuck's name, would I do such a stupid fing as that?" Lola asked. "It could blow up and kill me."

"Us, you mean," said Jonah.

Lola looked at him and narrowed her eyes. "…me."

"No, that couldn't happen," Max said, smiling and suppressing a laugh at Lola. "It's not going to blow up. It's far too steeped in ritual and magic for that. It could, however, try and defend itself."

"Yoo want me to wind it up?" Lola asked. She looked down at the Eight Ball which had been placed on the pool table.

"Exactly, young lady," Jonah said, gesturing towards the ball on the table with a fixed smile plastered across his face, as if he were an assistant on a cheesy quiz game. This unsettled her more than the prospect of provoking a highly volatile magical artefact. Lola did, however, remember the last time the ball launched at her.

"Why?" asked Lola. "It's already tried to kill me once."

273

"To overload its owner," said Max, looking down at the ball.

Lola scowled even harder. "And wot will that do?"

"It may just help Carl," Max advised. "Someone has hidden him in a different time zone and we need to help him get back to us."

"It takes a lot of energy to muck about with time," Jonah added. "And we should know," he said. Max nodded sagely back at him.

"The times we've mucked about with it," Jonah laughed hard at his joke and starting coughing. He stopped and wiped tears away from his eyes. Lola just stared with penetrating eyes and didn't crack a smile.

"A super-strength blow to it will give the signal that we mean to harm it," Max said.

"And it won't blow up?" Lola asked.

Max shook his head. "But it will try and defend itself."

"Like it did before?"

"Yes, but this time you are in control, well...more control of your power. And, we will be waiting," Max gave a wicked smile.

"That gives me so much confidence," Lola sighed, walking over to one of the tables and picking up a stool. She carried it next to the pool table and put it down. She then jumped up onto it and stood above the table, holding her cue over it with the end pointing down at the ball.

"Yoo sure about this?" Lola asked as she raised her cue above her head, waiting to strike down hard.

"Yes, Pitchfork," Max said.

Lola took in a deep breath. She felt her heart beating hard as she crashed her cue down superhumanly hard onto the ball. There was an almighty crashing noise as cue struck ball, like thunder and lightning echoing throughout the pub. Lola's arms actually hurt from the power of the blow.

She looked down at the ball. There didn't even seem to be a dent on it. There wasn't even a dent on the table, which confused Lola.

"Why ain't the table 'urt?" Lola asked. Jonah cast a frustrated look at Max.

"We enchanted it," said Max, leaning over and looking at the ball. He scowled.

"Oh," remarked Lola. "Shall I do it again?"

"Yes," Max answered and leaned back from the table.

Lola smashed down her cue even harder than before. The same thing happened. Lola jumped off the stool, leaned over it and tapped it with her nail.

"Looks like it's dead," she said. "It ain't doin' nuffink,"

Max smiled to himself. "This is the area where Carl disappeared. To keep him out of his real time zone takes a lot of energy. So much so, the control over the Eight Ball is weakened."

Lola took this as a hint to do it again and so she did. This time, a bolt of red light shot out from the ball and went through the door leading to the toilet, cloakroom and outside. It was the area where Eric had been formerly dumped in the cloakroom and it flew straight into him – making him pulse in and out of visibility.

Lola squeaked: "Oo...did ya see that red stuff?"

Jonah walked over to the door and touched it. "Yes, we did."

"Woz that good or bad?" Lola asked. "It looked kinda pretty but that could mean bugger all, right?"

"It was good," said Max. "Think of the Eight Ball as an egg and the red stuff as the white of an egg. We've caused a crack in the egg," Max explained to her gently – perhaps a bit too gently as she gave him a look that would've turned a giant to stone.

"But I fought the Eight Ball was a...y'know...a portal door type fing – not a time type fing," Lola said, feeling annoyed that all this stuff just kept getting stranger to her – not that much of it had made any sense to her in the first place.

Max laughed to himself but didn't show it to her.

"It is a very powerful magical artefact whether a good fake or not. In many ways it really doesn't make a difference at this point. The real Eight Ball is designed to open a 'portal door type thing' as you describe it, but because of its natural level of high and powerful magic other powerful spells can be grafted onto it or it can be used as a battery, if you like," Max explained.

"Oo...like a piggy back?" Lola grinned at Max and he grinned back.

"I like piggies," said Lola and Max smiled at her indulgently.

"So, the time spell used on Carl is most likely drawing its

275

power from this Eight Ball," Max said.

"Uhh…" Lola said. "Why would the Eight Bally thing agree to this?"

Max smiled. "The Eight Ball is not alive. It's been enchanted and laced with booby traps. It is basically good and evil and can be used by either side. It is why it is so dangerous. Something that can straddle both sides is unnatural to magic law and order," Max explained. "It should be removed from this dimension." Lola pouted while thinking about this and it still didn't make a huge amount of sense to her. Who were all these evil people and why didn't they have anything better to do with their time, she thought. Maybe if they just took up a hobby, none of this would happen.

"That 'red stuff' just might disrupt the spell that's holding Carl," said Max. "And help him in some way – because he is going to need all the help he can get getting back here."

Lola smiled wickedly and smashed her cue down on it again and again in a frenzy.

"Come on reddy stuff…go help Carl," she panted, as more red stuff flew out of the Eight Ball.

46

Carl stared at the cue hovering next to Eric. Why on earth had it decided on Eric to be a Vampire Killer? The man was at best inebriated and at worst permanently terrified. What possible use would he be to him?

"Eric?" Carl said, as Eric prodded the hovering cue and giggled at it. Eric turned his head towards Carl and tried to focus.

"Eric," repeated Carl. "This is your cue. You've been chosen to be a Putney Vampire Killer." Eric stared at him for a moment and then burst out laughing – more of a high-pitched, hysterical whinny than a sane laugh. Carl chewed his bottom lip and ran his hand over his short hair. Christ! Carl thought. What the hell was he going to do with him? Carl was even more confused that Eric was in the same time as him. Why on earth had Eric been sent into the future with him? Why? Why would Fergus send him forward in time? And here he now was, drunk and armed with a hovering cue. How was Eric going to protect anyone? He couldn't even protect himself.

Eric prodded the cue again and giggled again. Bollocks! thought Carl.

"Eric," Carl said softly, as he walked closer to him. Eric put a finger to keep Carl away. Carl held up his hands to show he was no threat.

"Eric," Carl whispered. "We have a real problem here." Carl took a step closer. Eric raised his other finger.

"Stay back!" Eric cried. "Stay back, I mean it!" Carl groaned and took another step forward. Eric turned and grabbed the

277

cue and as he did that the pub's lights flashed on and off repeatedly. Carl looked around him and at Eric, holding onto his cue.

Eric laughed and then he passed out, with his cue still in his hands.

"I wish Maisie was here," Carl sighed. He thought of going into the kitchen and entering into his infinity cube but he knew that the Time Police were waiting for him. They could be catching up with him at any moment. Seventeen thousand offences? How was that even possible?

What would happen when they did catch up with him? He knew that it wouldn't be that long before they did.

He hoped that the others had got his message about the Umpire's boat. He couldn't just keep watching the news to see if events had changed.

He knew that he really needed Maisie and the Staff Guardian. If anyone could get him back to his correct time, it would be them. However, the last time he saw them they were also on the run from the Time Police. Carl wondered where the two of them were. There was nothing for it. He would have to risk the infinity cube. Maybe it was a trap. He would have to risk it.

Carl looked over at Eric, passed out and gripping his cue. Why? he thought again. What possible use could this man be to anyone?

Carl turned around and headed towards his kitchen, shaking his head. He felt like a man walking to his doom but he had to. There were no other options. He walked by Tara, who still didn't see him or Eric.

Eric had a silly smile splashed across his face. He was lost in a dream about a giant gin bottle and he felt thirsty. As he felt this, a glass from the counter raised up into the air and floated over to a gin bottle. A measure was poured and it floated back next to him.

Carl took a deep breath and opened his kitchen door. Here we go, he thought. Here we go.

278

47

Marilyn, Bert, Johnny and Lola hovered above hundreds of jumping, jeering tiny angry female pirates. It was quite hard to make out the words they were jeering but it didn't take a huge amount of imagination to understand the thrust of it – 'die you bastards die' was possibly the closest.

Sophie felt panic sweeping throughout her entire body. She looked over to Pete, who was still unconscious and at this point was under no threat from the pirates. Thank God they were leaving him alone. What on earth was she meant to do?

"They're cute," Bert said, turning around on his cue to look at Marilyn. Marilyn still seemed extremely uncomfortable being on the back of Bert's cue.

"No, they are not," said Marilyn. "They are a dangerous plague. You cannot defeat them with aggression or violence. All you can do is remove them or incapacitate them."

Johnny was still invisible and, by extension, so was Sophie. She was on the back of his cue, one arm held tightly around his midriff with the other holding the pool rest.

"Sophie," said Marilyn. "In your own time, dear."

Sophie closed her eyes and swallowed hard. Do what? This was so far out of her normal world of late mornings and cappuccinos. She remembered drinking too much and sleeping in late. Ah sleep, she thought. Would I ever sleep again? Then it dawned on her – sleep! Yes…Sleep!

"Sleep!" she shouted. "We need to knock them out!"

"Marvellous," said Marilyn, who lit up another cigarette on the back of Bert's cue and blew out a long cloud of smoke. "I love it when a temporary Vampire Killer discovers how to

279

neutralise a pan-dimensional indestructible plague. I can almost feel a song coming on."

"Soo-per," said Bert, imitating Marilyn. Marilyn raised an eyebrow and tapped Bert on the shoulder.

"Don't get saucy with me, cabbie," Marilyn warned. "Or they'll be no tip, mate."

Bert cackled and Johnny laughed. Sophie chewed her nail and was thinking hard about how to actually knock out hundreds of tiny pirates.

"Let's just use our cues," suggested Johnny. "You know... think go to sleep and send out a zap," he added. "Kapow... sweet dreams ladies."

"Yoo fink that'll work?" Bert asked. "And then wot do we do wiv 'em?"

"Put them into a burlesque show," Marilyn dryly suggested and took another drag on his cigarette.

Johnny, Bert and Sophie all pulled out cigarettes, lit them and smoked while looking down on the jumping, violent pirates.

"We could make a fortune," Bert mumbled.

"I could make the costumes," said Marilyn.

"I could publicise them," said Johnny.

"I could try to explain it to the authorities...and to your girlfriend," Sophie added. Johnny cleared his throat and Bert hoarsely laughed.

Johnny decided to take the initiative. He thought a 'sleep zap' command to his cue and it sent out a bolt of energy at a pirate. Unfortunately, the pirate doubled in size. Marilyn just took another drag on his cigarette and sighed.

"Which part of 'you can't attack them' was difficult for you?" Marilyn asked.

"Oh come on..."Johnny insisted. "Putting someone to sleep is not attacking."

Sophie rubbed her nose and bit her lip. "Well, if we can't put them to sleep with magic then maybe we need to put them to sleep with other means."

"Such as...?" Bert asked.

"Well...to start with, they're here dressed as pirates, God knows why..." Sophie said.

"Yeah, why are they pirates?" Bert asked.

"Boats, water, invasion...it's a sick joke," Marilyn explained. "That's why."

"Maybe...we get them drunk...pirates...rum..." Sophie said. "Perhaps, even give them some boy pirates to think about."

"What?" Johnny asked.

"Well, loads of women...no alcohol and no men...it's enough to drive any female crazy."

The men all dragged on their cigarettes together.

"What do you have in mind?" Marilyn asked.

"How about a floor show?" Sophie whispered and Marilyn's eyes lit up.

"I like the way you think, baby," he said. "Leave it to Auntie Marilyn."

48

Carl walked into his kitchen. He really did not want to do this but he knew he was running out of options. The infinity cube perhaps was the only way he could contact Maisie and that crazy Staff Guardian and find a way back to his own time zone.

Carl slowly walked over to the kitchen table and sat down. It was here he had seen all those strange aliens and another version of himself from a different dimension. He had been given the time lollipop but, as incredible as it was, it was not the solution to returning to his own time zone.

Maisie had told him that his ability was more witchy and he did not need a physical enhancement super power. So, here he was alone and now it was time to see if his short lesson with Maisie had helped him in any way.

Carl closed his eyes and started to breathe in and out slowly. He felt his body starting to slowly relax and he could smell lavender. Strange, he thought. He and Katie had a large lavender bush in their garden. He tried not to think about Katie as he went deeper into a trance but she came to mind. Katie, I'll find you, he thought. I will. Hang on – you're not forgotten. You're not alone.

Carl went deeper and deeper into a trance. He suddenly felt his body buzz and pulse as if there was an energy separating itself out from his physical body. Whoa! He could feel his body almost stretch and expand. He opened his eyes and was staring straight into the ceiling.

"Ahh!" he screamed. What the fuck? It looked as though the tip of his nose was touching the ceiling. He raised his right arm to push himself away from the ceiling but all that happened was that his arm went through it.

"Ahh!" he screamed again. He thought to himself, where am I? What's going on? And as he did he flipped 180 degrees and found himself looking down at his body, which was sitting up and looked peaceful. He could also see that there was a long white cord connecting the two of them.

Carl's mind raced and he felt a sense of panic rising in him. Was he dead? Would he be here forever? Stay calm… stay calm…this must be part of your ability. Stay calm…just keep calm.

Carl was more than aware that something had gone slightly wrong and he had not entered the infinity cube but had, it seemed, separated his etheric body from his physical one…but was still connected to it by a life cord. He had heard about this kind of thing from paranormal TV shows. I'm having an out of body experience, he thought. This is an astral projection. Cool, part of him thought, while the other was clinging onto not freaking out.

Carl hovered above his body and looked at the connecting cord. As far as he could remember from the TV show, you could travel through space and time in the astral or etheric body and your cord would always connect you. If, for some reason, the cord was severed then you would remain separated and your spirit would leave your physical body for good. Dead, in other words.

Carl felt himself starting to feel a little bit calmer and more excited – the same way he felt in the cube. If this was one of his abilities then he should be able to adapt to it much faster than someone randomly having this kind of experience – better than that bloke on that TV show, who quit being a plumber and went to Peru to become a Shaman.

So, what was the point of being in his etheric body? He was still in this time zone and he couldn't touch anything. It was doubtful than anyone would even see him. However, he knew that the etheric body was not bound by physical rules and regulations. It obeyed a much faster and versatile energy. Carl also remembered that aggressive thoughts were too heavy and didn't help you operate one little bit in this realm. He had to keep his thoughts light and, if not light, then at least neutral.

OK, thought Carl. OK…why? What can I do with this? What?

He hovered and thought hard. Who do I need to see first? Who? It was the exploding boat. He had to stop the Umpire's boat from exploding. He had to warn the others and make sure that they did something to stop it.

Then there was the naked man, Eric. He had just become a Vampire Killer. How? Why? He still wasn't wearing any clothes and he was unconscious. Carl sighed and found himself floating up and out through the ceiling, up through the upstairs flat and up, up, up into the sky.

Yes, this helps, Carl thought. This really is helping, as he saw The Pig & Phoenix disappearing into the distance.

49

Fergus stood outside the pigeon room. His eyes were entirely white and they were glowing brightly. His skin began to seem scaly and his hair whiter. The dark red light he channelled had both a physical and a mental effect on him. He felt different, stronger and, if he could even remember the distinction, less human.

Where his body had been naked before, a layer of armour was starting to grow and cover him. The armour was scaly, dark silver and reflected light. It covered him from his feet to the top of his head. All that could be seen were his white eyes.

The squealing was growing louder in the room. Fergus raised his hand and the squealing stopped. He turned towards the stairs and looked down them. Somewhere down there, the cue was hiding from him. The cue had been fighting him but it was not yet strong enough to leave him entirely. He had managed to control it to some degree, hijacking its power for his own desires. It had been the power of the cue, a power that he had misused, that had led him to directly contact the Quilloks.

Fergus had loved Carl like a brother but the jealousy he felt over Katie had been overwhelming. Then the dreams began and he felt a presence around him. The dreams told him of a way he could have Katie – in another world, in another time and in another dimension. There she would love him; there they would be happy.

Fergus had initially thought they were merely dreams – something he had to process and deal with – but when Carl married Katie, he was devastated. He was torn between the love of his friend and the burning jealousy he could no longer contain. On that day of their wedding he listened to the dreams and the promise they made him.

Fergus listened and learned how to corrupt his cue. He learnt powers he never imagined he could have. He learnt methods and rituals through very powerful thought balls with so much information contained in them it took years for some of it to unfold. Some of them were just unfolding now. Deep, dark information that had been swirling around in his subconscious, not realised but driving him onwards on a path chosen for him. All it had taken was a crack in his heart and they, the Quilloks, had found him.

The great and glorious Putney Vampire Lodge – the great and noble flagship where Max, over 40 years ago, had banned the Quilloks into another dimension. Max had been an underage teenager pretending to be older than he was and had been an extremely talented Vampire Killer. The Quilloks raged against Max and the Lodge and had no notion of the human time that had passed. To them, to the Queen of the Quilloks, it had just happened and she wanted revenge. Fergus had been the vehicle that could make it possible. The Lodge, the great and glorious Lodge had fallen into neglect and that was where the weakness was found.

The Quilloks had been banned into a dimension that was extremely close to that of earth's dimension but they could not enter into it. They could, however, penetrate the barrier from time to time – operating in the etheric and using people as hosts, like an overcoat. However, the energy needed for this was enormous and human bodies could not withstand the change in the energy. So, modifications had to be made.

The Quilloks found that vampires were a closer match for them than humans. Their frequency was denser and they were more agile. However, the same problem happened. The bodies burned out. The Quilloks actually started to slow down the vampire problem in Putney by burning out so many bodies and this in turn 'helped' the Lodge. The vampires themselves ran from Putney – bringing the problem to a near halt. In fact, most supernatural problems ground to a halt. Max soon moved on to another Lodge and had a fast promotion to

Guardian class. Max, however, always made sure that wherever he was, his Guardianship included Putney.

The Quilloks had used the vampires as a vehicle to enter into the earth plane but the bodies barely lasted a night. The walking dead provided the doorway between the two realms but it was merely a crack. There were some humans so deep in despair and rage that their frequencies matched the density of the Quilloks, but their bodies could not withstand the possession.

Then there was Fergus. He was a custodian of a cue – a cue with an incredible dormant power. For some reason the present custodians had not been told about the extent of their power and this ignorance played into the hands of the Quilloks. The Pig & Phoenix became vulnerable to the Queen's watchful eyes and vengeance.

The Queen had felt the jealousy of Fergus and had used that frequency as a way to manipulate him. She entered his dreams, fed him venom and eventually seduced him into corrupting his cue. She had promised him another world – another world where Katie would love him and where she would forget Carl. There was a price. There was a catch.

In dreams she taught him the power of his cue and how he could force it to bend to his will. He learnt dark enchantments, rituals and spells which he used on the cue which, unwillingly, was forced into service like a slave. It had provided the energy to teleport Katie to Fergus but she had never materialised. She never appeared. He remained on the earth plane and she simply had been taken. Fergus's fate had been sealed. He had betrayed his Lodge, his friend and himself. He had been tricked and the price he was offered to be with Katie was enormous. It was one he accepted.

50

Eric opened his bleary eyes. He slowly raised his head and realised that yes he was still naked and yes he was in a pub holding a pool cue. He had had dreams like this in the past but this looked like a reality. He whacked his thigh – yes, it was real.

His mind raced with the things that had recently happened. A lot of it seemed as though he was in and out of consciousness with a lot of different people in different costumes trying to be nice to him. He remembered a wheelbarrow. He remembered Carl. "Ahh!" he shouted and the floor seemed to shake.

He looked around and the pub was empty apart from a woman (Tara) sitting on a chair at the bar. She clearly had no idea that he was there or maybe she was at that point in her life where a naked man in a pub shouting had no meaning to her. Perhaps this is what happened to people who frequented pubs regularly – they became angry nudists.

These strange thoughts rushed through Eric's head really as a way of distracting him from the real problem of the words 'Vampire Killer'. That little man, Carl, had told him he was a Vampire Killer. Eric felt the need to giggle again rising in him. Eric quickly looked around him and felt that he really, really needed to do something about his nudity. His house was about five minutes away. There was no-one to borrow any clothes from and he didn't have his phone on him. More importantly, he felt the need to escape and, it seemed, he had the perfect opportunity to do so.

Eric slowly stood up, put the cue down on the bar and started to back up slowly. He turned and ran towards the back door. He looked behind him only to see a floating cue following him. Eric yelled and the fruit machine opposite him blew up. Eric hit the deck, his heart pounding in his ears. He raised his head to look over at the smoking machine. This time the woman had run over to it and was freaking out. Eric called over to her but she still did not seem to hear him.

Eric stood up and decided he was still going to run for it. He looked nervously around him and saw that the toilets were nearer to him. He took a breath and ran there as fast as he could. He slammed the door behind him and looked around the gent's loo. There was a hand towel machine – the one with the large roll of material inside. Eric launched himself at it and started to take it apart in a frenzy. As he did this, there was a repeated thumping at the door.

"Go away!" he shouted but the banging continued. "Go away!"

He pulled the material out and ripped it violently. He then wrapped the material around him like a loincloth and ran towards the door.

"Who is it? What do you want?" he demanded but there was no answer. The banging got louder. Suddenly there was a smash and the tip of a pool cue broke through the door.

"Leave me alone!" Eric yelled as the cue forced its way through the door and hovered next to him.

Eric's eyes almost popped out of his head. He reached out his hand to touch the cue and as they connected there was an enormous glow of violet light. His body started to shake and it also started to randomly change shape. He changed from a cat into a dog into Lola and then into Carl. He also felt his eyesight being restored. He turned and looked in the mirror and saw Carl looking back at him. This time he didn't faint. This time he took up instant religion and prayed to whatever god or gods were listening to deliver him from this madness.

51

Carl floated up and up and out of planet Earth's atmosphere and then he stopped. He looked about him and saw that the white cord was still attached and stretched miles and miles all the way back down onto Earth. He looked at the planet and saw how beautiful it was. It was strange to him to think of all the chaos below when up where he was it seemed so peaceful. He didn't know why he was astral travelling and stopped here but, just like his experience in the infinity cube, he wasn't freaked out at all. It felt normal, as if it was something he had always done. There was really no concept of time to him – just overwhelming peace.

Carl was looking down at the Earth when he felt a strange sensation in his astral body. There was a tremor – then a shake. Carl felt as if eyes were on him. He turned around and looked into the beauty of space. He turned around again – nothing...but he had the feeling...he knew. He just knew.

He attempted to calm his mind. The lighter his energy the faster it would vibrate. Fear and anger would lower his frequency. Keep calm, Carl, he told himself over and over again. He closed his astral eyes and when he opened them he saw the most beautiful vision. There were seven beings, hundreds of foot high, in seven different colours of the rainbow. Their shapes were more like moving clouds than anything else. Carl was transfixed.

They moved towards Carl and surrounded him. He felt blissful and connected to everything. A sense of oneness overwhelmed him. He was one with everything that ever was or ever could be. There was no time. There was only now and separation was an illusion.

Just as they had surrounded Carl, they moved away from him. Carl reached out his hand in a futile gesture to try and touch them – to bring them back but they remained in their place and then suddenly began to fade away.

No, Carl said in his mind. Then the colours were gone and Carl was looking into space. His feelings were a mixture of sadness, wonderment and confusion. The feeling of bliss was passing and sadly becoming a memory.

"Stay where you are. You are under arrest," came the voice of a Time Police ship. Carl raised his hands and turned around to see a gigantic ship in front of him. It seemed they were able to arrest people in their astral bodies as well.

Maisie, where are you? Carl asked in his mind. Help me! I need help.

With that thought, Carl was flung at lightning speed across space and time – his cord still attached – and found himself thrust into the flight deck of the stolen Time Police ship.

The Time Police ship was, quite simply, overwhelmingly gigantic and the flight deck enormous. Carl arrived in what seemed like a space battle. Maisie was sitting in the co-pilot seat – her face intense with concentration – while the Staff Guardian had her feet up and was filing her nails. Blasts were striking the side of the ship, shaking it violently as four creatures sat tensely in chairs at posts – as eclectic a bunch as had previously been in his kitchen. The southern belle (the one he had seen before) seemed to be working furiously at the communications post and there was now a centaur in a leather jacket, a pair of floating eyes in dark glasses and a spinster from the 1930s wearing round glasses. They were all frantically occupied. A red alert siren was hollering throughout the ship with the ship's voice calmly repeating: "Warning, this ship will self-destruct in two minutes."

Carl ran behind Maisie – shouted at her – jumped up and down. He walked into her body and out again – and then decided that if he could ever scrub a memory from his brain, that would be the one. He shuddered...and then shuddered again.

"Hello!" he shouted, as the ship got hit again and again with blasts. "Maisie! Maisie!" Carl shouted but no-one could

291

hear him. "For fuck's sake – Maisie!"

Maisie had a head set on and contact lenses that were showing all kinds of schematics and calculations. She jolted to one side as another blast hit the ship.

Carl looked out of the window and saw nine ships of all shapes and sizes firing down on the Time Police ship. Jesus Christ! Carl thought.

Carl looked over at the Staff Guardian, who was barely paying attention to anything about her. Surely she would see him. She had to. Carl ran over and stood in front of her.

"Hello," Carl said. "Hello, can you hear me?" Carl asked. The Staff Guardian continued filing her nails. Carl sighed and looked around him despairingly.

"Of course I can hear you," said the Staff Guardian. "What do you take me for...human?" She raised her eyes and looked directly at Carl. Maisie, meanwhile, looked over and saw the Staff Guardian talking to nobody. However, she was getting used to this kind of thing. The other day she came across her floating upside-down and drinking a martini with what looked like a red cushion. It actually turned out to be an ambassador from Sirius who had got lost on his way to a party on Earth 80,000 years ago.

"What can I do for you?" The Staff Guardian asked.

"I need to get back to my own time," Carl explained.

"You need to get back into your body first," she said dryly, pointing at the life cord. "I'm not the only one with an axe who can chop cords, y'know." The Staff Guardian patted her axe.

This information alarmed Carl. Holy shit – his cord was stretched across time and space.

"But there aren't many of us," she added. "Don't worry."

"Everyone's in danger. I've been sent forward three hours in time and it's crucial I get back to my own time zone," Carl burbled at her. She looked as though there was a bad smell under her nose coming from a smelly dog. She wrinkled her nose.

"Would love to help but we're a bit busy," she said.

Maisie looked over, as if sensing something in the air.

"Warning. This ship will self-destruct in one minute," the ship's computer stated. Carl licked his lips nervously and looked over at Maisie.

292

"We need to get everyone out of here. This ship is about to destruct!" Carl yelled, panicking.

"Oh that," the Staff Guardian said. "No, don't worry – it's been stuck like that for days. It'll go back to saying self-destruct in ten minutes soon."

"What's going on?" Carl asked.

"Oh…y'know. We're harbouring a wanted fugitive or three," the Staff Guardian said.

Maisie, concentrating hard and destroying a small ship, spoke without looking over. "Who are you talking with now, you bonkers battleaxe?"

"Quiet, witch or I'll implode what's left of what you call a brain!"

Maisie snorted hard. "Blah…blah…blah…yeah, yeah, yeah. Whatever."

The Staff Guardian growled. "So annoying…'whatever'. Can't stand humans using that word! Whatever…whatever… Ugh! What does it even mean?"

Maisie grinned to herself. "Yeah…yeah…whatever…"

"So mature," the Staff Guardian snarled.

"Well, if we're talking about maturity, how old are you…? Two million years, is it?" Maisie asked, while blowing up another ship.

"It doesn't really matter how old I am because I will always look better than you, prune face," the Staff Guardian snapped. The pair of eyes and the Centaur turned to one another. The Centaur shrugged as if to say, I was better off in jail.

Maisie replied while blowing up yet another ship. "So, who are you talking to, nutter?"

"Oh…it's nothing…y'know…just your friend, Carl, in his astral body."

Maisie almost leapt out of her seat. "What? Carl…here?" She turned her attention away from the battle and a ship swooped by and fired, blasting the centaur away from his post. The southern belle rushed over. Luckily, he was just dazed. They looked at each other and the southern belle batted her eyes and the centaur seemed to blush.

"What have I taught you…never let your attention wander…" the Staff Guardian sighed.

"Carl…Carl…where are you, mate?" Maisie shouted. Carl

shouted where he was but Maisie couldn't hear him.

"He's over here and you can't hear him...honestly!..." The Staff Guardian said indignantly and drummed her fingernails at her work station.

"What's he doing here?" Maisie shouted as the ship's computer went back to stating that the ship will self-destruct in ten minutes.

"He's stuck three hours in the future and he needs our help."

Carl nodded quickly.

"We have to help him," Maisie pleaded. "He needs us"

Carl nodded even faster.

The Staff Guardian shook her head. "Err...in case you haven't noticed, witch, we are slightly busy right now."

"Yeah...but we have to help him!" Maisie felt a sense of extreme urgency. She so wanted to see her friend and to help. Her life had changed so much since she had been 'abducted' by the Staff Guardian. She had lost sense of time and space but not her sense of duty to her friend.

"Well...hurry up then!" the Staff Guardian commanded.

Maisie leapt into action like a creature possessed. She piloted the ship expertly. To think that she had been working in an estate agents and now here she was taking a stolen time ship into battle. She used to be such a peaceful witch! The Staff Guardian generated a glass of wine from thin air and took a glug. She nodded as Maisie destroyed three other ships. Then, just as she was charging another one, it turned and ran – leaving two more. The Staff Guardian burst out laughing. "For a flakey ole secretary, you're not bad in a fight."

Carl looked on with respect and a bit of concern. Was this the same woman?

"She's come a long way," the Staff Guardian whispered to Carl. "When she first started she stalled the ship four times. We couldn't stop laughing."

"Are you telling Carl about my stalling?" Maisie shouted.

"Yes," the Staff Guardian replied flatly and glugged another glass of wine.

"I'll never live it down," Maisie sighed. She turned and looked seriously at the Staff Guardian. "Look, duck, we need to help."

294

The Staff Guardian looked as if she had just accidentally drunk a glass of acid and scratched her head. She nodded and Maisie ran over and hugged her. The Staff Guardian cringed and patted Maisie on the back.

"So, what do we need to do?" Maisie asked.

The Staff Guardian smiled. "Well, we've got a stolen time ship and we need to get this human's time stream into some kind of order."

"Easy," said Maisie.

"Oh yes...of course it's easy for you. Let's drop knuckle-head back to his time zone. Don't you realise there are many different realities. This boy being projected three hours into the future would have sent his friends and the world onto a different path. Just thrusting him back may be the one thing we shouldn't do. Ever think about that?" the Staff Guardian asked both of them.

Carl didn't seem to mind being insulted at all and took to heart the warning.

"The fact of the matter is this. For three hours you didn't exist," the Staff Guardian said. "That's a lot of penalty points." The Staff Guardian laughed her head off.

Carl sighed. "Seventeen thousand offences, apparently."

On hearing this, the Staff Guardian laughed so hard she fell off her chair and wiped away some tears.

"Ooo...that is hilarious," she hooted. "I'm not even sure what the punishment is for that. That's one of the largest list of charges I've ever heard of."

Maisie looked at the Staff Guardian. "What's going on? What's he saying?"

The Staff Guardian explained and Maisie frowned. "Blimey," she exhaled. "I thought a few dozen parking tickets were bad."

Carl asked what she had meant about not existing for three hours. The Staff Guardian conjured a glass of champagne and put on a very wise and profound face. She climbed back onto the chair, slapping away Maisie's offer of assistance.

"The Time Police take deliberate non-existence as a very serious crime. It's up there with time hiccups. Hiccupping through different time zones is also frowned upon," she said imperiously.

"Like time pop lollipops?" Carl asked with a cringe. The

Staff Guardian nodded with a wicked smile. Carl cringed again.

"What's he saying?" Maisie asked and the Staff Guardian waved her hand as if to say 'not now'.

"The trouble is, little human, that because you were taken out of those three hours, those three hours have existed without you. So, we need to get you back when the others catch up with you. I can't just plonk you back. Do you see?"

Carl looked mortified. "But they need my help."

"I do admire arrogance, but maybe you should have a little bit more faith in your friends and not think that everything revolves around you?"

"Oo, talking about yourself again?" Maisie scoffed. The Staff Guardian clicked her fingers and Maisie collapsed to the floor. The Staff Guardian clicked her fingers again and Maisie's astral body floated out from her unconscious body.

"I do so hate three way conversations," she said dryly.

Maisie ran over to Carl and gave him a hug and for the first time in a while he felt better.

"So, what does this mean?" Carl asked.

"It means you haven't existed for three of their hours and if we send you back at the moment you disappeared, you could undo anything they've done in those three hours. Changing the course of history forever."

Carl looked concerned. "But my body is still on earth. Time is still moving forward...Oh my God...Eric! Someone came forward in time with me."

The Staff Guardian looked at Maisie. "It's never straightforward, is it?"

Maisie nodded in agreement and gave Carl another hug.

"But remember this. Those three hours will have to be lived at some point," the Staff Guardian whispered conspiratorially.

"We'll help you out, mate, alright? Leave it to us."

"Us?" The Staff Guardian asked.

"Yes, us you old bag," Maisie replied. The Staff Guardian gave Maisie a look that would have withered the faint-hearted.

"Let's go get your body, knuckle brain. Then maybe I can get back to having some fun."

"You mean, causing trouble," Maisie sighed.

"Exactly," the Staff Guardian said and conjured up a bottle of

296

champagne. "To the axe, to the Earth and to alcohol. Onwards!"

52

The boathouse was in turmoil. Johnny and Sophie were hovering above dozens of tiny aggressive female pirates, shaking their fists and mooning at them. Some were trying to climb on top of each other to reach them. Some had attacked each other and as a result were starting to increase in size. Others had noticed this and were copying. Punches, kicks and sword fights were breaking out amongst high-pitched threats of death and screams.

Despite being invisible, the pirates seemed to know exactly where Johnny and Sophie were. This worried Johnny more than a little. He was learning that being invisible to humans did not mean invisible to all creatures! For some reason, all he could think about were house prices.

Bert, under the instruction of Marilyn, had just flown over to the other side of the club house, where there was a large empty hall space. They were, of course, followed by a large group of jeering, screaming pirates. Marilyn leaned over and whispered to Bert. Bert pulled a 'whatever you say' face and they flew over to the bar.

Marilyn pointed at dozens of small shot glasses and bottles of rum and they flew to the table. The lids popped off the bottles which then hovered and filled up the glasses. Marilyn seemed pleased with this and then turned towards the open hall. He took a deep breath and then within seconds there appeared the illusion of a vaudeville stage – red velvet curtains and the glow of dusky yellow up lighting. There was a drum roll and the pirates stopped what they were doing and turned their attention to the stage. A deep voice boomed out:

"Arh, hello my dahlings and welcome to the Putney Pirate floor show, arh."

So cheesy, thought Bert. So very, very cheesy.

The pirates seemed suspicious and began to walk slowly towards the stage, as if trying to ascertain the nature of this new potential enemy. Some sniffed the air and some snarled.

Marilyn pointed at the glasses and they floated towards the front of the stage and plopped down on the floor.

"For your entertainment tonight, arh, we have, all the way from Rum Island, the one and only, the eye-poppingly gorgeous, the Parrot Pirate Party Players...arh."

Bert cringed.

The curtain shot up and raucous strip music boomed out. The pirates near Johnny and Sophie looked transfixed at the stage as dozens of hot male pirate strippers walked out on stage provocatively.

Suddenly there was a high pitched squeal of the word 'rum' and the female pirates stormed towards the stage. "Rum....Rum." The glasses were picked up and they seemed as large as beer barrels in the arms of the pirates. "Rum... Rum," they squeaked.

Some sat on the floor, glugging rum and watching the strippers on the stage, who were in the middle of removing their shirts. "Woooo!" one screamed and glugged down some more. Within minutes the pirates were grabbing the rum out of each other's arms, swigging it, shoving each other and whistling at the men. It was like Putney High Street on a Friday night. All that was missing were stilettos and vomit.

Sophie and Johnny took the opportunity while the pirates were absorbed in the strippers to fly over to Pete. He was still unconscious. Sophie looked at the watch.

"It's exactly the same as the ones Fergus gave me," she said guiltily.

"What's he planning?" Johnny asked. "Any ideas?"

"No," Sophie whispered. "I wish I did know. I wish I could help more."

"They're for some kind of mind control but to do what?" Johnny whispered back.

Sophie bit her lip. Fergus must know by now that she hadn't given all the watches out. If this was mind control then

299

he would know who was wearing one and who wasn't. He hadn't tried to call her and that also made her nervous. He must know that something had gone wrong and that she, in his eyes, had failed him.

"Don't feel so bad," Johnny said. "We often do things out of fear."

"Have you?" Sophie asked. Johnny didn't speak at first but then answered, "Haven't we all?"

Applause and wolf whistles broke out as the strippers whisked off their trousers to reveal gold G-strings.

Oh God, thought Bert and rubbed his eyes. That image would be with him for a long time.

Marilyn floated over some more glasses of rum and they were eagerly grabbed and devoured. Many of the pirates were starting to fall asleep and some others were now impersonating the strippers and taking their own clothes off, which perked Bert up a bit.

It took a further ten minutes of strippers, rum and slurred yelling before the female pirates got completely pissed and passed out.

"Fank the bloody Lord for that!" Bert cried. "I'm gettin' sore," Bert said referring to his cue.

Marilyn grimaced and jumped off the cue. "I know what you mean."

53

Lola folded her arms and glared at Max. "This is borin'," she moaned. "I 'ate just waitin'. Wot are we waitin' for?" she pouted and ran her fingers through her fringe and shook her hair.

"Patience isn't really one of your virtues, is it?" Max said.

"Fuck that," she snapped. Lola had been stopped from smashing her cue down on the Eight Ball after her frenzied attack. Max had decided that enough was enough and they weren't going to get any more out of the ball. Lola had actually been enjoying herself and had forgotten that she had been left out of the van excursion with the others. Now she was alone with the two Guardians and she was getting restless. As a way to alleviate the boredom, she began to hop-scotch up and down the pub and shouting 'bingo' every time she turned around. Jonah walked to the bar and poured himself a large vodka. Max gestured that he also needed one – urgently!

Lola hopped and scotched her way over to Max. "Wot about them watches?" she squeaked.

"What about them, Pitchfork?" Max asked, crossing his arms and taking a swig of the clear drink.

"Well...shouldn't we be doin' somefink wiv 'em?" Lola demanded, her eyes looking at him with a mixture of annoyance and suspicion.

"What do you suggest?"

Lola thought about it for a moment. "Couldn't I smash me cue down on 'em? It might 'elp."

Max laughed loudly. "How on earth would that help? You'd

301

break them."

Lola pouted. "It didn't 'urt the bally thing."

"That's because the bally thing is much tougher than the tick-tocky things." Max smiled. Jonah shook his head, releasing some dandruff onto his shoulders.

Lola was frustrated as to why nothing was being done with the watches. They were clearly important and they clearly had some kind of power but they were sitting in a box doing nothing. She had asked if she could hold one but was told a resounding 'no' from both men. She also asked if she could look in the box and was given the same reply.

The box was currently resting on the pool table. Lola slowly grinned.

"'Ow about a game?" Lola asked, pointing to the table. Max narrowed his eyes and breathed out slowly. He refused but Lola insisted, making her eyes as large as she could muster. He sighed and agreed.

"If I win, I get to 'old a watch," she said as she walked over to the table. Max shook his head. "No," he refused bluntly.

Jonah throatily laughed and then stopped. He looked out from behind a curtain onto the road and saw that people were starting to queue up outside.

"Punters," he said. "Lots of them."

Max looked over to Jonah. "We could really use an illusion of a full pub with bar staff." Jonah nodded.

"Do we know what happened to the staff?" Jonah asked in a hushed tone.

Max coughed. "You know it's much better never to ask Marilyn, chap. They all show up eventually."

While these two talked to one another, Lola quickly opened the box, took out a watch, put it in her pocket and put the box down on a chair next to Jonah. She smiled innocently at Max, which made him deeply suspicious.

Lola hit the side of the pool table and the balls started to pour out. She placed the triangle on the table and started to arrange the balls. Max asked where his cue was and she pointed over to the side of the bar.

"You expect me to play with a normal cue?" Max asked.

Lola shrugged. "There are two magicky fings downstairs. D'ya want one?"

Max crossed his arms. "Yes, Pitchfork. I would like to play with a magicky cue."

"I suppose ya want me to go and get it."

Max put his hand on the pool table and nodded. Lola looked put out, then turned on her heel and stomped off towards the bunker, muttering to herself.

Lola marched down the stairs and pushed open the door. She stomped towards the vault, where the two remaining cues remained. She clicked on the lights and approached the cue rack.

"Fuck!" she cried, almost jumping backwards. One of the cues (Eric's) was quickly pulsing in and out of visibility. Lola regained her composure and reached out her hand towards it. She tapped the flashing cue. It was there...and then it wasn't. She smiled. She tapped it again and giggled. This time, she reached out her hand and grabbed it. It began to flash faster and then she saw her hand was disappearing with it.

"Wow," she whispered and felt a buzzing in her pocket. She pulled out the gold watch and had a chance to look at it. It seemed like a normal expensive watch except that it was buzzing and for some reason the hands were starting to accelerate forward. She held the flashing cue in one hand and the buzzing watch in the other.

Three barmaids in three different pubs stopped what they were doing and stared forward.

Lola looked at the watch and saw that the hands were moving faster forward.

"Cool," she whispered to herself.

She looked at her flashing hand and noticed that the flashing was spreading up her arm and the watch hands were spinning uncontrollably. It would, perhaps, have been a sensible thing at this point for Lola to have put one or other of the objects down but this notion did not occur to her. The flashing transfixed her and she wanted to see how much more of her would start flashing and what she would see when it got to her head. Both objects felt cold, which surprised her. She thought they would be getting hotter but the reverse was true. They were getting colder; much colder.

Lola shivered and a huge smile broke out over her face as

303

her shoulder began to flash. She giggled. The flashing was almost at her head. Lola's mind wandered for a second and she thought about money – bags of money. As most of her thoughts were about getting married, Johnny and killing vampires, she was a bit surprised when the image of bags of money popped into her head. Recent images of Max telling her off popped into her head and she liked that.

"Shut up, Pitchfork," she said to herself, impersonating Max. "You can't do that, Pitchfork," she added, pulling a face.

The flashing was almost at her head – the watch hands were spinning around at high speed. Lola giggled again and then the flashing started on her head.

The first thing she saw was Eric, standing in the men's loo with towelling around his groin and holding a cue and then she flashed back to the vault. She began to quickly pulse between the vault and the gent's loo and watched as Eric turned physically into her and then into Carl. Eric, it appeared, was not able to see her.

Lola then found herself looking at a barmaid, another barmaid and then yet another one (who also didn't see her) in three different pubs as she flashed back and forth. Once again, she thought about money…money…bags and bags of it. She flashed to Eric, back to the barmaids and then she saw Fergus…and he saw her. Lola tried to let go of the cue but she couldn't. The pulsation was accelerating. Her whole body was trapped and when the flash pulse returned her to Fergus, she saw a creature that was somewhere between human and demon. With each pulse he walked a step closer to her. She flashed back to the barmaids and then back to Eric and then back to Fergus, who reached out his hand and grabbed her wrist. Lola shrieked and tried to pull away but his grip was too strong.

She started to pulse between the vault and Fergus only, whose hand she could see even in the vault. His white eyes stared at hers and a wicked grin passed over his pointed teeth. He began to pull at her arm and she began to pull back with her considerable strength.

"Fuck off!" she shouted. Fergus smiled at her and tried to pull her to him. Lola grimaced. His strength was incredible, then so was hers. With an immense force, Fergus pulled

Lola out of the pulsation and she stumbled towards the pigeon room and missed smashing the watch as she crashed into the door. High pitched squealing turned into a frenzied cacophony and Lola gasped, backed away from the room and turned around to face Fergus. He stood in the half light and smiled at her.

"Well, well, well," he whispered as Lola raised both her fists. "Well, well, well," he repeated as he walked slowly towards her.

54

Becky had just taken an order for a glass of white wine and a pint of lager when she stopped what she was doing, stared ahead with an empty glass in her hand and didn't move.

A young female customer seemed concerned about the barmaid standing behind the bar and tugged the sleeve of her boyfriend. He turned to his girlfriend and she gestured towards her. Becky didn't move.

The couple now stared at her, trying to work out whether it was joke. They called to her but Becky did not respond. Other customers took notice and exchanged bewildered looks.

The same thing had happened to two other barmaids in two separate pubs. They had frozen still while serving customers. They stayed this way for about one minute and then, at exactly the same time, the three barmaids turned away from the bars they were working at and walked towards their managers' rooms. Each was followed by 'heys' from customers and fellow staff but none of them responded.

As each woman entered the empty rooms, their expressionless faces merely stared ahead. They each approached a large safe and opened them. Thousands of pounds of cash was stashed in the safes. It was still only early in the day but by the end of the night each pub would have about fifty thousand pounds in cash more – as would dozens of other pubs in Putney.

The women filled the cash into bags, closed the safes and each quietly left the pubs with bags over their shoulders and headed in the direction of The Pig & Phoenix.

Max was sitting on the side of the pool table and he was

now concerned. Lola was taking too long. He also looked outside the pub. There were growing crowds of people – waiting. Why didn't they just go somewhere else? Max thought and then his mind turned back to Lola. A dark feeling swept through him.

He picked up the box with the watches and looked inside. One was missing. "Idiot girl," he whispered. Max stormed off towards the vault at great speed. Jonah looked up from his drink, raised an eyebrow and took a glug.

Max ran into the vault room where the two cues were and saw that one was flashing. Max's eyes narrowed and he cautiously approached it. "What have you done, Pitchfork?" he whispered. It was precisely this kind of thing that made him believe that all of the Putney Lodge would be better off with their powers stripped. They were irresponsible, untrained – a danger to themselves and to everyone else around them.

Max picked up the cue with both hands and gripped it hard. He growled in pain. His hands began to pulsate in and out of visibility. There was a fluctuation in time and a portal had been opened between God only knew where. Why one of the cues was involved, Max didn't know but he knew he had to close the portal. Sweat began to pour down his face. Images of money and Eric flashed into his mind. Max was now in incredible pain. The flashing was beginning to slow down and then he saw Lola in his mind…and Fergus. Max closed his eyes and groaned. He had to close the portal. Lola would have to fend for herself. A tattoo on Max's right arm began to glow and it turned bloody.

The flashing began to slow down and then Max opened his eyes and sighed.

Instead of closing the portal – he began to open it. "Silly, silly little Pitchfork," he whispered.

55

Outside the boathouse and along the riverbank, thousands of people were gathering to watch the start of the Boat Race. Anyone perhaps with the ability to see through a projected illusion would have seen one man carrying another man and two men and a woman carrying large sacks each. What they saw was a group of police officers removing a drunk man from a building.

They quickly approached the three-quarter silver painted van and Marilyn slid the door open. Bert, Sophie and Johnny, who was carrying Pete, climbed inside. Pete was plonked down on a box. He fell back and his head and shoulders nestled into the netting of a floor length gold ball gown. The others put down the large sacks carefully. Marilyn climbed into the driver's seat and put down his sack on the passenger seat – also carefully.

Sophie looked at Bert and pulled a worried face. Bert returned it.

"Wot we gonna do wiv these pirate birds then?" he asked in the direction of Marilyn, who was just starting the van.

Marilyn turned around to look at Bert.

"Hmmm…" he replied. "Problem."

Johnny turned his head from looking at Pete and shot Marilyn a glance. "What do you mean, 'problem'?"

Marilyn began to move the van, moving slowly through crowds of people. His destination was The Pig & Phoenix. More and more people were arriving and he was moving incredibly slowly.

"They are not from this world and they do so like to

misbehave themselves," Marilyn said. He beeped his horn and people began to move.

"What happens if they wake up?" Sophie asked, looking down at the sacks containing snoring pirates.

"We have to make sure that as long as they are our guests, they don't," Marilyn replied.

"How do we make sure they don't wake up?" Johnny asked, sounding nervous.

"We have to make *sure* they don't," Marilyn stated, beeping his horn again.

"We also have to try and wake up that man before he slobbers over my crinoline!" Marilyn growled, seeming more perturbed by that prospect than the prospect of an awaking plague of tiny psychotic female pirates.

Bert, Sophie and Johnny stared at the sacks, watching for any signs of movement. Incapacitation was the only option they had to keep them subdued. How long would the rum last, Sophie wondered? As they had learned that if they attack each other, they grew in size, they couldn't afford to lock them in anywhere.

Sophie looked over at Pete and saw that his watch was glowing. Sophie nudged Johnny, who looked alarmed. Johnny gestured to Bert, who shook his head, as if to say 'now what?'

"Marilyn," Johnny said.

"Yeeessss?" Marilyn asked, beeping his horn again. He then added: "Look at this…everyone's in jeans. Where's the glamour?"

"Marilyn…his watch is glowing!" Johnny cried and began to go slightly invisible. Sophie still wasn't used to this. She clutched her chest. "Oh my God," she blurted out. "Oh my God."

"Yeah, that's his power. He can hide really well, when there's trouble," Bert said and cackled.

Johnny gave a fake laugh. "Well, you only got speed because you're so slow and creaky."

Bert pulled a 'watch it' face but broke into a smile. "I wonder what yours is," he asked Sophie.

"Hey…I….I…don't even know what's really going on," she stammered. "I'm just temporary, anyway. Whatever that even means."

Bert nodded in sympathy. "Yoo know wot? I don't know wot it's all about neither. I woz gonna be goin' to Portugal and look at me now."

Johnny's ears pricked up. "You were?" Johnny asked. "When were you going to go to Portugal?"

Bert chastised himself for letting his secret slip. He looked guilty for a moment. "Well, yoo know me Mrs is over in Portugal and she wants me wiv 'er."

Johnny looked sad. "I didn't know Mrs Bert wanted you over there."

"Yeah…but…"

"This is more fun?" Johnny asked. Bert smiled and laughed. "Hell yeah."

The three of them burst out laughing.

"Bert, after you saved the universe, you can always go to Portugal." Johnny said sympathetically.

Bert smiled. "As long as I can take me cue," he said, as the van pulled up outside The Pig & Phoenix.

They all got out. Johnny picked up Pete and put him over his shoulder. The others carried the sacks. There were crowds of people standing outside the pub.

"Blimey," declared Marilyn. "The beer isn't that good," he said to the others as they pushed their way through the crowds towards the door. Marilyn knocked slowly twice and quickly three times. Jonah came to the door, a face like a drunk toad.

"Max and the girl have disappeared," Jonah said. Just at that moment, three women showed up behind them. They had blank expressions and each one was carrying a bag.

They all held out the bags and starting saying at the same time. "For Carl, for Carl, for Carl," over and over again. Marilyn raised an eyebrow.

"Great," he moaned.

310

56

Lola stood with her fists raised and glared at the demonic form in front of her. Fergus was taking steps closer to her and Lola had nowhere to back up to. The only door was behind her and the noise of inhuman squealing was painfully loud. Lola turned around for a moment to look at the door. It sounded as if hundreds of creatures were swarming behind it – some smashing into the door and slashing at it.

"Stay back," she warned, turning her attention back to Fergus.

Fergus chuckled and the noise was bone-chillingly vile. It was a sound she had never heard before and it unnerved her – the sound of a frozen soul. He kept moving forwards.

"Where's your cue?" he whispered.

"I don't need one," Lola replied. Fergus smiled and his pointed teeth glinted in the half-light. His white eyes seemed to look right through her as his black lips curled in disdain.

"How brave," he mocked, moving closer towards Lola, who pulled a face of disgust as she looked over his body. His naked body was covered in an armour of scales and there was also a vile and acrid stench in the air.

"Yoo don't frighten me. I'll kick yer arse, ya bitch-face hooker!" she shouted at him. Fergus roared with laughter.

"It's almost a shame to have to kill you," he said. "But my Queen does demand her sacrifices."

"She can fuck off 'n'all!" Lola defiantly took a step forward.

Fergus was now only a few feet from Lola. He stopped and his face seemed to morph into a mask of malice. He raised his hand forward and let out a blast of dark red energy at Lola.

It blasted her full in the chest and sent her flying backwards into the door, cracking it and increasing the squealing noise behind it. Lola fell to the floor, deeply winded but her super-strength had saved her from being killed. Lola slowly pushed up onto her feet, coughing and rubbing her chest. She raised her eyes to Fergus's and she frowned.

"I've 'ad worse period pains," she groaned and coughed.

"Well, well, well," Fergus whispered. "You have strength. But without your cue, you won't last." Fergus blasted Lola again and threw her across the hallway. She smashed upside down into a wall and fell down onto her back. Lola groaned loudly, her nose bleeding and with a cut in the back of her head.

"You cannot last long," Fergus taunted. He stretched out his hand and Lola levitated into the air. He threw her across the hallway again and she suddenly froze in mid-air.

A voice came from behind Fergus. "I don't think so, chap." Fergus spun around and saw Max standing on the stairs, armed with a cue – Fergus's cue, pointing at Lola. Fergus curled his lip at Max.

"This is just becoming better and better," Fergus sneered.

Max took a step closer towards Fergus. Max looked him up and down and he frowned.

"You're Quilloks," Max stated, taking another step forward. Fergus almost seemed to be smirking.

"You shouldn't be able to manifest in this world," Max said. "I saw to that."

Fergus, in anger, turned his attention back to Lola, frozen in mid-air, and threw a bolt of energy at her. Lola screamed.

"Drop my cue," Fergus commanded.

"Your cue? So…this is what happened to you, Fergus," Max said. "I'm so sorry. I didn't recognise you."

"It is you who should be sorry." Fergus reached out his hand and gestured towards his cue. Max felt it twitch in his hands and he saw Fergus straining. The cue remained in Max's hand.

"Before it was your cue, Fergus, it was mine," Max barked. "I was its former custodian."

Max took a step closer, his cue aimed at Fergus. "How dare you try and corrupt it."

"Try? I have."

"Its power is too strong for a foot soldier like you to control," Max snarled, his blue eyes burning with anger.

"You underestimate my power," Fergus hissed.

"I know a stupid puppet when I see one. Where is your Queen?" Max demanded.

"That is none of you concern," Fergus replied and slowly smirked.

Max walked closer towards Fergus. "Oh, everything that creature does is my concern."

Max heard the squealing coming from inside the room. He frowned, trying to recognise the noise.

"What on earth is in there?" Max growled. "Great Lodge, man, what have you done?"

Fergus smiled wickedly. "Oh, you'll find out soon enough."

Max scowled at Fergus. "Don't be a fool. You're being used. The Queen of the Quilloks is a treacherous creature. Whatever she promised you, I assure you, is a lie. Look at you…you're barely human."

"It is my honour to serve my Queen," Fergus said devotedly.

"She is a demonic creature who will see every human dead!" Max bellowed. "I banned her and her kind into another dimension and yet here you are. What is in that room?"

Fergus threw his head back and laughed and generated a bolt of energy in his hand. "This one will kill her," Fergus whispered. "Put down my cue or she will die."

57

Eric looked at himself in the mirror and saw the face of Carl looking back at him. As days had gone he had had better. His brain tried to process the image of the man staring back at him. His heart pounded and his throat felt dry. He pressed his face up against the glass and looked at his eyes. He turned his face left and right, looking at his new reflection. He raised his hand and lowered it. Whatever kind of nervous breakdown he was having he appeared to be in control of his body – whatever it looked like.

Eric turned his attention to the cue. It was beginning to pulsate in and out of visibility. The pulsation got faster and faster and Eric saw his hand fading in and out of visibility. Eric's eyes bulged as he saw his hands, arms and body pulsate with alarming speed.

As the pulsation moved up to his head, Eric found himself one moment in the toilet and another in a basement room, holding the cue in a cue rack and then in the bottom of the stairs in a house. He began to pulsate between all three, making him dizzy and sick. He found himself unable to let go of the cue and his body was accelerating between three different locations. With all his strength, he pulled the cue as hard as he could.

Everything stopped spinning and he was trying hard to catch his breath. He opened his eyes and looked around. He was at the bottom of a flight of stairs. It was dark and there was a strange smell in the air. Eric heard a crashing noise upstairs and before he knew it, his cue was pulling him up the stairs. His hand was stuck!

Eric found himself in the body of a man he once bought a house from, in a loincloth made from a toilet's hand towel and being dragged up a flight of stairs by a flying pool cue. Eric knew he had gone mad.

There was an enormous crash and a woman's scream. He then heard two male voices talking as he was pulled up the stairs. He came up behind a tall man, armed with a cue aimed at ...at...God only knew what that thing was. His heart pounded violently and he felt incredibly sick. He just wanted to vomit. He wanted this nightmare to end.

His cue pulled him up beside Max. Eric's cue sent out a bolt of violet light to the other cue, which pulsated in Max's hands. Max turned to Eric.

"Carl?" he asked.

Fergus hissed in Eric's direction. "What are you doing here?" Fergus looked Eric up and down – seeing Carl dressed in a loin cloth.

Fergus threw a red energy bolt at Eric. Eric's cue threw out a violet bolt and the two exploded in the air. Fergus yelled in frustration. He then turned his attention back to Lola.

"Both of you, put down your cues or I will kill her," Fergus threatened.

"And then I'll kill you," Max warned.

"Are you willing to sacrifice your friend?" Fergus asked, challenging the Guardian standing before him.

"We are all willing to sacrifice our lives. Isn't that right, Carl?" Max asked.

Eric just stared ahead at the large fish demon and giggled nervously. Max turned and gave Eric a cross between a withering glare and a quizzical look. Eric just nodded quickly and felt his knees begin to shake.

Fergus threw a bolt of energy at Lola. Eric's cue let out a bolt of energy and exploded with Fergus's. Fergus roared and turned to Eric, throwing a bolt at him. Max intercepted this attack with his cue and Fergus bared his teeth at them both. Eric, terrified, let out a yell – making the whole building shake – loosening plaster on the walls with the light swinging backwards and forwards. Paintings fell off the walls in every room, shelves fell over, chairs swept into the air and crashed into the walls. A howling whirlwind began on the lower floor

315

and it started to smash and crash around. Blasts of wind forced their way upwards and Max found himself holding onto the banister to keep himself from being blasted into the wall. The wind did not seem to affect Eric at all and he stood there, looking utterly bewildered and terrified.

Fergus tried to stand against the wind, his eyes closed and keeping his legs fixed firmly on the ground. Lola was still frozen still in the air and was conscious. Her hair was blown violently across her face and she was trying to breathe but the force of the air against her face was making it almost impossible.

The strength of the wind got stronger and the whirlwind was making its way upwards. Max tried to stagger towards Fergus with his cue outstretched. Fergus extended his arm and tried to send out a blast of energy. It missed Max and hit the wall, just missing Eric. Eric screamed again and this time a lightning bolt shot out from the ceiling and smashed into Fergus's chest, throwing him into the wall. He yelled as he hit it and crashed to the floor.

The two cue tips began to glow stronger as the whirlwind got closer to them – bringing a furious gale with it.

"Carl...stop the bloody weather!" Max yelled. "For God's sake, chap. Stop it!" Max shouted as he turned and headed towards Fergus, his cue outstretched.

"This ends here," Max whispered as he approached Fergus. Fergus raised his eyes and saw Max coming at him. He outstretched his hand – and sent a bolt of energy into the pigeon room door. Max glanced quickly over and saw the door begin to shatter. It was clear to Max that there was an enchantment covering the door. It had already taken a severe pounding and yet whatever was in that room was being firmly held there.

"Don't be an idiot, Fergus!" Max shouted. "You don't have to do this. You can still fight her."

Fergus smiled and sent another bolt into the door – cracks starting to appear with sparks of red energy.

"Why would I fight my Queen?" Fergus hissed. He sent another bolt of energy into the door and a massive crack appeared. The squealing intensified.

"Dear God, man. Stop this!" Max yelled, aiming his cue at

316

Fergus, taking a step closer.

Eric looked around at the situation and it made no sense to him at all. He threw his hands over his ears and hoped it would all go away. He felt the wind swirl around him but it did not affect him. The squealing…that terrible, terrible squealing!

Max was standing over Fergus with a cue pointing down at him. Fergus smirked up at him and he turned and created a hovering ball of red energy in his right hand. It grew bigger and bigger.

"This is for your little friend," he whispered. Fergus threw a bolt of energy at Lola. Max ran over towards her and jumped in front of it. It hit him full in the body. His eyes closed as he grabbed Lola and pulled her to the ground. They slumped down together and Lola could hear Fergus laughing.

Lola and Max looked at one another as the wind howled around them, the squealing echoing in their ears. Max was barely conscious and his eyes were starting to close. She took the cue that he was still clutching and with both their hands on it, sent an enormous energy bolt at Fergus, as he was starting to stand up. It hit him full in the face and he flew backwards into the cracking door.

There was an enormous cracking noise. It looked as though the door was about to split apart.

Lola looked over and saw Carl just standing there with his hands over his ears.

"Carl!" she shouted. "Carl!" But Eric was in a world of his own. "Get the fuck down!"

Lola crawled over Max and crawled into the wind towards Eric. As she did, she heard a loud, thunderous splitting noise. Her instincts told her to get to her friend as quickly as she possibly could. She pulled herself along into the wind.

"Yoo stupid twat, get down!" she growled and she got closer to him. Within seconds she was able to grab his ankle and yank him down to the ground just as there was one gigantic, ear-shattering explosion.

Wood, bricks, plaster smashed and crashed across their heads. Lola covered Eric's head and she felt a whooshing noise over her body.

Whatever had been in the pigeon room was now released and had smashed its way out of the side of the building.

317

She turned her head to the side to see if she could see Fergus – but she couldn't. She could see a large hole where the door had been. She turned her head to look at Max. His eyes were closed. Lola looked at Eric – his eyes were also closed and the wind started to calm down. Lola staggered to her feet, aiming Max's cue around her as it to catch any potential enemies.

She turned and she twirled but there was no-one there. She walked over to the smashed door and she looked into the room. It was dark and it stank of death. Lola held her breath and she stepped into the room. She looked about and had no idea at what the hell she was looking at. The walls seemed to be covered top to bottom in organic, colourful geometrical patterns of varying sizes. The room seemed to be dying, as if something had been born from it and its purpose was now over.

"Fuckin' fuck," she whispered and she twirled slowly, looking at it. She heard groaning and ran back to see that Max was shakily trying to get to his feet. He collapsed again and groaned.

"Yer too old for this," Lola said, sitting next to him. Max closed his eyes and groaned.

"Come on, ya old bastard, get up," she whispered to him. Max moaned and didn't move.

Lola leaned over him and with her index finger tapped his noise twice. "Beep...beep..." she said. Max's eyes shot open.

"What on earth are you doing?" he asked croakily and with a huge sense of indignation.

"Playin' beep beep..." she answered in a very matter-of-fact voice.

"Why...what...what on earth is beep beep?" he asked. Lola reached over and tapped his nose again and said: "Beep, beep." Max grabbed her hand and held it.

"I think you may actually be insane," Max whispered to her.

"That's wot Johnny says," she replied and nodded earnestly at him.

58

Crowds gathered in their thousands around the river – people eating ice-cream, drinking alcohol, pushing children in prams. There were film crews interviewing celebrities and all along the road were vans with large transmitters on top of the roofs. It was heaving and the weather seemed to be holding – so unusual, as many people muttered to each other. It probably won't last, others commented.

It was coming closer to the start of the actual race. The reserve Boat Race had already taken place with Cambridge winning. People crammed together all along the top of Putney Bridge and every balcony in eye's view was packed with people. Many eyes were fixed onto the large screens showing the event and there was an enormous buzz of talking and laughter.

The two crews positioned themselves to begin the battle. The Umpire's boat was lined up behind them and cheers went up as people began shouting for their team. "Come on Oxford!" "Come on Cambridge!"

Both coxes had their arms raised, indicating that they were both not yet ready. Crew members were taking off items and handing them over to a waiting boat. Shortly, the Umpire spoke into a microphone, asking if both crews were ready.

Cambridge's cox put their arm down but Oxford's remained up.

"Oxford ready?" the Umpire asked again.

To anyone looking at the Oxford eight, it would look as though eight strong men and a small female cox were waiting to take their first stroke. This was not the actual case. If

319

anyone who was blessed with strong magic was looking they would see something very, very different. They would see Sophie sitting in the position of the cox. They would then see, Marilyn, Johnny, Bert, Pete, Tara and the three other barmaids sitting in place of the Oxford crew.

Jonah was instructed to stay behind in the pub. He also believed he was the right Guardian to remain. Who else could guard an army of sleeping female pirates and a gang of angry punters outside the pub trying to get in? They had seen Johnny, Bert and the others go inside and this seemed to outrage them. (They also saw them leaving and this seemed to anger them even more.) Many were banging on the doors, demanding to be let in. It appeared that Carl had sold tickets to a barbecue – a barbecue that wasn't happening.

Jonah swaggered over to the bar, poured himself a large vodka and gulped it down. He poured another one and looked at the sacks on the floor. Some of the sacks contained a plague of female pirates and the others, tens of thousands of pounds in cash. Hmm…he thought and glugged down his drink. He took out the Eight Ball in his pocket and it was glowing. From what he knew of the Eight Ball, this was not a good sign. He ideally wanted to talk to Max about it but Max had disappeared. It wasn't the first time and it wouldn't be the last, he mused. Max was one of the toughest Guardians he had ever come across…and he was always disappearing (and returning). He was more at home in a battlefield than anywhere else. As for Marilyn – well…Jonah wrinkled his nose. "Bleuh!" he grimaced and poured another drink. He reached into the sack and pulled out one of the pirates.

'Hmmm…' he said. "How did you get here, then?" he asked before putting the pirate back in the sack and turning his attention to the watches. He had more pressing things to deal with.

Sophie looked nervously around her. It had seemed like a reasonable idea at the time, she thought. As she glanced around, she was convinced people could see who they really

320

all were but no-one noticed. Not even slightly! She didn't know the first thing about coxing or boats. She wasn't even that keen on water. She still had her arm in the air – she didn't know why. She was frozen with nerves.

Sophie frantically looked at Marilyn. Marilyn had Sophie's cue rest in the water like an oar with one hand, with a cigarette in the other while wearing a black beret and sunglasses. Johnny, Bert and Pete also had cues in the water but Pete and the other four women were still in a trance. Each had the gold watches on but Pete was now the custodian of a cue, whereas the barmaids were armed only with a wooden spoon, which they held as oars. It seemed that the remaining cue had wanted to join in the proceedings and had forced its way out of the basement and shot into (the unconscious) Pete's hand. What cues see in their custodians had always been a matter of debate at Lodge dinners and this choice would have put many a member in a flap – especially after a few brandies. Marilyn was under the impression that the Great Putney Lodge was suffering from a breakdown. They were now too far gone into this drama to question these choices but later he would. Oh yes...!

When Marilyn and the others had returned to The Pig & Phoenix Jonah had some of his own news to reveal to them. Jonah had been analysing the gold watches. If a term had to be applied to him then he would be an engineer. A magical artefacts engineer. Whereas many were happy to just use magic artefacts and not ask where they came from or why or how they worked, somebody actually had to make the 'damn things'. Jonah could take things apart and put them back together again. He equated it with plumbing.

Jonah had managed to take apart one of the watches and look at the magical components. Unfortunately, it had made the Eight Ball a bit frisky. The Eight Ball had started to glow and, if he was honest, he thought he had triggered off a serious defense mechanism. He kept his fears from the others and hoped that Max would return – soon.

He handed over a watch to Marilyn and informed him (in a somewhat patronising voice) that if he wore it, the others wearing one would follow his telepathic commands. Marilyn inhaled deeply, as if a slug monster had touched his favourite ball gown, and put the watch on. First it burned and then it itched. He thought to the others to follow him and Marilyn started an impromptu conga line. He informed Jonah he was just checking to see if it worked and Jonah sighed and poured another drink. While congaing around the bar, faint thoughts drifted into Marilyn's head.

Marilyn, as well as being an expert in illusions, was extremely good at telepathic communications. He couldn't feel much coming from the five 'zombies' but beneath it...just beneath them...he could feel a presence. He stopped in his tracks and closed his eyes.

"What is it?" Johnny asked but Marilyn shooshed him. He stood still and squinted.

"I'm getting something," he whispered.

"I thought you had a cream for that," Jonah said flatly but Marilyn didn't rise to the bait.

Marilyn sat down on a chair and focused hard. Images flashed into his head of the Boat Race – of an explosion and of Pete. He saw Carl being arrested and bags of money.

Marilyn turned to Jonah. "What are these watches?"

"Mind control devices," Jonah replied.

"Is that all?" Marilyn asked. "Are you sure?"

Jonah crossed his arms and stared at Marilyn. "They are primarily..."

"Primarily?" Marilyn interrupted.

"Primarily mind control devices," Jonah said. "Like all magical objects they can always have a secondary function."

Marilyn walked over to Pete, who had a cue stuck in his hand.

"Who is this man?" Marilyn demanded. "Why does he have a watch...and more importantly, why has he been given a cue?"

Sophie walked over to Pete and stopped. "I know him. He works with boats and teaches people to row. He was also meant to be driving the Umpire's boat today."

Marilyn tried to take the watch off but couldn't. "It's stuck, you bloated slug!" Marilyn hissed at Jonah.

"I know," Jonah replied. "I'm working on that".

"So, wot d'ya fink is goin' on?" Bert asked.

Marilyn sighed and the zombies copied him, which made

322

Johnny laugh. Marilyn shot Johnny a glare and he looked down at the floor.

"Well, I'll tell you what I think. That blob should be chopped up and fed to a large, hostile tortoise and…we need to get onto the river."

The others all exchanged looks. Johnny was the first to speak. "OK…umm….why? Why do we need to get onto the river?"

Marilyn inspected his nails and sighed. "Because Pete was meant to be blowing up the Umpire's boat and probably the two crews with him, that's why."

"Blow up?" Sophie asked nervously.

"Yes…Boom!" Marilyn replied. The zombies all said 'boom' after him.

"Boom?" asked Bert.

"Yes, boom," Marilyn answered. "Those watches are designed to explode."

Johnny walked slowly backwards, aware that he was going slightly invisible. "Wouldn't it make sense if we don't go onto the river? Why would we actually go onto the river? Shouldn't we be finding out where Lola and Max are?"

"If she's with him, she'll be fine," Jonah replied.

"But where are they?" Johnny asked. He was rapidly turning invisible.

"That I can't tell you. I haven't had time to do everything," he grumbled.

"But it's Lola," Johnny protested.

"And she's a Vampire Killer with a very aggressive former Vampire Killer and Guardian," Jonah said.

Johnny had turned completely invisible.

"Johnny is right," Bert said. "Why should we go onto the river?"

"To put a spanner in the works, that's why," Marilyn explained. "Jonah, you have to find a way we can get these watches off…in twenty minutes."

"Twenty minutes!" Jonah exclaimed.

"Yeeeessss. It seems a bit familiar, doesn't it? A watery sacrifice…in front of millions of people?" Marilyn turned to the others. "The world's horrified reaction could feed an army of demons for a hundred years."

323

Bert scratched his head. Suddenly Portugal seemed tempting again. He turned to see where Johnny was – but that was pointless. Sophie bit her lip.

"You want to take a load of bombs onto the river where a sacrifice is being planned?" Sophie asked.

"Yessss," Marilyn replied gleefully, his eyes glinting with determination.

"Could I suggest that we don't?" Sophie asked.

"You could," Marilyn replied, his eyes now looking into the middle distance as if he were completely in a world on his own.

"But it would be pointless?" Sophie asked.

"Yessss," Marilyn said as he broke into a wicked smile.

Bert sighed and lit up a cigarette.

The Umpire asked if Oxford was ready. Marilyn nodded at Sophie and indicated to her to lower her arm. Sophie really didn't want to but she did...very slowly. Her heart was pounding in her chest and her breathing was becoming heavy.

Marilyn looked at the driver of the boat – Pete's substitute. Marilyn had to use his considerable skill as an illusionist to project the image of Pete to everyone outside of the Umpire's boat (but not inside – they had already replaced him) and the enemy absolutely had to see Pete doing his duty. If everything went to plan there were some considerable illusions yet to come. His mind also drifted to the actual Oxford crew. Oh dear, he thought. Such nice boys.

Sophie shook down to her feet when the Umpire called: "Attention...Go!"

The two boats shot off with Oxford storming away on the outside. All Sophie saw were the cues in the water propelling the boat forward at alarming speed. Oxford was going into an incredible lead.

"This is rather jolly," said Marilyn, taking a drag on his cigarette. Bert and Johnny held onto their cues tightly as they vibrated with considerable ferocity. The other crew members looked blankly ahead.

"This is mental," complained Bert.

Sophie looked up into the sky and noticed that large, dark red clouds were beginning to form. She had never seen clouds like that before. She gestured to Marilyn to look upwards and he did. He took another drag on his cigarette.

"Hmm…that didn't take too long, did it?" Marilyn remarked. He closed his eyes and said in his mind: "Jonah, you large swollen oaf, have you done it yet?"

Jonah thought back to Marilyn. "You're always in a rush. Calm down."

Marilyn opened his eyes, almost as if in a rage. "Calm down," he hissed. He thought back urgently. "It has got to be now…I mean NOW."

The crowds looked up at the sky and began to point. There was a large explosion of thunder and there were screams.

Lola had managed to pull Max to his feet. He wasn't too happy being assisted by such a petite girl, but he had been injured. He knew that he needed some attention to his wounds but he also knew that he didn't have the time. He looked over at Eric/Carl. Eric had fallen unconscious and had turned back into his actual form. Max staggered over to him.

"Do you know who this is?" he asked. Lola wandered over and looked down at him.

"Yeah," she said. "It's wheelbarrow man."

"Of course he is. Who the hell is wheelbarrow man?" Max demanded.

"I rescued 'im earlier from slashy spider things. I put 'im in a wheelbarrow."

"That doesn't really answer my question," Max growled. He was aching from head to toe and his concern was rapidly rising.

"He has a cue," Max stated. "The seven are coming together and fast." Max looked around the debris. He stared into the empty pigeon room. He could smell the acrid stench.

"Wot woz in there?" Lola asked. "Smells like me mum's

325

cookin'."

"It's a birth pod. Like a womb," Max said seriously. "This isn't good, Pitchfork."

"Wot came out of it?" she asked, looking up at the older man. He looked so battered and scratched. In fact, they all looked battered and scratched. For a moment, all she could think about was how she looked and wanted to brush her hair.

He reached down and held her chin. "Something I had hoped I would never see," he said gently.

Lola looked concerned. "Grey hair?" she asked earnestly. Max chuckled for a moment and removed his hand.

"No...far worse than grey hair, Pitchfork. Far, far worse. Creatures that can span dimensions. Creatures that can end humanity," he sighed.

"That's not good, is it?" Lola asked. Max patted her cheek and said: "No, it isn't."

Lola smiled sarcastically up at him.

"Behave, Pitchfork," he whispered.

Eric murmured and the two turned their attention to him. "We all have to get back to the pub," Max ordered. "Bollocks... the portal. We have to close it before the Time Police show up."

"Time Police?"

"Yes, chap," he replied. "They've never really been very fond of us lot in Putney. Follow me."

Max reached down, picked up Eric and headed down the stairs.

Jonah looked at the watch in his hand and shook it. Marilyn had just given him twenty minutes before rushing off to the river with the others. Was that all the time he had? Jonah took it apart again at lightning speed and analysed it. He could see that it operated as a basic mind control device but what he could not work out is how it was staying on its victim's wrists. He couldn't even see where the explosives were. It infuriated him as much as he admired it. Very crafty! Very clever! All the magic he had come across in the last day or so was clever. It was as if someone had grafted and twisted things around. Things were hidden, disguised and had double usages. He knew he would come to understand it – he just didn't think he could break the mystery in twenty minutes.

Jonah closed his eyes and thought through the problem. All eight watches were meant for bar staff. One was on Marilyn's wrist, three on the barmaids, Lola had taken one and that left three. Pete has been given another watch separately. As for Tara, she was merely under Marilyn's mind control. The barmaids had been told to steal money from their different pubs and bring it to The Pig & Phoenix. Although large quantities of cash were always good in Jonah's mind, there could be no good reason for thousands of pounds being delivered by an enemy's minions.

Jonah's mind wandered back to some of his shifty mates in the past. Why would they send a ton of money to an enemy? His mind went over the problem. The only thing he could think of was to set someone up. How would bringing a ton of cash to Carl be even slightly a problem? The Lodge was magical and there would be a magical solution to such an ordinary obstacle. It would only be a problem if Carl wasn't a Vampire Killer with magical protection. Or if the Lodge was no longer magical. But if the world was blown up or taken over by vampires, who would care about a bloke in jail? (Marilyn had told him what he saw.) Jonah shook his head. He looked back at the watch. This was the problem he had to sort out. How do I get you off their wrists?

However, his mind kept coming back to the barmaids. Something had gone wrong. Why did they show up now? What had happened? Something had interrupted their programming. His mind pondered it. It has coincided with Lola's and Max's disappearance. They had to have something to do with it. Lola had taken a watch and the barmaids had appeared. That little Vampire Killer was part of the solution.

Jonah looked at the watch and held it.

"Bloody hell chap, where is everyone?" Max roared, staggering towards him with an almost naked man over his

327

shoulder. Lola was holding two cues – Eric's and Fergus's.

"Who's that?" Jonah slobbered, pointing at the unconscious Eric.

"Wheelbarrow man," he replied before plonking Eric down on a seat. Eric's head fell backwards and knocked against the wall.

Lola shot up behind Max. "The house gave birth to monsters and we almost died," she squeaked.

Jonah nodded. "Oh good," he murmured. "More important things, Wing Commander, Marilyn and the others are masquerading as the Oxford boat crew – including three watch-wearing, brainwashed barmaids who arrived with one hundred grand in cash for Carl."

"I see, chap," Max said matter-of-factly.

"Not to leave out a watch-wearing, basically unconscious man dressed as a pirate who is now also the custodian of a cue," Jonah added, referring to Pete.

"Well, chap – this man (pointing at Eric) also has a cue. I swear this Lodge really has gone senile," Max snapped. "The cues are spewing out Guardian level powers to any old passer-by. He has the ability to morph his appearance and create weather. Well, to be fair…he doesn't seem to be aware he has these abilities. To be really fair, according to Pitchfork, he hasn't really been conscious most of today."

Jonah screwed up his nose as if to show that he wasn't impressed by this news.

"Oh yeah…and there's also a plague of drunk, indestructible female pirates in those sacks. We've got to find a way to keep them unconscious," Jonah said, competing with Max for who had the worst information to tell the other. "Oh, and the gold watches also happen to be very powerful bombs and just so happen to be stuck to their wrists – including Marilyn's. We have about ten minutes to find a way to get them off before the world witnesses a Boat Race they'll never forget."

"Marvelous," Max replied. "Oh, by the way…Fergus, missing Fergus…the former cue custodian – is alive and well and has turned into a Quilloks."

"Oh," Jonah chuckled. "That's nothing. The Eight Ball is glowing and I think I triggered a self-defence mechanism. I

328

suggest we bring the ritual forward as quickly as possible."

"We were in a house that gave birth to something really, really nasty," Max boasted.

"How nasty?" Jonah demanded.

"Very," Max replied. "And they broke free."

"There are some very angry people outside demanding a barbecue," Jonah whispered.

"Good God, chap! Why didn't you mention that!" The two of them cackled and Lola looked at them as if they were deranged.

Jonah looked over at Lola. "Young lady, please come over here. I need your help."

"I'd watch it, if I were you. She's one of the most dangerous women I've ever met, chap," Max growled at Lola and she pulled a face back at him. She wandered over to the bar (not in the direction of Jonah) and looked down at the sacks. She heard snoring and peeked inside.

"Wot the fuck are them things?"

"Do what Jonah says, Pitchfork!" Max barked. "Time is ticking, chap."

Lola stomped over to Jonah and sat down with him at the table. He handed a watch over to her. Lola held it and looked quizzically at Jonah. "Wot?" she asked.

"Tell me what happened after you nicked a watch from the box," Jonah asked.

"I didn't nick it, I borrowed it," Lola replied defensively. Jonah shook his head slowly and gestured for her to get on with her story, which she did. Jonah looked as though a light-bulb 'pinged' above his head. He looked around to see where the two cues were. Max had placed them on the bar. So, one was Fergus's – or had been Fergus's. Jonah grinned to himself. Silly fool. Did he really think that he had the ability to turn a cue away from good? What a mug. As for the Quilloks, he had never expected to hear from them again. What were they after? Revenge? Pathetic.

Jonah picked up the two cues and brought them over to Lola. Lola explained that the cue had been pulsing in and out and visibility when her hand got stuck on it, while in her other hand she held a gold watch.

"It must have something to do with your strength ability. I am guessing it allowed you to accidentally create a portal between different people in different locations and time and force it open," Jonah said. "A very interesting skill, young lady."

"I dunno 'ow it works, though," Lola admitted.

"All in good time. You're already streets ahead of where you should be. You all seem to have developed abilities in an alarmingly short space of time. In the case of this man," (pointing at Eric), "and this 'Pete', there hasn't been any training at all. We don't even know what Pete's ability or abilities are. We'll have to wait and see."

Jonah handed Lola a watch and Eric's cue. Lola grabbed them and held them as she had done before but nothing happened. She stressed that previously the cue had already been flashing, and when she held it she had pulsed in and out of different locations.

"Yes," Jonah said. "But you weren't up here with us, were you? You were downstairs. Precision is very important. Magic is like engineering, young lady. You need good knowledge, talent and precision. You altered..."

"Interfered with, more like," Max said.

"...altered a very strong magical link and created a time portal."

"...a complete menace," Max said loudly. Lola huffed at him.

"That was talent. That was potential. She could be a superb engineer," Jonah protested.

"She didn't know what she was doing," Max argued. Lola nodded her head.

"It's true, I 'ad no idea at all," she added earnestly.

"Doesn't matter, Max," Jonah said. "Talent is talent. Raw, yes...at this stage. It would be a shame if it wasn't nurtured – if it wasn't allowed to be." Jonah and Max exchanged a serious look and Max looked away, looking troubled for a moment.

"Why's 'is cue linked to all this?" Lola asked, pointing at Eric. "Why not mine or Johnny's?"

Max stroked his beard and leaned forward. "Well, Pitchfork, first of all, flashy magical things usually mean the item involved is in a time flux or paradox. And, you and Johnny had been given your cues already, hadn't you? There were some unused cues just waiting for some insane custodian to team

330

up with them. Conscious or unconscious, it doesn't seem to bother the cues who they choose!"

"Time anomalies aren't always the cause of portals," Jonah said flatly.

"9 times out of 10, chap – they are," Max said.

"Are not."

"Are!" Max snarled. "And...what's more, when people muck around with time, time will always find a way to correct itself... eventually."

"I agree with that but what I am saying is OTHER things cause portals too," Jonah insisted.

"So, Eric's cue woz in anuvver time zone?" Lola asked, trying to keep the conversation on topic.

"Yes," Max answered. "In possibly two time zones...present and future."

How things could be in two time zones confused Lola and she thought hard about it.

Jonah sighed and the two of them started debating the issue of portals once more.

Lola bit her lip and interrupted them. She explained her movements with Eric earlier on in the day. She explained how she had plonked Eric in a wheelbarrow and left him in the utility room. Later on, when she had smashed down her cue on the Eight Bally thing, the reddy stuff had gone in the direction of the utility room.

Max grinned wickedly at Jonah. Jonah sniffed indignantly. "It's time, Pitchfork."

"Red energy is not always an indication of time," Jonah stated and crossed his arms. Max grinned broadly. "How many times have we discussed this? You know this from your former cue." Max scowled at Jonah and Lola frowned – mostly because she was still trying to work out what had been going on. Why colours were involved also confused her. Each of their cues generated a different energy colour. Maybe that was important too.

"So, the Eight Bally fing shoved Carl out of our time to try and screw us over and the reddy stuff shoved Eric out of our time too."

Max nodded. "The 'reddy stuff' came from the Eight Ball, Pitchfork. When we forced it out from the Eight Ball, the Lodge

331

re-directed it to where it was needed. You fight fire with fire sometimes. We used the same energy against itself. Whatever time zone Carl went to, Eric was also sent to by this Lodge. If he was sent to the future, then that's where and when the Lodge and the cue chose him as a custodian. God only knows why – he seems completely useless."

Lola looked as though she was bewildered. "I'm confused," she said.

"YOU don't know enough to be confused," Max said dryly. Lola opened her mouth to release a torrent of abuse but Jonah interrupted her.

"So... Even though Eric's cue was given to him in the future, once the cues are linked together, they are linked through time and space. The magic of the seven cues is very strong, young lady. Or even the magic of six cues and a cue rest...or even five cues and a cue rest..."

"Anyway," Max said, speaking over Jonah's digression, "... all this faffing about seemed to have caused a bit of a time problem," said Max. "And we all know who loves a time problem, don't we...Time Police."

Jonah snorted at the name. "They won't be coming here. A temporary portal is such a minor offence – hardly worth lifting their little finger over."

Max folded his arms. "They're become quite fascistic, chap. You should keep up to date. You also know our history with them – especially with you know who. SHE never liked Time Police."

The two men sat there with folded arms. Max stroked his beard and Jonah dusted some dandruff off his shoulders.

Max began to stride around forcefully and Lola's eyes lit up. She liked it when Max got all dominant and forceful and a girly grin played across her mouth. She went to her happy place again and imagined him climbing up a ladder and hammering nails. She was broken out of her fantasy when Max said:

"It's a time rift. You know it and I know it. Yes, we can re-open it and all the former links and connections will be there. We'll have to risk it. If the worst comes to the worst...SHE is always downstairs...in the vault."

Jonah shuddered. "You know she can't be relied on. She is

stark raving mad!"

Max looked worried for a moment. "That's true."

"And she never forgave you," Jonah grinned wickedly and Max scratched the back of his head, looking a bit guilty.

"So, are we goin' forward in time or wot?" Lola asked.

"No, Pitchfork," said Max. "It's tricky and very dangerous. Remember, you were dragged through the portal. It's not so easy to push through one. No, we open the portal and you get the watches off the 'Oxford crew'. The watches we have should be neutralized...should be."

Lola picked up her cue and took the two other cues plus the watch over to Eric.

"Bring 'im downstairs," she said. "We're gonna need 'im."

59

Carl sat next to Maisie, who was piloting the stolen Time Police ship. The Staff Guardian had become terribly bored of looking at Maisie's body slumped on the floor while her astral body was yapping away to Carl and decided to fix the problem. She snapped her fingers and Maisie shot back into her physical body. The Staff Guardian materialised a glass of a blue liquid and gave it to Maisie to drink. Maisie pulled a face of disgust but took it and drank it. First she went deaf... then she staggered over to the 'spinning' console and clung on for dear life and then... she could see Carl in his astral body. Maisie smiled at Carl, whacked her chest and coughed out some smoke. She shook her head, clearing some of the deafness, sat at her console and for the first five minutes could only speak backwards in Swedish.

Carl felt a huge sense of urgency and couldn't understand why it was taking so long to get back to the planet Earth. He looked over at the Staff Guardian. He swore the horns on her Viking hat were getting bigger each time he glanced back at her. She was staring and scowling at a screen.

"Morons...MORONS!" she yelled at the screen. "You're next...and you!"

Maisie was focused on her task at hand and then seemed to look very concerned.

"Oi! Nutter!" she yelled. The Staff Guardian broke away from her fist-shaking and glanced over.

"Now what? Can't find the steering wheel?" she mocked.

"Err...no..." Maisie replied sarcastically.

"What is it?"

Maisie ran her hands over her controls and breathed in deeply. "I hate to tear you away from your ranting but...we have a bit of a problem, duck."

The Staff Guardian stood up from her chair, swung her axe over her shoulder and came over to Maisie's side.

"Earth isn't that hard to find," the Staff Guardian taunted, conjuring up a bottle of champagne. She turned to Carl and said: "Why anyone would actually want to find it is beyond me."

Maisie fixed her with a stare. "Just look at the screen."

The Staff Guardian peered at the screen. "What?"

Maisie stood up and pointed. "Look!"

Carl and the Staff Guardian both leaned forward to get a closer look. Carl did not understand what Maisie was going on about and...then...he saw them.

"Fuck!" he cried.

The Staff Guardian glugged straight from the champagne bottle and wiped her mouth. She moved Maisie out the way and sat down in her chair. She tapped a few times on the control panel and looked back at the screen.

Hundreds of Time Police ships – possibly thousands – on their tail.

The Staff Guardian tapped a few more times and an image of the Earth came up on the screen. There was a shimmering shield of dark blue starting to appear around it.

"Oh dear..." said the Staff Guardian. "That doesn't look too good. Sorry, little human, but we will have to abandon your mission."

Carl felt panic pulse through his astral body. "You can't! Please...you can't...Maisie..."

"This isn't good, Carl," Maisie whispered. "What the hell is that blue thing?"

The Staff Guardian smiled. "That is a planet being put into quarantine."

"You're smiling? You're actually smiling?" Maisie snapped.

The Staff Guardian laughed. "It happens...deal with it."

Maisie grabbed the Staff Guardian's arm. "What does this mean?"

The Staff Guardian rubbed her chin. "It means don't bloody go there, witch."

"Please…we have to…" Carl begged. This was a nightmare. He had to get back to his friends. He had to find Katie.

Maisie looked at Carl compassionately. She let go of the Staff Guardian's arm and said in a low voice. "Are you afraid, oh great looney?"

The Staff Guardian sniffed. "Nice try, witch, but I know who is putting the Earth into quarantine…and you don't mess with them."

"Who?" demanded Maisie. "Someone more powerful than you? Surely not?"

"No!" the Staff Guardian cried. "But one battle at a time. There are thousands of ships pursuing us…or didn't you notice?"

Maisie looked back at the screen, which was showing the Time Police ships. "Can we outrun them?"

"Hmm…" muttered the Staff Guardian. "Possibly…"

"Possibly!" Maisie yelled.

"Yes…possibly."

Carl rubbed his astral eyes and inwardly groaned.

"I beg you…please…just get me back and then…leave…"

"Oh, yes…let's outrun a homicidal Time Police fleet and then let's have a toasted baguette…possibly a skinny latte."

Maisie licked her lips and breathed out. "Please…can you drop Carl off?"

The Staff Guardian looked at her nails and took another glug of champagne. "Can I outrun a fleet of Time Police, navigate my way through a quarantined planet, drop off bonehead and get out in time for lunch?"

"Yes!" Maisie cried.

The Staff Guardian looked around at her crew. "The odds are against us, witch." She started to walk around the bridge. "Can I? Should I risk my crew for this…barely conscious mortal?" she said, gesturing towards Carl. Carl nodded eagerly.

The crew looked nervous and most were shaking their heads. "You're right…I should!" The crew groaned.

The Staff Guardian bellowed: "Everyone to your posts! Some of us may not make it! Onwards…Huzzah!" she cried.

Maisie grinned at Carl and looked at the screen. Her face

336

then turned deadly serious.

The Time Police were starting their attack.

60

Max, Jonah (carrying Eric) and Lola moved downstairs. Lola placed Eric's cue in the rack and put hers next to it; as there had been previously two cues side by side (Pete's and Eric's) they needed another one to try and replicate what had previously happened. Lola then handed Max his former cue and he seemed genuinely delighted to be holding it. It had clearly meant a great deal to him. Within moments, he gently put it down on the floor next to him before stepping forwards towards the cue rack.

Max had only just closed the time portal. He truly hoped the Time Police wouldn't notice that they were about to open it again. He had to do it – linear time was running out. The Boat Race was about to begin and Marilyn needed to get the watches off his and the others' wrists. He hoped Marilyn knew what he was doing. Max was not keen on telepathic communication and wasn't that talented at it. He could send some information and receive others – a bit like a fuzzy radio signal. Max tried to think to Marilyn but without a response.

"Can't get a fix," Max said to Jonah.

Jonah sighed. "He's probably going over the top and burning up a lot of fuel. You know what he's like – silly ole tart. Anyway, the ole trout doesn't stop buzzing me."

Lola butted in and instructed Max to bring Eric over to the cue rack and she placed his hands around the cue. They fell off. She put them on again and this time he gripped them. Lola also put one hand on the same cue and held the watch in her other hand. She turned to Max.

"Come on, buttercup," she whispered. Max raised his

eyebrows.

"Do NOT call me buttercup," he cautioned.

"Come on Sex God," she teased. Max shot her a glaring look and decided it was better to ignore the remark altogether. Max told Lola that as soon as she started to see images of the barmaids, Pete or Marilyn, she was to instruct the watches to come off their wrists.

Max had figured that Lola's 'interference' (and 'interference' it was in his mind) had broken or overridden whatever mind control had been exerted on the barmaids and on Pete. It was entirely possible that Lola did have a natural gift for telepathy and mind control and her super strength extended to a super-powerful mind. Oh, dear Lord, Max thought. May the great Lodge Masters protect us all.

The cue started to flash and Lola felt herself going lightheaded and being pulled towards a vortex. She saw an image of Katie, only for a moment. She seemed anxious – desperate to get a message across but Lola felt her mind torn away and she was up in the clouds – crimson red clouds – and she heard screaming.

The Oxford crew was surging ahead of Cambridge when the rain began to belt down. It wasn't ordinary rain. It was cold; so very cold and it was turning to hail. Some people in the crowds were making a run indoors, while others hadn't noticed because of their unfeasibly gigantic umbrellas. Sophie felt the freezing water and hail hit her face and it hurt.

People were still cheering and waving flags. The noise of the helicopter buzzed overhead and she could hear the Cambridge cox shouting instructions. They were also reacting to the coldness of the rain. Marilyn noticed this and felt agitated. He looked at the gold watch on his wrist and tried to get it off. No luck. 'Come on...come on!' he cried to Jonah.

They were passing by the boathouses at incredible speed.

Marilyn looked up at the sky and it was now a dark red. He knew it was only a matter of moments before the bomb

339

watches exploded. It was also only a matter of time before they'd be passing into Barnes. Great Lodge, thought Marilyn. Their zombie problem is the worst in Europe!

Lola saw herself enter into the crimson clouds and pulse back into the pub. The inside of the crimson cloud was so, so cold. She tried to hold her attention there and she could see the shapes of...what were they? Her general reference points were not the strongest of her skills but she knew she had seen that shape before. There were lots of them sitting in the cloud, leaning over the edge. Fuck me, she thought. They look like them mermaid fings. There were hundreds of them and they all seemed poised to leap out of the cloud, armed with spears, their scaly faces contorted into a permanent look of malice and rage. They were about seven foot tall and seemed incredibly strong. They had the upper torso of a humanoid and the tail of a fish. They also had vampire fangs.

Max was holding onto Lola's arms, as he watched her pulse in and out of invisibility – he wasn't going to lose her again! He asked her if she had seen the barmaids, etc. but she said she hadn't. She described what she was seeing. Max sighed and whispered: "It's an invasion force". Max knew it was an invasion force that had been building up in Sophie's house, being nurtured and grown! They were half in this dimension and half in another and they were waiting for the explosion; they were waiting for the fear of all the people watching around the world. The combination of millions of people experiencing shock and fear at the same time would be an enormous food source for them – making them strong enough to pour into this dimension.

Jonah felt the Eight Ball burn in his pocket. He took it out and he looked at it. "This is not good," he said to Max. "Looks like its water has broken and it is going into labour."

"Bollocks, chap," Max said as he turned to look Jonah in the eye. Jonah nodded at him, as if to acknowledge that this was one of 'those' times.

"If we don't do the ritual now, this thing will go off," Jonah

340

whispered.

"We can't open a portal of that size now," Max warned. "God knows how many millions of those things are waiting to come through. Those waiting in the clouds are just a handful. Opening a portal could bring death to this planet."

"If we leave it any longer there won't be a planet left to worry about," Jonah protested. "I know magic and this thing is going to explode and a nuclear explosion would seem mild by comparison."

"This is the Queen's doing!" Max bellowed. "She's played us every step of the way!" Jonah nodded and took a swig from a hip flask. "We have to open the Eight Ball portal. We have to take that risk and we need Marilyn, chap...and you stuck a bomb on him."

Jonah took another swig of whiskey. "I've been wanting to do it for years."

Marilyn knew that when they hit the Putney/Barnes border the bombs would detonate. This ritual was designed for the jurisdiction of the great Putney Lodge. They were moments away from being blown up but they mustn't let the Quilloks know that they knew that. The Queen would be expecting an explosion and he didn't aim to disappoint her. Could they stop the boat, turn and run and avoid all of this? No. The watches were going off no matter what, and Marilyn wanted to make sure it was done as close to his terms as he could manage. He also needed to take it to the edge because right now he needed the extra time. He tried to get the watch off his wrist again and it wouldn't budge. All those wearing watches had gone into sync with one another. They had become one big bloody bomb.

He knew that right now the Quilloks Queen and Fergus would be thinking that Pete was on the Umpire's boat and that there was going to be one almighty explosion. Marilyn hoped they hadn't seen through their plan, that they hadn't picked up on his brain waves linked into the watch web. The arrogant confidence of evil in its own superiority was often its

341

downfall and the Queen was arrogant. He remembered her well.

Johnny and Bert exchanged looks. Both of them were thinking the same thing…they had the chance to bolt and get out of here. Johnny (who was half invisible) found himself staring at the watch on Marilyn's wrist. Bert looked down, avoiding the hail. He thought about Portugal and Mrs Bert and sighed. Sophie just wished she had stayed in bed.

They were getting closer to the Barnes border.

"They have really bad zombies," Johnny whispered to Bert.

"I know," Bert said, fretting. "I've seen the newsletter."

Marilyn interrupted their conversation. "When the watches come off, you two know what you have to do."

Johnny and Bert nodded, although no-one could see Johnny do that – he had gone invisible yet again.

Lola tried to home in on the watches. All she could see were huge crimson clouds containing hundreds of warrior mermaid creatures. She could feel the evil permeating her skin. She was cold, so, so cold. Evil, she thought, was not hot or burning like Hell was described – it was cold. It was frozen. It was where love had stopped and only hate remained.

Max was urging her to find the watches – quickly!

Lola felt overwhelmed by the feelings of coldness and darkness. How could she act quickly? What would Johnny say?

Johnny.

Her thoughts turned to Johnny and she felt a warmth in her heart. She focused on that.

An image of the boat pulsed into her mind. She smiled.

She focused on Johnny again and the image became clearer. Max was able to see the image with her in his mind's eyes.

"Now, Pitchfork! NOW!" Max demanded. "Get the watches off them," he growled. "Do it!"

Just as the boat approached the Barnes border the watches fell off, and all those who had been wearing them slumped forward, apart from Marilyn. Johnny and Bert quickly snatched up all the watches – which wasn't so easy for Johnny but Bert had speed on his side. Johnny aggressively and urgently thrust the ones he had collected to Bert, who flung his leg over his cue and sped up into the sky and the crimson clouds at lightning speed. Johnny, who was invisible, chugged over to the Cambridge crew and fired a light blue bolt at them – making them capsize. There were gasps from the audience and Johnny felt a pang of guilt. He was, after all, a Cambridge supporter and could have gone either there or Oxford – if he had wanted to.

The Oxford eight stopped dead at the Barnes border just as Bert swooshed up into the clouds. The first thing Bert noticed was the sheer size of them. There were ten gigantic crimson clouds – each one five times the size of the London Eye and uniform in shape. They hovered in the sky, shoulder by shoulder, blocking out the sun.

"Bugger me backwards," Bert whispered and he charged into one of them.

Bert flew at the first cloud, which had the texture of a membrane and it wasn't that hard for him to penetrate. His combined speed and the energy of the watches allowed him to do so. It was a thin veil between this dimension and another one and it was scary how easy it was to tear. He dropped a watch as he tore through the cloud, into the next, the next, the next, dropping the watches (spacing them out so all the clouds would be destroyed). All the Quilloks saw was a blur and then there was a series of massive explosions, following Bert as he thrust through the final cloud and stormed down back towards the Oxford boat.

Marilyn was standing up in the boat. As he watched the beginning of the explosions, he concentrated hard and extended his hands up towards the sky. This was going to take one hell of a lot of energy and he wasn't sure how much he had left.

The audience standing on the side of the Thames and on the TV would have seen the Cambridge crew capsize, the Oxford crew stop (for no apparent reason) and the large

343

crimson clouds turn into huge hot air balloons advertising 'The Pig & Phoenix' and also Marilyn's singing act performance there later in the day.

Sweat broke out on Marilyn's brow as he looked up and saw what was really happening.

"Tricky little tadpoles, aren't they?" he said to Johnny, who had returned to the boat.

All Johnny could see were the balloons. "You're performing tonight? What...what???"

"I believe in optimism," Marilyn whispered.

"And self-promotion," Johnny whispered back.

"You need a positive mental attitude in this game, mate," Marilyn said before frowning. "Hmm...we appear to have a problem."

"Just the one?" Johnny asked, looking upwards. What Johnny couldn't see were about one hundred mermen vampires falling into the water.

"Hmm..." Marilyn said as the Umpire's boat pulled up alongside them. Marilyn looked towards Sophie. "Get ready," he ordered. Sophie looked completely alarmed.

"For what?"

"Battle," Marilyn said.

"W...what?" Sophie asked quietly as Marilyn grinned at her.

Marilyn then closed his eyes and thought to Jonah: "We have a breach."

"Abeach...what?" Jonah replied telepathically.

"No, you slug. Abreach...a breach!"

Sophie was about to mount her cue rest when she noticed that Pete was opening his eyes.

"Marilyn!" Sophie cried. "Marilyn, LOOK!"

Marilyn turned to look at Pete, whose eyes were now open. He looked around – clearly confused. His brain just could not register what was going on. He looked at the cue in his hand, which had begun to glow a vibrant orange. The colour passed into Pete's body and soon he was glowing orange. Marilyn stroked his chin with his finger as he watched Pete's legs slowly turn into a tail of a large fish.

"Interesting..." Marilyn whispered. Sophie's jaw dropped to the floor.

Lola opened her large brown eyes and turned them on Max. She smiled weakly – looking exhausted. He smiled at her and patted her on the shoulder.

"Well done, chap." Lola grinned at him and took a very deep breath and blew her fringe out of her eyes.

Jonah cleared his throat. "I think we should be moving down to the Church, don't you?" He pulled out the Eight Ball from his jacket and showed it to Max. It was emitting a deep crimson colour, which was beginning to spread out from the tiny object. Max looked taken aback by this and scratched his beard.

"We need Marilyn, chap," Max said to Jonah. "Opening the portal needs three Guardians – not two. We have to get him NOW."

Jonah nodded back to Max in a way as if to say: 'Yes, I bloody know that!'

"Good – all the cues have been assigned – we have a chance," Max said, talking more to himself than the other two. He seemed pleased with this information, almost comforted by it.

"That one hasn't been assigned. It's been rescued. AND... don't forget the cue rest," Jonah reminded Max in a slightly haughty tone. "There's eight of them. There's not meant to be eight of them."

"Before it was Fergus's, it was mine. It's come back to me," Max whispered.

Jonah looked as if he may actually be sick. "Oh, good-o. Shall I book you two a room or would you just like to be alone?"

Max spun the cue around his head and shoulders expertly. Lola's eyes lit up and she grinned.

"Wow," she said.

"Don't encourage him, young lady. Really – it's for the best that you don't."

Lola looked at Max spinning and twirling the cue. He then stopped to attention.

"Tell Marilyn to meet us at the church," Max instructed Jonah.

Jonah sighed and closed his eyes and tried to think to Marilyn. However, he couldn't get through. He tried again.

"Busy line," Jonah said flatly.

Max nodded angrily; furious with the situation. Jonah turned to Lola and had the look of a man contemplating jumping off a cliff.

"Whatcha lookin' at me like that for?" Lola asked.

"Oh dear Lord, NO!" Max cried. "No...no...no!"

Jonah sagely nodded his head. "Yes," he said to Max. "It is probably the only way."

Marilyn stared at the image in front of him. Pete had transformed into an seven foot orange merman. His cue has taken on the appearance of a trident and his hair had grown. His eyes were glowing a vivid orange and his teeth had become pointed.

Sophie was staring at the creature in front of her. Too scared to move, too scared to scream.

Marilyn saw that about one hundred Quilloks were in the Thames and moving towards the boat and the crowd.

Pete reared up on his tail and let out a deep, booming yell. Marilyn took a step forward and booted him off the side of the boat. There was a huge splash and the boat rocked.

"Get on with it, mate," he said. It was too late for him to try and cover up the sound of that yell, which seemed to have had a rather quieting effect on the crowd, who had turned their attention away from the Cambridge crew being pulled out the water and into boats and onto where an unearthly yell had come from.

Marilyn told Johnny and Bert to get back into position and steer the boat into the middle of the Thames.

Pete swam down to the bottom of the water and sat there, perched on his tail. As days go this was certainly the most

346

bizarre he had ever encountered. He knew he had been at Eric's earlier on in the day and now...here he was.

Pete's cue had taken control of him in a rather sharing way. It had communicated with him not so much in words but in feelings, and had explained that this was very necessary and that it was very sorry for any trouble caused. Using a thought ball, the cue had communicated the entire situation to Pete and that, yes, it was necessary under these circumstances to turn him into a mini-Neptune. The cue had chosen him for his love of all things watery and a deep desire to beat up a very annoying work colleague.

Pete's eyes glinted in the water as he saw twenty Quilloks swim his way. He held his trident cue forward and let blast an enormous bolt of light orange energy. Ten of them were stunned unconscious immediately and began to sink to the bottom. The other ten turned their attention on Pete and swam furiously towards him. The other eighty were going their separate ways and heading towards the bank.

Johnny and Bert had managed to steer the boat to the centre of the river. The TV stations were filming the Oxford crew turning into the centre of the Thames and sitting there for no apparent reason. Commentators were going crazy; people were yelling for them to continue the race.

Marilyn turned to Sophie and said: "Get on the back of Johnny's cue. I'll get on Bert's. And don't forget your cue rest."

Sophie nodded. She found herself moving like a robot towards Johnny, who was now hovering above the boat. Marilyn got on the back of Bert's cue as Johnny helped Sophie on his.

Marilyn looked down at the boat. He told Sophie to use her rest. "You know what to do."

Sophie hadn't a clue. She merely pointed her rest at the Oxford boat with the barmaids in it and it started to move forwards all on its own – much to the cheering of the crowd.

The four of them flew higher up and watched as the boat entered into Barnes, at which point there was an unspoken feeling that it was now the responsibility of the Barnes Lodge to sort out the problem. Marilyn was aware that, if they were to actually get through this, flowers would need to be sent. Possibly a card.

347

The crowds cheered on and the boats followed the 'Oxford crew'.

"Down there," Marilyn ordered. He pointed at five Quilloks surfacing behind the boats. Bert zoomed down, yellow bolts blasting out from his cue. All five got hit and they sank dead to the bottom.

Marilyn was feeling the drain of all the illusions he had had to maintain. He was keeping himself and Bert invisible, as well as disguising the barmaids as the Oxford crew and trying to make the Thames seem relatively calm and demon free. He needed to keep that illusion going as long as he possibly could. Johnny, he knew, would have no problem at all remaining invisible.

Pete had been coming up behind the Quilloks, who were trying to take down the boats, and blasting them with his trident. The shock waves of the blasts were making the water incredibly choppy. One of the boats following the race almost capsized. Johnny chugged down on his cue and Sophie instinctively sent out a stabilizing energy that just saved it.

Bert and Marilyn skimmed along the top of the water at incredible speed, as Marilyn kicked a Quilloks in the head.

"You don't always needs magic, mate," he whispered to Bert.

Bert's super speed meant that Marilyn could repeat this non-magical assault at least fourteen times, as Bert shot other further bolts from the cue, taking further enemies down.

Johnny saw that some of the Quilloks were trying to enter into Barnes territory. He knew they must not get to the 'Oxford crew'. He flew as quickly as he could forward and told Sophie to stop them. Sophie was acting from pure instinct. She knew she wanted to stop seven Quilloks and what her cue rest created amazed her. It shot out a huge energy net which dropped from the top of the water to the bottom and tangled them up in it. Their spears could not cut it and they also sank to the bottom. Sophie smiled. As terrifying as this was, it was also exhilarating. She was invisible. She was flying. This couldn't be real – could it? She felt a strength enter her body. Whatever happened, she hoped that she would be allowed to remember this. A time when she felt brave; a time when she had courage.

Bert swooped down over her head. Jesus – he couldn't see them.

"Oi!" Sophie shouted. Bert skimmed back down to the surface of the water. He turned back to wave at his invisible comrades and was knocked off his cue by a Quilloks leaping out of the water.

Bert felt his feet being pulled down into the water. He had barely any air in his lungs as he found himself being dragged downwards. Bert moved about as quickly as he could to shake off the Quilloks but the creature would not let go. Panic and survival took over Bert. He thrashed and kicked but nothing helped. He felt his last bit of strength leave him when the grip on his leg was released. He opened his eyes, and in the murky water he saw Marilyn smacking the Quilloks around the head with his cue. Marilyn pointed the cue upwards, put one arm around Bert and zoomed up and out of the Thames. Bert took an enormous gasp of air.

"Tricky little darlings, aren't they?" Marilyn said, placing the cue beneath the two of them expertly. He had placed Bert back on the front of it. "I prefer being driven, mate."

"Little? They're bleedin' enormous!" Bert cried.

"Focus, cabbie. We have work to do. Down there!" Marilyn pointed. Bert was back in the saddle within moments and zapped three more Quilloks.

Max, Jonah, Lola and Eric stood outside the church on Putney Common. Jonah had two sacks of snoring tiny female pirates over one shoulder and the glowing Eight Ball in his pocket. It was really starting to burn and the red light was almost covering his entire body. Max had his arm gripped tightly around Eric's shoulders – who was still, mostly, unconscious.

Max turned to Lola and said: "I assume, chap, that this church may actually explode if you walk into it."

"Why?" Lola asked innocently.

Max sighed and resignedly shook his head.

Jonah took the first step forward towards the door. "Ok, Max.

You go and remove anyone in there. I'll get started with...you know what." Jonah gestured towards Lola. Max actually threw a hand over his face for a moment – it was beyond comprehension what they were going to have to do.

Max walked into the church, leaving Eric propped up against a wall. They had managed to find him a pink bathrobe, which was far too small for him.

Jonah stood outside, and within a few minutes a string of people, including the vicar, came wandering out in a trance-like state. Max looked at Lola and pulled her by her arm.

"Watch it!" she shouted. Max let go of her arm and stomped into the church and up to the altar. He thrust his hand into his inside jacket pocket and pulled out his Lodge book. He looked at Lola again, who had now entered into the church. Max rolled his eyes and let out an even longer sigh. He looked over at Jonah, who was now standing next to him at the altar. He put the tiny pirates on it and nodded to over to Max.

"Let's just wait a few more minutes," Max said.

Jonah shook his head. "Look at me. I can barely contain this energy. Soon, I won't be able to."

Max shook his head in anger, disbelief and annoyance.

"I know it's against everything you believe, Max. But we have to make this sacrifice."

Max growled loudly. Lola folded her arms and pouted.

"Are yoo two gettin' married or somefink?"

Max shoved his hand in his other pocket and pulled out a ritualistic knife. Jonah put his hand in his pocket and pulled out an identical version.

"Lola, come here," Max ordered. Lola looked nervously at both of them.

"Why?" she asked.

"Just do as you're told, woman!"

"Up yours," Lola said, raising her cue. "Wot ya gonna do wiv them blades?"

Jonah stepped forward. "We're not going to hurt you, young lady."

"Don't fuckin' look like it!" she shouted.

Jonah took another step forward. "You've got it all wrong. We're going to promote you to Guardian class. Lola, you're

350

going to be a Guardian."

Lola's jaw dropped and she fixed them both with a piercing look.

61

The stolen Time Police ship rocked as a blast hit it. Maisie flew out of her co-pilot seat and skidded across the floor. There were injured crew members scattered about the bridge as the Staff Guardian piloted the badly damaged ship.

Thousands of ships were pursuing them. Dozens were firing on them.

Carl was frantically looking around him. He heard a loud American voice boom out across the ship: "You are under arrest...you are under arrest!"

The Staff Guardian laughed furiously as she returned fire. "Up yours!" she hollered.

Carl stared at the screen in front of him. He could see the Earth getting closer. There was also the dark blue shield wrapped around the planet...but the shield wasn't quite complete – there was still a gap in it.

"Can we get through?" yelled Carl.

"No idea!" the Staff Guardian shouted back.

Maisie got back to her feet and staggered back to her seat. She started firing on the ships that were surrounding them. She looked at the gap in the shield.

"Jesus...it's closing!" she shouted as the gap began to get smaller. "We're not going to make it! We're not going to make it!"

62

Pete back-flipped out of the water, throwing his trident and harpooning three Quilloks at the same time. He landed back into the water with considerable grace before retrieving his trident and pursuing more vampire mermen.

The hail still bolted down from the sky and most of the crowd had dispersed into the surrounding pubs. Marilyn felt he was beginning to lose the signal with the Oxford boat and with the power of his illusion. He felt that they must be at Mortlake by now. The simple fact was that they had already gone through the finish line and were still continuing on at alarming speed. The 'Oxford crew' weren't stopping any time soon, much to the entertainment and concern of a watching public.

Bert swooshed and twirled and Johnny chugged over the river, killing the remaining Quilloks vampires. Between them all, they had managed to destroy all the vampire mermen that had fallen into the river. Marilyn was very pleased. He sent a thought to Jonah and was a bit put out when he couldn't get through. He also knew that something would need to be done about all the dead mermen in the Thames. Hmm...he thought to himself. Very tricky. He also thought about the real Oxford crew that would have to be returned at some point. Very, very tricky. There was also the small issue of Carl's bar staff. Hmm...

Johnny was personally very concerned that he was visible to vampires. Although, technically, he was mostly dead, he was still fearful of being killed. It was true that the power of his cue gave him a life force and allowed him (some) invisibility but he really wanted another (better) ability too. Invisibility just seemed to mean he could hide from humans. He supposed he should be grateful that he didn't have to be sleeping in a vegetable patch any more. It was also true that he was becoming a very good sharp shooter with his cue and he felt very connected with and trusting of it. It was like knowing you could dive out of a plane without a parachute and survive. Hmmph! He still wanted another ability, though. One that meant he could get away from supernatural enemies!

Bert hadn't enjoyed himself so much in years. There was something for flying at an incredible speed. It was thrilling. He was amazed that a man of his physique and age would be getting up to this kind of thing. He croakily laughed. If only Mrs Bert could see him now. She wouldn't perhaps be so critical. What would the boy think? Bert wrinkled his nose. The boy never left his attic. Well, he will do after this, Bert thought. He can go and live with his mother!

Sophie's heart was still pounding. She was also cold and soaking wet. The hail was still pelting down. Her logical mind thought that once the Quilloks ships had been destroyed, normal weather would resume. However, the weather seemed to be getting worse, in spite of their success.

"Why is it still raining?" Sophie asked Marilyn. Marilyn looked around. The girl was right. The weather wasn't lightening up. It seemed to be getting worse.

Marilyn tried to think to Jonah once again and there still was no response.

"We're going back to the pub," Marilyn said.

"What about my friends in the boat? What's going to happen to them?" Sophie asked.

Marilyn shook his head slowly at her. "They are the least of my worries right now."

The four of them began to fly back to the pub. Johnny turned to Marilyn and asked, "What about that man, Pete?" Johnny gestured with his head towards the river. Marilyn looked over his shoulder and saw Pete flipping somersaults out of the water under the cover of torrential rain.

"He seems perfectly happy where he is," Marilyn said before adding to Bert: "Drive on, cabbie."

Lola glared at Max and Jonah. She held her cue threateningly and pursed her lips. This information was most definitely not computing. Lola truly believed that they wanted to sacrifice her on the altar in some kind of blood-letting ritual. She blew her fringe out of her eyes for the fifth time and looked fiercely from one to the other again and again.

"Bollocks," she said, flatly and menacingly.

Max leaned back on his heels and let out a huge laugh. "Bollocks? BOLLOCKS?" he bellowed at her. Jonah turned to Max and raised his hands in a pacifying way. He then turned to Lola and tried to put on the most benign expression he could think of. He actually just looked mentally ill and Lola became even more suspicious.

"Young lady," Jonah said, taking a step towards her. "We need to promote you to the status of Guardian, so that we can have three Guardians open the portal and possibly save the world. You know…the nice planet with the green trees…"

"Or destroy it," Max chipped in. Jonah shhhd!

Lola's mind was in survival mode and this information was not getting through. Lola pointed at their ritualistic knives.

"Wot yer doin wiv them blades? Yoo gonna kill me?" Lola squeaked at them. Max held the knife handle out towards her.

"Believe me, Pitchfork, there have been times when I would've loved to have killed you but now is not one of them, and trust me, and I mean trust me, I do NOT want to promote you to Guardian class! Initiates train for years to become Guardians. This is an honour you do not deserve." Max glared at her, his blue eyes looking as if they could actually explode.

Lola pursed her lips even more tightly together. "Yoo should watch ya blood pressure. A man of yer age could drop dead… at any second…like a big, fat, dead duck." Max mouthed the word 'duck' to himself in disbelief. He banged his head on the altar slowly.

Lola slowly lowered her cue. She could tell that Max was genuinely angry with the idea of promoting her to being a Guardian. This knowledge made her let out a high-pitched giggle. (She also felt a sense of relief that they didn't want to kill her! It had been a strange day – many things had tried to kill her.) Jonah covered his ears and winced. Max closed his eyes and looked furious.

Lola started to walk closer towards the two of them. "So, I get to be a Guardian then?" she asked with a sense of mischief in her voice. Max threw a hand over his eyes and rubbed them. Jonah smiled as politely as he could and nodded at her.

"Yes, you do. We also have to make you one as quickly as we possibly can," Jonah said as nicely as he could and urged her to come forwards.

Lola reached the altar and placed her cue on it. She could hear the female pirates still snoring. She wondered when they were going to wake-up. How long would the enchanted rum last?

"Young lady, we need you to lie down on the altar," Jonah said.

"That sounds just a bit dodgy to me," she replied suspiciously.

"Get on the altar, Pitchfork," Max said and put on a huge, false smile. "Please."

Lola grinned at Max and then giggled. "Haha...yoo 'ate this," she squeaked and jumped up onto the altar. Max smiled sweetly at her through gritted teeth.

Jonah told her to lie down with her head towards him. He was going to suggest her head facing north but he thought it may actually confuse her. Jonah then told her to close her eyes. This took a little bit of persuasion but after a bit of eye opening and giggling, she did comply.

Jonah and Max stood on either side of her. They raised their left hands and each cut them with the knives. They allowed the blood to drop onto Lola's eyelids, which she wasn't that impressed with.

The two men began to chant and drop blood down her body. Their blood began to glow a golden colour and it was absorbed into her body. Their chanting became louder and louder as they stood next to her abdomen. They raised the knives above their heads and thrust the blades deep into her stomach. Lola lurched forward – screaming.

Marilyn and the others flew onto the roof of The Pig & Phoenix. Marilyn wanted to take a look at the lay of the land. He lit up a cigarette in the pouring rain and looked around. Sophie walked over to him and tapped him gently on the shoulder.

"Shouldn't we go inside or...?" Marilyn took a deep breath in through his nose. He seemed to Sophie as if he had gone into a trance. He seemed to wince, and he held his stomach. He seemed surprised and turned his attention to the others.

"Hmm," he said. "I think we need to get down to the common...quickly."

Sophie looked down the side of the building and at the crowds that were still angrily standing there. She thought that by now they would've gone somewhere else but there is something very determined about an outraged, English crowd. The torrential rain just seemed to make them more determined to stand there and complain to one another.

"Shouldn't we leave someone here...I mean...this place... shouldn't it be protected?" Sophie asked.

Marilyn seemed pleased with this level of concern from Sophie and patted her on the shoulder.

"This Lodge, normally, can take care of itself, I assure you," Marilyn whispered. "It is an extraordinary place. What you see with your eyes is only part of it."

Sophie smiled weakly and pushed her glasses back up onto the bridge of her nose. "Shall I stay here or not?"

"No, if it wants us...it knows where we will be," Marilyn answered. "If it wants you, it'll know where to find you."

Sophie looked over to Johnny and Bert, who were still standing over their cues. She looked up into the sky. It had turned a dark crimson red and a massive gale blasted down the Lower Richmond Road. Sophie turned her back into it and crouched down.

Marilyn stood resolutely firm and stared into the distance.

"We go...now," he said, turning towards Bert and Johnny, who were now soaking wet and looked battered from the wind. "But first," he whispered, "I need to change."

357

Lola took deep breaths and looked down at her stomach. There were two blades sticking into her and the pain was intense. There was no blood, however.

She looked over at Max with eyes of betrayal and rage. She looked over to Jonah and she felt an urge to kill him.

"What you are feeling is the death of your former self," Jonah whispered and began to read from the Lodge book.

"You die as an initiate so that you can rise as Guardian," Max whispered.

Lola snarled at them. "Yer all off ya fuckin' tits," she hissed at Max.

"Shut up, Pitchfork," Max said. "We've all been through this. Stop moaning."

Lola growled. As she did, she felt the pain in her stomach subside. She looked at her stomach and the blades were beginning to leave her stomach of their own accord, as if something inside her was pushing them out. She watched as the blades were finally and completely pushed from her stomach and fell to each side of her on the altar. Two beams of white light shone out from where the blades had pierced her. The wounds healed up and in their place were two small tattoos – the numbers 44.

Lola sat up and looked down. She rubbed her belly. "I 'ate tattoos," she said. "Me mum will kill me."

Max sighed. "You've just become a Guardian, you ungrateful girl."

"Wot the fuck is 44?" she demanded. She rubbed her belly, almost trying to get the tattoos off.

"It is the number of the Guardian," Jonah replied.

"It means the rising of your consciousness," Max said. "Oh, the irony."

Lola rubbed her belly again. "Yoo fuckin' stabbed me!" she cried, leaping off the altar.

"If we told you we were going to do that, you wouldn't have done it," Max snapped.

"No fuckin' shit," she growled. "It don't look nice! 'Ow can I wear crop tops now?" Lola pouted.

Max walked over to her slowly, pulled her arm and brought her face up to his. "Stop whining, Pitchfork," he whispered.

Lola stared into his eyes and pulled her arm free. "I'm a

fuckin' Guardian...yoo can't tell me wot to do."

Max looked as if he could actually explode. Of course, she was right. Lola was now the same level as he was. She was a Guardian...Oh dear Lodge Masters. He let go of her arm and breathed deeply in.

There was so much to being one. She would have so much to learn and Max believed her to know so very little. However, he had to concede that her abilities were Guardian class. The Putney Lodge and cues had given ALL their custodians extreme abilities in a very, very short space of time. Max was a stickler for order, rules and discipline. He followed rules often without question. What was happening in Putney, in his view, was close to chaos. He had a very good idea why it was happening and there was little he could do about it.

He had been contemplating stripping them all of their powers, if they survived this day. He looked over at Lola and was now looking at a fellow Guardian. There were moments he thought she was actually mad. He didn't know whether she was very brave or generally had no concept of endangerment. She was fearless and now she bore the mark of a Guardian. The Eight Ball ritual could only be carried out by three carrying that mark and the mark could only be given to one who had developed sufficient strength and power that they could withstand the transition from initiate to Guardian. Max remembered his time. It had taken him years to work on his abilities and strengths. His cue had worked with him, slowly.

His transition had been frightening, painful and exhilarating. Lola just seemed to be angrier and now even more powerful. What niggled Max more was that he knew that as she was the same class as himself, he could not strip her powers – alone.

The powers she had developed with her cue would remain with her forever. She would soon need to hand back her cue as it would be seeking out another initiate to work with. (He hoped at a much slower rate.) He thought about the other Vampire Killers. All of them, (including the unconscious ones!) had Guardian level powers. Each one could withstand the transition. Of course, there was so much more to being a Guardian. There were examinations, training of others,

359

mentoring of others, moral responsibilities and duties. He tried to imagine Lola teaching. He tried to imagine her at a meeting of the Guardians. What on earth would the Masters say? Eyebrows were definitely going to be raised – higher than they had ever been raised before.

Jonah cleared his throat, trying to get Max's attention.

Max was about to say something when a massive gust of wind smashed through the church doors.

Jonah held out his hand. The Eight Ball was emitting a huge red light. It was now covering Jonah's body.

Max was about to say something when another gust of wind blasted through the Church, making the doors bang loudly. Max looked out through the stained-glass window. The sky was turning black. Something was coming. Lola saw that Max seemed taken aback.

Lola looked down at Eric. "It's probably wheelbarrow man having a bad dream."

Max glanced down at Eric, muttering in his sleep. Maybe he was controlling the weather. Great Lodge – maybe he was more dangerous asleep than awake. He looked over at the sacks of female pirates. Please don't wake up, he prayed. Not yet.

He looked back out of the window just as a bolt of lightning struck it – making the glass shatter across the floor.

He picked up Eric, grabbed Lola's arm. "Come with me," he said. "We've got to open the portal now!"

63

Fergus kneeled down and averted his eyes from the Queen in front of him. He could sense her rage as if it were his own. Her fury and hatred pounded in his head.

He slowly raised his eyes to look up at her. Her eyes were white and soulless. Fergus had made a deal with the Devil and there was no return – no redemption, no salvation. He was Quilloks now. He glanced at the other hundreds of Quilloks surrounding her. Had they also been human once?

He remained kneeling.

The Queen spoke to him and as she did, lightning shot out from her mouth and struck the walls of the gigantic cloud ship. The walls looked organic – alive even. The ship shuddered and rocked.

Fergus observed his Queen. She was twice the height of her guards and her scales were gun metal grey. She wore a pendant around her neck, which was the shape of the Eight Ball. It was glowing red. She had a fish tail, and when she stood up it turned to long, scaly legs with black claws for toes.

The failure of the Boat Race massacre had displeased her. The energy of the bombs, the shock of a watching world would have created enough energy for all the vampire ships with the vampire mermen on board to break permanently through the thin walls of the Earth dimension. It should've been so very easy.

The Lodge was meant to have been weakened. The Vampire Killers were meant to have been has-beens and never-was-es. Yet THEY had stopped the explosions. They had killed her vampire Quilloks. She had thought that once

361

her hybrid species had broken through, it would only be a matter of time before they would create such a dense atmosphere of fear, death and pain that she could just open a portal door and walk in.

This plan had failed. No explosions. Worse, the antics of the Oxford crew had brought much amusement to millions. She looked over at the membrane wall and the image of the crew passing under Richmond Bridge flashed on it, pursued by boats and a helicopter and people laughing.

She held the Eight Ball around her neck and smiled demonically at Fergus. Her smile was symbolic of their pact to him. Fergus knew that karma was very precise. Just as he had betrayed Carl, Katie and the Lodge, he himself had been betrayed. He had never seen Katie again. The Queen had held her prisoner within the same prison dimension, occasionally taunting him, fuelling his despair and rage.

Katie. He would have done anything for her. He would have done anything to protect her. His loyalty had always been to her.

The Queen hissed loudly and spoke softly. "The ritual begins," she said. "They have started. Prepare the ships."

Fergus looked at the membrane wall and saw the image of the church on the common. The sky had gone black, as if it was night, and it was raining hard. His thoughts turned to Carl.

Carl had discovered his own infinity cube.

Impressive. Did he know what powers could come his way? Did he know what an infinity cube was?

When Fergus had left the Lodge, the cues were used for games of pool and for stabbing the occasional vampire through the heart. They knew very little about their cues. The Lodge had bizarrely been neglected by other Lodges and by the Guardians. It was as if it had been put in hibernation.

When he had made a deal with the Queen, he had learnt so much.

She had accelerated his learning to an incredible speed. He learnt about magic, time travel, artifact engineering. He had been away for an earth year and had learnt the equivalent of decades of study. Fergus had learnt to harness his abilities while using his cue as a power source.

Stealing his cue had been part of the deal. The Queen had hoped that breaking up the seven cues would weaken their collective power. She thought if one was corrupted then the others would be poisoned through their powerful link. She thought Fergus would be strong enough to destroy them and she wanted revenge! Revenge on Max. Revenge on his cue. Revenge on the planet that banished her! She had watched and waited and along came Fergus. Too delicious. She had laughed to herself over and over at her plan. The delight in using a cue custodian as the destroyer of the earth – the delight in corrupting one who was meant to be a Protector and the Protector of Max's cue.

When Fergus did return to the earth plane, his powers had grown so extensively he could be ranked at Guardian level, if not higher. As he re-entered the earth plane, the link between the cues did strengthen – very quickly. However, just as one cue custodian grows in power, so do all others. In her pursuit of revenge, this minor detail was overlooked.

Fergus thought about his cue. He no longer was in possession of it. He knew his Queen was displeased and he knew the consequences of her displeasure. Self-preservation was very much a human trait. There was a part of him, therefore, that was still human and he wanted to survive. How much longer he would have his extensive powers without his cue, he didn't know. He would have to act fast.

He looked at his Queen. Not even the mighty Putney Lodge could stop her. Thousands of ships were poised to break through the portal when the Eight Ball ritual started. He looked at the Eight Ball around her neck. He lowered his eyes and closed them.

64

The sky was pitch black when Marilyn and the others landed outside the church. The streetlights had not come on. Marilyn could see people inside the pub on the corner looking out the window and looking at their watches. He could imagine the conversation: "Dark, innit?"

The streets were empty. The storm and the lightning had sent people into their homes and into pubs. Many were following the antics of the Oxford crew – which had long gone through Richmond and was still going.

Marilyn turned and looked at the church as another bolt of lightning hit the wall. His neck tingled. He knew that feeling so well. Vampires. Old school vampires. He looked over the common towards the cemetery. He turned to Bert, Johnny and Sophie.

"Get ready. Don't let anything get into the church," he said to them.

Sophie squinted and saw hundreds of dark shadowy figures coming towards them. They raised their cues and Marilyn lit up a cigarette. He was wearing a long red wig and a glamourous silver sequined ball dress. His make-up was exquisitely done and he wore knee-length silver-heeled boots. Oh yes, he was ready for battle.

Max, Jonah and Lola stood over the altar and put the glowing red ball in the middle of it. Jonah's eyes were closed. It was clear that he was still containing the energy of the Eight Ball and it was painful. The three of them linked hands and the glowing red colour passed around all three of them. Jonah felt a sense of relief as he shared that energy. Lola's extra-human strength meant she could take on more than the others and it was not a good feeling. She felt a pang of admiration for Jonah, who had been holding the energy in him with very little complaint.

Lola opened her mouth to say something but red light came out of it. She wanted to talk but all that came out was a symbol in red. No sound at all. She looked at the symbol floating in the middle of the altar and Max glared at her. He shook his head. She was curious that she had tried to say 'Max' but that symbol had come out. He raised his leg and with his foot he kicked the symbol away from the altar and it disappeared. His look at Lola said: "DO NOT ever do that again." She felt an urge to giggle and part of her wondered what that would look like.

Jonah took in a deep breath and he looked down at the Lodge book next to the Eight Ball. He opened his mouth and a string of symbols in red came out of his mouth and entered into the Eight Ball.

Max read from his Lodge book and a string of red symbols floated from his mouth and entered into the Eight Ball. The Eight Ball was still flashing but it began to get faster.

Max nudged Lola and he gestured for her to read a certain line from the book. She read it and symbols came out of her mouth – which she found truly amazing. Wow…was all she could think. Her symbols were also red and they entered into the Eight Ball.

They repeated this process, the symbols progressing in colour from red, orange, yellow, green, blue, indigo and violet. When the final colour entered into the ball, the ball levitated in the middle of the altar and it started to spin furiously. All the colours could be seen in it and as it got faster and faster the colours blurred into a white light. The Eight Ball began to crack.

Max dropped Lola's and Jonah's hands. He turned to Lola. "Now we find out if it's the real Eight Ball or not."

365

Marilyn took a deep drag on his cigarette and watched as hundreds of vampires began to approach them. They were old-style vampires. None of them were pretty and they weren't angst-ridden. Very few were wearing black leather jackets and even fewer were wearing hair product. They weren't hybrid vampire Quilloks warriors but they were still vampires. They were dangerous and they could kill.

One of the side effects of performing the Eight Ball ritual was that it attracted vampires within a ten mile radius. It was entirely possible some of them were from Haringey!

"There are hundreds of them," whispered Sophie, holding her cue rest out in front of her. "We can't kill them all."

"We protect the church," Marilyn ordered. "The ritual must continue."

"But you're wearing a ball dress," Bert protested, looking Marilyn up and down.

Marilyn took another long hit on his cigarette. "Do you think I'd be dressed like this, mate, if I couldn't handle myself?"

Bert considered this for a moment and nodded in acknowledgement.

"Here they come," Marilyn said, as he extended an arm forward.

Sophie took a deep breath and prayed. Johnny hoped another ability would manifest and Bert thought about his stomach. It was churning.

65

Lola stared down at the Eight Ball. To think all this fuss was over that little bit of plastic-looking crap. Could that thing really bring about the end of the world? It all seemed so pointless to her.

Here she was – a Guardian. What a laugh! She was a Guardian and she was part of the Eight Ball ritual. Her new status meant she could now go to dinners and everything! She wouldn't be left out anymore. Lola felt a sense of pride and was mentally choosing an outfit to wear to a posh dinner when she noticed the crack in the ball was widening – intense white light was exploding out of it. (She had thought that any light coming out of it would've been red and sparkly like before).

Max looked at the white light for as long as he could before averting his eyes. He took a deep breath and picked up his former cue. He held it tightly.

The white light touched his mind and questions and thoughts burst forward. He didn't know whether they were his questions. It felt like his thoughts but he wasn't sure. He thought about the cue in his hands. Yes, it had once been his and it had taught him well. There had been other custodians since his time but it was presently assigned to Fergus and Fergus's custodianship had never been revoked. It had been Max's decision not to do this. Max could have severed the cue from the other six. He could've severed Fergus's custodianship. He hadn't.

It had been Max who had decided to keep the present-day Putney Lodge custodians in the dark about many things. He

367

had had to. There had been no choice, he justified to his mind.

The Great Putney Lodge at all costs had to be protected and keeping its profile low throughout the Lodge network had been and was, unfortunately, necessary. Having easily removable custodians had also been necessary, but they had become distinctly less removable. It was this strange group of misfits who now stood between a possible inter-dimensional demonic invasion force of thousands and the end of the world. Max fought an urge to laugh. That lot! Hah!

Where was the other one? Where was Carl? What had happened to him? Max guessed he must've got lost in time. Maybe he would be the only survivor; trapped somewhere – trapped...where wheelbarrow man had been.

Max flicked his eyes over to Lola. Eric had been sent forward in time by the Lodge to follow Carl. Lola had opened a portal where Eric had been. Carl had to be on the other side of the portal! There could be a way to get to him.

The white light entered Max's mind further. It now felt like a powerful and intelligent force in his head. Max had experienced this before in his life, but it had been a long time ago, when the seven cues had combined to bring forth the white light.

The seven colours had now once again combined.

As the white light began to explode out of the crack in the Eight Ball, it began to spin around the ball and expand. Lola had her eyes firmly shut when Jonah and Max reached for her hands, forming a circle around the ball.

Lola found she could start to hear thoughts in her head. She wasn't entirely sure what it was she was experiencing. She saw pictures and moving images she was sure had nothing to do with her. She found herself understanding that the white light would contain any evil the ball blasted out. This was not the problem, she felt Max think. Whether the Eight Ball was real or not was irrelevant. It was the opening of the portal that was the danger. This was when the earth became vulnerable.

Lola felt Jonah thinking about the invasion force coming. Max and Jonah found themselves thinking about dinner dresses. Lola began to feel Max's thoughts about the Lodge and he her thoughts about him climbing ladders in a mining helmet.

Lola began to receive information about the cues and the Lodge. She was connected to these two Guardians. The two men had worked together for years but Lola's mind was something new to Max and Jonah. Max felt as if he was getting electric shocks from her while being assaulted by strange images of a TV chef.

Lola felt a sense of relief that all cues and the cue rest had been assigned. Max was feeling that if Fergus was still a custodian it didn't seem to matter. If Max had performed the ritual separating Fergus and his cue when both custodian and cue had been absent, the cue would've been lost forever. It would've been destroyed in the process. The power of the Seven would never be, or so he thought.

Max supposed that the cue in his hands was incapacitated. It could not serve Fergus, as he was evil and corrupt. He could, he supposed, sever it now and free it up. Free it up to choose another custodian. Would there be time?

"Yes," Lola thought to him. "For fuck's sake, do it, buttercup."

"Do NOT call me buttercup!" Max replied back to her. Jonah laughed out loud.

The Eight Ball was encased in expanding white light. The inside of the church was filled with blinding white light as Max began to whisper an incantation. It was fortunate he was in a church with two other Guardians! A separation ritual needed both these things. Great Lodge, did they need some good fortune!

Max felt the cue shake violently in his hands before it broke away and flew straight through the church window and out into the sky.

"Fly...be free!" Lola cried.

Max's nostrils flared with indignation.

369

66

The stolen Time Police ship hurtled its way towards the planet Earth. The bridge was swamped with smoke – the crew were unconscious apart from Maisie, the Staff Guardian and Carl. Maisie's nose was bleeding and she had a gash across her forehead. The horns on the Staff Guardian's Viking helmet were now gigantic. She roared with laughter as she blew up four Time Police ships. Hundreds were close behind.

The gap in the shield wrapped around the Earth was now a tiny slither – they were only moments away from it.

The Staff Guardian plotted the course directly for it as another two blasts smashed into their ship.

Carl closed his eyes and prayed.

Bert and Johnny raised their cues and held them towards the hundreds of vampires swarming their way. Bert thought he saw something streak by them – like a large stick. Whatever it was, it was moving at incredible speed and went right up into the air.

Bert looked over towards the church and found himself distracted by the incredible light beaming inside it. A light which seemed to be contained within its walls; it didn't flood through the broken window and onto them. It was all part of the magic, he figured. He understood so very little of it. Marilyn had told them that Lola was in there. When he asked 'why?'

he'd been shhd.

Bert turned back and scrutinized the distorted faces of the vampires before him. Some were old, young, ugly and even pretty. They were all, however, a deathly white colour and many were baring enormous fangs. The older the vampire, he had been told, the longer the fangs. Some of them must be ancient, he thought.

He had never been up this close to so many vampires before and one thing he really realized was that they stank. It was a combination of a sewer and bad breath. It wasn't the fighting that would be the problem – it would be how long he could hold his breath to fight them with. Bert reached into his pocket and pulled out some chewing gum and quickly stuffed some pieces up his nose. Johnny noticed this and held out his hand. Bert gave him a couple of pieces and Johnny copied. Sophie just seemed to be staring ahead of her and Johnny felt a pang of pity for her. Poor girl.

"Sophie," he said. Sophie turned to look at him; her eyes seemed terrified. She was so different to Lola, who marched into everything like a crazed warrior, oblivious to the notion of being harmed. She was more vulnerable and Johnny felt a chivalrous energy sweep through him.

"Get on the back of my cue," he said. Sophie scuttled over as Johnny lowered his cue and it began to hover. Sophie threw her leg over and sat on it. Johnny then got on and she put one arm around him.

"Aim for their hearts and their heads," he said to her. Sophie nodded and was grateful she wasn't going to face the vampires on her own.

Marilyn inhaled deeply. "Ready, kittens?" he asked the others.

"No," they all replied together.

"Tough titties," Marilyn said, "It's time to dance."

Marilyn kicked a leg forward and a massive silver bolt shot out from his stiletto. The energy bolt went through the hearts of at least ten vampires, who fell to the floor and went up in smoke.

"Meet my sexy silver boots of death, corpse-walker scum!" Marilyn cried.

Bert's face was hard to describe. Fear, bewilderment and

371

admiration came close. He gawped as he watched the Guardian high kick silver energy bolts at hundreds of vampires from his stilettos.

The vampires, who were about fifty feet away, began to run at them.

Holy shit, Bert thought. There are too many of them.

Bert threw his leg over his cue and hovered next to Johnny and Sophie.

Sophie raised her cue rest in her arm and held it forward like a jouster.

"Let's do it," she whispered, as she felt courage pour into her.

Johnny took a deep breath and shouted, the only clichéd thing he could think of... "Charge!"

The three of them stormed forward into the oncoming army.

As the Vampire Killers swept through the sea of vampires, blasting them, kicking them, blowing the heads off the ones trying to get into the church, Marilyn hovered up into the air, spinning around and around, releasing a multitude of blasts from his heels. Bert was sure he heard him cackling with laughter (possibly even singing), but could not be sure with all the noise going on.

Energy bolts were blasted from the cues and Bert had the edge with his phenomenal speed. He swept through them, around them and knocked them down.

Vampires exploded, went up in smoke, heads were decapitated, as cues and cue rest blasted and staked wave after wave of vampires. Bert checked out the destruction they had caused. The common was becoming emptier, as they killed wave upon wave of vampires. He felt exhilarated and proud. He felt a connection to all previous Vampire Killers and a connection to all the other custodians. He felt the tradition enter into his bones and he knew what it was to be a member of the Great Putney Lodge.

He looked over into the horizon with the pride of a job well done... and noticed that thousands more vampires were storming their way.

Thousands!

"Oh my God," he whispered. "Johnny!" he shouted. "Look... LOOK!"

372

Johnny, who was hovering high above the vampires (he had learnt from his own death that vampires could leap very high, thank you very much), looked to where Bert was pointing. Oh, shit! was the only thing he could think of. He would normally have thought about running for it but he thought more about protecting Sophie, and this was a strange thing for him to be so concerned about another.

Sophie looked over into the distance and could not believe her eyes. She had never seen so many people, let alone vampires, pile onto Putney Common before. What was worse, some of the vampires were flying.

Bert and Johnny swallowed hard. Now, this was definitely something new! Hundreds of flying vampires were coming their way. Flying vampires were known only to inhabit Camden. What were they doing down here?

Bert looked over towards Barnes and saw what he hoped would not happen – zombies – hundreds of them, lurching their way.

Oh fuck, he thought. Oh, fucking fuck.

67

Lola looked at the white light for as long as she could and had to turn her head away. The noise of battle outside drummed through her head and what was that smell? God!

She thought she heard a noise coming to the left of her and she looked down. Eric was stirring. He was slumped in the pink bathrobe next to the altar with his cue glued firmly in is hand. His cue had become very protective and would not be budged! Eric opened his eyes and Lola mentally prepared for the screaming and the shrieking and was thinking of zapping him unconscious with her cue again but there was something different about his eyes. It was like looking at a different person.

Max and Jonah were still linked into Lola's mind and they followed suit and squinted over at Eric, shielding their eyes from the light.

Eric stood to his feet, the pink dressing gown barely halfway down his thighs, and he began to spin the cue around his head like an expert Vampire Killer. Hmm…Max thought. Lola picked this up and said out loud: "Hmmm."

Lola was not sure what was going on. It didn't feel like the same person in front of her but he didn't feel evil; just different.

The Eight Ball was splitting further and further apart – blasting out more and more white light, bathing the Guardians, Eric and the female pirates in it and filling every inch of the church. The building began to violently shake as if it could not contain the power of it any longer.

Plaster fell from the ceiling and smashed onto the altar. A

huge cross fell over, crashing onto the floor, and the floor was vibrating. Lola almost fell over but Max pulled her up and close to him.

Eric stood to his feet and he stood proud and tall. Max scrutinized him as much as he could and he knew Eric now felt familiar. In the past the presence had been diluted. This was concentrated.

Eric looked up to the ceiling for a moment and then turned towards Jonah, Max and Lola. He smiled warmly as he began to levitate. Jonah and Max nodded towards him, as if they recognized him. Lola pouted and covered her head as another piece of plaster hit her shoulders.

Eric levitated past Jonah and Max and floated outwards towards the broken window. He floated over Lola's head. She looked up and wished she hadn't. Ugh! She would never get that image out of her head! She watched him float out of the window and then she couldn't see him anymore. Thank God! Looking after him had been a right pain in the arse.

Max's jaw seemed to have dropped slightly and Jonah looked almost dewy eyed. Lola held onto the altar as the church shook faster and faster.

What was the squeaking noise? she asked in her head. She tried to get a fix on where that annoying noise was coming from. She looked left, right, up and down and then she realized…it was coming from behind her.

She turned around to see that some of the female pirates had awoken and had made their way out of the bag.

They seemed to have hangovers. They were angry and the bright white light wasn't helping their mood.

"Maaaaax," Lola said.

"What?" Max growled, holding onto the altar.

"Look," Lola replied. Max did as she asked.

"Bollocks," he whispered. He had said that a few times today already. It probably wouldn't be the last.

375

68

Marilyn high-kicked dozens upon dozens of energy bolts at the oncoming vampires, sending them back to the hellhole they came from. He was bellowing out a well-known show tune or two as the vampires exploded beneath. "HAH!" he yelled below. "This is nothing, babies. Wait until Auntie Marilyn really gets going!"

He was high kicking and twirling when he suddenly stopped.

Flying vampires…hundreds of them…

Marilyn's instincts were to create an illusion to frighten them away. He felt his energy reserves; they were low. Maybe…maybe soon he would get the energy back again to create something but not right now. Now, it was hand to heel combat.

A swarm flew towards Johnny, Bert and Sophie. Marilyn saw Bert move around the enemy as a blur but Johnny and Sophie were visible to these vampires.

Marilyn thought about why Johnny would be invisible to humans but not vampires. Surely the cue would make him invisible to the enemy. Unless, Johnny perceived humans as more of a threat? Marilyn felt a strange stirring of suspicion but before he could give it any more thought, he found himself knocked to the floor. Dozens of vampires surrounded him, fangs bared and eyes full of hunger.

"I better not have laddered my tights, mate," Marilyn whispered, bearing his teeth back at them.

Bert stormed towards a batch of twenty flying vampires. They were flying above tree-top level without any kind of device. They were quick and agile and they made a strange moaning noise.

These vampires seemed younger. In fact, they looked like Goths. Perhaps they had been turned back in the mid-1980s. It was hard to tell with lots of black clothes and eye liner; perhaps they were retro-Goths who had been recently turned. Anyway, it was a pointless train of thought. They were the enemy– even if they looked as though they were a bunch of depressed teenagers. Bert thought about the boy up in the attic. They seemed the same age and this played on Bert's mind for a moment but not for too long. A smile broke across his face – he was going to enjoy this.

Bert saw a gap between their formation and zig-zagged between them. The first male vampire (possibly female, it was hard to tell) got a punch straight across the jaw and he fell straight down onto a clump of zombies, knocking them to the floor.

The zombies obviously thought this was some kind of aerial pizza delivery system and instantly began to tuck in. They also then decided that they didn't like vampire at all and left the half-eaten vampire on the floor before they lurched forwards towards the church.

Zombies are not really known for their intellectual train of thought, although there had been cases of highly intelligent zombies within the area of Barnes. Barnes village had long suffered a zombie infestation (plus zombie cultists) and over the years the Barnes Lodge had acquired the greatest collection of zombie folklore anywhere in the world. Technically, their Lodge should have stopped the zombies coming over the border into Putney. However, Putney should have stopped mind-controlled barmaids disguised as the Oxford boat crew entering into their territory, which they had been very busy trying to sort out in the public eye of the media! So, up yours, was the closest interpretation of this gesture.

The remaining Goth vampires growled at Bert. Although they were fast and agile they did not have the speed and dexterity of Bert. One female Goth hissed at Bert and spat at him as he dashed past her.

How ladylike, thought Bert before he turned at high speed and blasted her in the chest with an energy bolt. Another pizza delivery fell to earth!

This outraged the others. They bared their fangs and hissed in unison. Bert flew up as high as he could, pursued by the others on his tail. One of them was much faster than the others but she was no match for Bert's speed. Bert suddenly stopped and as she flew by him he kicked her in the stomach and she went cascading downwards. Marilyn had been right; sometimes you don't need magic. Bert grinned to himself. Should he be enjoying this so much?

He flew upwards and upwards and began a head-first descent onto the vampires beneath him at alarming speed. His cue sent out dozens of energy bolts and vampire after vampire fell down to earth.

May all under-tippers have the same fate, Bert thought as he looped the loop and plunged downwards towards the next batch.

Max looked down at the tiny pirates and some of them clocked him peering at them. One gave him the finger and jeered at him. Another one mooned him and slapped her butt. One scratched her head, looking seriously hung-over and angry as if trying to work out where the fuck she was and why. As a basic plague force that could be programmed to take on any form, thinking was not their specialty; more point them in the right direction and run – preferably to another planet.

Max had seen this type of thing before. He knew that the only way to deal with a force you can't fight is to immobilize them by knocking them out or by removing them from your particular dimension.

Lola raised her cue and aimed it at one of them. Max grabbed her wrist, stopping her. "No, Pitchfork. You can't fight them. Physical strength is useless with them."

Lola almost fell forward as the shaking of the building was becoming more violent. Max pulled Lola towards him to stabilize her as a piece of plaster hit a pirate. She doubled in size.

Lola whistled to her cue and it shot next to her side. She broke free of Max's grip and swung a leg over her cue. She swooped down and picked up the sacks, also grabbing and pushing the loose pirates in them.

"What are you doing? We're in the middle of a ritual!" Max shouted over the noise of the crashing plaster and the battle outside.

"Ain't me bit over? Do ya still need me or somefink? Time is money!" Lola shouted back at him. Max had to think about this for just moment. No, she wasn't needed for the immediate moment. The ritual needed three to open and close the portal. Whatever she was planning to do she had better do it quickly. Removing the threat was completely the right thing to do. What that maniac was planning to do with the pirates he had no idea and in many ways didn't want to ask. He couldn't order her around. She was able to make these life and death decisions now and he had to abide by them.

"Don't attack them, don't shoot them and don't let them hit each other. They grow when they are attacked. And get back here as quickly as you can. We don't have much time," Max warned her. Lola looked at him dismissively.

"I didn't know ya cared, Max," Lola teased.

"I don't. You're a menace. Now bugger off," he huffed.

Lola flew off, ducking falling plaster and flew out of the smashed church window. Jonah was holding onto the altar.

"You make a charming couple," Jonah chuckled, batting his eyelashes at Max.

"Sod off," Max grunted at him. Jonah laughed as he was thrown backward.

The light was blinding and it began to form a massive crack across the ceiling of the church. The portal was beginning to open.

"Marilyn, where are you? Get in here," Max thought to his fellow Guardian.

"Sorry...a bit busy at the moment," Marilyn thought back. Marilyn was hovering in the sky, flicking his hand and releasing pink light circles from a bracelet which had a rather unusual effect on vampires. It first of all turned them pink. Their heads then expanded to three times their normal size then rapidly shrank to the size of a golf ball. This was followed by a small popping noise as their heads did, indeed, proceed to explode.

Marilyn had been thankful a cue custodian in a fluffy pink bathrobe had helped him out of a tricky situation. In fact, he could have sworn he recognized the man. There was something about the eyes; the confidence which seemed so familiar. He exuded a calm energy that few Guardians ever had.

It had been known that in times of great danger, one of the seven would return by inhabiting the body of a custodian. It also took a very particular type of custodian for this to happen to. Either a very noble and self-sacrificing character who would willingly act as a host or someone who was slightly vacant, for whatever reason best known to themselves.

Yet there was a much darker side to the ethics of hosting and it was considerably frowned upon within the Lodge community. In the times of the great Vampire Wars, there had been experimentation involving mind control. These experiments had been carried by both by evil and not so good alike. A mind would be broken and as it broke it splintered. Each splinter would be host to a different personality that would not be aware of the others. Each personality could be independently programmed to perform a different role. Combined with dark magic, magicians could load a victim's mind with the spirits of those who had passed on and communicate with them as and when they needed them. They could also memorise entire books and spells and operated as a Victorian computer database. Huge amounts of information could be hidden and easily accessed by the victim's handler. The host would not even be aware they held such information.

The ethics of these experiments meant they had been outlawed throughout the international Lodges. But there were those who believed the laws were for the sheep and the laws of the rabble did not affect them.

Their victims had similar characteristics and if you knew what to look out for you could recognize them. One of them would be that magic would seem to seek them out in one way shape or form. Strange things would seem to happen to a

380

normal person. Another one was a peculiar twitching of the eyes and shifting of the shoulders but only a trained eye would notice it.

It was entirely possible that if one of the seven had taken hold of Eric, it would be because Eric had been mind-controlled at some point or was being mind-controlled. It would also be hard to say how many personalities he could potentially possess. It was good to know there was possibly one of the seven down there but it revealed something possibly more sinister. Was Eric still being mind-controlled and by whom? It was also possible that the recent events had been sufficient cause to affect his mind and they – the Putney Lodge – were, in fact, responsible. Questions would need to be asked.

Marilyn spun around and around shooting out pink light as Lola shot by him, holding two sacks over her left shoulder.

"Oi Oi," Marilyn shouted after Lola.

"I'm a fuckin' Guardian," Lola shouted over her shoulder. "Woo hoo."

"Yesss," Marilyn said. Four Guardians were better than three. Marilyn looked down at the church and saw a light show going on inside. He knew that the portal was opening and that it would have to be shut almost immediately. The Eight Ball, fake or real, would need to be sent through it and the doorway sealed quickly...before anything decided to take advantage of the opening. Tricky, he thought. Very tricky.

69

Maisie was holding onto consciousness and she tried to breathe through the billowing smoke on the bridge. She fired repeatedly on the Time Police onslaught which was closing in like a pack of predators pursuing wounded prey.

The Staff Guardian had a look of steely determination and then she frowned. The gap in the shield had closed. She knew what it meant to hit the shield. It meant destruction.

Lola flew very high up and over towards the Thames. The rain pelted down and the sky was black. Lola hovered over the water and could barely see what was beneath her. The weight of the sacks was increasing and Lola knew what that meant. They were fighting each other to get bigger.

Lola was acting on instinct and it told her to remove the threat from the church. How she was going to stop them, she didn't know. She knew that it was only a matter of time before they became huge. How big they would become she had no idea.

Lola felt a pull in her being towards the Thames. She felt a connection there; a sense of comradeship; a place of help. She had felt a change since the ritual. Her perception had heightened. She felt a sense of knowing she couldn't explain and she knew the Thames was where she had to go.

It was so very dark and the weather was so very cold. The air had a demonic taste to it and it was the first time her sense of taste had been used in this way. She could taste evil. It had a distinct flavour. She also found it was true that good had a certain taste to it. She could taste it now – below.

The wind whooshed against her and rain splattered against her face and hair. She flew down over the murky Thames and heard the rain splashing and pattering on the water. Wind also howled around her and she sped across the water's surface. The sacks were getting heavier and she felt the material begin to tear.

Her instincts told her she was close…but where?

The material in the sacks ripped further and she felt fists starting to punch her in the back. Arms and legs were kicking and punching and they were strong blows.

One blow struck Lola in the neck. She lost concentration for a moment and swerved on her cue. She couldn't fight back as she was trying to stay on the cue. Another blow and then another. The weight was increasing faster and faster. Jeering and biting followed. The biting was vicious.

"Just yoo fuckin' wait!" Lola growled over her shoulder. "I'm 'avin' ya!"

The ripping and tearing increased and then it felt lighter as dozens of larger pirates fell down into the Thames.

For a moment they disappeared quietly under the water. She swooped over the water's surface, searching for any sign of life. Maybe they would drown, she thought. The triumph of hope over reality didn't last too long.

Within moments much, much larger pirates were swimming on the surface of the water. They must've been about six foot tall by now and they were heading towards the bank.

Just as one reached the bank, there was an enormous roar as a seven foot Poseidon leapt out of the water with five pirates clinging onto him.

Wot the fuck? she thought.

"There is still a dimensional tear in the sky," she heard Marilyn's voice in her head.

"Huh?" she replied. "A portally fing?" she asked.

"No, a tear-y thing," Marilyn snapped. "Open it and shove the dah-lings through."

"'Ave yoo seen the size of 'em?" she thought back as she

383

flew down towards the Poseidon thing, which did not feel evil to her at all. "Yoo shove 'em through!"

"Busy, mate," Marilyn thought back. "You're a Guardian. Get on with it."

How the fuck was she going to stop something she couldn't fight?

She swooped towards the Poseidon thing who was throwing the pirates around, making them grow.

"Oi, fish man person," Lola said. Fish man person stared at her but not threateningly. He held a trident cue in his hand and, as a Guardian, Lola recognized that he was a cue bearer. Lola was vainly pleased she hadn't been turned into a large fish man. Before she had joined the Vampire Lodge she had had no idea such a thing could happen. Would that happen to her later? How would she attend posh dinners if it did?

The fish man was throwing even more pirates around.

"Yer gotta stop attackin' 'em. It just makes 'em bigger," Lola said. Pete was still able to understand everything that she said and had actually been enjoying himself as a mini-god of the water. These pirates were proving to be a problem.

"We need to get 'em up into the sky," she said. "There's a tear-y thing up there and we need to shove 'em though it."

Pete had no idea what she was talking about but he knew instinctively she was an ally. As a cue custodian his abilities had expanded in line with the others and at a considerable rate. His cue had assigned him aquatic powers. He could breathe under water and move with incredible dexterity. As the Quilloks were fish demons, an ally in the waters had clearly been deemed necessary.

When the next pirate attacked him, he touched her head and threw her forwards. As she flew through the air she transformed into a large fish. He repeated this numerous times.

'Ow the fuck is that gonna 'elp? Lola thought.

"Pitchfork!" Max thought to her. "Get on with what you're doing and get back here."

"But he's turnin' pirates into fish!" she thought back.

"I don't care!" Max bellowed at her. "It's almost time!"

The pirates were swarming over Pete and he was

transforming them into huge fish, who then proceeded to ram each other...becoming bigger. Soon all the pirates had been transformed into another shape but their aggression and purpose was still the same. There was a difference, they were contained in the water – at least for the moment.

Pete opened his mouth, finding it hard to speak.

"Go and open the tear-y thing," he said with a glimmer of humour in his voice. There was a sound of gargling in it but only faintly.

"Wot ya gonna do?" Lola asked.

"You just watch," he said in a deep voice. Lola rolled her eyes and flew up towards the sky. Jonah had said she had a talent for portal things – her super strength affording her certain abilities.

She flew up high in the sky and she scrutinized her surroundings. As she looked, she could actually perceive a rip in the sky about 100 feet long where the clouds had been. It was sealed but it was weakly sealed. It was a fresh cut. Lola took a deep breath and thought to her cue to open it up. Her cue tip let out a bright emerald light which reached out and touched the rip. She was delicate so as to open it as little as possible. God only knew what was behind there – anything was possible. It was not that she wasn't ready for it but she had learnt there are enemies you can't attack with strength.

The light penetrated the tear and it started to open.

"Fish man," she shouted. "Get on with it!"

Pete was being surrounded and attacked by dozens of fish but there was another ability that a mini-god of the waters had and that was dominion of those in water. Pete raised himself to his full height on the surface of the water, held out his trident and roared loudly. He thrust his trident in the direction of the fish, let out an enormous orange bolt of energy and the fish pirates went still.

He extended his other hand towards the water and the water started to spin and spin and spin. Pete concentrated and the water began to rise in the spiral up towards the sky, up towards Lola who was concentrating on holding the tear-y thing apart.

His trident let out another bolt of energy towards the

385

passive fish surrounding him and they began to move in single file towards the spiral. One by one they journeyed into the spiral and one by one they were sucked up towards the sky.

Lola saw the spiral behind her and she knew she had to get it to connect with the opening. Lola focused on bringing the tear-y thing closer to the spinning water, which was not connecting. She looked down the funnel and saw that some parts of the fishes were turning back into pirates. It appeared Pete's transformation ability didn't last that long.

Lola focused harder and she saw that some of the pirates were trying to make their way out of the spiral.

Oh no, fish bitch, she thought. Yoo ain't goin' nowhere!

Lola pulled the tear-y thing closer and closer and just as a group of pirates were about to break free, the spiral and the tear-y connected.

"Push," she shouted down to Pete.

Pete roared, pointed his trident at the spiral and pushed the water upwards with incredible force.

Lola watched as the water went gushing through the tear, taking the pirates with it. There were jeers and yells and screaming as one by one the pirates were sucked through. When all the pirates were taken, Lola thought to her cue and a bright emerald light shot out of it. Lola was speedily repairing the hole. God, how many holes were there over the planet?

Lola watched as the tear knitted itself together. Just as it was about to close one giant fish about fifty feet long pushed its head through it, trying to rip it apart again. Lola's eyes narrowed and she flew closer up to it. She brought her small body up to it, smiled sweetly and pulled her fist as far back as she could take it. The fish actually managed to give an expression of surprise as a super-strong tiny fist punched it straight back through the tear. She blasted the tear with as much light as she could, seeing through the crack that many of the fish creatures were the size of houses and trying to get back through.

"Yoo really stink!" she growled at them, smelling her hand and wrinkling her nose. "This better wash off."

She used her strength to hold her cue as it blasted the

hole. She thought it would never end and then...the tear repaired. How long for? That she didn't know. She was new to all of this. Maybe once a tear always a tear.

Lola looked down towards the Thames beneath her and turned around on her cue and flew downwards. She could see the fish-man in the water and swooped down to his side. The rain was still so intense that everything seemed blurred.

"Fank yoo, fish man," she said.

Pete nodded back.

"Umm...I've got to go and save the world now," she said and added: "and then choose a dress."

Pete looked out over his watery domain. He turned to face Lola.

"I shall come," he whispered. Lola thought about this for a moment and then nodded.

"OK Fishy man...but keep up," she said before taking off into the sky and storming back to the church.

Pete rose to his full height on the water and looked at his trident and up at the sky. He instinctively knew that he controlled all waters and as long as he could touch it, he remained in this form. It was raining heavily and he watched it hit his scaly skin. He pointed his trident into the rain and pulled a stream of it towards him so that it was suspended in mid-air in the shape of a large ball. He watched it for a moment before turning it into ice and then into the shape of a chariot. He levitated himself upwards and brought himself down onto it.

Pete pointed his trident forward, the chariot rose upwards into the air and the fish-man rode the skies towards the church.

70

Johnny and Sophie were standing back to back, as a swarm of zombies had them surrounded. Sophie's cue-rest blasted out netting made of light that trapped her enemy and pinned it to the ground. She didn't seem to have an ability that actually managed to shoot a destructive bolt but the netting worked as a trap until another of the custodians could kill her captives. Dozens were trapped across the battle field and many of them were dead.

Sophie felt fully alive, fully focused and the concept of anything other than the moment she was in didn't exist. She felt courage and she felt a connection to all the others. She glanced upwards and saw Bert swooping about overhead. More flying vampires had arrived. It seemed that Bert's tactic was to get them onto the ground and hope that the zombies would wipe them out. He was so fast that he looked like a blur in the rain – the never-ending cold rain, plastering her hair against her face.

The light was getting brighter from the church – almost engulfing it. The more light there seemed to be the more enemies seemed to arrive. The Putney Vampire Killers were just a few against thousands…with more arriving.

Johnny blasted vampires and zombies again and again. His mind was on automatic pilot, aiming and shooting as wave upon wave kept coming up against him.

Marilyn was involved in a full-out fist-fight between six zombies. He threw a punch that knocked the jaw off one zombie before turning to another and kicking his heel through its thigh. He then head-butted another one, grabbed a blade from his garter-belt, taking the head off a smaller zombie at lightning speed, and smashed the heads together of two others.

Marilyn wanted to get into the church to help the others with the ritual but he couldn't get in there. He was halting dozens of vampires and zombies from getting into the church. Where was Lola? The light was getting bigger and brighter – the portal was about to be fully opened. They could not risk it being open for longer than a few seconds. Fake or real, it made no difference. The ritual for the Eight Ball Portal created one of the most vulnerable portals on the earth. It could not and must not be allowed to remain open for long. It would be like blood to a shark. All nearby dimensions could bleed in. This Eight Ball had been laced with dark magic and it was a danger in itself – regardless of its authenticity.

Max and Jonah were holding onto anything they could as their legs were being pulled off the ground and upwards into the light. The portal was almost fully open. Max thought to Lola but could not get a response. He shouted out loud for Marilyn.

The two men looked upwards and saw the portal opening up. The size of the portal was going to be immense – hundreds of feet across – and unprotected. The light was brighter and brighter and the wind pulled at them violently. Max lost his grip and was violently pulled upwards. Jonah released one of his hands and caught Max's foot. The strain was immense.

"You ain't going anywhere. You still owe me a fiver," Jonah shouted.

"Rubbish," Max shouted back. The force of the pull was incredible, sucking the air out of his lungs.

"Bloody woman..." he growled.

"Yoo talkin' about me?" Lola shouted, holding on to a statue nearby, almost upside down.

Max turned his head against the wind and saw Lola. "Pitchfork! Get over here."

Bit by bit, grabbing any object she could hold on to, she brought herself over to Jonah. With one hand she held herself down and reached up and grabbed Max's other foot. Jonah and Lola dragged Max back down towards them and they gripped onto each other tightly. Lola was not amused by the proximity of both men.

Max pulled his ritual book out from his pocket. The wind battered the pages as he turned to the correct place.

"Repeat whatever I say," he shouted.

Max began a series of words Lola didn't understand but she blindly copied them as best she could. He then tore at his sleeve to reveal tattoos, grabbed Lola's arm and placed his on hers. Lola felt a burning sensation and looked down at her arm. When Max took his arm away Lola could see that she had been left with a replica of a symbol. Another tattoo! It looked like a sun within a snake but she couldn't be sure.

Jonah exposed his sleeve and raised it to the sky, followed by Max and Lola. The three symbols on their arms began to glow with a golden light. The light emerged from their arms and combined above them in a large, formless shape. Lola watched as it seemed to turn into some kind of golden snake – it was huge. It opened its fangs and screeched towards the portal. Max looked down at the book again and began to read. Golden symbols came out from his mouth. He looked at Lola to urge her to copy and she did. She was amazed once again to see the floating symbols come out of her mouth instead of words. Jonah followed suit. Max read again and Lola copied. The symbols followed the snake upwards into the light. Lola looked upwards, squinting, but could barely see anything.

The walls were shaking, the light was blinding and there was a constant roaring noise in her ears. The three of them clung onto each other, with Lola's strength holding the two men downwards as furniture and statues went flying upwards. The Eight Ball that had been suspended in mid-air shot up and disappeared.

Lola held on and on. The pull was too much. It was too powerful. She felt her strength would not be enough and then…it stopped. Everything stopped. The light disappeared. Everything went quiet in the church.

The three of them released each other quickly and stepped away. Max looked around with cynical, questioning eyes. Jonah looked around as well.

Lola could hear the battle going on outside. Whatever had happened, it hadn't stopped that.

"Well, is it over?" Lola chirped.

Max and Jonah looked around and then at each other. The Eight Ball had gone. It had not broken. They had managed to contain the ball and remove it before it could break. If it was the real one, and it had broken, legend said there was a definite outcome to that. It being a fake had worried Max even more. The effort to create it and manipulate the Lodge Laws was extremely worrying. Max knew the Queen of the Quilloks was behind it. Had she managed to get through to the Earth dimension? Had they closed the portal in time?

Had anything got through? If so, where was it?

The real Eight Ball had been created by a human to find a way to end the fight between good and evil. A weapon made with good intent. How many people had died as a result of good intentions? But this human had been bitten and turned into vampire as he created it and legend had it that the Eight Ball could be wielded by good and evil alike. It had been so powerful it had been removed from the Earth dimension and hidden, or so the legend went. The ritual had to open a portal large enough so that nearby dimensions didn't get their hands on it.

"I don't know, Pitchfork," Max replied.

Max also turned his ear to the noise of battle outside and his instincts pulled at him. He didn't have a cue but he grabbed a metal pole from the ground and headed outside. Jonah followed suit. Lola looked up at the church roof – what was left of it anyway – and she shrugged. The rain was still belting down and the clouds were dark. She thought she saw something in the clouds – perhaps she did. More flying vampires?

Lola watched Jonah kick open the door, sending a handful of vampires flying. Some also pushed their way into the church. Come on, bitches, she thought to herself. She whistled to her cue and it shot into her hand.

71

Maisie and Carl stared at the closed shield around the Earth. A ferocious pulse wave blasted out from the shield and hit the stolen ship, shaking it violently. Maisie fell forward onto her console – her eyes almost closed. Carl rushed to her side. There was little he could do. He was in his astral body!

The Staff Guardian extended her arms forward, releasing a huge beam of light – an identical colour to the dark blue shield which shot out through the ship, into space and into the shield. Her face contorted as she chanted under her breath and a small crack opened in the shield. The stolen ship swept through – followed by twenty Time Police ships before the crack closed – leaving behind the rest of the fleet.

"Tally...bally...ho!" she cried and hooted with laughter as she plunged her ship towards south west London.

Fergus sat at the feet of his Queen. She had beckoned him over to her side and he had quickly obeyed. She smiled a vile and cruel smile as she looked at a membrane screen showing the battle.

"It is done," she hissed. "And it is all down to you. To your betrayal of your friends, your beliefs and your planet."

Fergus looked at the image. His features showed no emotion at all.

"How does it feel?" she chuckled. "To be responsible for so much death and destruction?"

"I live to serve you," Fergus said blankly. "The Earth means nothing to me".

"And your reward?" the Queen asked in a mocking tone.

"I live only to serve you," said Fergus.

"Good," hissed the Queen. She raised her scaly hand to the Eight Ball around her neck.

"It's time," she added.

Bert swept through the sky, relentlessly shooting vampires to the ground. He had lost track of the numbers – it just seemed to be endless.

Eric, in his pink dressing gown, and Marilyn in his torn ball dress, seemed to sum up the Putney Lodge to Max. Great Lodge! He was curious as to who or what was inhabiting Eric's body. He had an idea who it could be and the 'entity' was good but then his thoughts went darker as he thought about the Eight Ball. If it had been the real one (and it had broken) then the inability to tell good from evil was meant to be one of the effects of it breaking. How long the effects lasted for, no-one knew. When good cannot tell evil from itself, evil shall reign. This was why the Eight Ball was so feared.

Jonah was laying in deep to a dozen vampires and was destroying them with expert precision. The numbers were dwindling around them but there were still hundreds.

Bert was flying high up in the sky when he thought he had seen something and then...he was hit by an energy bolt and he fell off his cue. He was plummeting down to earth, turning around and around in the air, passing by jeering vampires, who hissed at him. He saw a giant fish-man, in what looked like a chariot, come by the side of him, equaling his velocity. The fish-man extended his arms and grabbed Bert and pulled him into his chariot.

Bert's cue had followed him and shot straight into his right hand. He extended his cue at the fish-man threateningly.

"Who are yoo?" Bert demanded.

"Pete," the fish-man replied.

"Pete?" Bert asked. "Strange name for a fish...thing."

393

Pete smiled and drove his chariot through the air. He extended his cue, pointing it into the rain and turning it into ice-spears. The spears flew through the sky, piercing the hearts of flying vampires. Bert hung on as the chariot spun around and swooshed down towards the ground.

Sophie had managed to pin down hundreds of vampires and Johnny was zapping them as she did so, working well together. In the near distance, Lola had emerged from the church, punching and kicking her way through vampire after vampire. Her thoughts had turned to Johnny and she felt a pang of concern. Was he OK? Was he alright? Was he lying somewhere injured?

Sophie was zapping a vampire, when one sprang out from nowhere, knocking her to the ground. Huge fangs came towards her neck, when Johnny decapitated it. He pulled Sophie to her feet and she gave him a hug.

"Oi," Lola barked. "Wot's goin' on 'ere?" as she stepped over a huge pile of zombie corpses. A vampire flew down at her and she punched it half way across the common.

"What?" Johnny asked, as he ducked down and stabbed a vampire in its heart. Sophie turned around and shot out another net over two zombies.

"Are yoo chattin' up me fiancé?" Lola demanded.

"Me?" asked Sophie with slight alarm and panting.

"Yeah. Well, just watch it..." she said, pointing at her. She then grabbed Johnny and kissed him and then ran off towards Max and Jonah. She had a feeling they needed her and she was now a Guardian, after all.

Bert and Pete flew through the sky, zapping and impaling vampires, while on the ground the others fought hard and quickly, dispatching the vampires and zombies with quickening speed. Marilyn high-kicked the head off the last-remaining zombies and looked at the Guardians and Vampire Killers around him. They had wiped out an army of zombies and vampires between them. The Eight Ball ritual had been performed and he, like Max, was internally holding his breath.

The others made their way over to the side of the Guardians. They were soaking wet and covered in mud and gunk. Pete landed his chariot next to Max, who merely raised an eyebrow.

"Alright, chap?" he asked. Pete nodded.

"Nice chariot," Max said.

"Thanks," Pete replied.

Lola looked around her and stopped at Johnny and Sophie. She frowned directly at Johnny who shrugged questioningly back at her. Lola pouted and turned her attention to Max.

"Is that it, then?" she asked.

Max inhaled and breathed out. "Believe it or not, Pitchfork, that seemed too easy."

Lola almost spluttered out the words: "Yoo wot?"

"Yeeesss," added Marilyn, looking down at his boots and seeming pleased that they were in good condition.

"That was easy?" Sophie added.

"Hmmm," said Jonah.

Bert coughed. "Yoo expecting more?" he asked.

Max looked up at the skies. "Those clouds are no ordinary clouds. They're hiding something," he said softly. "Look at them."

All the others turned their eyes upwards.

"They look like clouds," Lola said.

"Look again," Max said and Lola scrutinized the clouds. Then she saw something. It was like a flash of light and her instincts told her that it was bad news.

As Bert looked up a blast of icy wind hit him in the face. The temperature was severely dropping. He shivered and noticed that Sophie was shivering too. It began to feel as if a gale force was blasting across the sky and the common.

Marilyn narrowed his eyes and kept them focused on the clouds. The clouds that were beginning to disappear as the wind howled.

Max just stared up into the sky, not moving a muscle.

As Johnny looked up, he saw the clouds being blown away and then...he saw them.

Where there had been clouds, Johnny could see huge flying objects materialize. It was hard to tell how many there were of them. Hundreds? Thousands. For as far as Johnny could see, the sky was full of gigantic, hovering craft – blocking out the skies and emitting a dull red glow. Johnny could sense their evil and it made him shudder. This was unlike anything he had perceived before. It was very dark and

395

very threatening. Their numbers were overwhelming.

To Lola, the ships weren't like anything she had ever seen. If she had to describe them – they looked alive or as if they were made of some kind of flesh and blood.

"The Quilloks royal fleet," Max said. "This is an invasion."

The others kept their eyes on the skies above.

"What are we going to do?" Sophie asked. "There are thousands of them."

"…and there's nine of us," Bert said and swallowed hard.

"They don't have Pitchfork, do they?" Max barked, turning his attention to Lola. Lola stuck out her tongue at him. "Hardly seems fair on them."

"Oi!" Lola squeaked at him.

"Why are they 'ere?" Bert asked before gulping. "Who are they?"

Max took a deep breath. "They are the Quilloks and their Queen is seeking revenge."

"For what?" Sophie asked with a great amount of tension in her voice.

"On me…and on this planet," Max replied matter-of-factly.

"What did you do to her?" Sophie asked.

"I banished her from this planet into a nearby dimension," Max said. "I think she took it rather personally."

"Seems to have found a way out," Marilyn remarked. "You never were that good at banishments."

"Not now, chap," Max warned.

"I thought you said you sent her to that prison dimension," Jonah chipped in.

"I did," Max replied.

"Hmm…"Marilyn murmured.

"What?" Max snapped.

"Just saying…you banished her and here she is," Marilyn said.

"It was a long time ago when I was a young man," Max replied.

"That must've been ages ago," Lola said earnestly. Jonah cackled at this.

"Watch it, Pitchfork!"

The four Guardians bickered for a moment longer before they heard Sophie say: "Oh my God…look at that!"

396

All of them turned their eyes upwards. One of the ships was separating from the others and was dropping down slightly in the sky. It then stopped. It changed from a dull red colour into a vibrant red and it began to pulse at a slow pace. An opening appeared in the front of the spherical craft. From it lowered a long object that looked like a huge slide, also in the vibrant red colour. It dropped miles down towards the earth and onto the common. It must've been about fifty feet wide. It landed on the other side of the common to the Guardians and Vampire Killers and it was massive.

Johnny stared at this slide and noticed that something was pouring down it. It was red – it looked like blood. He shuddered again.

There was a high-pitched, piercing tone throughout the air and all of them covered their ears, apart from Pete, who seemed to be able to withstand it.

Lola thought that her ear-drums would explode. And then it stopped.

Once again they all looked at the slide and back up to the ship. Lola could see tiny figures begin to glide down on the red liquid at a measured speed. Lola could see that there must've been about twenty of them. There was a large figure at the front, with a smaller one behind.

"Wot is this?" Lola asked to Max.

"Looks like a procession, doesn't it?" Max replied.

"Is that the Queen?" Lola asked, her mind thinking for a moment that she wasn't correctly dressed to meet royalty.

Max nodded, not taking his eyes off the procession. He breathed steadily in and let out a long, quiet breath. His eyes did not move from the tall, scaly creature gliding down the red liquid. He understood the symbolism of this too well. She could have easily transported down to the planet surface but this was making a statement. This is your blood, humanity, and there will be more of it.

The nine of them watched as the Queen and her procession arrived on the other side of the common. There were about twenty of them. The Queen was the tallest – even taller than Pete – and then behind her was Fergus. They stood still and looked over at the nine.

The nine moved shoulder to shoulder. Those with cues

397

held them in their right hands and they slowly walked over as one united force towards the Quilloks.

They arrived in front of the Quilloks and they were able to take a look at the Queen. Lola thought she looked well minging and there was that horrendous smell again. The smell of pure evil. The Queen walked forward towards the nine.

"Hello, Max. So good to see you once again and under such charming circumstances," she hissed.

"You haven't aged a day," Max said back flatly. "Then with fish-demons it's rather hard to tell, I find."

"Demon?" the Queen chuckled. "Goddess and liberator to humankind," she smiled, showing her pointy teeth.

"Of course, what was I thinking?" Max said.

"And who are all your lovely little friends?" she sneered.

"They are the ones that are going to remove you from this planet. And this time I'll find a much cosier dimension for you," Max smiled sweetly at her. "If you survive."

The Queen threw her head back and laughed. The hissing noise made Sophie's toes curl.

The Queen's eyes looked over to Pete and she stopped for a moment.

"And who is this?" she whispered.

Bert nudged Pete and whispered, "I fink she likes yoo."

"No way, mate," Pete whispered back. "Don't even think it."

Max looked over to Pete. "This is one of the custodians."

The Queen smiled again.

"Let me see," she said as she began to count. "You appear to have a few cues missing," she mocked. "Well, I know what happened to one of them." She turned and beckoned to Fergus to come over to her side.

"I'm sure you've met before," she hissed as Fergus walked over to her side.

"He used to be one of yours, I believe. Careless, Max, so very careless of you and your Great Lodge," she cackled.

"And careless of you, my dear...seeing as he no longer has a cue," Max replied.

"It is of no matter. The damage has been done. Your planet is going to be destroyed and it is all down to your pride, Max. As your planet burns, I want you to know that."

"Thoughtful, as ever. And as before, it is your pure arrogance and blind ambition that is your undoing," said Max.

The Queen laughed coldly.

"I have thousands of ships waiting to invade your planet. Look at you. You cannot possibly defeat me," she taunted. "You do not even have the power of the seven."

As she walked nearer, Max saw that she had an Eight Ball hanging around her neck. He felt chills going down his back. Was that the real one? How on earth had she got hold of it?

"Oh...you like my little trinket, do you?" the Queen sneered. "You wouldn't think so much trouble could be contained in such a little thing."

"I have to say that I admire all the effort you've gone to. I'm actually rather flattered," Max said icily.

"Don't be," she hissed. "I am going to enjoy watching you all die."

The Queen raised her hand and brought it slowly down. "Let it begin," she ordered.

72

Sophie looked up at the sky. A Quilloks ship dropped down lower to the common and it released a laser blast on the ground near the nine. The Queen began to laugh heartily. Bert and Lola jumped on their cues and flew upwards towards the ship. As they got nearer, they saw that some of the other ships were beginning to move closer to the Earth. The invasion was beginning.

Bert swept up towards the ship the Queen had come out from and he shot bolts from his cue at it. It penetrated some of the sides but didn't seem to make much of an impact. Lola flew out further, avoiding laser blasts as she flew around one of the ships. It was gigantic and there were hundreds of them. She let off a series of blasts from her cue, the blasts matching her super-strength. Lola managed to cause damage to the left side of one of the ships and she could see explosions. She smiled to herself.

Lola flew around to the other side and blasted that. Again she caused damage as laser bolt after laser bolt missed her. She looked at the ship she was attacking and it stopped firing at her. She had managed to stop that one – for the moment at least. She flew towards the ship where Bert was firing but his bolts were making little damage. These ships were incredibly tough. However, they were also stationary. If and when they decided to move over the earth, she could not stop them. The world could be destroyed. Was that all they could do? Fire lasers? Did they have other tricks up their sleeves?

Lola flew next to Bert and fired at the ship from behind him.

"Tough bastards, aren't they?" he shouted to her.

"Nah," Lola shouted back. Her blasts hit the side again and caused damage. As long as they remained still...she could get them all. Yes, there were hundreds and hundreds but she was determined.

With that thought ten of the ships started to break away and began to slowly move.

Bollocks...thought Lola. She couldn't pursue all of them. If Bert's cue didn't damage the ships then it was likely the other cues couldn't as well. She looked and saw that other ships were beginning to move as well.

Johnny, Pete and Eric remained on Putney Common. Johnny looked at the Queen and his heart shuddered. She exuded complete evil. He could feel that throughout his soul. His eyes looked at the Eight Ball around her neck. That must be the real one, but how had she come by it and what were her plans?

As Johnny's eyes looked at the Eight Ball, Eric looked over at Johnny and then back to the ball. Eric walked over to Johnny.

Max glared at the Queen and she stood still, smirking and then laughing as she watched the efforts of Bert and Lola in the sky.

She grabbed Fergus by the arm and threw him to the ground.

"Pathetic," she hissed. "Your time has come too."

Fergus turned his head up towards the Queen. She raised her hand and he saw an energy ball forming. This was to be his end. What had he done?

As the Queen raised her hand higher, Sophie looked at the trees behind Fergus and she saw there was something flying towards him at tremendous speed.

Fergus put out his hand to block the energy ball and as she released it, it was blocked. Fergus's cue had returned to his hand.

Max raised an eyebrow and shook his head.

"Fickle, aren't they?" Marilyn whispered to him.

"The Great Lodge has gone senile," Max said back.

Fergus looked at the cue and back to the Queen. She growled in rage.

"How sweet," she whispered.

401

Fergus got onto his feet and aimed the cue at her. He sent a bolt of energy at her and she merely absorbed it.

"Really?" she whispered. "You think you can harm me? No-one can harm me. Not even the power of seven."

"I will kill you," Fergus said darkly

"And then what? Re-join your little gang? They don't want you any more than I do."

Fergus fired another bolt at her and she laughed.

"Pathetic," she hissed.

She raised out her arm towards him and he began to levitate. She then flicked her hand and he was thrown violently down at Max's feet. Fergus raised his eyes and met steely blue ones.

"We'll talk about this later, chap," Max said coldly.

Eric moved over to Johnny's side and said in a very calm and wise voice: "Why isn't she using the power of the Eight Ball?"

Johnny, who was still looking at the Queen, turned to Eric and looked at him quizzically.

"She is, isn't she?" Johnny said back. "Or am I missing something?"

"No, the Guardians opened a powerful portal to remove the ball from this world and she brought through this fleet when it was open. She tricked us."

"So?"

"Well, the story is that the Eight Ball can be used by good and bad. It says that if bad has it then good will not be able to tell the difference between the two and chaos will erupt."

"And?" Johnny asked, really not knowing why he was getting this lecture at this particular moment in time. There really was a lot going on. "Looks quite chaos-y to me."

"When you look at her, what do you feel?" Eric asked.

Johnny didn't need long to answer that. "I feel sick. She is pure evil."

"So...you can tell the difference – even though she has the Eight Ball?"

Johnny nodded. He then had a realisation. If he could tell the difference then she couldn't be harnessing the power of the Eight Ball.

"So...she hasn't figured out how to use it," said Johnny.

402

"No. But look at what she has tried. She has tried creating vampires and hybrids but they are close to the solution but not the key," Eric whispered.

"And what is the key?" Johnny asked, turning to look Eric fully in the eyes. They looked so wise and so old.

"You are," Eric stated. In that moment, Johnny, once again, turned invisible.

73

Lola telepathically communicated to the other Guardians, "Oi, they're fuckin' movin'!"

Marilyn, Max and Jonah winced.

"Volume," Marilyn thought back.

Max looked down at Fergus and pulled him to his feet.

"Get up," he commanded. Fergus stood up and looked down at Max.

"Stand there," Max pointed next to him and Fergus obeyed. "No-one kneels to that creature."

Fergus cast his eyes down and nodded.

"That was my cue. Bloody look after it," Max barked at him.

Lola pursued one of the ships that was starting to move, firing bolts after it but there were too many of them moving off. Why weren't the others up here with her and Bert? What were they doing down there?

Bert and Lola worked as a team, chasing one of the ships and then another. They found themselves flying through the middle of about six of them when a force-field went up around them, generated by the combined ships. They tried to fly out between the ships but they were trapped. Lola flew around and around, with laser bolts chasing after them. The force-field began to shrink, closing in on them. They were running out of space fast. Lola blasted again and again at the force-field but it was useless.

She saw the force-field closing in and she could not see a way out. Her thoughts turned to Johnny and her friends left down below. She flew over to Bert's side and stuck out her tiny chin defiantly as their trap got smaller and smaller. Bert

404

thought about Mrs Bert and Portugal.

There was nowhere left to go. The next shots could get them.

Lola inhaled and did not flinch. Bert gulped.

Lola saw one of the ships' guns aim right at them.

And the ship exploded before them. Followed by another and then another.

Lola looked at Bert and he looked back. They took no time to make their exit.

Lola flew forwards and saw before her an enormous triangular ship.

"Die, fascists, die!" came the voice over a loud-speaker. It was a posh woman's voice and it sounded slightly tipsy. Lola then heard another female voice say: "You are completely barking mad!"

"Shut-up, witch!" the posh voice said.

The triangular ship was about five times the size of the Quilloks ships and its firepower was awesome.

Lola then heard another voice: "This is the Time Police. You are under arrest. Return the ship immediately,"

"Never!" the posh voice cried.

The triangular ship vapourised another ten Quilloks ships. The loud-speaker was still on and she could hear the woman laughing.

"They're down below, Carl," she heard the second voice say.

Carl? Lola's heart leapt. Was Carl on board?

Another twenty giant ships materialized, identical to the triangular ship, and they began to fire. "You are under arrest. You are under arrest."

"Bugger off," the posh voice said. The stolen ship took a series of powerful blasts – it now looked thoroughly smashed about. The Time Police ships continued firing but didn't stop the stolen ship from firing and pursuing Quilloks ships that were breaking away. Thirty more ships were taken out and then ten more. Lola could hear cackling over the airwaves.

"They really are the scum of the universe," she could hear the posh voice ranting. "Now you, time to sod off my ship!"

"Love ya, Carl! Good luck!" cried Maisie.

Lola looked over at the ship and saw a small transparent

figure float out of it, on some kind of transparent cord. Lola had never seen anything like that before.

It floated towards her as laser bolts went through it.

Hmmm... Lola thought as she tried to work it out and came up with zero.

The figure got closer and closer to her and she could see that it looked like...*Carl!* But he wasn't solid. The astral body of Carl got nearer to Lola and she had now a permanent perplexed look as she chewed her bottom lip. She looked over to Bert, who didn't seem to see anything at all.

"Are yoo seein' that, Bert?" Lola asked.

"Seein' wot, Pix? There's a lot goin' on!" he said huskily.

"The floaty body fing. The fing that looks like Carl," Lola said and pointed in the direction of what could be described as a transparent Carl balloon.

"Errr...nah. Yoo sure?"

"Yeah, course I'm sure," she said back.

Lola flew towards the floaty balloon Carl and she saw that it was...well, a copy of him? Something to do with him?

"Carl! Oi! Carl!" Lola shouted as she flew nearer to him. She saw that he tried to open his mouth but no sound came out. She did, however, hear something in her mind.

"Pixie!!!" it shouted as he zoomed by her and plummeted to the Earth.

Lola turned to Bert. "Yoo really ain't seein' this?"

Bert shook his head and Lola chased down after Carl. He was heading past the common and towards The Pig & Phoenix, as if a stretched elastic had been released and was snapping him back.

406

74

The Queen looked at the sky and hissed. Her ships were disappearing! Her attention was turned away from Max and the others and she stared up at the sky.

Eric turned to Johnny and whispered to him: "The Eight Ball was created by a warlock who was *both* alive and dead. He was not the living dead like a vampire. Through magic he managed to walk the bridge between the two worlds. The Eight Ball can only be wielded by one who can walk the two paths."

Johnny turned to Eric. He knew! Oh God, he knew!

"You walk the two paths. You are a great warlock."

Johnny turned white and leaned in nearer. He whispered: "No...I am not a great warlock. I accidently fell into an enchanted vegetable patch."

"There are no accidents," Eric said.

"There really are," Johnny insisted.

"You are the only one that can wield the power of the Eight Ball. You are the only one that can destroy it."

"M...me? No...really...no," Johnny whispered.

Eric walked around to the other side of Johnny, so that he was standing between Johnny and Pete.

"We will distract her and you will take the Eight Ball," Eric said.

"What!" Johnny cried.

"Now is the time," Eric ordered.

Pete turned his head, looked at Eric and did a double-take. It *was* his mate. What was he doing here? Had the whole world gone mad?

407

"Eric?" Pete asked.

"Yes and no," Eric replied. "Just follow what I do," he said, grabbing Pete by one arm and Johnny by the other. Pete looked up at the sky and then back to the Queen. She was hissing up at the battle above. Fury was an understatement. She turned slowly and looked at Max. He smiled at her darkly and her eyes burned with rage.

Max raised an eyebrow mockingly and the Queen snarled at him.

"Oh dear... not all going to plan?" Max asked in saccharine-sweet voice.

The Queen's eyes darted over to the huge slide and she was preparing to move back to it.

The three Guardians stepped forward.

"I don't think so," Jonah said.

The Queen stopped in her tracks and laughed.

"You think you can stop me?"

"Yeah," Marilyn said. "Actually, we do."

The Queen looked up at the sky and saw more and more of her ships being vaporized. The twenty-one triangular ships were decimating her fleet.

The Staff Guardian was having immense fun blasting everything Quilloks out the sky and the Time Police were delighted to find an illegal Quilloks fleet in the Earth dimension. It wasn't technically a time breach, but they decided that the crazy police ship hijacker was far too much work, and that the Quilloks were easier prey. And they really, really wanted to let off some steam.

The Quilloks fleet was no match for the power of the Time Police ships. Only a handful of the Queen's ships were remaining.

"Die! Die! Die!" The Staff Guardian cried out before turning the stolen ship around and heading at full speed away from the Earth just as all the remaining Quilloks ships were wiped out. The Time Police followed their battered prey and disappeared out of sight.

"Time Police," the Queen hissed. "They have no right!"

"Really? What about Carl? Where did you send him in time?" Max demanded.

"You'll never find him," she replied with a cold dark laugh.

408

"The power of seven can never be."

The Queen was about to make her exit towards the slide when Eric stepped forward, pulling Pete and Johnny with him. She stopped in her tracks and looked Pete up and down, barely noticing Johnny. She smiled a cruel but slightly seductive smile at Pete.

"Well, well, well," she whispered. "What do we have here?"

Pete locked eyes with her, and took a step forward.

75

Lola followed the astral body of Carl, which was now hurtling at phenomenal pace up the Lower Richmond Road. She watched it disappear straight through a wall and into The Pig & Phoenix.

Lola flew onto the roof and went into the pub via a door and then ran down the stairs.

"Carl? Carl?" she shouted as she ran into the bar area of the pub. There she saw Carl standing next to a table, looking like a ghost.

"Wot the fuck 'appened to yoo? Are ya dead?" Lola squeaked.

"Good to see you too, Pixie," Carl answered. She could now actually hear him. She could actually talk directly to him.

"Wot the fuck is this?" Lola said, swiping her hand through him.

"It's a long story but I am sooo pleased you can see me."

"Wot...?? I don't understand," Lola said with frustration.

"OK. The nasty big queen sent me forward in time. I then went into a trance and left my body as a ghost. I then met up with some...err...*friends* on a time ship and they brought my ghost body back in time," Carl explained.

Lola looked at him for a moment, her mind trying to process the information.

"Wot the fuck?" Lola snapped.

Carl actually smiled. "Yeah, it's complicated. I need to get back to my body, which is forwards in time, and then back here," he said with a sigh. Lola sighed too and then her mind wandered.

410

"Did I tell yoo that I'm now a fuckin' Guardian?" Lola smiled. "It's great. I 'ave all kinds of mental powers and that big bearded bloke can't tell me off or nuffink."

Carl nodded. "Wow...that's great, Pixie," Carl said, resigned to her often going off-topic.

"I can tell yoo wot to do...hah!" she said. "I'm also really good with portally fings. I've been sucked through 'em and patched 'em up. That wheelbarrow man got pulled through one."

Carl's eyes lit up.

"Really? But he was with me...he was forwards in time," Carl said.

"Well, he ain't now. He's out there wearin' pink and floatin' about – with nuffink underneath," she said and shuddered. "Me eyes!"

"Pixie, focus..." Carl said. "When and where did he get pulled through?"

"Well...first we fought it woz yoo cos he looked like yoo...but it's all gone fuckin' mad today," Lola growled.

"Pixie...how did it happen?" Carl asked and Lola briefly explained, as best she could.

Carl narrowed his eyes in concentration.

"So, there is a time portal here. You...we...could re-open it. If wheelbarrow man could come through, then so can I."

Lola wrinkled her nose, thinking about it.

"S'pose...yeah...let's do it. I'm a fuckin' Guardian, I can do wot I want!" Lola cried and hurtled downstairs into the basement. Carl sank through the floor and met her below.

Lola put her cue in the cue rack and held onto it with one hand. She focused on Carl and began to concentrate.

Lola found herself going into a trance state and she opened her internal eyes. She saw a tiny speck of light and she willed it to open. As it started to open, she saw a swirling vortex and within it she saw Carl's body in the kitchen. She now tried to mentally force the vortex to remain still. It took an amazing amount of mental strength – helped by her incredible magical strength.

Carl looked around Lola and saw that an actual physical vortex was opening up next to him. He smiled.

"Pixie, I'm going to find my body and come back here. I'll be quick," Carl said as he jumped through the vortex.

Lola felt the incredible strain of keeping a time portal open and contained. She felt that it just wanted to split apart and expand and expand and expand.

Come on, Carl, she thought.

Carl found himself floating upstairs, entering back into the bar and hurtling as quickly as he could towards the kitchen. There he leapt full force back into his body and came to with a gigantic jolt, as if he had fallen twenty feet from the air onto a mattress. He gasped and lunged forwards – trying to gather his senses.

He breathed deeply and reached out for his cue, which he grabbed. All his instincts told him to run...run...run.

Carl ran as fast as he could out from the kitchen, through the bar and then down into the basement. There he saw the vortex. It had definitely shrunk. Crap!

He shoved his hand through it, reached through and felt... well...like someone's thigh. Oh God...it was Lola's – she would torment him over this forever.

Lola looked down at Carl's hand on her thigh and she raised an eyebrow. She focused harder on the vortex and with so much effort, she managed to push it open. Carl literally squeezed himself through it. For once, he was grateful he was pretty short.

He collapsed on the floor next to Lola and took a long, deep breath.

"Carl, yer know I'm an engaged woman," she said.

Carl grinned. "Yeah...I know."

"I won't tell Johnny about this," she sniffed and added: "Yer quite safe."

"Thanks, Pixie," he panted as he patted his own body down. He could feel once again and he was back in his own time zone.

"Don't mention it...Now, come on ya bitch...we've got arses to kick."

76

The Queen seemed to be fascinated by Pete, as if she couldn't quite figure out what he was.

Pete took a step forward towards her. She looked him over.

"You are a custodian," she hissed. "And one who has taken on such a splendid form. Shame you will have to die."

Eric nudged Pete, who seemed to look slightly sickened by this strange flirtation.

"I'm sorry...you have to...err...be going," Pete said and cleared his throat. Marilyn raised his eyebrows. Max almost choked.

The Queen stepped forward again.

"You could come with me," she said. "This planet is doomed."

"Go where? Your fleet is destroyed. You have failed," said Max.

Eric leaned over to Johnny's ear.

"Invisible now," he ordered.

Johnny closed his eyes and began to will himself invisible, but he couldn't.

"Do it, or I'll tell Lola you fancy Sophie," Eric threatened and on that threat Johnny couldn't have turned invisible faster.

"Go get it," Eric whispered.

Johnny found himself walking behind the Queen. Her minions she had come with were now obviously scared. Johnny crept by some of them as carefully and as quietly as he could.

He found himself behind the Queen. Her being exuded pure evil and he hoped he would hold his nerve. He was

413

terrified she would turn around and grab him and well…kill him? He was actually technically dead-ish.

As the Queen was focused on Pete, Johnny reached up towards the back of her neck where the Eight Ball was held on a chain.

He moved his hand closer and closer and he could feel himself shaking. Oh God…oh God…why me? Oh God.

His hand was now centimeters away. He took a deep breath and grabbed it! The chain snapped off the Queen's neck and he held the Eight Ball in his hand. As he held it he felt an enormous pulse of energy fly through his body. It was so strong that it threw him about half way across the common. When he landed, it then threw him all the way back again straight into Pete, who went flying straight into the Queen and knocked her onto her back with him on her.

"Ahh!" Pete bellowed, horrified at his physical proximity to the Queen.

Jonah moved forward and pulled Pete off her.

Johnny's hand seemed to have glued itself around the ball and he could not open his hand.

The Queen leapt to her feet and pointed at Johnny.

"What are you?" she hissed. "This is impossible."

The Queen looked genuinely scared and began to back away. She looked over to see if the slide was still there and she ran towards it. As she began to move, Fergus pointed his cue at her and let out a solid stream of energy. Johnny pointed his, followed by Bert, Pete and Eric.

The Queen seemed to be trapped for a moment in the streams of light that were plunging into her. She smiled a wicked smile.

"Where is your power of seven now?" she mocked, as she started to move towards the slide.

As she turned her back, she felt another stream of light hit her and then one more. Seven!

She turned around and saw that Lola and Carl had also joined in. She was held in the streaming of seven colours and they were beginning to build more and more in their brightness, until they formed a gigantic pulse of white light.

The Queen began to scream louder and louder. Then around the seven custodians, the three Guardians formed and they began to chant.

Sophie stood on the outskirts, looking in with her cue rest in her hands. She felt it begin to buzz, so much so that she had to let it go. Sophie watched it fly over to the white light, where it was dissolved.

"I'll banish her this time," Marilyn said.

"Don't start," Max threatened.

The white light spiraled up into the sky, as the Queen's body seemed to be stretched upwards with it.

Her screaming got louder.

Max looked her in the eyes and said: "Enjoy your new home. I've had many years to perfect banishments. This time, you won't be coming back."

And with that, Max uttered another word and the white light shot into the air with the Queen and her minions in it.

Johnny looked at his hand with the Eight Ball in it. The power he was feeling from it was getting more and more intense.

Max looked over at Johnny and seemed confused and alarmed. He knew whatever he was seeing should not be happening. It looked as though Johnny was actually absorbing the energy of the Eight Ball.

"Keep the energy going, no-one stop!" Max shouted.

He ran over to Johnny and grabbed his cue from his hands.

"Sophie, get over here," he ordered. Sophie ran over and Max thrust the cue into her hands.

He grabbed Johnny and threw him into the centre of the light streams, so now the cue energy was focused on Johnny.

"I can't open my hand," Johnny said.

"I'm so sorry chap," Max whispered to him.

"Keep the light on him," he demanded. Lola was about to put her cue down.

"You too Pitchfork!" Max bellowed .

"Yoo can't order me about!" she yelled at Max and stopped pointing the light at Johnny. Max marched over and grabbed her cue from her. Lola was about to punch him as hard as she could but she looked at Johnny. He was becoming absorbed into the white light and he was trying desperately to open his hand.

"The Eight Ball has to be banished!"

"Yoo ain't banishin' Johnny!" Lola shouted.

Carl dropped his cue too, as did the others.

"You don't understand, the planet is going to be destroyed if we don't banish it now!" Max roared.

"Great Lodge, we all have to make sacrifices. If you can't handle that then you are not worthy of the cues you possess," Max seethed.

Lola ran over to Johnny and tried with all her strength to open his hand. She could see that the light was now passing into Johnny's body.

"Oh my God!" Lola cried. "It's goin' into ya!"

Jonah walked over to Lola's side. "Let's both try," he said to her. Lola smiled at him with genuine gratitude.

Jonah and Lola started to pull on Johnny's hand with all their combined strength. It seemed as if nothing would move his fingers and then there was some give.

"Aim now," Jonah said. "Do it." The custodians didn't listen to Jonah. Lola looked at the others and said.

"Do it. I ain't gonna let 'im go," Lola squeaked.

The others reluctantly pointed their cues at Johnny and Lola. The pain on their faces was apparent. Max was using Lola's cue and Sophie, Johnny's.

Carl looked on and felt a deep instinct come over him. His time in the infinity cube and his time in his astral body had changed him. He was aware he had so much more to learn and do and he was just at the beginning but he had changed. He was wiser somehow.

Carl went over to Johnny and put his hands on his shoulders.

"Trust me," he said.

Carl closed his eyes and within a moment had stepped out of his physical body and was standing next to his own body. He stepped into Johnny's body, which was a surprise for both of them. Carl could feel what Johnny was feeling. What was interesting was the amount of energy Johnny had absorbed. It had an intelligence to it. The energy was adding information into Johnny's mind.

Carl thought down to Johnny's hand and willed it to open. He took his entire energy there and began to force it apart.

Lola saw that Johnny's hand was starting to open. She

416

reached her little fingers in and gripped it. The light began to diminish at her touch and some of the light passed into her but Lola was not half dead and she could not wield the Eight Ball. Lola pulled with all her strength to budge it and Carl pushed from inside Johnny's body.

Lola was not going to let go again and she tried to get it out from Johnny's hand but it seemed to be stuck to it.

"Fuck!" she cried. "Fuckin' fuck!"

With all her superhuman strength, she managed to finally yank it free from Johnny's hands. She whistled for her cue and it shot to her hands.

"Carl," she said. "Come wiv me."

Lola shot up into the sky and headed towards the Thames. Carl followed right behind her.

Lola aimed towards the tear-y thing she had just opened and closed before. And once again hovered in front of it.

She handed the Eight Ball over to Carl. Carl looked down at the object. It was hard to believe it was so deadly.

"I'm gonna open the teary-y fing and yoo shove it through, OK?" she shouted.

Carl nodded.

Lola aimed thought to her cue and once again the light began to pulse out and make a tear in the sky. As the tear opened, Lola looked over at Carl.

Carl flew over to the tear – he really wanted to have a look at it and it was incredible. As he looked into the void, he turned and looked back at Lola. He then looked at the object in his hand – the tiny thing that had caused so much death and destruction. He scowled at it and chucked it through the tear.

Lola immediately began to patch up the tear again as quickly as she could. She looked at it for a moment and then turned to Carl.

"Eight Ball down," she whispered and smiled broadly.

77

Fergus looked at his hands and saw that they were returning to normal human hands. He felt ashamed. Deeply ashamed.

He looked up into the sky and saw that Carl and Lola were flying back. He looked around at the bodies and the mess around him.

Carl landed next to Fergus and looked at him with a mixture of emotions.

"Where is she?" Carl demanded.

Fergus looked down at the ground.

"I don't know," Fergus replied. This was not the answer Carl wanted and he grabbed Fergus by the neck.

"The Queen lied to me. I thought I could control her but she…she played me from the start," Fergus wheezed, trying to get Carl's hands off his neck.

"Where is Katie?" Carl snarled, squeezing Fergus's neck tighter. "Is she dead?"

Fergus shook his head. "I don't know. The last thing I knew was she had been taken to a prison planet."

"Where is this prison planet?" Carl demanded.

"Not in this dimension," Fergus rasped, trying to breathe.

Lola marched over to Fergus. "Wot the fuck was all the money about?"

"Money?" Carl asked.

"Yeah…loads of women showed up at the pub with fahsands of pounds. All chantin' yer name."

"What?" Carl asked, releasing Fergus.

Fergus looked around at all the faces glaring at him as he rubbed his throat. "There's a dimension near here. Pretty

418

much identical to here except you are dead. I was going to start again with…another Katie. This time I would be rich. Perhaps I would have a chance."

Carl glared at him. "So, you just abandon my wife in a prison and start again with a look-a-like," Carl growled. "You steal money from here and take it there. Class."

"Why were they asking for Carl?" Bert asked.

Fergus shook his head. "Something must've interfered."

"Or you wanted me to take the blame. Set me up and fuck off out of it!" Carl shouted.

"The Queen…she…manipulated everything," Fergus whispered.

"Yeah," said Carl. "You just keep telling yourself that."

"Evil is very seductive," said Marilyn. "I once dated…"

"Not now chap," Max chided. Max's blue eyes scanned the horizon and he let out a long sigh.

"We've got a lot of clearing up to do…" he said.

Max pointed a cue to some of the bodies and they began to dissolve.

"Mopping up is the dullest part of the job," he complained. "Come on…get to it."

The others followed Max, leaving Carl and Fergus together.

Fergus stood back for a moment. He was returning more and more to human form and he was naked. Carl stood over him and pulled him up by his throat.

"Do you have any idea?" Carl's voice was strained. "You…fucking…" Carl threw a punch across his jaw.

"Where is she? WHERE? Just tell me!" Carl yelled at him.

"I don't know!" Fergus shouted back. "I would do anything for her!"

"Like abandon her? She would not want you to have done this! Look at it!" Carl shouted, his arms gesturing towards the bloodbath on the common. "That bitch almost destroyed the earth…because of you!"

Carl had tears welling in his eyes. "I should skin you alive…"

"If I could take it back…" Fergus started.

"…well you fucking can't. You can't take back any of this."

"I will try…" Fergus whispered.

"Do me a favour," Carl whispered back. "Just fuck off…

just..." Carl closed his eyes, turned his back on Fergus and walked away.

Fergus stood up and watched Carl walk off. His eyes glistened as he stood up. He still had some of his Quilloks abilities and he stretched out his hand to the side of him.

Johnny looked over and watched. He saw that reality around Fergus's hand seemed to oscillate and expand.

"Carl...I'm so...so sorry," he whispered and with that he disappeared.

Johnny and the others were close to one another. He turned to Lola and said. "He's gone. He's just disappeared out of existence."

Lola threw her hands to her hips. "Just 'ow many fuckin' tears in reality are there? It's a mess this planet!"

Jonah sighed. "He's trackable."

Marilyn nodded. "Yeah...gone to that parallel world. It's rather nice there."

Max said: "Wasn't that when you accidentally dated yourself?"

Marilyn smiled. "Hmmm."

Max walked over to Johnny and looked him up and down as if assessing him. "Well...it appears you are alive."

"Of course," Johnny said, trying to be casual.

"I mean completely alive," Max said. "You kept that well hidden. Well done."

Lola threw a look at both of them. "Whatcha mean?"

Johnny looked sheepishly at Lola. "I'll explain later."

Carl's mind was whirling with all the things that had happened. He walked forward zapping bodies and watching them dissolve.

Their worlds had all changed forever. Lola was a Guardian and he was a time criminal. He knew he had to repay some hours back and he didn't know how he was going to do that yet. But he still had his time pop lollipop and he had an infinity cube —well, a broken one...and one he had very little idea how to use. He hoped Maisie was OK. He owed her so much and he wanted her back safely.

For a short while all of them cleaned up the common from dead bodies. The church was a mess and Boat Race Day had been ruined. What was he going to do with the money

Lola had mentioned? He would have to find a way to get it back to wherever it came from.

Carl's mind turned to Katie. Katie was out there somewhere and he would find her!

"Katie's alive," Carl said to his friends. "I'm going to bring her home."

Lola walked over to him. "I saw 'er in a mirror. She is alive... well, she woz. Y'know wot I mean. A few hours 'ave passed..."

Carl gave her a hug. "I know what you mean."

As soon as the last body had been zapped by Eric he turned to Max and whispered: "I'll be back when you need me." Max smiled and clapped him on the back. "Cheers, old man."

Within moments Eric's body had collapsed to the floor. Lola rolled her eyes. "Anyone got a wheelbarrow?"

Pete began to return to his human body and, luckily, he was wearing clothes. He looked stunned for a moment but like most cue guardians he seemed to take it all in his stride.

Jonah looked around the common and the sky was becoming lighter. "Time for a drink," he stated.

"To the pub," Max said. Instead of flying they all walked up the Lower Richmond Road together slightly battered and bruised.

"Any news on the Oxford crew?" Johnny asked.

"Such lovely, lovely boys," Marilyn sighed.

"We need to get on with the mind wipe, film set rubbish," Jonah said, carrying Eric over his shoulder.

"Yes...just the usual blurb...a film crew was filming a vampire film on the common...special effects...blah, blah, blah," Max barked.

Sophie and Bert walked holding arms like old friends down the road with Pete walking behind.

Johnny and Lola walked hand in hand.

"How about a weekend break in Rome?" Johnny asked. He was fully alive! At last – weekend breaks! No more sleeping in the vegetable patch. Lola jumped into his arms and kissed him. "I'm a fuckin' Guardian!" she squeaked. Johnny smiled.

"Yes, you're a fucking Guardian," he said.

"We'll find her." Bert slapped Carl on the back. "Don't worry."

"I know...I've got a plan." Carl grinned. "And I will need your

421

help."

His friends grabbed their cues and banged them on the ground twice.

21484179R00236

Printed in Great Britain
by Amazon